Managing and Maintaining Microsoft® Exchange Server 5.5

D1401118

PUBLISHED BY
Microsoft Press
A Division of Microsoft Corporation
One Microsoft Way
Redmond,Washington 98052-6399

Library of Congress Cataloging-in-Publication Data
Managing and Maintaining Microsoft Exchange Server 5.5 / Microsoft
    Corporation.
        p. cm.
    Includes index.
    ISBN 0-7356-0528-9
    1. Microsoft Exchange Server.   2. Client/server computing.
    3. Software maintenance.   I. Microsoft Corporation.
    QA76.9.C55M345   1998
    005.7'13769--dc21   98-20388
                                                                  CIP

Printed and bound in the United States of America.

2 3 4 5 6 7 8 9   MLML   3 2 1 0 9 8

Distributed in Canada by ITP Nelson, a division of Thomson Canada Limited.

A CIP catalogue record for this book is available from the British Library.

Microsoft Press books are available through booksellers and distributors worldwide. For further
information about international editions, contact your local Microsoft Corporation office or contact
Microsoft Press International directly at fax (425) 936-7329. Visit our Web site at mspress.microsoft.com.

Acquisitions Editor: Anne Hamilton
Project Editor: Maureen Williams Zimmerman

Contributors

Thank you to all the field consultants and support engineers who contributed their time, expertise, and wealth of experience to make this book possible.

Enterprise Services—Americas
Brian Boruff

Microsoft TechNet
Tim McBride

Editorial
Bob Haynie, Thomas Hoffman, Michael Ohata

Contributing Consultants and Engineers
Michael Aday, Joe Baltimore, Ursula Bazik, Paul Bowden, Jason Brandt, Kali Buhariwalla, Ken Charlton, Matt Finger, Sara Holcomb, Ken Kubota, Peter Nilsson, Perry Owen, Joseph Pagano, Laura Payne, Eric Savoldi, Erik Swart, Soner Terek, Steve Townsend, Maureen Tracy Venti

Contributing Groups
Microsoft Consulting Services New Jersey, Microsoft Information Technology Group (ITG), ITG Messaging Services (Escalation Management Team, Messaging Platforms & Gateways Team, Network Accounts Management Team), Premier Support Team Central, Premier Support Team West, Microsoft Technical Support

Technical Review
Nitin Bhatia, Joanne Bromwell, Jed Dawson, Dan Grady, Cheen Liao, Todd Luttinen, Kristina Marx, Mark van der Merwe, Mahesh Nasta, Rob Sanfilippo, Bill Skilton

Additional Contributions
Mark Adcock, Max Benson, Lou Chaney, Daniel Chu, Tom DeFeo, Craig Johnson, Kristin Kinan, Barbara Moatz, Joe Palermo, Jim Reitz, Stuart Schifter, Sheri Spencer, Brian Valentine, Deb Waldal, Zev Yanovich

Production
Laurie Dunham, Jerry Dyer, Nancy Jacobs, Sharon Limbocker, Peter McKinnon

Indexer
Richard S. Shrout

Project Editor
Maureen Zimmerman

Contents

Part 3   Disaster and Recovery Planning

Appendix

Introduction

Managing and Maintaining Microsoft Exchanger Server 5.5, Best Practices from Microsoft Consulting Services is designed as the companion volume to *Deploying Microsoft Exchange Server 5.5.* Created as a resource for anyone with an Exchange 5.5 system in place, this second volume is a natural next step for administrators and systems designers who have worked their way through the first book. In it they will find information on managing, securing, and optimizing the system they have just deployed. Both volumes are designed for information technology (IT) and information systems (IS) professionals, both condense and organize the broad expertise of field consultants and support engineers, both offer the benefit of consultants' real-world experiences.

You should use this book as a supplement to the Microsoft Exchange Server 5.5 product documentation and the *Microsoft Exchange Server 5.5 Resource Guide* in the *Microsoft BackOffice Resource Kit, Second Edition.* The resource guide contains a wealth of information, ranging from high level (Exchange Server architecture) to fine detail (addressing and routing, and a discussion on Collaboration Data Objects—CDO—and the Exchange Forms Designer). The resource guide is the encyclopedia of Exchange, and the book you are reading now often refers you to it for general and background information.

No single book can cover every post-deployment topic for a product as complex as Exchange Server, and it was a challenge just selecting areas to cover. But even more challenging to the design of these two volumes was the "problem" of sorting information and procedures into either the deployment or production environments. Obviously, many administrative procedures should be built in during deployment, just as many choices made during deployment will affect the texture of administrative decisions made afterwards. In truth, the two phases are so closely intertwined that separation is often arbitrary.

This book focuses on what to do after the rollout—how to fine-tune the messaging system, how to understand and plan for messaging traffic, how to design and implement a working support structure, how to avoid the perils of disaster through backup and recovery planning, and how to tune and optimize. Throughout, the text balances concepts with procedures. This book and its companion, *Deploying Microsoft Exchange Server 5.5,* are designed to explain in general and instruct in particular. Use this information to *do* things.

What's in This Book

There are four parts, each with several chapters.

Part 1: Exchange Messaging Operations

This section begins with a direct continuation of *Deploying Microsoft Exchange Server 5.5*. The earlier book included a chapter on developing a deployment audit; this book completes the audit process by extending it through hand-off to the operations team. After you have completed an audit, you may want to move right into a study of messaging operations and how to administer them (Chapter 2). If this, in turn, inclines you to try to optimize the number of users/server, Chapter 3 gets into the nuts-and-bolts calculations, explaining gains and trade-offs. These calculations must, of course, take into account directory replication and background traffic (Chapter 4) and how performance tuning deals with this traffic, backbone design, and connector choice.

Part 2: Supporting Microsoft Exchange

Based on an extensive project during which Microsoft Consulting Services developed and implemented a 3-tier support structure for a large company, the chapters in Part 2 show how to divide support tasks logically, how to apportion responsibilities, and how to control support issues effectively. In short, this section shows how careful planning can give you the greatest return on your support dollar *and* can increase user satisfaction by providing efficient, rapid response.

Part 3: Disaster and Recovery Planning

What can bring down your Exchange system and what can you do to prevent it? If you can't prevent it, how do you recover information and services and restore communication? The more you rely on a messaging system (and some companies communicate almost exclusively through e-mail), the more important it is to protect against failure and to provide for speedy, certain recovery. This chapter offers a three-part discussion of this complex information. A chapter on concepts (Chapter 9) looks at what you are trying to accomplish and what options and methods are open to you. An extensive chapter of frequently asked questions (Chapter 10) answers thoroughly just about every specific question you can think of. Chapter 11 wraps up this topic with information on error numbers and maintenance utilities.

Part 4: Optimizing and Tuning the System

This is a grab bag of helpful ideas and procedures. First is a quick overview of backup/recovery basics. The material is covered in several other places in the book, but this chapter looks at this important topic in the context of setting up regular procedures and strategies. Next is a chapter on a rare problem (message storms), followed by an examination of Exchange *client optimization* that starts at the beginning—how to identify and define client needs and limitations—and proceeds through various strategies for achieving peak performance. The book wraps up with a common situation: how to assess, plan for, and deploy hot fixes, service packs, and upgrades. In sum, after things are running day to day, you can turn to this section for ideas on how to keep them running smoothly.

Additional Information

Appendix A lists references and resources referred to in the book or used in its development: support offerings, Web sites, white papers, and Microsoft Technical Support Knowledge Base articles on Exchange Server and *upgrading* to Exchange 5.5.

The last thing in the book may be the first thing you'll want to take advantage of: a time-limited Microsoft TechNet sample CD-ROM that includes a representative selection of one issue's contents *and* the utility mentioned in Chapter 13 on message storms. For a book such as this one, drawn from first-hand accounts and experience, TechNet is an obvious companion tool: it is *the* support resource for professionals in the trenches. Each month, it provides subscribing IT professionals with in-depth information on evaluating, deploying, managing, and supporting Microsoft products and technologies.

Conventions Used

Convention	Description
ALL CAPITALS	Acronyms, filenames, and names of commands.
bold	Menus and menu commands, command buttons, property page and dialog box titles and options, command-line commands, options, and portions of syntax that must be typed exactly as shown.
Initial Capitals	Names of applications, programs, servers, windows, directories, and paths.
Italic	Information you have to enter, first occurrences of special terms, and book titles. Used also for emphasis as dictated by context.
`monospace type`	Sample command lines, program code, and program output.
Q123456, Title: XGEN: How to Deploy Microsoft Exchange Server 5.5	Knowledge Base article titles. Search for them on Microsoft TechNet or at http://support.microsoft.com/support/a.asp?M=F using the "Q" number (no spaces).

PART 1

Exchange Messaging Operations

This section begins with an outline of the messaging systems audit process in preparation for hand-off to the operations team. Chapter 2 moves into a study of messaging operations and how to administer them. Chapter 3 discusses the nuts-and-bolts calculations of optimizing the number of users/server. This leads you to Chapter 4, covering backbone design and how performance tuning deals with directory replication and background traffic.

CHAPTER 1

Handing Off the System to Operations

Systematic auditing begins during deployment and makes sure that all your design work has been incorporated into the final system. This is discussed in Chapter 15 of the companion book *Deploying Microsoft Exchange Server 5.5*. After the system is in place, the auditing process continues into operations. This chapter provides a framework for organizing the review and assessment of the messaging system and to identify and address potentially troublesome areas.

Operations Auditing Process

You can use the template in this chapter to organize your audit. Because environments vary, messaging operation specifics can make some issues moot while increasing the importance of others. No audit template can ever be 100 percent accurate for all cases, even ones with identical configurations and deployment plans, so use this document to start outlining your auditing efforts.

Handing over the operations for a complex product such as Exchange in a large organization requires specific maintenance processes and work items. The audit group identifies these processes, assesses them against the template in this document, and adds job-specific issues to calculate the time and resources needed to complete the audit and to ensure the operations team's readiness to manage the system.

Each section of this chapter begins with a description of what you should document:

> ***What should be in this section:***
>
> *A summary of the documentation that you should produce at this stage of the audit.*

Operations Ownership Transfer Process

What should be in this section:

A review of the process that engineering and deployment personnel will use to transfer server ownership to operations personnel. Suggest improvements and create a risk analysis for the failure to develop the plan.

Server Backup and Recovery Process

What should be in this section:

A complete backup plan that should be submitted to the audit team for review. At a minimum it should ensure that:

- *Backup services encompass the systematic and periodic backup of file, mail, and utility server data.*

- *Data recovery services enable the restoration of entire server volumes or the reinstatement of purged end-user data files that reside on their home server.*

- *Data recovery services provide for on-demand recovery of system and end-user data from core infrastructure server permanent storage to removable storage media.*

- *The scope of included servers is noted.*

- *The process has a complete schedule including a schedule for reusing media.*

- *It contains a defined treatment plan for backup media, including offsite storage.*

Exchange backups do not disrupt messaging on the Exchange-based server, although the process does boost I/O and CPU usage above normal operation levels. If you schedule backup for periods when few interactive processes are accessing the server, you can minimize the number of clients affected by slower Exchange response times.

It is also strongly suggested that you have backup and recovery processes for:

- *The Windows NT registry*

- *The master boot record*

- *Server disk administrator configurations*

Windows NT Registry

Include the Windows NT registry in backups. Some third-party backup packages require you to specify that the registry be included. The backup tool that ships with Windows NT cannot back up remote registries over the network (it handles only the local system registry), but some full-service retail backup programs can. Remote registry backup should not pose a problem if local tape devices are used, but additional security issues may require base configuration changes if remote tape devices are used. Research those changes and document them here.

Windows NT Master Boot Record

Back up the master boot record whenever partition information changes for primary or extended partitions. Back up the partition boot sector whenever an administrator formats a volume, installs Windows NT in the volume, or converts a volume from the file allocation table (FAT) file system to NTFS. For more information, please refer to the *Windows NT 4.0 Server Resource Kit*, in the *Resource Guide*, Chapter 5, "Preparing For and Performing Recovery." Look for the section Replacing the Master Boot Record and the Partition Boot Sector.

Disk Administrator Configuration

The Windows NT Disk Administrator controls the Windows NT disk configuration concerning mirroring, volume sets, and other disk fault tolerance parameters, and allows the user to save this information if recovery is required. The Disk Administrator, **Partition, Configuration** menu allows you to back up the current disk partition and volume information, which can aid in recovery. Policies should be in place to ensure that all changes to Windows NT disk configuration information are backed up and saved.

Disaster Recovery

Develop for each Exchange server a complete disaster recovery plan that includes:

- An up-to-date emergency repair disk for each mission-critical computer.
- The three Windows NT initial install boot disks.
- A full backup of files on the server.
- A full backup of the server registry including security accounts manager (SAM).

- A current copy of the disk administrator configuration.
- Onsite hot swappable hardware and hardware spares (where necessary).
- A 9,600-baud modem on each server connected to the same Component Object Model (COM) port on all servers.
- A manual for each server, outlining steps to take if a server goes down or the system is disrupted by a catastrophic event.
- Training for operations personnel on what to do if a server goes down or the system is disrupted by a catastrophic event.

Each mission-critical server should be configured for debug as detailed in the section Blue Screen Recovery below and should have the appropriate Windows NT and Exchange symbols loaded. All Exchange servers should be configured for dump files and automatic restart. Paths can be set in the computer **System Properties** dialog box.

For more detail on disaster recovery see Part 3 "Disaster and Recovery Planning."

Blue Screen Recovery (Catastrophic Server Failures)

Make sure that each server's hardware configuration documentation includes firmware levels and that its software configuration documentation includes information about service packs, hot fixes, and third-party drivers. Microsoft support engineers need this information so they can install the proper debugging symbols before analyzing a memory dump, so having it handy can reduce server downtime.

Configure servers to write a memory dump file to disk in the event of a blue screen error. This allows the server to be brought back into production, if possible, and records vital troubleshooting information for support personnel. **Control Panel** (click **System** and then **Recovery**) contains other administrative options for support that can be configured for automatic reboot, event log recording, and administrative alerts.

Support personnel should be familiar with these Microsoft Knowledge Base articles, also available on Microsoft TechNet:

- Q129845, Title: Blue Screen Preparation Before Calling Microsoft
- Q123750, Title: Debugging Windows NT 3.5 Setup STOP Screens

Status Monitoring

What should be in this section:

How Exchange servers are monitored. This information can help resolve operational issues related to the Exchange architecture. Consider:

- *Exchange server monitors*
- *Simple Network Management Protocol (SNMP) monitoring of the message transfer agent (MTA) and related queues on Exchange servers*
- *Third-party solutions*

To be effective, monitoring should use Exchange link monitors, SNMP traps and monitoring consoles, and third-party solutions to capture the status of the connecting local area network (LAN) and wide area network (WAN) segments in the architecture.

Suggested Values for the Performance Monitor

The following table of performance monitor values shows a sample (with a 10-minute alert interval) for creating alerts.

Performance monitor object	Counter	Threshold
Logical disk	% Disk Time	>80%
Memory	Page Faults/sec	>20,000
Memory	Pages/sec	>5
MSExchangeIS Private	Average Local Delivery Time	>3,000 (milliseconds)
MSExchangeMTA	Work Queue Length	>200
Network Interface	Pkts Rcvd/sec	>20,000
Network Interface	Pkts Sent/sec	>400,000
Network Segment	% Network Segment	>30%
Paging File	% Usage	>80%
Processor	% Processor time	>80%
Server	Errors System	>0
Server Work Queues	Queue Length	>4
System	%Reg Quota in Use	>80%

Message Routing (Exchange Link Monitor)

Use the link monitor tool shipped with Exchange server (or an equivalent) to monitor message routing by "polling" remote Exchange servers every 15 minutes. This verifies that all connecting components between the systems are operating correctly, or notifies an administrator if a response is not received in the allotted time. The tool notifies the administrators through Windows NT administrative alert or e-mail, or by calling a program such as a third-party paging program for unattended operations. If third-party tools are used, the polling can also sample round-trip delivery times between the sending and receiving systems and log them for trending purposes.

In addition, the RC should monitor MTA queue lengths (performance monitor counter) or Windows NT application event logs for MTA resource events related to queue threshold exceptions and should automatically notify appropriate personnel of exceptions to normal operating conditions.

Windows NT Server Services (Exchange Server Monitors)

Exchange Server also ships with a tool called server monitor, which checks the status of Windows NT server services running on computers with Exchange installed. If a service is found inoperative, server monitor can issue Windows NT administrative alerts and automatically restart the service or the entire server. It can also monitor Windows NT application event logs for events that indicate that key Exchange services are no longer running.

Performance Monitor Threshold Exceptions

Tools must be deployed that notify an administrator when performance thresholds have been exceeded, so that corrective action can be taken.

Windows NT Alerter

Configure Exchange servers to send Windows NT administrative alerts to Windows NT workstations in an administrative location (a central site or one with a high population of administrative personnel) monitored 24 hours a day, x7 days a week (referred to as 7x24).

Performance and Capacity Planning

What should be in this section:

Status-monitoring data such as automated reports that show servers with declining performance. Collect and store this information for long-term performance and capacity planning, which is an integral tool for identifying and evaluating relationships between organizational growth and messaging system architecture growth. Develop a process and criteria for identifying problem servers and/or networks so that engineering changes can be recommended and completed. Identify the people responsible for long-term performance trending.

Refer also to Chapter 3, "Calculating Users per Server," for an overview of capacity planning concepts and areas to assess as you scale your organization's system for more users.

Incident Tracking and Escalation

What should be in this section:

A review of and comment on the risk of improperly documented escalation processes. To guarantee smooth server operation, thorough documentation must identify support escalation issues and resolution processes. Documentation should cover the escalation process and mechanisms for capturing problems to avoid repeat issues and ensure consistent patch application. This must be completed no later than the deployment, ideally before deployment begins.

The escalation process should have at least three phases: problem capturing, internal escalation, and external escalation. It must assign each issue a severity level and an owner, provide contact information for the issue owner and onsite personnel, and identify the affected server name and relevant system information. Customers with a Microsoft Premier Support contract (strongly recommended) should also document the SRX number associated with the problem report and relevant Microsoft Technical Support (MTS) personnel contact information.

Capturing Problems

Many sites use specialized database tools for tracking critical problems inside their architectures, and these systems should be able to correlate the Microsoft Premier Support case number (if any) to the internal problem identification number.

Internal Escalation

This section of the document should review the process for internal escalation and detail the process by which issues are transferred from internal to external support personnel.

External Escalation

Your organization must understand the external escalation process and how to track the status of the issue even after it has been received by external escalation personnel. Customers with an MTS agreement should escalate an issue to Microsoft Premier Support by calling 1-800-936-3100 and providing the Premier ID. The customer support manager should have a complete list of the organization's Premier contacts and their Premier IDs.

When opening a support incident with Premier Support, you must assign a severity to the incident. The table below explains severity levels:

Severity level	Definition
A Critical	■ System, network, server, or critical application down. Situation severely affecting production and/or profitability. ■ High-impact problem in which production, operations, or development are proceeding but production and/or profitability will be severely affected within several days. Severity A situations are so critical that to resolve them it is acceptable to: ■ Interrupt other work and commit personnel to overtime to provide additional information to Microsoft. ■ Apply the solution provided by Microsoft within a half day of receipt.
B Urgent	■ High-impact problem. Production is proceeding, but is significantly impaired. ■ Time-sensitive issue important to long-term productivity. Severity B situations are so critical that to resolve them it is acceptable to: ■ Start gathering information for Microsoft within one day of receipt. ■ Apply the solution provided by Microsoft within one day of receipt.
C Important	■ Important issue, but one that does not have significant impact on current productivity.
D Monitor	■ Issue requiring no further action beyond monitoring for follow-up if needed.

1. Inform the Microsoft Premier Technical Account Manager of Severity A and B incidents so that the issue gets into the system and can be escalated.

2. Ask the Microsoft Premier Support Engineer to escalate the issue if acceptable progress is not made after all requests made by the Microsoft Premier Support Engineer have been completed.

Routine Systems Management Checklist

What should be in this section:

A review of the schedule and processes for routine system management. This information should be clear and detailed. The sample checklist below, which summarizes items that should be checked regularly, complements the standard, complete documentation.

Demand-Driven Procedures

- Distribution list management based on user requests.
- Public folder management based on user requests.

Daily Procedures

- Examine performance monitor counter exceptions.
- Use server and link monitors to monitor exceptions.
- Back up critical data.
- Check for buildup of transaction log files.
- Check available disk space and the alerter service.

Weekly Procedures

- Review event logs.
- Check for message tracking log buildup.
- Verify public folder replication status.

Monthly Procedures

- Validate backup.

Periodic or Infrequent Procedures

- Perform information store maintenance.
- Verify mailbox and public folder use.
- Verify storage limits.

Troubleshooting Resources

Make these resources available to all support personnel:

- The first customer contact form prior to contacting Premier (Q155545, Title: XGEN: First Customer Contact Form for Exchange).
- The additional troubleshooting tips and resources found on the Microsoft Exchange Support Site at http://support.microsoft.com/support/exchange/.
- The hot fixes, bug reports, Alert, and News Flash services found on Microsoft Premier Service Desk. For more information on Premier Technical Services, see http://www.microsoft.com/Enterprise/support/techservices.htm.
- Exchange Books Online installed on all administrator workstations (Windows 95 or Windows NT).
- TechNet CD-ROM on the network or through individual licenses.
- Internet access to the Microsoft Technical Support Knowledge Base (or in TechNet).

Relevant Knowledge Base Articles

Microsoft Windows NT

- Q158744, Title: How to Automate Network Captures with Network Monitor
- Q129845, Title: Blue Screen Preparation Before Calling Microsoft
- Q148954, Title: How to Set Up a Remote Debug Session Using a Modem
- Q164931, Title: Using Regedit to Backup Your Windows NT Registry
- Q130928, Title: Restoring a Backup of Windows NT to Another Computer

Microsoft Exchange Client

- Q163576, Title: XGEN: Changing the RPC Binding Order
- Q148284, Title: XCON: When and How to use the Mtacheck Utility
- Q159298, Title: XADM: Analyzing Exchange RPC Traffic Over TCP/IP
- Q177763, Title: XADM: Troubleshooting Failure to Generate Offline Address Book

Microsoft Exchange Administration

- Q170361, Title: XADM: Troubleshooting a Rapidly Growing Information Store
- Q159485, Title: XADM: Troubleshooting Setup Problems Joining an Existing Site
- Q128325, Title: XADM: Reclaiming Disk Space for the Information Store
- Q170334, Title: XADM: Troubleshooting Intrasite Directory Replication
- Q159298, Title: XADM: Analyzing Exchange RPC Traffic Over TCP/IP

Microsoft Exchange Connectors

- Q147704, Title: XCON: Troubleshooting Tips for: Exchange MTA Not Starting

General

- Q161495, Title: XADM: Setting Up Exchange View-Only Administrators
- Q150564, Title: XADM: How to load Exchange Symbols for DR. Watson

Remote Debug Capabilities

For debugging Exchange and other user mode applications, WINDBGRM (which comes on the Exchange CD-ROM) must be running on the machine and you must have normal Remote Access Service (RAS) access to the net. To get the machines ready for the Windows NT kernel debug, prepare them in accordance with Knowledge Base article Q148954, Title: How to Set Up a Remote Debug Session Using a Modem.

Onsite Configuration Review

Process and Tools Used

What should be in this section:

Review a sample of the system configurations onsite. The tools that you might use in the review are listed below.

Your audit team should obtain administrative access to the organization's Windows NT Server domains and Exchange sites to gather configuration information on the pilot or production systems deployed. Use these tools:

From Windows NT Server Installation

- Event Viewer
- Server Manager
- User Manager
- WINS Manager
- NBTSTAT
- PING
- IPCONFIG
- Network Monitor

From the *Microsoft Windows NT Server Resource Kit (Supplement 2)*

- SRVINFO
- NLTEST
- WINSCL

Recommendations Summary

What should be in this section:

A complete list of the recommendations that you have made during the audit process. This will give your team a clear list of action items.

Sample Exchange and Windows NT Backup Schedules

Windows NT Backup Schedule Sample

Type of backup	Day of week	Time of day
Incremental	Saturday	10:00 P.M.
Incremental	Sunday	10:00 P.M.
Incremental	Monday	10:00 P.M.
Incremental	Tuesday	10:00 P.M.
Incremental	Wednesday	10:00 P.M.
Incremental	Thursday	10:00 P.M.
Full	Friday	10:00 P.M.

Exchange Server Backup Schedule Sample

Type of backup	Day of week	Time of day
Incremental (log files)	Saturday	7:00 P.M.
Full (Exchange database)		
Incremental (log files)	Sunday	7:00 P.M.
Full (Exchange database)		
Incremental (log files)	Monday	7:00 P.M.
Full (Exchange database)		
Incremental (log files)	Tuesday	7:00 P.M.
Full (Exchange database)		
Incremental (log files)	Wednesday	7:00 P.M.
Full (Exchange database)		
Incremental (log files)	Thursday	7:00 P.M.
Full (Exchange database)		
Full backup (log files and Exchange database)	Friday	7:00 P.M.

CHAPTER 2

Messaging Operations and Administration

This chapter provides a framework for better Exchange system management through a better understanding of messaging operations within a large enterprise. This material also appears in the *Microsoft Exchange Server 5.5 Resource Guide*. It's included here to provide continuity in completing your handoff to the operations team.

It gives the messaging operations group useful guidelines on functions, staff, and utilities. Based on an assumption that system design, architecture, and deployment have been completed successfully, this document examines general areas of messaging operations in some depth. It concentrates on messaging operations in a large enterprise—a company with at least 20,000 messaging users distributed across multiple locations. Smaller organizations might also be able to use this information if they scale it down effectively.

These operations are discussed: internal and external messaging, server operations, system monitoring, first-, second-, and third-level support, daily operations, and escalation procedures.

Messaging Operations

This section offers a general discussion of messaging operations.

Departmental Staff

A typical messaging services department has a single director. The number and type of staff that report to the director vary widely, determined by the size of the enterprise messaging system and its number of users. This discussion considers an enterprise with 45,000 messaging system users and a single Microsoft Exchange system. A typical support department for this setup would have a director of messaging and two reporting managers: messaging operations and messaging system engineering.

Operations should handle the day-to-day supervision of the Exchange messaging system: monitoring, troubleshooting, and logging problems and procedures with the system. Reporting to the manager of messaging operations are messaging operations technicians and possibly a supervisor of network accounts. In some organizations, network accounts management falls in the network infrastructure department—which usually handles Windows NT account management—so the two groups should agree on and follow a single procedure for creating Exchange mailboxes.

Engineering requires enough staff to handle complex system problems (often escalated from operations) and the evaluation, measurement, and planning of forthcoming technologies. The engineering team should also measure system performance and plan enhancement.

A 45,000-user messaging system, monitored 24 hours a day, 7 days a week (24x7), would most likely have this staff:

Messaging Services Department Staff Organization

Director (1)

   Manager, messaging operations (1)

      Senior operations analyst (2)

         Associate operations analyst (0-1)

      Operations analyst (3)

         Technicians (17)

   Manager, messaging system engineering (1)

      Senior operations engineer (2)

         Associate operations engineer (0-1)

      Operations engineer (2)

Attract and keep good people at the operations analyst, senior operations analyst, operations engineer, and senior operations engineer positions, people who learn the company's network, business, and political infrastructure. A high rate of turnover or attrition in positions described below means more time spent training new staff and less time spent improving the messaging system.

Director Provides messaging technology vision based on technology capabilities and business need. Coordinates activities of messaging operations and engineering groups. Represents all aspects of the enterprise's messaging system to internal and external sources.

Manager, messaging operations Ensures that the messaging system is functioning at peak performance and, when performance declines, identifies the reason before users are affected. Ensures that all messaging operations technicians and operations analysts have the tools they need.

Manager, messaging system engineering Drives the team toward constant analysis and design with the goal of improving system performance. Ensures the team has all necessary tools and training to handle problems escalated from the operations group.

Associate operations analyst Installs, configures, and documents new production servers in the messaging environment. Performs rudimentary troubleshooting of messaging system problems.

Operations analyst Installs, configures, and documents new production servers in the messaging environment. Troubleshoots system problems and documents them in the system log.

Senior operations analyst Helps mentor new operations analysts and substitutes as operations analyst when required. Handles escalation issues not resolved by operations analyst and technicians. Ensures that the daily log is a useful repository of troubleshooting information.

Associate operations engineer Performs rudimentary analysis on input from operations group. Brings ideas and recommendations to other members of the engineering team for further discussion.

Operations engineer Performs detailed analysis on input from the operations group. Handles escalations from operations group, performs troubleshooting, and completes follow-up. Evaluates product features for inclusion in the messaging system.

Senior operations engineer Evaluates released and unreleased messaging systems. Provides detailed test plans for features to be implemented. Attempts to minimize impact of next generation releases of Exchange. Handles extreme escalations from Microsoft Technical Support and works with them when required.

Messaging operations technician Handles daily message system monitoring and reporting. Records events properly in the daily log, ensuring that all events that transpire during the shift are logged and reported to appropriate personnel. Handles escalation requests from the standard helpdesk department.

Monitoring

When To Watch

Most global enterprise messaging operations must be watched 24x7 for obvious reasons. National enterprises may be able to scale back the number of shifts or provide skeleton shifts for off-hours monitoring.

How To Watch (Methods)

This question also has many possible answers. Out-of-the-box utilities can be used to build a monitoring system. Also many third-party tools are being brought to market that allow monitoring of messaging systems, some of them outside the scope of this chapter.

For large messaging systems, set up some machines running Windows NT Server and instances of Performance Monitor (perfmon) that display statistics for each of the objects and counters mentioned below. Perfmon can consume a lot of screen space, so use large-screen (at least 17-inch) monitors. A basic Windows NT Server machine can be configured for these tasks. A good start on a monitoring computer is one with a single, fast-speed processor, 64 to 128 MB of RAM, 2 to 4 GB of disk space (sometimes used for storing log traces temporarily), and a large-screen monitor.

The monitoring area described above can fit in a 15-by-15-foot space. Typically, there are two messaging operations technicians at this monitoring station, one who can go to a server console if necessary. Configure perfmon instances with alerts that audibly or visually notify technicians when predefined thresholds are passed. Do not rely on a warning system that requires a technician to watch a set of screens.

What To Watch

Messaging operations involve making sure that messages are delivered to messaging system users within stated service levels. Typically, the most critical monitoring area is queue length on the message transfer agent (MTA) process machines. System problems usually manifest themselves in very lengthy message queues. What you watch depends on the functions performed by the Exchange server in question. Typically, in a large enterprise, Exchange servers take on specialized roles such as user mailbox server, public folder server, messaging hub, and Internet mail server. Perfmon application objects and counters recommended for monitoring are documented in the sections Blueprint for Regular Monitoring and Blueprint for Troubleshooting.

Acceptable Thresholds

Which perfmon thresholds are *acceptable* varies by company. Assess and document normal system usage, then establish a baseline against which to set threshold values.

Who Will Watch (Staffing)

To staff a monitoring area, you need people who are motivated to learn more but at the same time are happy to perform routine tasks such as checking current system status. This is the challenge of developing a good monitoring staff. Look for individuals who learn quickly, are amenable to shift work (first, second, and third for 24x7 monitoring), are good at following procedures, can see how to improve procedures, and have good communication skills. Technical expertise should be in Windows NT Server, Exchange Server architecture, and Exchange Client operation.

Metrics

What To Measure

Look for items that help you to tune system performance and develop trend data for capacity planning. Measure:

- Number of mailboxes
- Number of distribution lists
- Number of messages delivered per time period by destination area (such as over the Internet)

- Storage size by mailbox by department
- Greatest number of senders
- Greatest number of recipients
- Gateway/bridgehead traffic

Remember that measurements burden the system. Don't measure too many items or too frequently.

Acceptable Service Levels

To set acceptable service levels, you must first understand the message system's infrastructure. A company with a fiber optic network probably will have higher acceptable levels than a company with many dial-up links.

A typical service level statement, such as "Intra-company Exchange messages from one user to another will be delivered in X minutes or less," sets user expectations. This can help reduce support calls because it instructs users to wait X minutes (the acceptable service level) for a message to be delivered before assuming there is a problem.

Be conservative when stating service levels. Allow the operations group time to react to a problem. For example, if the network consists of very high bandwidth links that are rarely used above 35 percent, Exchange systems can be designed and implemented that deliver messages almost instantaneously anywhere. Even with this type of performance, however, avoid issuing service level statements saying, "…messages will be delivered in under 30 seconds." This does not allow staff enough time to identify a problem and react. Set the level at 10 minutes or less. As important as messaging is in today's enterprise, 10 minutes is still acceptable to users and allows monitoring staff to become aware of a problem and begin reacting to it.

The next section expands on the items presented so far, providing more detail where appropriate, especially on monitoring and troubleshooting.

Blueprint for Regular Monitoring

We have not yet attained that evolutionary stage where the data center contains nothing but machines running the business systems and other machines that oversee them as they do it. With a little work, however, you can reduce the amount of manual checking that occurs. This section of the chapter attempts to provide a generic Exchange daily operations guide.

Daily monitoring ensures that all critical Exchange Server services are running properly. The procedure is to check the performance of Exchange and other established monitors on a regular basis so that problems can be found and resolved or escalated to the next defined support level.

The messaging operations technician monitoring the system handles the phones and updates the messaging operations daily log. If a computer requires troubleshooting, the technician on duty dispatches another technician to handle it.

Frequency

Critical servers (mailbox and gateway/bridgehead) should be checked every 10 to 15 minutes. Other, less-critical servers can be checked every 30 to 45 minutes.

Reporting

All incidents must be documented. Reliable, thorough documentation grows into a knowledge base for your enterprise messaging system, one that support personnel can query to resolve problems quickly and without "reinventing the wheel."

The on-duty technicians should keep written records of any interaction with the servers—pertinent details, status/error messages, and observations.

Each day the daily log report should be sent to messaging operations staff and management or posted to a known site where it can be checked.

Methods

The tables that follow define the Performance Monitor setting for each type of Exchange Server in the enterprise.

Perfmon configuration for a standard mailbox server

Object	Counter	Scale	Instance
MSExchangeMTA	Work Queue Length	1.0	N/A
Processor	%Processor Time	1.0	0 (,1,2, 3 if multi-proc)
Process	%Processor Time	1.0	MAD
Process	%Processor Time	1.0	DSAMAIN
Process	%Processor Time	1.0	STORE
Process	%Processor Time	1.0	EMSMTA

Chart settings: Update interval = 120 seconds, Vertical maximum = 100, Chart type = Histogram.

Perfmon configuration for an Internet Mail Server

Object	Counter	Scale	Instance
MSExchangeMTA	Work Queue Length	1.0	N/A
Processor	%Processor Time	1.0	0 (,1,2, 3 if multi-proc)
Process	%Processor Time	1.0	MAD
Process	%Processor Time	1.0	DSAMAIN
Process	%Processor Time	1.0	STORE
Process	%Processor Time	1.0	EMSMTA
Process	%Processor Time	1.0	MSEXCIMC
MSExchangeIMC	Queued Inbound	1.0	MSExchangeIMC
MSExchangeIMC	Queued Outbound	1.0	MSExchangeIMC
MSExchangeIMC	Queued MTS-IN	1.0	MSExchangeIMC
MSExchangeIMC	Queued MTS-OUT	1.0	MSExchangeIMC
MSExchangeMTA Connections	Queue Length	1.0	Internet Mail Service Server

Chart settings: Update interval = 120 seconds, Vertical maximum = 300, Chart type = Histogram.

Perfmon configuration for a bridgehead server

Object	Counter	Scale	Instance
MSExchangeMTA	Work Queue Length	1.0	N/A

Chart settings: Update interval = 120 seconds, Vertical maximum = 100, Chart type = Histogram.

Expected Server Behavior

The following descriptions are based on a large, complex enterprise messaging system with over 45,000 messaging system users. Results can vary widely in different environments, and the descriptions are offered as probabilities, not inviolable rules. Results are affected by many variables such as network infrastructure, messaging system user profiles (light, medium, or heavy user), and Exchange system architecture.

- **MSExchangeMTA, Work Queue Length**—The level should rise and fall in an acceptable range of 0 to 50. When messages are stuck in the queue, the counter does not change or stays above the upper range. Watch for "artificial floors" on the MTA queue, a state wherein work queue length remains at or above a non-zero integer. This can mean that the queues contain corrupt or stuck messages or that messages have been sent with the deferred delivery option in Exchange clients.

- **MSExchangeMTA, Messages Delivered per Minute**—This counter measures the rate of the number of messages being delivered by the MTA to the information store. Normal load is 10 to 40 messages per minute. If this number is constantly under 5 per minute when pending items are in the MTA queue, it is likely that the server is under severe load or one of the processes has a problem. If this number is extraordinarily high (greater than 200 per minute) for an extended amount of time, it is likely that a message is stuck in the MTA queue.

- **Exchange Services Processes**—This is the object: Process, Counter: % Processor time, Instances: DSAMAIN, EMSMTA, MAD, and STORE. No object should be at 0 or at 100 percent *all* of the time. An object always at 0 percent indicates a "dead" process. Check service control manager to verify that the service is running. An object always at 100 percent usually indicates that something is out of order. Check other services and the event viewer to find out what.

- **Paging File, % Usage**—Make certain that the usage is in a reasonable range, generally 15 to 35 percent. When usage exceeds 60 percent, usually something is wrong. If the usage constantly exceeds 90 percent, there is a problem with one of the processes, the server needs a RAM upgrade, or the paging file was incorrectly allocated during setup.

- **LogicalDisk, Free Megabytes, Instance: E**—This is the amount of free space on the transaction log drive. Monitor this object to ensure that the drive does not fill up with .LOG files. Normally, the .LOG files are removed whenever an online backup is performed. If the .LOG files are not being removed, verify that the backups are being done correctly and completed successfully (see the section Exchange Backup under Exchange Maintenance later in this chapter).

- **MSExchangeIS, Active Connection Count**—This measures the number of logons to the store service and should be greater than zero. If the server has active mailboxes and zero connections, there is a problem. Use a test account to see if you can connect to the server.

- **MSExhangeDS, Pending Replications**—This measures the number of replication objects yet to be processed.

- **MSExchangeDS, Remaining Replication Updates**—This measures the number of objects being processed by the directory service. This number usually starts at 100 and decreases to 0 within 1 to 3 minutes.

Blueprint for Troubleshooting

User Notifications

Before taking any action that can cause a long-term interruption in service, attempt to inform users of the problem and that it is being worked on. Update the daily log and any other applicable status applications.

If the affected server still can send messages to mailboxes, use an announcements-type mailbox or the server's test mailbox to send the message. Name the mailbox something like "Messaging operations" so that users read the message.

Performance Monitor Counter Configurations

The perfmon counter configurations described in the previous section are for normal operating conditions. When monitors detect an anomaly in the messaging system, you must "focus" monitoring on the problem servers. These more focused perfmon configurations are described in the following tables. Run these instances of perfmon on any server where you suspect a problem because the added detail is useful in troubleshooting. Do not run them constantly because they increase system load. These secondary monitors are intended to chart items that change over time until the trouble has passed.

Perfmon configuration for detailed, secondary monitoring for all server types

Object	Counter	Scale	Instance
Processor	%Processor Time	1.0	0 (,1,2, 3 if multi-proc)
Process	%Processor Time	1.0	MAD
Process	%Processor Time	1.0	DSAMAIN
Process	%Processor Time	1.0	STORE
Process	%Processor Time	1.0	EMSMTA
MSExchangeMTA	Work Queue Length	1.0	N/A
MSExchangeIS Private	Messages Delivered/Minute	1.0	N/A
MSExchangeIS Private	Messages Sent/ Minute	1.0	N/A
MSExchangeDS	Pending Replication Synchronizations	1.0	N/A
MSExchangeDS	Remaining Replication Updates	1.0	N/A
MSExchangeMTA	Messages / Sec	10	N/A

Chart settings: Update interval = 5 seconds, Vertical maximum = 100, Chart type = Graph.

Secondary perfmon configuration for Internet Mail Service servers

Object	Counter	Scale	Instance
Process	%Processor Time	1.0	MSEXCIMC
MSExchangeIMC	Queued Inbound	1.0	MSExchangeIMC
MSExchangeIMC	Queued Outbound	1.0	MSExchangeIMC
MSExchangeIMC	Queued MTS-IN	1.0	MSExchangeIMC
MSExchangeIMC	Queued MTS-OUT	1.0	MSExchangeIMC
MSExchangeMTA Connections	Queue Length	1.0	Internet Mail Service Server

Chart settings: Update interval = 5 seconds, Vertical maximum = 100, Chart type = Graph.

Exchange Services

Although Exchange services are set to start up automatically when the server is rebooted, there will be times when you need to start them manually.

Service Start Order

The startup order for the Exchange services is:

1. System attendant
2. Directory
3. Information store
4. Message Transfer Agent
5. Event Service
6. Internet Mail Service
7. Key Management server

Service Dependencies

Because there are dependencies between services, starting a service that depends on a second service will start the needed services. For example, if the information store is requested to start before the system attendant and the directory, the Windows NT service manager will start the system attendant and the directory.

The Exchange dependencies are:

- Directory service depends on the system attendant.
- Information store depends on the directory service and system attendant.
- Event service depends on the directory service and information store.

- Messaging transfer agent depends on the directory service and system attendant.

- Internet Mail Service depends on the system attendant, directory service, information store, and messaging transfer agent.

Service Start Application Log Events

Each service logs an event to the application log when startup has completed.

Service start application log events

Service	Event source	Event number
System attendant	MSExchangeSA	1000
Directory	MSExchangeDS	1000
Message transfer agent	MSExchangeMTA	9298
Information store	MSExchangeIS Public	1001
Information store	MSExchangeIS Private	1001
Internet Mail Service	MSExchangeIMC	1000
Key Management server	MSExchangeKMS	1001

Starting and Stopping Exchange Services

If you must shut down a server and restart it, stop the system as cleanly as possible and inform users that mail may not be accessible while the problem is being resolved.

This section refers to Exchange services in several ways. For example, the Microsoft Exchange information store is also called the "Store" and "MSExchangeIS." Here are the various names for each of the Exchange Server services:

Exchange Server service common names

Name source	Name
Service Control Manager Name	Microsoft Exchange system attendant
Command Line Name	MSExchangeSA
Other	SA or MAD
Location	D:\EXCHSRVR\BIN\MAD.EXE
Service Control Manager Name	Microsoft Exchange directory
Command Line Name	MSExchangeDS
Other	Directory
Location	D:\EXCHSRVR\BIN\DSAMAIN.EXE

Name source	Name
Service Control Manager Name	Microsoft Exchange information store
Command Line Name	MSExchangeIS
Other	Store or MDB
Location	D:\EXCHSRVR\BIN\STORE.EXE
Service Control Manager Name	Microsoft Exchange message transfer agent
Command Line Name	MSExchangeMTA
Other	MTA
Location	D:\EXCHSRVR\BIN\EMSMTA.EXE
Service Control Manager Name	Microsoft Exchange Internet Mail Service
Command Line Name	MSExchangeIMC
Other	SMTP Gateway
Location	D:\EXCHSRVR\CONNECT\MSEXCIMC\BIN\MSEXCIMC.EXE
Service Control Manager Name	Microsoft Exchange event service
Command Line Name	MSExchangeES
Other	Event Script Service
Location	D:\EXCHSRVR\BIN\EVENTS.EXE
Service Control Manager Name	Microsoft Exchange Key Management server
Command Line Name	MSExchangeKMS
Other	KM service or security service
Location	D:\SECURITY\BIN\KMSERVER.EXE
Service Control Manager Name	KeyToken
Command Line Name	KeyToken
Other	Token
Location	D:\KEYTOKEN\KEYTOKEN.EXE

The system attendant, directory service, information store, and MTA are commonly referred to as the "Core Four."

Built-in Recovery

The directory, information store, and MTA all have built-in startup recovery methods that are automatically invoked if the service does not stop cleanly.

The directory and information store both go through JET recovery, which replays the last transactions against the database if the database is not synchronized with the transaction logs. It normally takes 3 to 5 minutes to replay a 5-MB log file.

Not all of the transaction logs are replayed, only those that haven't been flushed to the database.

If the MTA service does not stop cleanly, it performs an MTACheck at startup that checks and repairs the MTA database files, which are the DB*.DAT files in D:\EXCHSRVR\MTADATA.

The application event log shows when a component goes into recovery mode.

JET Recovery Event Log

- EDB #18: JET recovery started.
- EDB #71: Logged for each file replayed by the recovery.

MTACheck Event Log

- MSExchangeMTA/Field Engineering #2119: MTACheck start.
- MSExchangeMTA/Field Engineering #2206: Once for each internal MTA queue checked. The MTA queues are:
  - XAPIWRKQ
  - OOFINFOQ
  - REFDATQ
  - MTAWORKQ
- MSExchangeMTA/Field Engineering #2207: MTACheck completed.

The MTACheck will save the process results in the file D:\EXCHSRVR\MTADATA\MTACHEK.OUT\MTACHECK.LOG.

It can take from a few minutes to a few hours to run the MTACheck, depending on the number of files in the MTADATA directory.

You can run the MTACheck manually, but not remotely. It must be run from a console command prompt. The syntax for MTACheck is:

D:\EXCHSRVR\BIN\MTACHECK /v /f *logfilename*.**LOG**

where **logfilename** is the name of the file you want to create (for example, 032296a.log).

Special Components

Some sites in an Exchange environment have the Key Management component installed. Although the service is set to **automatic,** it is necessary to verify the service has started. For security purposes, the Key Management (KM) service requires that the KM diskette be inserted in the floppy disk drive for the KM service to start properly.

Stopping Exchange Services

Before rebooting a server, stop Exchange services to help ensure a clean stop of the Exchange databases.

If the system is in a controllable state, *manually* stop *each* Exchange service before issuing the **Shutdown** and **Restart** command. Stopping them one by one greatly improves the chances of restarting the server successfully and makes it easier to determine where a problem originated if a service cannot be controlled. It is easy to create a command file, say STOPEXCHANGE.CMD, that contains the necessary NET STOP *<service name>* commands to completely stop all Exchange Server services. For example, to stop the four basic Exchange Server services, use the following four lines in a .CMD or .BAT file (not case sensitive):

```
Net stop MSExchangeMTA
Net stop MSExchangeIS
Net stop MSExchangeDS
Net stop MSExchangeSA
```

Be patient when stopping services. If a service has been running for a long time, it may take a long time to stop. This is especially true of the information store and directory, which must flush transactions to the database and close threads when the services are stopped. For example, a directory on a new server may take 10 to 15 minutes to stop.

Use performance monitor to verify the service being stopped is still attempting to stop. If the process time for the service drops and stays at zero, it is very likely the service is in an uncontrollable state.

Service Start Failures

If a service will not start, troubleshooting is required. First, determine which service is not starting. Use **Control Panel** and click **Services** or **Net Start** to show the active services:

Control Panel and **Services** shows only completely started processes.

Control Panel and **Net Start** shows all completely started processes and any process attempting to start.

Always check the application event log for errors. Any service failure should log at least one event, which provides a starting point for troubleshooting.

Validated Permissions

Each of the Exchange services requires network connectivity to start. The account being used to start the service is validated for each service startup.

Information Store and Directory Service

If the information store or directory service is the problem, check to see if they are in a state of recovery, which can take from 5 to 50 minutes, depending on the number of .LOG files. Check the event viewer to verify that recovery is taking place.

System Attendant

If the system attendant will not start, something is fundamentally wrong with the computer. Check the event viewer to ensure that the network and related services are not causing problems. The network-related services must be running before system attendant will start.

MTA

Most of the problems that cause MTA to fail to start are related to the contents of a message. If MTA will not start, try stopping the information store prior to starting the MTA. If the MTA then starts, start the information store and monitor the server. Always check the event viewer to get additional information. If there is a problem with one of the files in the MTA database, an entry will be made in the application log. It could be necessary to remove a file from the database if it is causing problems.

If the MTA doesn't communicate with adjacent MTAs, wait at least 10 minutes. The MTA is designed to reset the association and retry the connection after 10 minutes. Stopping and starting an adjacent MTA might cause the process to "wake up" and recognize that the restarted server is available.

If the MTA service starts but messages remain in the work queue, use perfmon or the Exchange Server Administrator program to determine the destination. This will provide the information you need to continue troubleshooting.

Internet Mail Service

If Internet Mail Service fails to start, check the HOSTS file. The Internet Mail Service server must know each target server. The hosts file is C:\WINNT\SYSTEM32\CONFIG\ETC\HOSTS. If you are using Domain Name Service (DNS) for your Internet Mail Service name resolution, use a command prompt and the NSLOOKUP TCP/IP utility to determine if you are having DNS problems. More documentation of the NSLOOKUP command can be found by typing **NSLOOKUP**, waiting for the ">" NSLOOKUP prompt, then typing **help**.

Last Resort

Be sure to try starting the service several times before giving up. Sometimes it helps to wait a few minutes before starting a service. This is especially true if a service depends on another service. Check to make sure that the dependent service is fully started.

Booting the server can be useful. Sometimes the machine is simply in a state that requires a reboot. Programs and subsystems may require cleanup that only a restart will fix.

If all else fails, run the service as an application. Many times this will work. Although it isn't a perfect solution, it is an acceptable short-term workaround and usually provides more detailed error reporting. Run it this way only until the service start problem is resolved.

Service names and binaries locations

Service name	Executable
System attendant	D:\EXCHSRVR\BIN\MAD.EXE
Directory	D:\EXCHSRVR\BIN\DSAMAIN.EXE
Information store	D:\EXCHSRVR\BIN\STORE.EXE
Message transfer agent	D:\EXCHSRVR\BIN\EMSMTA.EXE
Internet Mail Service	D:\EXCHANGE\CONNECT\MSEXCIMC\BIN\MSEXCIMC.EXE
Key Management server	D:\SECURITY\BIN\KMSERVER.EXE

Service Stop Failures

If a service is in an uncontrollable state, the process must be terminated before the service can be brought online.

If a service stop is aborted, it will leave the service in an unknown state. Use SRVINFO and the event application log to verify the state of a service.

To force a process to terminate, use KILL.EXE or PVIEW.EXE. Both of these work only at the console, but KILL.EXE is a character-based application and can be used in an RPROMPT session.

KILLing Services

Before KILLing a service, check perfmon and the event viewer for additional information. If the service shows some activity for the service being stopped, it may just be a matter of time before the service stops. If the perfmon shows zero activity for a period of time (say 10 minutes), the service is most likely uncontrollable.

By stopping the uncontrollable process, it *may* be possible to cleanly stop the other services.

If the KILL utility is used against the information store or directory, JET recovery will occur when the service is started. Monitor the event viewer and perfmon when such a situation occurs.

Killing the MTA forces the service to run a MTACheck at the next service start.

When using the KILL utility, it's easiest to specify the service by using its .EXE name. It is also possible to KILL the process based on the process ID. The process ID is assigned by Windows NT and isn't a fixed identifier. TLIST.EXE shows each process and its process ID.

Services and their process names

Service name	Process name
System attendant	MAD.EXE
Directory	DSAMAIN.EXE
Information store	STORE.EXE
Message Transfer Agent	EMSMTA.EXE
Internet Mail Service	MSEXCIMC.EXE
Key Management server	KMSERVER.EXE

Verifying Active Processes

Use TLIST.EXE to verify the process has been successfully terminated. If it is still active, try KILL.EXE a couple more times. Always give the server a couple of minutes to terminate a process.

TLIST.EXE is a character-based application and can be used in an RPROMPT sessions. TLIST.EXE is a utility on the *Microsoft Windows NT Server Resource Kit.*

Sample TLIST Output

```
c:\winnt\system32>tlist
0 System Process
    2 System
   30 smss.exe
   44 csrss.exe
   36 winlogon.exe          Winlogon generic control dialog
   50 services.exe
   53 lsass.exe
   77 spoolss.exe
  113 benser.exe
  120 beserver.exe
  137 LOCATOR.EXE
  148 RpcSs.exe
  151 AtSvc.Exe
  157 snmp.exe
  164 SYSDOWN.EXE
  176 CPQMGMT.EXE
  180 MAD.EXE
  186 NetIQmc.exe
  127 dsamain.exe
  278 store.exe
  286 emsmta.exe
  363 metrics.exe
  540 logon.scr             Screen Saver
  501 rprompt.exe
  499 remote.exe
  333 cmd.exe
  313 TLIST.EXE
```

When the process cannot be terminated, the server must be rebooted.

Location: Utilities

KILL.EXE, TLIST.EXE, and PVIEW.EXE are found in the *Microsoft Windows NT Server Resource Kit.*

Testing and Monitoring

If a server is having problems that require the services to be cycled, continue to monitor the service after it is online. Problems sometime will recur, especially MTA and information store problems.

If it is undetermined if the server is behaving normally, log on using the server's test account and send some test messages. Verify with the target recipient that the test messages have been received.

Sending messages between the test mailboxes using delivery receipts is a useful way of verifying server-to-server communications.

Exchange Maintenance

Exchange Backup

Back up the Exchange databases regularly. The recommended frequency is a weekly full backup and a daily incremental or differential backup. Backups affect server performance, so do them during times of moderate to low load.

An online backup (with the Exchange services running) makes a copy of the databases and purges any unneeded transaction logs.

Without backups, there is no way to recover from a database failure. If the transaction log drives are using the recommended setting (circular logging disabled), they will eventually fill with transaction logs. They will not fill up if circular logging is enabled.

Backup Methods

The actual files backed up by an online backup depend on the type of backup selected. A **Normal** backup method is the default setting.

Backup methods summary

Backup methods	Description
Normal	Copies the databases and uncommitted .LOG files to tape. Purges committed .LOG files.
Copy	Copies databases to tape.
Incremental	Copies committed .LOG files to tape. Purges committed .LOG files.
Differential	Copies committed .LOG files to tape.

Normal Backup

When a **Normal** or **Copy** backup is performed, the Exchange directory database (DIR.EDB), the Exchange information store databases (PRIV.EDB and PUB.EDB), and any needed .LOG files are copied to the tape.

While backup is taking place, new database changes can occur so JET maintains a "patch" file that logs these latest changes. The patch file is backed up at the end of the process along with the transaction log files.

At the conclusion of the backup, any unneeded .LOG files are purged.

The **Normal** method has all of the latest data on the tape but is time consuming. It backs up the entire database, so it can take a considerable time to complete.

Copy Backup

A **Copy** backup creates a mirror image of the databases and all associated database .LOG files. It does not purge the .LOG files.

Incremental Backup

An **Incremental** backup backs up only the transaction .LOG files, not the databases themselves. The committed .LOG files that JET no longer needs are purged. To restore from incremental backups, you need the most recent **Full** backup tape and all incremental tapes up to the restore date.

Differential Backup

A **Differential** backup backs up only the transaction .LOG files but the committed .LOG files are not purged at the end of the process. To restore, you need only the **Full** backup tape and the latest differential tape.

Services Required for Backup

To back up an Exchange Server, the directory *and* the information store services must both be running on the server. If one of the services is not running or is unresponsive, the backup fails.

Permissions Required for Backup

To do a backup, only Backup Operator permissions are required. However, to log on to the console, Server Operator permissions or better are needed. NTBackup uses the permissions of the current logon to do the backup. Third-party backup utilities run as Windows NT services that get their permissions from their service startup parameters—typically these are set to the Exchange service account.

NTBackup

Exchange Server includes a modified version of NTBACKUP.EXE. The standard NTBACKUP handles only Windows NT files. The Exchange version is aware of the Exchange organization and database components (the directory and information store).

Exchange Restore

In the event of a major catastrophe, it may be required that Exchange databases be restored from tape. Two scenarios require restoring the information store and directory: if the Windows NT Server crashes and has to be rebuilt from the ground up or if the information store or directory becomes corrupt beyond repair or recovery.

Individual mailbox restoration on Exchange Server can be a long and arduous process that requires extra hardware and staff-hours. You must set a policy for individual mailbox restoration or you may be totally overwhelmed performing mailbox restores.

The Exchange client and Outlook client provide several options to guard against accidentally deleting messages. By using the deleted items folder and either emptying it manually or only when the client is closed, users can protect themselves from simple mistakes.

With Exchange Server 5.5, users and administrators can take advantage of a feature called Deleted Items Retention. This allows administrators to configure public and private information stores to retain deleted items in a special reserve. With Outlook version 8.03 (or 8.0, 8.01, or 8.02 with the proper client extension installed), end users can retrieve items that they have deleted over a certain number of days (configured by administrators). This feature can serve as a simple, non-negotiable restoration policy. Deleted items are retained for, say, three days, then purged from the system. Of course, you can make exceptions for the occasional corporate officer whose mail gets accidentally deleted.

Other successful enterprise messaging services departments have implemented a standard chargeback to departments requesting individual mailbox restorations. These charges range from $100 to $250 for each mailbox restored.

Developing a Messaging Operations Toolkit

One of the common threads that runs through all successful messaging operations departments is the ongoing development of a messaging operations toolkit.

Follow simple guidelines when developing a toolbox. First, make sure you *need* a tool. Often people try to develop tools that come with Exchange. Second, if Exchange does not supply it, look in the resource kit or for third-party solutions. Many times, resource kit utilities coupled with third-party utilities can be used to build a comprehensive tool set. If you simply can't find the functionality you need, develop the tool yourself.

Daily Log

As part of your messaging operations toolkit, develop a method by which your operations staff can report events and procedure outcomes. The daily log becomes the repository for knowledge about your messaging system. Over time, if it is added to diligently, it becomes a knowledge base that less experienced users can query when troubleshooting.

If it is to serve these purposes, the daily log should have these characteristics: it should be easily accessible from any desktop system, it should have adequate storage capacity for growth, it should enable users to generate reports of daily log activity, and it should be easily searchable using text strings as search criteria.

Solutions in use at successful enterprise messaging operations centers include Web-based entry and searching systems, and Exchange electronic form-based implementations. In either case, the backend database and its design and maintenance will make or break the daily log system. If you don't index the database properly or keep its record count manageable, you will find no shortage of complaints when messaging operations staff look in it for troubleshooting information.

Web-based implementations have an advantage over other implementations in that few (or no) client configuration changes need be addressed. A URL link is given to users of the system, and the Web server handles data presentation. Other implementations, especially those based on electronic forms, require logging on to the computer being used and creating a messaging profile for access to the appropriate public folder or forms library on the Exchange backend. These steps are sometimes enough to discourage use of any daily log system. Ease of use and access is key to successful daily log systems. The daily log system should be as easy to use as a notebook and pen for recording events. This helps ensure that people will use it frequently and correctly.

Checking

The daily log system is a useful repository of the performance of your enterprise messaging system. In addition to performance data, the daily log can be used to establish problem resolution times and audit trails for verification of service level agreements.

All messaging operations technicians should check the daily log, particularly at the beginning of shifts, to learn about the events of the preceding shift. Methods for checking the daily log vary, but common ones are reports generated by an automated process and a simple, Web-based query interface to the daily log database.

Report Distribution

A daily log report that shows all log entries for a given day should be distributed to messaging operations management and engineering, with event and procedure severity levels clearly indicated so as to elicit appropriate response. Messaging operations engineering can assist with those issues that require escalation out of the messaging operations regular staff.

The most effective report distribution media is e-mail, but e-mail, of course, may go down. If the messaging system is not working, no one receives the daily log reports to notify upper level messaging operations personnel of problems. If the messaging system has been down for a while, then upper and lower levels already know about it and the daily log report is most likely extraneous. The daily log report is a method for messaging operations management to know what is happening in their system during regular operations.

Incident Reporting

The details of each server incident should be recorded in the daily log system. Each incident should include the date, time, operator's user ID, and a brief, but effective description of the incident. If any error messages were encountered, be sure to include them in the details section.

It is best if incidents are reported as they happen. However, this is not always possible if numerous problems are occurring in parallel. At a minimum, all messaging operations operators should record dates and times of incidents and transfer them to the daily log when time permits but no later than the end of their shift. Here's a sample:

```
[public]
Severity B
joeuser
Location
14 Mar 1997
14:25:33
MSG-33 Message transfer agent (MTA) service stopped unexpectedly.
Running MTACHECK. ETA to normal service is 14:45:00. Users should be OK
to log in and send mail. Delivery times to other destination servers may
be negatively impacted.
```

This is succinct, yet informative. The technician has documented a relatively severe ("A" being the highest) event by telling what happened, what is being done to rectify it, an ETA to normal service, and what the end-user community will experience.

Descriptions of Useful Utilities

Any successful messaging services department will develop any number of utilities for making operations easier. Typically, a product is not produced to satisfy the great number of needs of differing environments right out of the box. Subsequently, implementers of technologies will build supplemental tools and utilities for making the product that much more effective. Below are some descriptions of tools and utilities that can be developed if the need arises. Remember that some of the listed utilities are provided out of the box by Exchange Server.

Mailboxes

In most Exchange Server implementations, the mailbox object is both the most numerous and most critical, so you must be able to address needs and problems with mailboxes quickly and efficiently. The Exchange Administrator program covers most issues you are likely to encounter. Where Exchange Administrator does not, these tools are recommended:

> **Intersite Move utility**—In larger enterprises that implement Exchange in a multi-site configuration, when users move across site boundaries, it is not a simple matter to move that user's mailbox directory information and mailbox contents. Procedures should be defined that efficiently move user information and mailbox content data to the destination. This requires that end users take on some responsibility, storing mailbox contents in personal folders prior to the move and restoring the contents from the personal folders after the move. After mailbox contents have been stored in the personal folders, export the user data to a file using the directory export tool (part of ADMIN.EXE), remove the mailbox from the local site, and change the file that was exported to reflect the new site location. If necessary, you can then import the mailbox into the new site. After completion, users move any mailbox contents back to the new home server if they want to store them there. The *Microsoft BackOffice Resource Kit* has some utilities that automate much of this process.

Distributions Lists

Forms- or Web-based Distribution List Update utility In many large enterprise Exchange implementations, the number of distribution lists (DLs) often rivals that of the number of mailboxes. It is imperative that the messaging services department provide management in this area. There should be an easy-to-use, low-administrator intervention method for DL creation and modification.

DL Membership Display tool   Do you need a quick way to view the membership of a DL? A command line utility negates the need to run the administrator graphical user interface (GUI) tool.

Standard DL Build tool   Many enterprises maintain generic DLs such as Everyone, Accounting–All, and Corporate Campus. It can be very useful to have a tool that builds DLs based on user attributes, such as location or building name, while keeping generic distribution lists in a state of high integrity. This is important when blanket messages are sent out by executives. Make sure the Exchange directory contains accurate user information if you want to use tools that build DLs automatically.

Distribution List Update tool   A good DL update tool offloads a significant amount of the messaging system support burden.

Public Folders

Public Folder Ownership Fix tool   In many large enterprise Exchange implementations, the ownership and responsibility for public folders is delegated to the requester of the public folder. Ownership of public folders in Exchange Server takes the form of an entry from the global address list (GAL). In addition to the requester of the public folder, you should consider adding a second owner of the public folder—a global public folder administrator group. This group is a distribution list in your GAL, and by adding it as an owner of a requested public folder, you can track the status messages on the public folders. Now, the original public folder requester/owner has the ability and permissions to remove the public folder global administrator group from public folder owners' property. It is recommended that you develop a tool to reset this ownership and/or add the public folder global administrator group to those public folders from which the group has been removed.

Public Folder Reporting tool   Tracking public folder usage is important for numerous reasons such as capacity planning and successful load leveling across servers. Here are some items to watch:

- Search for all public folders owned by a given user or having other attributes, such as what forms are in the folder library and so on.
- Report of public information store database growth over a time period.
- Replication volume, by folder and time period.

- Folder owner report and query tool.
- Disk space used by the public folders or hierarchy.
- Report of access to public folders by user. Useful for determining when to replicate a public folder to a remote location to conserve WAN bandwidth.
- Report, by folder, of number of new postings and breakdown of post type (normal, attachments, forms, and so on).
- Report, by server, of number of new folders created.
- Report, by folder or tree of folders, of number of messages and total KB used.
- Report, by folder, of number of accesses per time period.
- Report and query of last access date and time, showing all folders not accessed in the last month.
- Report and query of the last date and time a folder had items posted in it, searchable as above.
- Security auditing tool to find all folders that have forwarding rules installed. This allows you to keep an eye on what messages go out on the Internet.

CHAPTER 3

Calculating Users Per Server

How many users can a single Exchange server host? This seemingly simple —and frequently asked—question is in reality complicated because there are so many reasons for asking it. Some administrators ask it because they have already invested in server hardware and need to evaluate current capacity; others, because they need information on which to base purchasing decisions and plan future growth and capacity. A number of users per server that works for administrative reasons might not suit server bandwidth restrictions, or one that works with available bandwidth might make backups too time consuming. And on and on.

The first half of this chapter discusses the performance issues that can help you answer this important question. The second half makes specific recommendations for planning an Exchange Server rollout and scaling it for increasing capacity.

Defining the Context of Capacity Planning

One difficulty inherent in this question lies in the basic units used to frame it: *user* and *server*. *Users* vary widely in their messaging, scheduling, and workgroup application usage, depending on how much they use e-mail, calendar, and public folder applications for business and personal activities. Your organization's corporate culture and geographical distribution of offices also affects the messaging system. Some users receive hundreds of messages each day; others, only one or two. Some users generate 50 messages a day; others, only a few per week. In any given organization, a small percentage of the users account for a disproportionate amount of the total server load.

Servers vary widely as well. Some organizations with large, centrally located or well-connected sites use a small number of high-end, multiprocessor computers with several gigabytes of RAM and dozens of disk drives. These servers host as many users per server as possible. Other organizations deploy hundreds of inexpensive, lower-end servers to connect many small, geographically-dispersed sites. Or an organization might consist of remote sites, varying in size and connection speeds, each with different server and end-user capacity requirements.

The only thing true for all organizations is this: they all want the most out of their messaging system in terms of hardware, maintenance and administration costs, and capacity.

Messaging Activity

To determine the number of users a server can support, you need to evaluate the two types of load that users place on the server: *user-initiated actions* and *background actions.*

User-Initiated Actions

User-initiated actions are messaging operations the server performs as a result of user activity, and they seem (or should seem) instantaneous from the user's point of view. When users open an unread message in their private folder in the server information store, the server performs these synchronous actions:

- Receives and interprets the open request

- Evaluates any access restrictions

- Retrieves the message from the database

- Marks the message as unread

- Updates the unread message count for the folder

- Marshals and returns the requested message properties to the client

- Generates a folder notification to the client, signaling that the message has been read

All of this happens in the time it takes for the remote procedure call (RPC) issued by the client application to return control to the client. From the user perspective, the entire action also includes additional client processing time required to draw the window and display the message properties. User-initiated activity accounts for the most significant load factor on Exchange servers that directly support users (versus servers that function as the backbone or gateways). User load is determined by the number of users actively using the messaging system per unit time and the kinds of actions they perform.

Background Actions

Exchange Server also performs background (or asynchronous) actions for connected and remote users: accepting, transferring, routing, and delivering messages; expanding distribution lists; replicating public folders changes and directory service information; executing rules; monitoring storage quotas, and performing background maintenance such as tombstone garbage collection (also known as online database defragmentation) and view index expiration. As long as these actions are completed within reasonable time limits, they do not affect users' perception of system speed.

Background load is also determined by the number of users on the server. In systems with many users, Exchange servers that function as gateways or intersite connectors can experience heavy background activity. However, if these servers do not directly host any users, they will not experience user-initiated activity loads.

Inequality of Actions

To model the load these actions put on the Exchange server, some administrators conveniently consider all user-initiated actions as equivalent and all background actions as equivalent. This is certainly not the case. Users copying a 500-KB message to their personal information store place more load on the server than users copying a 1-KB message. Sending an e-mail to a distribution list with 100 members creates more background activity than sending the message to a single recipient.

You can predict server load better if you look at combined activity over time. Examine the activity of a particular user group during a time period (say, a typical 8-hour work day), and add up its user-initiated actions (interaction with the server to send or read messages, look up recipients in the address book, and so forth). Measure its related background actions. Classify the user group's activity level relative to other groups. You can use this data to characterize user groups by the number of actions they perform per unit time and the server load characteristics (such as messages size) of those actions. This is what you need to predict system performance for various user communities.

Here's an example classification from the Exchange Performance team for low, medium, and heavy usage:

- On a daily average, a *low usage* user:
    - Sends 3 messages
    - Reads 5 new messages and 12 old ones
    - Makes 1 schedule change
- A medium usage user:
    - Sends 6 messages
    - Reads 15 new messages and 12 old ones
    - Makes 5 schedule changes
- A heavy usage user:
    - Sends 8 messages
    - Reads 20 new messages and 12 old ones
    - Makes 10 schedule changes

How heavily your organization depends on messaging for business communications has an impact on Exchange Server performance and the number of users that a server can host. Some companies, like Microsoft, run most communications through the messaging system, creating heavy usage. The same hardware performing the same functions can host 500 light users but only 150 heavy ones.

Server Load and Response Time

A server's hardware resources include one or more CPUs, primary memory (RAM), and one or more disk drives and their controllers (the I/O subsystem). To carry out user-initiated or background actions, Exchange Server uses these three resources to varying degrees. Performing a client open-message request requires several milliseconds of CPU processing time, one or more disk accesses, and enough memory to hold the code and data necessary to perform the operation. When each user-initiated action completes before the next starts, the server dedicates 100 percent of its hardware to each action, completing it as fast as possible with no wait for available resources and essentially idling between actions. Users enjoy minimal server and network response times. The server is *unloaded*.

When many users initiate actions close together in time or many background events occur, actions compete for server hardware resources, creating bottlenecks. The code that performs an action has to wait for available hardware. When the server is *under load*, actions can take longer to complete and users experience slower response times.

The relationship between load and response time determines the number of users a server can support. As the load on a server increases, the response times users experience change at some point from acceptable to unacceptable. You need to estimate where this crossover point falls for your organization.

Activity that causes load is not evenly distributed over time. Workday morning hours can generate the highest load as users spend time responding to e-mail or reading public folder information that arrived from the previous day. Lunch-time, evenings, and weekends experience lulls in messaging activity. Even if you ignore variations at this level and assume fairly uniform usage intervals, loads still vary over time because of individual differences in usage level and schedule.

Think of user-initiated actions as *quantum events*, which gather user load and evenly distribute it over time. For instance, most servers experiences bursts of activity at the beginning of the workday as users on the same server download new messages. If most of these users immediately read through their new messages, they cause another burst of activity. When an Exchange server hosts enough users, the *quantum effects* of individual usage patterns, schedules, and habits average out and should not represent a large percentage of the total user load on the server except in extreme situations.

Factors Affecting Performance

Hardware Resources: CPU, Memory, I/O Subsystem, Network Cards

The type and number of CPUs in a server dictate the performance potential for an Exchange Server environment. Computers based on the Pentium II processor offer better performance than computers based on the Pentium chip, and a 233-MHz Pentium performs better than a 133-MHz Pentium. Multiple-CPU computers outperform single-CPU computers, but not linearly: a server with two 233-MHz Pentium CPUs does not typically provide *twice* the performance of a computer with only one.

Paging is a result of memory contention that arises when two or more applications want to use system memory. If the system runs out of physical memory, it uses paging to write pages of memory to the hard drive and free up physical memory for the other process. When that process is done, it reads those pages off the hard drive back into physical memory for the original process to use.

Memory contention is tolerable until the system reaches a point where system resources (CPU time, bus bandwidth, disk time, and so forth) expend more effort passing pages back and forth between processes than doing real work. If you graph memory contention against average response times, you see a fairly smooth line from zero contention up to the point where response times increase dramatically, called the *thrashing point*. As memory contention increases past this point, response times increase exponentially. Temporary thrashing is tolerable in some environments, but you should work to avoid it.

Overall Exchange Server performance depends on the I/O subsystem. Take into account the type and number of disk controllers, the type of drives installed, and fault tolerance and RAID configurations. Use all available SCSI channels and add more, if necessary, to improve performance. Additional disk drives also increase performance, especially with random disk I/O, which Exchange Server public and private information stores use. Because all drives have mechanical limitations, adding more drives can efficiently distribute the workload. For more information, see The Limits of Unlimited Information Store in Chapter 8 of the companion book *Deploying Microsoft Exchange Server 5.5*.

For optimal network performance, consider your adapter type and network medium choices, such as twisted-pair wire, optical fiber, coaxial cable, and so forth. You can install a high-performance network adapter card in the server, using only the minimal number of network protocols, and multiple network cards to segment the LAN, if appropriate. Because network adapters provide widely varying levels of performance, carefully evaluate the bus type, bus width, and the amount of onboard memory.

Exchange-Related Factors

Connected Users Versus Total Users

When calculating users per server, estimate how many users will connect to the server simultaneously. You can put more user accounts on one server if you know not all of them will connect at the same time. For example, if two shifts of workers never log onto the Exchange server at the same time, you can host both sets on the same server. Hosting more users/server increases the server's background activity, but is usually better than having more simultaneously-connected users. Remember, however, that Exchange Server still performs some actions (directory updates, routing messages, and so forth) on behalf of users, even when those users are not logged on to the system.

Location and Use of Information Stores

Exchange users can store their messages in the server-based information store or in personal folders (a .PST file) on their local computer or a network drive. Even with personal folders, users have a server-based store to receive messages and process rules. But if users set their default delivery location to a personal folder and store most of their messages there, this offloads a lot of work from the server. Messages delivered to a user's server store mailbox still initiate inbox mail sorting rules, but the server defers execution until the user logs on.

Storing data locally can keep the server out of a lot of Exchange transactions. For instance, when users request data from their personal folders, the server does not have to read the attributes and data, write them into the buffer cache, mark the data as read, update the unread message count, and send the data to the client. If users save a copy of everything they send in the Sent Mail folder, the Outlook or Exchange clients can save these locally to a .PST file, offloading the server. When users delete messages, the client saves copies in the local Deleted Items folder instead of on the server. The Exchange server has less data on a continuing basis, which can simplify backups.

Types of Clients

When describing groups of users, also note the client protocol. Exchange Server supports a range of client protocols: Post Office Protocol version 3 (POP3), Internet Message Access Protocol (IMAP4), Messaging Application Programming Interface (MAPI), and Hypertext Transfer Protocol (HTTP) using the Outlook Web Access (OWA) client. Exchange also supports Macintosh and Windows 16-bit MAPI clients. Here's how each protocol can affect Exchange server loads.

MAPI

The feature-rich, Windows 32-bit MAPI client Outlook places the highest processing load on Exchange Server. Outlook provides access to the global address list, different views, and rules that other mail clients do not have, as well as access to public folders and electronic forms. The Calendar, Journal, Contacts, Task List, and Notes components also add server load, especially the Calendar, if used heavily (discussed later in this chapter). The OWA client supports some of these features and will add more of them as it matures. Currently, OWA users can access their calendar but they don't have a meeting wizard and cannot access other users' calendars.

The Macintosh and Windows 16-bit Outlook clients are also MAPI based, but they provide only a subset of the features available to the Windows 32-bit Outlook client. For example, 32-bit Outlook forms do not run on the Macintosh or Windows 16-bit platforms.

POP3 and IMAP4

POP3 and IMAP4 Internet standard clients are download- or receive-only protocols, accessing mail through POP3 or IMAP4 protocols, respectively, but sending messages through Simple Mail Transfer Protocol (SMTP). This can significantly affect Exchange Server performance because these clients receive messages from one server (hosting their mailboxes) and send messages through another server (supporting the Internet Mail Service), cutting the Exchange Mailbox Server processing requirements in half.

Because POP3 clients cannot store messages on an Exchange server, they store them on the client computer, reducing server storage requirements. This also reduces server processing requirements because the retrieval and message manipulation actions take place on the client. POP3 clients operate similarly to Outlook or Exchange clients working in offline mode. A client that has downloaded e-mail performs all of its processing against the local hard drive and the server is no longer involved in the manipulation and deletion of these messages.

IMAP4 clients can preview message headers before downloading, which can save remote users a lot of time by, for instance, deferring the download of a 5-MB file coming across a remote access connection.

OWA

For OWA clients, processing requirements (which can be very heavy) fall on the Internet Information Server (IIS) computer. Testing shows that when IIS and Exchange Server are on different computers, you can greatly diminish response time by putting more than 700 OWA users on a single, four-processor, 512-MB RAM, IIS server. Placing both IIS and Exchange on the same computer decreases the gain significantly.

An OWA user, when compared to an Outlook user, places less load on an Exchange Server that is not running on the same computer with IIS. This is because Outlook's more numerous features allow users to do more with the Exchange Server than OWA clients can.

Public Folder Usage and Replication

Public folders can have a dramatic affect on Exchange Server performance depending on folder size, frequency of user access, number of different views for each folder, number of replicas, replication schedule, and frequency of content changes. Large public folders consume a lot of the information store, and reading them requires more disk I/O. If many users access a folder frequently, the server is kept busy satisfying those requests. For each user, the public folder also keeps track of the expansion state of each of its folders and the read/unread state of each message.

Although public folder replication is fast (initial testing indicates that it takes only 61 seconds to replicate a thousand 1-KB messages between two servers), it proceeds in bursts because changes are batched and then replicated according to the schedule set by the administrator. Replication can be scheduled as frequently as every 15 minutes (with a setting of **Always**) and users accessing a folder when replication kicks in notice a sudden slowdown that lasts until replication finishes. Updating a lot of folders stresses the server more and extends replication-burst slowdowns.

Public folders can contain messages and free-standing documents. Free-standing documents have more overhead than messages because they are typically large, sometimes very large. For example, if you drag-and-drop a 1-MB file to a public folder, every time a user accesses that file, 1 MB of data is sent across the wire, and if repeated enough this can obviously affect server performance for every user. Another performance problem can arise from caching. On the way in and the way out, data also goes through the buffer cache, which contains the most recently used data that was read/written to the database. When a user opens the 1-MB public folder file mentioned above, 1 MB of other data is flushed out of the buffer cache. If a user then tries to access the flushed data, Exchange Server has to go to the disk to get it.

Users also notice if a site spans a slow link with a replica of a public folder on either side. This set of conditions can arise consistently because of the algorithm Exchange uses to connect a user to a public folder replica. When a user requests access to a public folder, Exchange checks the user's home server for the folder. If it finds neither a replica nor a pointer to a public folder server for all users on that Exchange Server, it checks other local servers. (This new feature—location field, commonly called *subsites*—gives Exchange administrators more control over user access to public folders.) If Exchange doesn't find the folder there, it routes the client randomly to any site server with a replica of the folder, and this route may cross a slow link.

For each user, Exchange maintains the read/unread state of each message and the expanded state of each folder in the hierarchy. It stores this information in the public folder on a specific server. Exchange has to continue routing the user to the same public folder replica to keep this information synchronized, so after the user is connected across the slow link, that connection is used from then on. Exchange administrators must design public folder strategies carefully, making use of the location field and correctly setting up the site topology, to avoid this potential performance problem. You can also see the section on public folder replication in the *Microsoft Exchange Server 5.5 Resource Guide.*

Exchange Server now supports Network News Transfer Protocol (NNTP), which also affects public folder use. First, NNTP makes it easy for administrators to set up a public folder to import the millions of messages found on the Internet, which can obviously increase storage requirements. Second, administrators can allow outside NNTP users to participate in public folders, and network traffic can soar if a lot of external users frequent the folders. Third, NNTP newsgroups can be 40 GB or larger. If possible, it is a good idea to put these public folders on a dedicated server to insulate your system from unpredictable loading.

Rules and Views

Rules are user-defined actions that a server performs: pop-up notifications when a message is received from a specific person, automatic relocation of messages into folders based on subject line, and so forth. Tests have shown that rule processing affects performance negligibly unless every user has dozens of rules set up.

Views require the server to store and track indexes. The most recently used ones are cached, but users may notice slower performance when accessing a seldom-used view. Still, this performance hit is minimal.

Electronic Forms

Electronic forms basically are handled as are all other messages, but the first time a form is used the client must download it into the local forms cache before executing it. This is a one-time hit, recurring only if the form changes. If a new form is sent to a lot of users and they all try to execute it at the same time, the hit can be significant.

Scheduling

The Outlook calendar and the former Schedule+ client use a hidden public folder to replicate the free and busy information. By default, this folder is placed on the first server installed in a site. Occasionally the administrator has to set up replicas to support a heavier user load, and these increase replication traffic and latency in updating the free/busy information. By default, all users in a site can view free/busy information for all other site users. The administrator has to set up free/busy folder replication between sites, and this functionality can affect Exchange Server performance. Are dedicated resources needed? As of this writing, Microsoft's IT department uses four dedicated free/busy servers (each with four processors and lots of RAM and disk space) to handle more than 40,000 users.

The real performance concern with the former Schedule+ client is whether the user works with a local schedule file. If yes (the default), Schedule+ is very responsive and efficiently updates the schedule information on the server periodically. If a user chooses not to work with a local schedule file, each schedule change requires interaction with the server. Schedule+ was designed to work standalone and not just against a server, so it always works with a local file first and then updates the server, rather than simply interoperating with the server. Single users not working with local schedule files notice performance loss; if enough users work this way, all users can be affected.

The Outlook Calendar is more integrated with the mail client and uses the same storage location as is used for the rest of the mail. When Outlook users working against Exchange Servers set their server-based mailbox as the default delivery location, Outlook stores all calendar information in their mailbox's "calendar" folder on the Exchange Server. This folder can be set up for offline use as well, in which case users' free/busy information is made available to others. If users select a personal folder (.PST file) as the default delivery location, all calendaring information is stored there and the free/busy information is not available to others. To share calendar details and free/busy information with others, users must make their server-based mailboxes the default delivery location.

MAPI Applications

It is hard to quantify the effect MAPI applications have on an Exchange Server because each one is different. One reason MAPI applications perform poorly is that they use RPCs inefficiently when communicating with the server. This can be avoided by batching functions so that they go to the server in one RPC. The Exchange Development team found this out when they designed the default *read note* so that it took 14 RPCs to retrieve and display a message. For one user this would not matter, but if 250 users on one Exchange Server each issue 14 RPC calls to retrieve and display a single message, the performance hit would be tremendous. The Exchange Performance team (which helped enhance RPC efficiency for Exchange code) redesigned the function to use only 2 RPCs.

All client/server application code should be written for performance. Even a single poor piece of code, when multiplied by enough users, can seriously degrade performance.

Connectors and Gateways

Connectors and gateways run on the server and contend with other Exchange processes for resources, including the store. They operate in bursts and can degrade performance temporarily.

Exchange Server is designed so that if a specific connector or gateway causes performance problems, you can easily dedicate a server for it or add a second instance of it elsewhere in the site. Exchange Server treats sites as units, so these options are transparent to users.

Directories, Replication, and the Bridgehead Server

A bridgehead server acts as the door in and out of the site's directory. When configuring an intersite directory replication connector, the administrator designates one server in each site as the bridgehead server responsible for swapping directory updates with its counterpart. Within a site, directory replication is proportional to the number of directory changes. It should affect performance noticeably only during migration to Exchange Server (when the directory is changing often) or in organizations where hundreds of directory updates happen every day.

MTA

The message transfer agent (MTA) primarily routes messages between servers. Even in single-server systems, however, it has other responsibilities such as expanding distribution lists and routing outgoing gateway or connector messages. It affects performance the most in multiple-server environments, but even in single-server setups it initiates some processing.

Exchange Server 5.5 improves overall MTA performance. Its database queue has been optimized to alleviate scalability issues, which Exchange 4.0 addressed by locking down database queue objects in RAM. Exchange Server 5.5 replaces all database queue access in the mainline with a far simpler and more efficient RAM-based queue mechanism. It uses the database queue format only when backing up secure queue information to disk during clean shutdown or for MTA check processing, to be mapped back into RAM on the next MTA startup.

Several other Exchange 5.5 features improve the MTA's use of the underlying file-system: file-handle caching, deleted-object file caching, and direct I/O for full buffers. File-handle caching and deleted-object file caching use a new per-object bitmap to collect and delete files at closedown. The Exchange Server 5.5 MTA also optimizes database server internals and MTA database usage to route more messages faster.

Upgrading to Exchange 5.5 improves MTA performance, allowing you to put more users on a server without increasing its load.

Server Scripting Agent and Routing Objects

Exchange Server 5.5 now supports server-side scripting through a scripting agent, which allows developers to create event- or time-driven forms applications using VBScript or JavaScript. These scripts are actually executed on the Exchange Server, so developers should write scripts that are efficient and optimized. To guard against the installation of bad scripts (one that checks every message in an information store every hour, for example), the administrator determines who can put them on a server.

The Exchange routing objects (Exchange Server 5.5 Service Pack 1) are a set of components that build on the event and scripting architecture of Exchange Server 5.5 to simplify the development of routing and approval applications. The components include a simple routing engine, routing objects, programmer's reference, and sample applications. Again, developers need to take care in writing these applications so that they do not negatively impact server performance.

Real-Time Collaboration

Exchange Server 5.5 supports Chat. Although the chat protocol is somewhat lightweight, the Exchange 5.5 Chat Service allows an Exchange Server to host up to 10,000 online meetings and real-time discussion clients simultaneously. If this sort of activity becomes so common that it affects system performance, isolate this service on a dedicated server.

The Outlook 98 client provides NetMeeting, which allows users to set up and schedule online meetings. This normally has no impact on Exchange Server performance, but it can consume bandwidth if there are many participants simultaneously using audio and video, and sharing applications.

Non-Exchange-Related Factors

Other Server Activities

The tests performed by the Performance team were done on a *pure* Exchange Server—Exchange Server installed on a Windows NT Server 4.0 computer that was a member server and had nothing else running on it. In the real world, this is seldom the case. In fact, Windows NT Server is designed to run multiple server applications on one computer and this can have an effect, perhaps even a dramatic one, on that server's performance.

It is too complicated to evaluate the performance intricacies of all Windows NT Server applications and how they might affect Exchange Server performance, but here is a rule of thumb: running applications simultaneously affects server performance only when the applications are resource intensive. For instance, using the server as a Windows NT Domain Controller, WINS Server, or DHCP Server in systems where few client activities request those services would not affect performance much. On the other hand, running Microsoft Systems Management Server, SQL Server, or SNA Server simultaneously can affect it significantly.

Network Quality and Connectivity

Client/server performance can be determined by the quality of the underlying network. Exchange Server provides better connectivity and performance on a 100-MB/second Fiber Distributed Data Interface (FDDI) ring than on a Token

Ring network or when attached to an overloaded Ethernet segment where lots of collisions occur. Consider WAN connectivity and quality, especially when calculating site boundaries and whether clients can access their Exchange Server across the WAN.

Finding the Limits

Exchange Server has no practical limit on users per server but other factors can (or should) restrict the configuration.

Until Exchange 5.5, the public and private information store databases could not exceed 16 GB apiece. On large servers, this often became the users-per-server ceiling, depending on how much server storage users were allowed, how much single-instancing of messages and attachments increased the server's logical storage capacity, how often personal folder stores were used and, to a lesser extent, how many rules, views, and finders users defined on the server.

Exchange Server 5.5 has an unlimited store, and planners now have to consider how much disk space can be configured in a single server and how long it takes to back up or restore data. Online tape backup hardware can achieve 25 to 40 GB/hour, with restore rates about half that. Even so, a large enough backup or restore can be very time consuming. See The Limits of Unlimited Information Store in Chapter 8 ("Advanced Backbone Design and Optimization") of the companion book *Deploying Microsoft Exchange Server 5.5*.

And there are intangible factors. You can put several thousand users on one Exchange Server computer, but do you feel comfortable doing so? If hardware fails (it happens), those several thousand users are all out of business. The new Microsoft Clustering Server available with Windows NT Server 4.0, Enterprise Edition can increase hardware reliability and possibly your peace of mind.

Intangibles aside, how do you determine how many users to put on each server? This section explains how.

Testing Methodology

There are four steps to calculating users per server:

1. Optimize the server (including hardware and the Exchange Server setup).
2. Classify users and set their performance expectations.
3. Use Load Simulator (for MAPI clients) or InetLoad (for POP3/IMAP4 clients) to test configurations against your user data.
4. Analyze the results.

Optimizing the Server

Should you stripe all your drives together or configure separate partitions for different server components? How much memory should you dedicate to the buffer cache? There are other questions, too. This section helps you answer them.

Optimizing Server Hardware

Three hardware features affect Exchange Server:

CPUs

CPUs perform at certain rates, beyond which you cannot optimize. Performance is determined by how many you have and what type they are. Microsoft performance testing found that Exchange 4.0 and 5.0 did not scale well past 4 CPUs and that Exchange 5.5 can scale up to 8 CPUs on Intel Pentium or Digital Alpha chips. Configuring above these limits does not boost Exchange performance and you might as well use the CPUs elsewhere. As for CPU type, faster is better: a Pentium 233 chip performs better than a Pentium 200, a lot better than a 486/66.

1. Windows NT Server accepts one optimization that affects how your server uses CPUs.

2. In **Control Panel,** open the System applet and click on the **Performance** tab.

3. Set the **Performance Boost for Foreground Applications** to **None**.

This boosts the system priorities Windows NT Server assigns to background tasks (all Exchange Server services are background tasks).

Memory

Exchange Server is already well-tuned for the most efficient memory usage, so there isn't much more you can do to optimize memory. However, Exchange Server uses all the memory you give it, up to the total size of your information store—if for some reason you want to commit the entire database to RAM. Exchange Server uses most of the memory you give it for a buffer cache, which holds writes to the information store for off-peak processing. An Exchange Server needs at least 24 MB of RAM, but boosting this to 64 to 128 MB improved test performance much more than upgrading CPUs.

▶ **To optimize Windows NT Server memory use to help Exchange Server**

1. In **Control Panel**, Network applet, set the server service to **Maximize Throughput for Network Applications**.

2. In **Control Panel**, System applet, configure a large pagefile for virtual memory. A rule of thumb is 125 MB plus the amount of physical RAM. For example, if the server has 64 MB of RAM, set pagefile size to (125+64) MB, or 189 MB.

Disk I/O Subsystem

The disk I/O subsystem can be optimized to good effect. First, some background information:

Server Transaction Logs

Exchange Server issues I/Os to the server disk subsystem to read data from disk into memory or to write data to permanent storage. For example, when you open your Inbox, the set of properties in the default folder view must be accessed for each of the first 20 or so messages in the inbox folder and returned to you. If this information is not already cached in memory on the server from a recent, previous access, it must be read from the server information store database on disk. In this case, the disk *read* I/O is synchronous to opening the mailbox.

Similarly, a message transferred from another server must be secured to disk until its receipt is acknowledged (this prevents message loss during system failure). In this case, the disk *write* I/O is synchronous to the background action of transferring and accepting the message.

The disk I/Os issued by Exchange Server are either *reads* or *writes* and *synchronous* or *asynchronous*. Although all read I/Os and asynchronous write I/Os can be considered *random*, many of the synchronous writes issued by Exchange Server are *sequential*. That is, to speed up actions which require synchronous write I/O, Exchange uses a special method of writing changes to disk known as a *sequential, write ahead transaction log*.

Transaction log architecture capitalizes on current disk drive design. Seek time (how long it takes the disk head to move from one position to another to read or write data) is the prime determinant in random disk I/O rate. If the I/O to the drive is sequential rather than random, seek time drops close to zero, dramatically increasing the number of disk I/Os per second the drive can support.

Placing the information store transaction logs on their own physical disk *with no other sources of disk I/O on the drive* is the single most important aspect of Exchange Server performance on all but the smallest, single-drive Exchange Server configurations. Second in importance is using the FAT file system because it performs best with sequential activity. (If the log exceeds 2 GB, you must use the NTFS.)

Removing other sources of disk I/O from the drive is important: although the transaction log is written to sequentially, other I/O requests will move the disk head away from the log file, increasing seek times. This is true even of *read* actions, many of which also involve writing to the server information store transaction log. For example, when you read a message, it is marked as no longer unread and the number of unread items in the folder is updated.

The Exchange Server directory service also uses write-ahead log architecture, but changes to the directory are so infrequent that giving it a separate, physical disk drive usually is not worth the expense. An exception would be servers on which large numbers of directory service modifications are made, such as servers used for large directory imports.

Random Disk Access I/O

Except for transaction log activity, Exchange Server disk I/O tends to be random. This includes the Windows NT pagefile, server databases, message tracking logs, and so forth. However, because server components work at separate tasks, they generate varying rates of disk I/O. For example, when a message is received from another server and delivered to a user, the MTA first secures the message to disk in its transient database, causing a single random write to the MTADATA directory. It then calls the system attendant, which makes an entry in the message tracking log. The MTA then notifies the information store that a message is available, at which time the information store receives the message from the MTA and writes the message into its own permanent database, generating synchronous write I/O to the information store transaction log as well as asynchronous read and write I/O to the information store database in the MDBDATA directory. During this time, page faults may also have occurred if the system is under memory pressure, adding additional I/Os to the Windows NT pagefile or executable files.

So you can boost server random I/O performance by using other system disk drives to enhance the I/O rate on the partitions where these random I/Os occur. Because sources of activity vary, combine the remaining disk drives together into a software or hardware stripe set to make the combined capacity available to whichever server component needs it.

What about the Pagefile?

The system pages when the processes running on the Windows NT server (including Windows NT itself) need more code and/or data pages than are present in physical memory.

If an Exchange server has only 24 MB for 50 to 100 users, it will have to page just to accomplish normal Exchange tasks such as handling user requests, moving mail off/on the server, and so on, making it a significant percentage of your total disk I/O. Paging is necessary because the working sets of all Exchange Server processes (and Windows NT Server) don't fit in physical memory all at once. If the site has only one server and little off-server traffic, the MTA has little to do (except expanding the occasional distribution list) and it can swap out, leaving more room for the rest of the server processes and reducing paging. Paging increases if the server runs processes beyond the core Exchange services (such as Internet Mail Service) or performs tasks such as importing directory objects, generating the offline address book, or starting up the server services.

If the Exchange server has enough physical memory that most pages needed by server processes fit into it at the same time, there is not much paging during normal operation. Even servers with 128 MB or more of RAM, however, will page, especially if the buffer caches (which are included in the information store/directory working set) are set too high for the amount of RAM in the computer. The Exchange Performance Optimizer tries to set these correctly.

Paging tends to occur in bursts, as when a large message moves through the system and memory pages must be paged out to make room for it and then paged back in after it is gone. And I/O is as a rule randomly distributed over the pagefile. This is why it is almost always best to host the pagefile on the stripe set. On computers with little memory, paging becomes a significant percentage of the I/O and a stripe set places all available I/O capacity at its disposal, usually speeding up the computer. Low-memory computers are often bound by the pagefile, but alleviating this requires more RAM, not more disk space.

Computers with more memory page less, except for bursts, startup, and so on. If your computer pages very little, you can host the pagefile just about anywhere—even on the transaction log drive because it won't be accessed often and won't interfere with the log's sequential activity when it is. But there is no reason to get fancy. To handle the bursts and simplify buffer settings, just host it on the big, random I/O partition with the databases.

Should you dedicate a disk to the pagefile? No. If you are paging, I/O performance is better when you combine that drive into the stripe set and put the pagefile there. If you aren't paging, it wastes a drive that could boost random I/O capacity if you added it to the stripe set. Putting the pagefile on the stripe set makes most of the disk I/O subsystem available to whatever portion of the system (pagefile or not) needs random access disk I/O capacity.

Running the Exchange Performance Optimizer

Poor server response time under load usually means a bottleneck in any of three critical hardware resources: CPU processing capacity, RAM, or the I/O subsystem. The first step is not to buy more RAM but to make sure the Exchange Server software is configured properly for your hardware configuration. Exchange Server runs on computers from the extremely small to the extremely large, but you need to adjust configuration settings to optimize Exchange for the hardware on which it runs.

The Microsoft Exchange Performance Optimizer automatically detects your server hardware and adjusts hardware-dependent configuration settings. Always run the Optimizer after installing Exchange Server on your server hardware and after adding or removing hardware. Without it, the system will run, but not as well as it should. Look for the topic on optimizing performance in the *Microsoft Exchange Server 5.5 Resource Guide* for more information on using the Performance Optimizer.

Using Load Simulator

User Definitions

When calculating users/server, you have to characterize user groups as accurately as possible. Capacity planning is not an exact science; it relies on intelligent estimates. If this is your first messaging system, you will have no baseline for system usage. If you have been using other messaging products, Exchange's functionality and its features such as public folders will be difficult to assess against network bandwidth. Luckily, you can use Load Simulator (LoadSim) iteratively, refining your estimates against various scenarios and observed usage patterns.

The following tables can help you classify users. The Exchange Performance team does not have all the answers nor is this is the final word on users/server. This is just some test data taken in a specific environment and offered as a rough guide.

The Exchange Performance team defined low, medium, and heavy users. Here were the initial states:

Parameter	Light	Medium	Heavy
Number of non-default folders	20	40	60
Number of messages per folder	5	5	5
Number of messages in Inbox	1	4	9
Number of messages in Deleted Items	1	1	1

These LoadSim parameters define the activity for each user classification:

Parameter	Light	Medium	Heavy
Hours in a day	8	8	8
Originate new mail (not reply or forward)	2x	4x	6x
1K text (ups1k.msg)	90	60	50
2K text (ups2k.msg)		16	10
4K text (ups4k.msg)		4	5
10K attachment (ups10kat.msg)	10	5	10
Excel attachment (upsXLatt.msg)		4	5

Parameter	Light	Medium	Heavy
Word attachment (upsWDatt.msg)		2	5
Embedded bitmap (upsBMobj.msg)		2	5
Embedded Excel Object (upsXLobj.msg)		2	10
Recipients per new/forward message	3	3	3
Add a distribution list to addressees	30%	30%	30%
Read new mail	12x	12x	12x
Send reply	5%	7%	15%
Send reply all	3%	5%	7%
Send forward	5%	7%	7%
Delete (move to Deleted Items)	40%	40%	40%
Move messages	20%	20%	20%
Load attachments on read mail	25%	25%	25%
Maximum inbox size (in messages)	20	125	250
Other old mail processing	5x	15x	20x
Schedule+ changes	1x	5x	10x
Messages received per day (computed average)	22.9	66.3	118.9

Server Definitions

The Performance team used these definitions for low-end, middle, and high-end servers during Exchange Server 4.0 testing:

Server type	Manufacturer	Processor	RAM	Disk configuration	Network card
Low-End					
Server A	Gateway 2000	One 486/66	32 MB	One 515-MB One 1-GB	Intel EtherExpress Pro
Server B	Compaq Proliant	One 486/66	32 MB	One 1-GB One 2-GB	Compaq Netflex II
Middle					
Server C	Compaq Proliant	Two 486/66	64 MB	One 2-GB	Compaq Netflex II
Server D	Compaq Proliant	One Pentium 90	64 MB	One 2-GB One 8-GB Stripe	Compaq Netflex II

(continued)

Server type	Manufacturer	Processor	RAM	Disk configuration	Network card
High-End					
Server E	AT&T 3555	Eight Pentium 90	512 MB	Two 2-GB One 24-GB Stripe One 16-GB	3 Com Etherlink III

Again, these are sample numbers only.

Running LoadSim

LoadSim runs only under Windows NT. Here are a few things to consider when running it:

- Make sure you have classified your users and set up the servers that you want to test.
- Install the actual Exchange Client on the Windows NT Workstations or Servers you plan to use as the LoadSim clients.
- Determine the acceptable response time for your users. Usually, 1 second (1,000 milliseconds) is a good number to use for this, but you may decide that 1.5 seconds (1,500 milliseconds) is adequate.
- Use LoadSim to define the test topology and generate the user import files.
- Use the Exchange Server Administration program to import those user definitions into your Exchange Server Directory. You must do this on every server you plan to test.
- Use LoadSim to define the initial state of users and public folders.
- Run the User Initialization and Public Folder Initialization tests against your server to populate the Exchange Server information store.
- Define some tests using the user classifications and run them against the different server platforms. For example, test 250 *light* users against a server defined as *medium*.

Each LoadSim pass runs for several hours and produces one number that is the 95 percent weighted average response time in milliseconds that each of the LoadSim users experienced during that test. Test several different user counts to generate several different data points and then graph the results. Some example results are shown in the next section.

Sample LoadSim Results

The following tables show some sample LoadSim results derived from testing performed by several vendors.

Note This information is subject to change without notice at any time. Microsoft is not responsible for the results of any changes, policies, or decisions made in reaction to, or on the basis of, this data, or for any conclusions drawn from it.

DIGITAL AlphaServer 4100

These LoadSim results show the maximum number of users Exchange Server 5.5 can support using the Exchange MAPI/RPC protocol on a Digital AlphaServer 4100 configured with one, two, and four processors. The AlphaServer systems were tested with Exchange Server 5.5 in a single-server configuration (that is, as a standalone server, supporting the given number of clients).

Server configurations used

System	Digital AlphaServer 4100 5/533
Number of CPUs	≤ 4
Disk controller	4 Adaptec 2940-uw SCSI adapters
Logical disk C:	NTFS 2-GB RZ28 VW
Logical disk D:	NTFS 4-GB RZ29B VW
Logical disk E:	NTFS 28 x 4-GB RZ29B VW NT stripe set Raid 0
Logical disk F:	NTFS 3 x 4-GB RZ29B VW
Physical memory	2-GB
Virtual memory pagefile	2,108,416-KB on F:\
Network card	DEC PCI Fast Ethernet DEC chip 21140 (DE500)

Results

Number of processors	1	2	4
Maximum users per server	4,500	8,000	10,000
95th percentile response time (ms)	454	608	509
Message recipients delivered	373,960	643,662	831,774
Total messages delivered	84,738	145,914	190,106

Compaq ProLiant 6000

These test results show the 95th percentile response time score of hosting 9,000 Exchange Server 5.5 users using the Exchange MAPI/RPC protocol on a Compaq ProLiant 6000 Server configured with four processors.

Results

Number of users	**9,000**
95th percentile response time score	336 milliseconds (ms)
Total messages delivered (8-hour period)	695,298
Protocol	Exchange MAPI
LoadSim canonical profile	Medium (typical corporate mail user)
Platform	Compaq ProLiant 6000
	(Four) Intel Pentium Pro 200-MHz, 1-MB Cache, 3-GB RAM
	(Two) SMART-2/DH Array Controllers
	(Eighteen) 4.3-GB Wide-Ultra SCSI Drives

Hewlett-Packard NetServer LXr Pro8

Hewlett-Packard Network Server Division in Cupertino, California, used LoadSim to generate workload that demonstrated the scalability of the LXr Pro8 running Exchange Server version 5.5. Exchange users were simulated with LoadSim running on 35 HP NetServer E series servers, each simulating 400 users.

Results

Number of users	**14,000**
95th percentile response time	344 milliseconds (ms) time score
Messaging protocol	Exchange MAPI
LoadSim canonical profile	Medium (typical corporate mail user)

System configuration

Component	Configuration
System make and model	Hewlett-Packard NetServer LXr Pro8
Processors	(Eight) Intel Pentium Pro 200-MHz, 1-MB cache, 4-GB RAM
Operating system	Microsoft Windows NT Server v4.0 Enterprise Edition + SP3
I/O subsystem 1:	Embedded Ultra-Wide SCSI Controller, (one) D4910A 4-GB Fast-Wide, 7.2-K RPM
I/O subsystem 2-4:	(Three) American Megatrend, Inc., 434 disk array controllers, (29) D4903A 4-GB ultra-wide SCSI drives

Component	Configuration
Disk files distribution	Drive C: Operating System, (one) 4-GB Drive, RAID0
	Drive D: DS, MTA and DS Log Files, (two) 4-GB Drives, RAID1
	Drive E: Windows NT Pagefile, (one) 4-GB Drive RAID0
	Drive F: Information store log files, (two) 4-GB Drives, RAID1
	Drive N: Information store database, (twenty-four) 4-GB Drives, RAID0
Network	(Three) HP J3171A 100 Base-TX

IBM Netfinity 7000

The IBM Netfinity 7000, available in rack and tower models, is a four-way symmetric multiprocessing (SMP) server featuring a 200-MHz Pentium Pro processor with either 1-MB of L2 cache or 512-KB of L2 cache, and up to 4 GB of memory. These test results show the 95th percentile response time score of hosting 10,000 Exchange Server 5.5 users using the Exchange MAPI/RPC protocol on an IBM Netfinity 7000 Server configured with four processors.

Results

Number of users	10,000
95th percentile response time	649 milliseconds (ms)
Total message recipients delivered	807,744 messages for the 8-hour period
Messaging protocol	Exchange MAPI
LoadSim canonical profile	Medium (typical corporate e-mail user)

Server Configuration

Component	Configuration
Processors	(Four) 200-MHz Pentium Pro, 1-MB L2 cache
System memory	3 GB
Disk controllers	(Two) IBM ServeRAID II Ultra SCSI adapters Version 2.40 firmware and device driver
Disk Drives (total)	Internal: (twelve) 4.51-GB disk drives, Expansion: (ten) 4.51-GB disk drives, (one) EXP10 rack storage expansion enclosure, all disk drives 7200 rpm.
Logical drive C	NTFS, (drive 1), RAID0, write-back, for OS, pagefile, MTA, DS

(continued)

Server Configuration *(continued)*

Component	Configuration
Logical drive D	NTFS, (drive 2), RAID0, write-back, for Exchange log files
Logical drive E	NTFS, (drives 3 to 22), RAID0, write through, for Exchange Mail database
Network adapters	Windows NT Server 4.0, Enterprise Edition with Service Pack 3
Exchange server	Version 5.5 (Build 1960.5)

NCR WorldMark 4300

These test results show the 95th percentile response time score of hosting 10,000 Exchange Server 5.5 users using the Exchange MAPI/RPC protocol on an NCR WorldMark 4300 Server configured with four processors.

Results

Number of users	10,000
95th percentile response time	422
Processor usage	62%
Message recipients delivered/day (computed)	791,296

Server Configurations Used

Component	Type	Quantity	Description
Server	NCR 4300/4	1	
Processors	Pentium Pro	4	200-MHz with 1-MB second-level cache
Memory		2 GB	
Network adapters	10/100 MB/S	3	
Disk host adapters	NCR PQS	2	4 SCSI channels per adapter
Disk subsystem	NCR 6282	3	2 with (ten)4-G drives, 1 with (six) 4-G drives

Sample InetLoad Results

LoadSim can help you find out how many MAPI clients you can host per Exchange Server. InetLoad is the corresponding tool to use for POP3 or IMAP4 users. The InetLoad test results below were derived by the Exchange Performance Team.

Test Results

Test Case	1	2	3
CPU	(Two 200-MHz Pentium Pro	(Four) 200-MHz Pentium Pro	(Four 200-MHz Pentium Pro
RAM	512 MB	512 MB	512 MB
Disk	(Seven) 9-GB RAID 0	(Seven) 9-GB RAID 0	(Seven) 9-GB RAID 0
Protocol	POP3/SMTP	POP3/SMTP	IMAP4/SMTP
Max. users	7,000	10,000	4,000
95th percentile receive times (ms)	775	940	844
95th percentile send times (ms)	160	117	105
95th percentile total (ms)	935	1064	949

The Art of Performance Analysis—Detecting Performance Bottlenecks

Your Exchange Server users complain the server is too slow. Do you need more hardware? If so, what type? More RAM? More disks? Another processor board? This section discusses which hardware components to buy and in what ratio to buy them.

Detecting performance bottlenecks is more art than science, but you can improve if you keep at it and pay attention. The first goal is to determine which of the three major server components (memory, disk I/O subsystem, or CPU) is the bottleneck. The first tool to use is the Windows NT performance monitor.

Memory

Does the system need more memory? Use performance monitor to see how much it is paging. Check Paging File: % Usage and Memory: % Available. If the paging file is over 50 percent used and if the percent memory available is less than 25 percent, more RAM is a good idea. RAM is normally (but not necessarily) added in 16- or 32-MB increments. Follow the manufacturer's suggestions.

Disk I/O

Is the disk I/O subsystem the bottleneck? Use performance monitor to find out if the server is being I/O bound on asynchronous I/Os to the Exchange Server database. Check PhysicalDisk: Disk Queue Length and PhysicalDisk: %Disk Time.

Disk queue length shows outstanding disk requests per physical disk, including requests in service. Multispindle disk devices (a RAID stripe, for example) can have multiple disk requests active at one time, so you want to look for disk queue length minus the number of spindles on the disk device. If that number is consistently high, you are disk-I/O-bound. It should average less than 2 for good performance.

Disk time is the percentage of elapsed time that the selected disk drive spends servicing requests. If this is a high percentage, it shows that your system is spending most of its time servicing disk requests and needs faster disk drivers or more of them.

CPU

Is CPU usage high? Here is where things get tricky because this can be true even when the disk and/or memory is the bottleneck. Check those two areas first and then check the CPU.

To determine if the system needs more processors, check performance monitor on System: % Total Processor and Process: % Processor - Process X. If total system processor usage is averaging above 75 percent, you probably need to add another CPU. (Review usage on all processors if you want a look at the symmetrical multiprocessing capabilities of the Exchange functions on a Windows NT Server.)

Tests show that Exchange Server 4.0 and 5.0 do not scale well past four CPUs. If you already have four CPUs and are still CPU-bound, you can upgrade processor type, add a server, or move up to Exchange Server 5.5.

C H A P T E R   4

Directory Replication and Background Traffic

This chapter continues the discussion started in Chapter 3 on capacity planning. It describes in greater detail Exchange Server backbone design, connector choices, directory replication, background traffic, and general performance tuning. You can find a version of this chapter with more information relevant to deployment in the companion book *Deploying Microsoft Exchange Server 5.5*. An updated version is included here because of its importance to capacity planning before *and after* deployment. Although the discussion is based on version 5.5, many of the principles apply to earlier versions.

Caution This chapter describes changes to the Exchange raw directory and Windows NT registry. Before you apply *any* changes to a live system, test them first in a lab environment. Document carefully any changes you make in a live environment.

For more information on directory replication, refer to the *Microsoft Exchange Server 5.5 Resource Guide*.

Basic Issues

Exchange Server is unique in how it integrates with the underlying environment and how it forms a collective of knowledge between the servers. Although Exchange can be deployed out of the box in simple environments, designers of larger environments may need to tune components to achieve maximum performance and efficiency. Getting the right design in place is crucial to the operation and support of the Exchange infrastructure. You can always make changes afterwards, but it is far easier when Exchange is deployed correctly from the day one.

Design questions:

- Should I have multiple sites or a single one?
- How do I know if my network will accommodate Exchange?
- Which connector should I use between sites?
- Which messaging topology should I use, mesh or hub-and-spoke?
- Should the directory replication topology match the messaging topology?
- What if I want to change it all afterwards?
- How can I know if the system is performing at its best?
- Can I control the number of system messages generated?

This section makes general recommendations and offers ideas on how to decide upon your design. It is based on field experience in different environments working with clients who wanted different functionality and performance. When you have worked through the process, don't worry if your result differs from the recommendations presented in this chapter: the solutions you derive will reflect the size and needs of your enterprise.

Backbone Design

Single Exchange Site Environments

Although you might think that only small Exchange installations deploy a single site, many sizeable companies enjoy the simplicity of having a single Exchange site that spans, sometimes, the world. So the first question to confront is: should you deploy one or more Exchange sites? It can be a relatively easy question to answer, for although a single-site configuration has some prerequisites such as authentication for the site services account and administration policy, in most cases it simply is a matter of how much network bandwidth is available.

Network Bandwidth for a Site

Site boundaries are perhaps the toughest topic for Exchange designers. The rule of thumb is that, to place Exchange servers in the same site, you must have an average of 64 Kb/seconds of available bandwidth. The problem with this is the same as with any rule of thumb; it doesn't cover all circumstances. Can you put 50 Exchange servers at each end of a 64-Kb link? If the available bandwidth falls below 64 Kb, will Exchange "break"?

Another problem is rooted in human nature. Ask the people in charge of the network if there is an average of 64-Kb available bandwidth and, normally, they will ask you to specify how much traffic Exchange will produce and at what times of the day. It is a perfectly reasonable question, and a lot safer than trying to derive an answer to yours, but it doesn't get you any closer to a decision.

To work through this problem, consider these Exchange site technicalities:

- Both the directory service and message transfer agent (MTA) components communicate directly with each other within a site.

- Any Exchange server can communicate directly with any other Exchange server in the site.

- Remote procedure call (RPC) produces errors if it can't get a response (directory service or MTA) within 30 seconds of making a request.

- If one Exchange server in the site is located at the end of a very slow link, this can slow performance of all Exchange servers in the site.

- Changes to the Exchange directory are replicated every 5 minutes (default).

- User-generated messages are sent immediately and cannot be scheduled.

- The knowledge consistency checker runs (every 3 hours, hard-coded) on each server, causing intrasite traffic (more on this later).

- Backup replication occurs every 6 hours, also causing intrasite traffic (more on this later).

Obviously, it is difficult to assess exactly how much intrasite traffic Exchange generates. This chapter can help you assess the situation generally. The first clue is, in general, don't be afraid of creating large sites—they can make system administration much easier. More decision-making help is in the sections that follow.

Domain Structures

Before you install the first Exchange server, you should have a clear strategy for whether you will install your Exchange servers in one of your existing Windows NT Server domains or if you will create a new resource domain. This decision for many companies depends upon whether the existing domain structure is "tidy" or whether it has grown organically over the years and is not simply and cleanly organized. In companies with a multitude of account domains, many Exchange designers tend to create a separate resource domain for the Exchange servers.

Separate Resource Domain

If you decide to build a separate Windows NT Server domain, deploy separate non-Exchange servers to act as the domain controllers (one primary domain controller—PDC—and at least two backup domain controllers—BDCs—for resilience). These are solely used for Exchange Server startup and process authentication. For best performance, deploy all Exchange servers as member servers. The resource domain should have a trust to each domain that holds user accounts (for mailbox mapping). This topology works well for companies that have user accounts in different domains but cannot implement trusts between them for security or political reasons.

Existing Accounts Domain

If you decide to use an existing account domain, install all dedicated connector servers as member servers. Now the question is whether to install mailbox and public folder servers as member servers or as BDCs. The latter choice can improve client performance, but there are other factors to consider. When an Exchange client logs on to the mailbox, its account credentials must be validated against the domain controller with the accounts database—even if the user is already logged on to the Windows NT domain. If all Exchange servers are built as member servers, clients logging on must wait while the Exchange server checks credentials. This wait is reduced if the Exchange servers are built as BDCs, but BDCs must participate with the PDC in domain replication and sometimes general client authentication, so too many BDCs in a domain can degrade Windows NT and network performance. If you configure Exchange servers as BDCs, allow for extra processing and memory overhead when you create specifications for the hardware.

Hub-and-Spoke Versus Mesh

If you decide on a multiple-site environment, you must choose between hub-and-spoke or mesh architectures. This is based mainly on the projected ultimate size of the system. If there will be more than 40 Exchange sites, use the more scalable hub-and-spoke. Mesh designs allow full use of the rerouting capabilities of Exchange, but when sites proliferate the routing tables grow exponentially until route calculation time and pressure on the MTA become unacceptable.

The best performing Exchange installations are generally hub-and-spoke. The hub site is usually a small collection of Exchange servers dedicated to message routing and directory replication. Spoke sites are located at regional offices and linked to the hub using a standard Exchange connector (site, X.400 or Internet Mail Service) with a piggy-backed directory replication connector. All hub servers should run Exchange Server 5.5, even if the spoke sites run previous versions. It has an enhanced message transfer agent capable of coping with much greater loads than previous versions.

Centralized Hub Sites

If all hub servers are in one location with high-bandwidth and high-availability links, it is called a *centralized hub*. This design works best when the network has a clearly defined central point and regional offices have direct network connections to it. This design increases site connector options because any server in the hub can act as the local messaging bridgehead.

Distributed Hub Sites

If you want to provide a local hub access point for satellite offices, deploy the hub servers over a wide-area, medium-bandwidth network. This design works best for companies with numerous separated large offices but no clear network center. This design can work well and can be more efficient than a centralized hub (by reducing directory replication traffic), but it does limit site connector options. If the design allows any Exchange server in the hub to connect to the spoke, the network may flood or RPC may timeout.

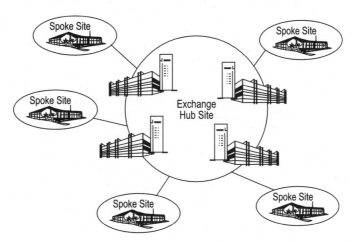

Number of Spoke Sites

Always try to limit the number of Exchange sites in the organization to simplify administration and reduce directory replication traffic. If a design requires more than 30 Exchange sites, these elements must be carefully tuned:

1. Schedule on the directory replication connector.
2. Address book views replication schedule (defaults to every 6 hours).
3. Public folder hierarchy replication.
4. Public information store status messages.

Expanded explanations of replication and public folder traffic are presented later in this chapter.

If a design requires a very large number of sites (over 200), make sure the correct tuning parameters are in place and deploy hotfix software if any Exchange 4.0 or 5.0 servers are running within the system. Contact Microsoft Premier Support Services to obtain hotfix software for installations with greater than 212 Exchange sites.

Choice of Messaging Connector

After you have defined site boundaries, you must decide which connector to use to link the sites. Your main choices are:

- Site Connector (using RPC)
- X.400 connector
- Internet Mail Service
- Dynamic RAS Connector

Some instances indicate a type of connector rather obviously. For example, if a company already pays for a public X.400 connection to a provider, the X.400 connector is an obvious choice for the Exchange network. Other instances require some decision-making. For example, if the enterprise has available only a couple of modems and standard telephone lines, you can approach connectivity in three ways:

- Use the Dynamic RAS Connector for point-to-point transfer.
- Use a dial-up connection to the Internet and use the Internet Mail Service.
- Deploy Windows NT routing technology that provides dial-on-demand connectivity, then deploy the X.400 connector.

Perhaps your greatest dilemma is when there is either a WAN using leased lines or dial-on-demand Integrated Services Digital Network (ISDN). In principle you could use either the Site Connector, X.400 Connector, or Internet Mail Service to link the sites together.

Use the Site Connector whenever possible because it is the fastest and provides the most resilience. To use it, a network must support synchronous RPC and Windows NT authentication. Although you can deploy a site connector in a Windows NT model where there are no domain relationships, you may have to implement one temporarily to carry the authentication while you set up the Site Connector. This involves setting up a two-way trust and assigning Exchange permissions for the local site services account in the adjacent site. After the connector is in place, you can remove the trust relationship.

The rule of thumb says that you should use the Site Connector when bandwidth is good, the X.400 connector when bandwidth is limited, and the Internet Mail Service when you link sites over the Internet. Fair enough, but what is *good* bandwidth? Many people are too timid when it comes to estimating available bandwidth, so they use the "safest" connector (X.400). This does use less bandwidth than other connectors, but it introduces resilience and security issues. You should also consider the amount of network latency. For example, satellite links, well-known for high latency, can cause errors to appear in the Event Log, even though the network has sufficient bandwidth to carry the data.

To help you compare connectors, the tables below show how much data is seen on the network when transmitting a message between two sites using each of the available connectors.

A simple plain text message—traffic includes binding and authentication of the MTAs

Connector	Traffic sent (bytes)	Traffic received (bytes)	Total frames	Comments
Site (RPC)	7,484	3,889	60	Secure connection, whole session encrypted
X.400	4,087	751	19	Message header and body part names in plain text
Internet Mail Service	6,962	1,376	30	Uses NTLM authentication and encryption

A simple plain text message—MTAs already bound

Connector	Traffic sent (bytes)	Traffic received (bytes)	Total frames	Comments
Site (RPC)	4,744	1,434	24	Secure connection, whole session encrypted
X.400	3,653	319	13	Message header and body part names in plain text
Internet Mail Service	6,962	1,376	30	Uses NTLM authentication and encryption

A message with a 304-KB attachment—MTAs already bound

Connector	Traffic sent (bytes)	Traffic received (bytes)	Total frames	Comments
Site (RPC)	342,302	19,629	471	Secure connection, whole session encrypted
X.400	332,366	12,279	454	Message header and body part names in plain text
Internet Mail Service	453,164	13,258	523	Uses NTLM authentication and encryption

As you can see from the tables, the X.400 connector is most efficient on the network. However, it does not provide the level of security that the other connectors offer. You will also notice that there is not too much overhead on the Site Connector as the size of the message increases. All RPC requests made by the Exchange MTA are serialized. If an MTA does not respond quickly enough, thread blocking can occur, preventing the local MTA from communicating with other servers, even on fast links. You will need careful analysis to ensure that Exchange Server performance is not degraded by slow network links. In general, messaging system designers, still favor the Site Connector for its resilience capabilities.

Directory Replication Connectors

The simplest arrangement is to layer the directory replication topology directly onto the messaging topology. If you decide to deploy "shortcut" messaging connectors, document them carefully and use them sparingly: if you deploy many of them in a large multiple-site Exchange system, the Gateway Address Resolution Table (GWART) can get extremely large, which puts significant overhead on route calculation, which can hinder message routing and delivery.

In a pure hub-and-spoke environment, stagger directory replication times between the hub and the spokes so that the whole environment is updated in one cycle.

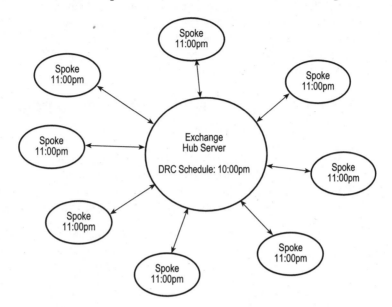

This figure shows each hub-to-spoke directory replication connector set to request updates at 10:00 P.M. and each spoke-to-hub directory replication connector set to request updates at 11:00 P.M. This one-hour gap ensures that the hub site has complete knowledge before the spokes start requesting updates. This is significant: reverse the request times and it would take two days to replicate new objects to the entire organization (assuming the replication occurred only once a day).

Setting Limits on the Backbone

To keep the messaging system fast and efficient, you must set a maximum message size. There are lots of opinions on this, of course, but 5 MB is a common maximum. When you choose a limit, there are various ways to impose it. If you have complete control of the Exchange environment you can set the **Outgoing Message Size Limit** on individual mailboxes, which allows certain users or agents to send larger messages if required. Although this limit can't be set at the information store level, you can automate the setting using ADSI. A different approach is to set the maximum message size limit directly on the MTA, thus limiting every user automatically.

Exchange system traffic is allowed to exceed the message size limit. For example, you cannot use it to restrict large messages in a replicated public folder. To enforce a restriction in this case, you would have to use a rule to affect a specific public folder.

Tuning a Messaging Bridgehead Server

Large Exchange installations usually deploy dedicated message switching servers in the hub site for performance reasons. In these scenarios the MTA process must take precedence over all other tasks in the server, Exchange and non-Exchange. To fully tune a connector server, you have to "break" the normal Exchange rules of hardware design and configuration.

CPU, Memory, and Network Interface Cards

Dedicated Exchange MTA servers are normally processor-bound. You will get far more performance out of a dual-processor 333-MHz Pentium II than you will from a quad-processor 200-MHz Pentium Pro. Current architectural limitations prevent Pentium II–based servers from supporting more than two processors. For mailbox/public folder servers, a Pentium Pro–based server offers higher performance because of the more tightly coupled L2 cache memory.

Dedicated messaging servers often need only 128 MB of memory because their information stores are small compared to those of mailbox and public folder servers.

If your hardware vendor supports multiple-failover network interface cards, it is a good idea to install them. This will ensure that the server stays running even in the event of a network failure.

Disk Configuration

Connector and mailbox/public folder servers differ in hard disk arrangement. Both types should use a quality Redundant Array of Inexpensive Disks (RAID) controller that supports hardware level RAID5 and RAID1. For mailbox and public folder servers, place the information store databases and transaction logs on separate disks; for connector servers, place both components on the same disk because the MTA does not pass messages through the store. To boost performance, distribute the \exchsrvr\mtadata directory over as many spindles as possible. The reason for this is that when the MTA is receiving a message, it is written to the hard disk as a .DAT file in the \mtadata directory and, after the routing decision has been made, the data is passed directly to the MTA of another Exchange server, thus bypassing the information store.

There are a few exceptions to the above rules. Connectors based on the Exchange Development Kit use virtual queues (MTS-IN and MTS-OUT) that *are* held in the information store, so for servers with these connectors (Internet Mail Service, Connector for cc:Mail, Connector for Notes, and most third party connector products), it is a good idea to place the logs and the information store on separate disks for performance and resilience. It should also be noted that the directory service acts as a client to the information store and passes incoming directory replication requests through the information store.

The write-back memory cache on a quality RAID controller can also be enabled to improve performance. Quality controllers have heavy parity ratio and a battery backup. If it allows you to set the read/write cache ratio, such as the Compaq SMART Array controller, configure it as 25 percent read and 75 percent write for maximum performance.

Performance Optimizer

After installation is complete, you can boost performance by running the Exchange Performance Optimizer and selecting the correct options for your server. If you don't run it, performance may be sluggish and the server may generate error messages in the application event log. For a pure Exchange messaging bridgehead server, deselect the **Private** and **Public Store Server** checkboxes and select **MultiServer**. This increases the number of available kernel threads and Request To Send (RTS) threads in the MTA from 1 to 3.

Take great care when selecting options within Performance Optimizer, such as **Number of users on this server**. For example, a hub server would not house any local mailboxes and so you might be tempted to select the **Less than 500 users** option, the lowest user range. Unfortunately, this setting appears in the MTA registry parameter *MDB users,* which sets the directory service cache size in the MTA. As a new feature in Exchange Server 5.5, the MTA can cache commonly used directory objects (such as mailboxes) instead of constantly reading from the directory when a message is routed. To set this registry key appropriately, specify a higher user range in the Performance Optimizer or manually tune it with the registry editor. A good rule of thumb is to set the *MDB users* value to equal one third of the total number of recipients in the global address list (GAL).

Manual Registry Tuning

Depending on the total number of connectors supported by the hub servers, you may want to change some MTA registry settings. Exchange Server 4.0 and 5.0 required specific registry adjustments when used as a message switching hub. For example, only 64 TCP/IP connections could be created by the MTA, which limited the total number of connectors that could be reasonably housed on a single server. The number of threads that the MTA could allocate was also based upon a registry value that required careful tuning on busy servers. The Exchange 5.5 MTA is much more dynamic, and you will find that many of the MTA registry keys are now redundant, although the Performance Optimizer will still change them. For example, the LAN-MTA parameters are now dynamically adjusted and allocated as needed, but the Performance Optimizer will still adjust the parameters when the **Connector, Directory Import** option is selected. So that you do not waste time attempting to tune redundant parameters, refer to the full list of active parameters in the section Active MTA Registry Parameters at the end of this chapter.

Some of the MTA registry values do not work as expected. For example, Performance Optimizer always sets the value for **Dispatcher threads** to 2, although the MTA when it starts allocates 6: 2 for the Router, 2 for Fanout, and 2 for Results. Therefore, the **Dispatcher threads** value that is visible in the registry should not be taken as the absolute number of threads allocated to this component. This value indicates how many threads each subcomponent can allocate.

You almost never have to alter MTA registry parameters in Exchange Server 5.5. The only common case is if you have more than 20 X.400 connectors on a bridgehead server, in which case you must adjust the *TCP/IP control blocks* to equal the total number of X.400 connectors.

MTA registry parameters can be found under

HKEY_LOCAL_MACHINE/System/CurrentControlSet/Services
/MSExchangeMTA/Parameters

Urgent Associations

The Exchange 5.5 MTA is the first version to assure that important messages are not held up behind lower priority ones. It creates an urgent association dynamically for a priority message as soon as it arrives in the queue.

Tuning a Distribution List Expansion Server

Many organizations want to take full advantage of distribution lists, a popular feature in Exchange. Companies that have a large number of lists, including large numbers of users, should deploy a dedicated distribution list expansion server within the hub site.

When defining distribution lists, you should place no more than 3,000 users in a single list, definitely no more than 5,000. Use nested lists wherever possible as this will increase performance. Although the messaging hub site seems like an ideal place to create your lists, Exchange allows the delegation of distribution list management (users nominated to maintain a list can modify its contents), which requires the list and its owner to be in the same Exchange site.

With nested lists, you should define the master list in the Exchange hub site, and its nested lists in the sites where their maintenance will take place. When users send messages to the master list, the nominated server in the hub site expands the entire list including nested lists, and then distributes the message appropriately.

To optimize a distribution list expansion server's performance, increase the MTA registry key *DL Member Cache Size* from its default of 15,000 to an appropriate number for the size of the organization. The default value allows the server to cache up to 15,000 distinguished names held within the distribution lists, which can include duplicate names for users held in more than one list. The cache is refreshed every 10 minutes (default), when a thread examines the *When-Changed* raw attribute of the list. If the list has changed since the last refresh, it is reloaded into the cache. If it hasn't, the thread remains, as the cached list is still up to date.

You can also tune the *Dispatcher threads* and *Transfer threads* registry parameters if the distribution list server is having difficulties clearing its queues.

Tuning a Directory Replication Bridgehead Server

The executable for the directory service is called DSAMAIN.EXE, and it is fully multithreaded and multitasking. Upon startup of the directory service, the program allocates threads to handle client requests and directory replication from other Exchange servers. The registry parameter **Max Threads** *(EXDS+NSP+DRA)* controls exactly how many threads can be allocated for the directory service process. The Exchange Performance Optimizer always sets this value to 50 no matter which options are selected. These threads are shared between the different directory service tasks:

- **EXDS**—Process that handles Lightweight Directory Access Protocol (LDAP) and DAPI requests.
- **NSP**—Name service provider handles directory requests from MAPI clients.
- **DRA**—Directory replication agent handles server-to-server replication tasks.

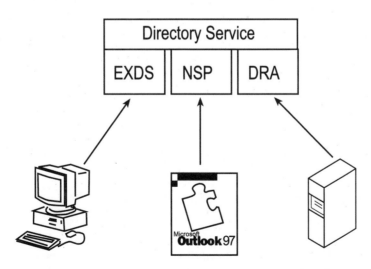

All of these sub-components compete for threads from the directory service. If the Exchange server contains a large number of mailboxes (more than 1,500) and is slow responding to client requests, increase this registry value by 30 to ease the bottleneck. Use Windows NT Performance Monitor to see how many threads are in use by the directory service (Object = Process, Counter = Threads in use, and Instance = DSAMAIN).

Although DRA threads are allocated out of the master pool, you can adjust the number reserved for this sub-component. If an Exchange server can't keep up with replication requests or if you have a dedicated Exchange server for directory replication (directory bridgehead), you can increase the **Replicator maximum concurrent read threads** registry parameter, doubling, for instance, the 10 set aside by Performance Optimizer. Remember: threads come out of the master pool, so you may need to increase the *Max Threads (EXDS+NSP+DRA)* registry parameter as well.

Directory registry parameters can be found under

HKEY_LOCAL_MACHINE/System/CurrentControlSet/Services /MSExchangeDS/Parameters.

Changing Directory Replication Connectors

The network infrastructure in an enterprise often changes, so it may sometimes be necessary to adjust Exchange to make best use of underlying networks. The most common requirement is to change directory replication connectors.

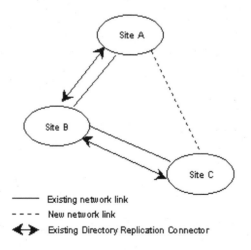

———— Existing network link

- - - - New network link

◀━▶ Existing Directory Replication Connector

Unfortunately, Exchange will not allow the configuration of triangulated directory replication connectors so the directory replication link must be torn down between sites before another can be established.

Rebuilding directory replication connector links is tricky. For instance, objects in the public folder hierarchy will have been replicated between the sites already. As long as you don't initiate any form of DS/IS consistency adjuster when the directory replication connector has been torn down, you should have no problems with any public folder replication or affinity when replication is formed again. Even public folder permissions are retained during a teardown.

Distribution lists present the biggest challenge. As soon as you tear down a directory replication connector, distribution lists lose any recipients that are no longer present in Address Book. You can avoid this by exporting distribution list (DL) membership out of the organization, simply by specifying the GAL as the export point. If the DLs belong to different sites, you must import the membership into each site individually.

Directory Replication Architecture

The Replication Model

Unlike a Windows NT Server domain, which maintains one central copy of the directory, in an Exchange site all Exchange servers are considered as masters and can modify any object within the site, regardless of where it was created. Between sites, all Exchange servers receive a read-only replica of all objects. The only exception to this rule is the address book views naming context, which is read/write between Exchange sites.

When a modification is made to the Exchange directory, a change notification is sent to all servers in the site, informing them that an update has taken place. It is then up to those servers to pull the updated entries from the notifying server. Change notification timings are controlled by registry parameters.

Change notifications are not used between sites. Instead, at a specified time, a bridgehead server sends request messages to an adjacent bridgehead server, which processes the requests and sends back the necessary response.

Background Traffic

There is no doubt that Exchange is a robust messaging product; however, for the product to notice inconsistencies, a level of background traffic (mostly directory replication and status information) will be seen between Exchange servers intrasite and intersite. Although Exchange can automatically detect and correct problems, enterprise-style installations may want to throttle this automatic facility if network resources and bandwidth are limited.

Invocation-Ids

Every directory service has a unique identifier called an **Invocation-Id** associated with it. To see the ID for a given Exchange server, run the Exchange Administrator program in raw mode (ADMIN -RAW), then drill down in the navigation bar and select the local server name. The right panel shows the directory service object. If you get the raw properties of, say, the directory service and select the **Invocation-Id** attribute, you'll see a 32-digit hexadecimal string that is the unique signature for the local directory service. It looks like this:

```
00F4355CE15AD111900800A02470DBE1
```

DSA-Signatures

Whenever an object is modified, the Invocation-Id of the local directory service is stamped against that object. The information is exposed through the **DSA-Signature** raw attribute on the directory object. These signatures provide the basic building blocks for intrasite and intersite replication. When a directory replication request is made to an Exchange server, the local DSA returns only objects stamped with its signature.

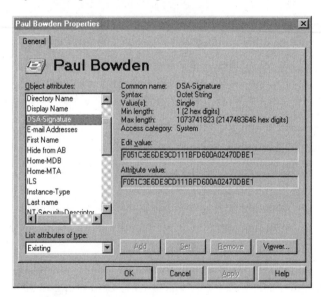

There are only two instances when an Exchange Server can inform other servers of directory data that it doesn't "own." The first is when a directory replication bridgehead server passes along information it has learned from connected sites.

The second is a little more complex. Imagine three servers in the site: A, B and C. If C is down, A and B replicate modifications to each other freely. If A is taken offline and C is then restarted, server B informs C of its own changes *plus* modifications that were made on server A. This scenario occurs only when Exchange services are started up, not if there is a break in communications such as a network fault.

Update Sequence Numbers

Whenever a change is made to the Exchange directory, the local directory service stamps the next available Update Sequence Number (USN) on that object. Starting at 1 and going up to 2,147,483,647, USNs are crucial to directory replication. Even so, USNs are not synchronized between servers in a site—each Exchange server maintains its own count, although the counts should be fairly close because directories should contain about the same number of objects.

Local directory services stamp one of their own USNs against all objects, regardless of whether they were created locally or replicated from another Exchange server.

To see the current USN of a given server, you must make a modification to the existing directory. The easiest way see the last USN is to modify a field on a current object like a mailbox, then look at its **USN-Changed** attribute.

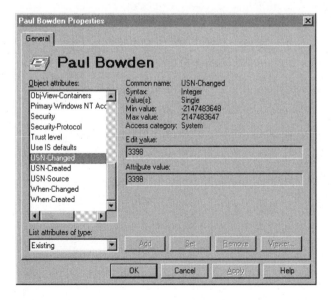

USN Fields

In raw mode, each directory object has a set of fields relating to USNs:

USN-Changed   The USN applied by the local directory service the last time this object was modified.

USN-Created   The USN assigned by the local directory service when this object was originally created in the local directory.

USN-Source   The USN assigned by the directory where the object was first created or last modified. This either relates to the USN assigned on absolute time of creation if local or the latest USN assigned on this object if replicated from another server.

Object-Versions

When a new object is created, it is stamped with version "1." Whenever it is changed, the directory service making the modification increments the version number. Replicated out to other directory services (untouched), version numbers are the directory service's primary tool for finding replication conflicts. If the directory service finds an object with the same version number but different **DSA-Signature**s, it knows the object has been changed independently on two different servers. The directory service resolves the conflict by saving the version with the latest time signature (**When-Changed** raw attribute).

Naming Contexts

An Exchange 5.5 directory has five naming contexts (Exchange 4.0 had four). Modifications always take place within a naming context. When a change takes place, a change notification is sent out for that context. For example, if you change two objects in different contexts on the same server, two push notifications are sent out to the other servers in the site. You can see the context names in the event log if diagnostic logging for directory replication is turned up:

Naming context identifiers in the event log

Naming context	Referred to as
Organization	/o=orgname
Site	/o=orgname/ou=sitename
Schema	/o=orgname/ou=sitename/cn=Microsoft DMD
Configuration	/o=orgname/ou=sitename/cn=Configuration
Address book views	/o=orgname/ou=_ABViews_

For example, a modification to a mailbox in the recipients container occurs in the site naming context. A modification made to an X.400 connector occurs in the configuration naming context.

Note   The Windows NT event viewer is a great troubleshooting tool that Exchange Server uses with directory replication diagnostic logging.

Local Modifications

When you use the Exchange Administrator program, you must log on to an individual Exchange server. When you select an object in the site naming context, the data is always retrieved from the logged-on server. When changes are made to the configuration naming context, the data may be retrieved locally (for example, from the X.400 connector) or pulled from the source server (for example, from the MS Mail (PC) connector).

When you create new objects or make modifications to existing entries, that data is written locally, even if the object's "home" is another server. This applies even when creating mailboxes on a server in the site that you are not logged on to. In this scenario, the mailbox is created only after replication has occurred.

REPS-TO and REPS-FROM

Each directory service retains a list of all other servers in the site with which it performs replication. These lists can be seen in raw mode on each naming context. The REPS-TO list is not too interesting, but the REPS-FROM list shows all of the other servers in the site that replicate to this one. More important, especially for troubleshooting, it shows the last USN received from that server. When looking at the REPS-FROM list for a particular context, keep in mind that the number reflects the last change made within that context, not the last change made on that server. Make it a habit to refresh (by pressing F5) the Exchange Administrator program before looking at USN numbers.

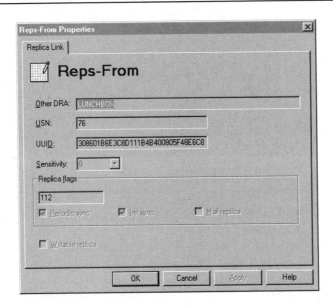

Directory Service "Channels"

Because directory services in the same site must authenticate to each other directly, a low-overhead communication channel is established between them and stays open for about 15 minutes. Data can flow freely over the channel without re-authentication between the servers. Directory service authentication generates roughly 8 KB of traffic.

Intrasite Directory Service Binding

When directory services communicate with each other, they do so through RPC. Because RPC itself relies on an underlying network protocol such as Transmission Control Protocol/Internet Protocol (TCP/IP), Internetwork Packet Exchange/Sequenced Packet Exchange (IPX/SPX), and NetBIOS extended user interface (NetBEUI), a registry parameter controls the prioritized transport list for binding. This is found under:

HKEY_LOCAL_MACHINE\Software\Microsoft\Exchange\ExchangeProvider

Value: RPC_SVR_BINDING_ORDER

Default: ncacn_ip_tcp,ncacn_spx,ncacn_vines_spp

To help Exchange reduce the binding latency, place the correct transport protocol at the start of the list and remove the others. If a remote Exchange server is temporarily down or there is a short-term network problem, the local Exchange server may waste CPU cycles and time (increasing latency) trying the other network protocols.

Objects Received from Remote Sites

It is always useful to see the last object replicated from a particular server or site. Just as you can look at the REPS-FROM list for contexts within your own site, you can also look at REPS-FROM information relating to other sites by calling up the raw properties on naming contexts in the read-only portion of your directory. This information should tell you about the last USN received from the remote bridgehead.

Object Replication

When an object such as a mailbox is modified, the entire object must be re-replicated. The directory service does not support field-level replication. This is a consideration if you are populating all of the fields for directory entries or if you perform bulk directory updates.

Manual Refreshing

When modifications are made to the local directory, they are normally seen immediately. If, however, changes are made through replication, you may need to refresh the window (by pressing F5) before you notice the change.

Tombstones

When an object is deactivated and marked for deletion from the Exchange directory, it becomes a tombstone entry. Because this is considered to be a change on the local directory, it is replicated to all other servers. Before being deleted, tombstone objects are kept for 30 days (the default) to leave enough time for the deleted object to be replicated throughout the organization. After 30 days, each Exchange server will expunge tombstoned entries, which does not involve additional replication.

Replication Traffic

Amount of Replication Traffic Generated

Let's return to the question: how much traffic does Exchange generate on the network? This is an important element in planning. Some Exchange designers try to minimize traffic by populating the fewest fields possible in the directory (display name, alias, and primary Windows NT account); others use the directory to its maximum potential. As a rough guideline, a mailbox created (or modified) with the minimum fields populated produces about 3.5 KB of traffic to all other servers in the site, and a fully populated one produces about 5.8 KB. These are rough figures and you can't multiply them when calculating directory replication traffic for multiple directory entries because data is bundled together.

Because servers within a site are presumed to have good bandwidth to each other, intrasite data is not compressed. Intersite, the local bridgehead servers can compress replication information before submitting messages.

Traffic Seen When Joining a Site

All Exchange servers in the organization must receive a complete copy of the Exchange directory. It is important to understand how this fact affects the network transmission rates, especially in cases such as adding a server to a large organization when it is at the end of a slow link.

In some companies, the overhead of replicating the directory to a new server over a slow link is too great. For scenarios such as these, other options are available such as building the new Exchange server on a high-speed network and then physically moving the server to its destination.

Intrasite Backup Replication Cycle

Regular backup traffic must be taken into account. Regardless of the amount of change, every server in a site initiates a full backup replication to every other server every 6 hours by default. This does not burden the network as much as you might think. Exchange Servers pass only delta information, and because all servers are kept close to up-to-date, this traffic can be fairly small in small sites. In large sites it may be significant, and you may want to change the bit mask to extend the interval between backup replication cycles.

A backup replication initiates this sequence of events between a local server and every other server in the site:

1. Local DSA requests an update for the organization naming context and waits for a response.

2. Remote DSA processes the request and sends any changes.

3. Local DSA requests an update for the site naming context and waits for a response.

4. Remote DSA processes the request and sends any changes.

5. Local DSA requests an update for the schema naming context and waits for a response.

6. Remote DSA processes the request and sends any changes.

7. Local DSA requests an update for the configuration naming context and waits for a response.

8. Remote DSA processes the request and sends any changes.

9. Local DSA requests an update for the address book views naming context and waits for a response.

10. Remote DSA processes the request and sends any changes.

Backup replication requests go to each Exchange server in the site. The local server updates its knowledge grouped per naming context, not by server. For example, if there are three servers in the site, the local server asks for the organization naming context from server B, waits to complete, then asks for the organization naming context from server C. After these have been received, it then moves on to the site naming context. If one of the servers is down for maintenance, the next task is attempted without further delay. DSAs have a fixed timeout of 35 minutes. If an adjacent server cannot be contacted within this time, an error 13 is raised in the event log.

Assuming that each naming context is already up to date, allow for about 20 KB of replication traffic for each server, each way. This can be significant in large sites. An Exchange site with 50 servers would see 47.8 MB of total traffic (# Servers - 1) 20 (# Servers) staggered over 6 hours. To see if this is acceptable, you must analyze the speed and topology of the network links dividing the Exchange servers.

You can adjust the backup replication schedule by changing the raw **Period-Rep-Sync-Times** attribute (each naming context has one of these) in the directory. The field contains 168 hexadecimal digits, each digit controlling a 1-hour timeframe, which means you can shift the cycle over a 7-day period. On some servers you may notice that the string is populated with 1s, which indicate the first 15-minute period of the hour; on others you may see 8s, which equate to the third 15-minute period. Click on the **Editor** button to see/set the time schedule for replication.

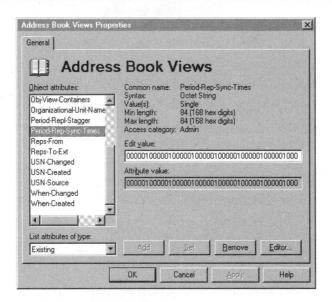

Intersite Backup Replication Cycle

There is no intersite backup replication cycle, but every 6 hours a single request message passes between bridgeheads asking for updates to the address book views context. The number of address book views request messages from each site depends on the total number of sites in the organization (# of sites – 1). This action can be controlled using the **Period-Rep-Sync-Times** attribute for the address book views naming context.

The Knowledge Consistency Checker

At each 3-hour interval the Exchange knowledge consistency checker (KCC) executes to verify that server knowledge is consistent throughout the site. The KCC runs on each Exchange server and verifies that all servers have knowledge about each other. The KCC checks the number of servers in the site that it knows about against the number of servers in the site that its partner has listed. If it finds that the local server does not have the same knowledge as the partner server, it establishes replication links to the new server. Partner servers are defined as the result of a *stricmp* calculation against the list of servers in the site. In general terms, the local KCC moves from one server to the next in numeric or alphabetic order. In a large, complex site, you can directly influence the KCC connections and latency by correctly naming your servers. The same amount of data is generated no matter how you name your servers, but you can use your knowledge of the underlying network to optimize the connections.

Failure to consider the underlying network when planning Exchange server names can increase overhead on your WAN and pressure on Exchange.

Consider this example of a poorly designed site. For simplification, the Exchange servers are literally called A, B, C, and so on. Black lines represent the network structure, and boxes represent Exchange servers.

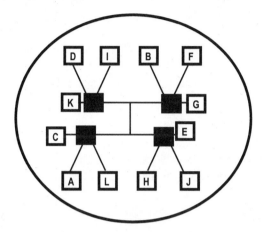

This structure will cause knowledge links to be established over multiple network hops and over the WAN. Using different server names could alleviate much of this unnecessary traffic, with corresponding improvement to network performance.

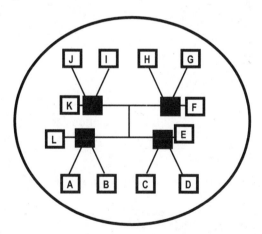

The last server in the site establishes its knowledge link with the first. When another Exchange server joins or leaves the site, full knowledge of that change should be propagated within a few hours. In this context, "last" and "first" do not refer to when the servers were installed, but to their alphabetic position in the configuration context.

When all servers are up and running, this ring is consistent. If a server goes down for some reason, its upstream partner continues calling it. If there is no response in 30 seconds, the upstream server gives up and binds to the inactive server's downstream partner.

The KCC also has a role to play for intersite knowledge. During initial replication, the KCC can create placeholders for other sites. These can be seen in the local Exchange Administrator program as an "empty" site name and configuration container. After these objects exist, the directory service populates them with the information contained in the directory replication response messages received from adjacent bridgehead servers.

Intrasite Replication Packets

The table below outlines the packets sent and received on the network during intrasite replication. Packet lengths can vary with different naming conventions; the values used here are offered as a general guide.

Intrasite replication traffic

Packet description	Length
Context change notification	214 bytes
Notification acknowledgment	118 bytes
Context pull request	246 bytes
Response to pull request	Multiples of maximum frame size
Context received acknowledgment	60 bytes

Replication Events

Each part of the directory replication process raises an event as it executes. If diagnostic logging is turned up, this information can be seen within the application event log. In the following table the DRA is the Directory Replication Agent.

Replication event IDs generated by the directory service

Event ID	Description
1068	Local DRA was told to pull updates from the remote server.
1070	Local DRA has been asked to supply changes to a remote server.
1071	Local DRA has calculated the number of objects to be replicated.
1199	Local DRA has compressed the replication message.
1058	Local DRA has successfully received an update for the context.
1099	Local DRA has received a request message from another site.
1101	Local DRA submitted a response messages to another site.

DRA Option Values

Whenever requesting directory replication, a DRA specifies the options criteria for the request. These can be seen in the application event log when diagnostic logging for replication is turned up.

Option values seen against events in the application event log

Option value	Description
3	Normal intrasite replication
4000	Manually invoked request updates
4041	Normal replication for bridgehead servers, or downstream servers requesting updates for remote site naming contexts from the local bridgehead in the site
4051	"Backup" replication cycle
C000	Manually invoked request for all objects

Intersite Replication Messages

The mechanics of intersite directory replication differ from those of intrasite replication. Activation is controlled through the **Schedule** tab on the directory replication connector on each bridgehead server. Be careful when setting the activation schedule. It is easy to select a one-hour time block, which would generate four update request messages per context within that hour and therefore four complete replication cycles. You should instead choose a single 15-minute block in the **Schedule** tab for each desired replication cycle. When the schedule becomes active, the directory service on the local bridgehead composes a number of messages and addresses them to the directory service on the remote bridgehead.

Intersite replication request messages

Msg	Contents	Size (bytes)
1	Request configuration naming context	144
2	Request site naming context	120

The total number of request messages composed depends upon the number of sites gained through this connector. If the directory replication topology is hub-and-spoke (20 satellites), each satellite bridgehead composes 40 messages on each directory replication schedule (2 x 19 other satellites and 2 requests for the hub site). All directory update requests are sent to the adjacent bridgehead in the hub site. The hub site responds to these requests on behalf of the other satellite sites. This means that if the hub site does not have full knowledge of a particular satellite site, it cannot pass on any more information than what it has to the requesting satellite.

If there has been no change to the requested context, a response message is sent saying so. If there have been changes, the objects are gathered, compressed (if necessary), and then sent in a single mail message per context (up to the packet size defined in the registry). A response message is sent for each request.

If there are problems with the underlying message transport, you will see many directory replication requests in the MTA queues. The bridgehead must *always* respond to requests, so when message routing resumes you will see many responses in the queues. If replication appears not to be working, don't request a full directory update between sites—the requests will just pile up, and when message routing resumes the responses will pile up. Failure to receive responses usually means a problem in the underlying message transport, not with replication. Most new Exchange administrators are not used to the pause between setting up a new directory replication connector and the population of the stubs. They therefore assume that directory replication is not working and try to manually request updates, which just makes the MTA queue up with more directory replication messages.

Manually Asking for Updates from a Remote Site

If you believe that your local Exchange site is out of synchronization or you want immediate delivery of recent changes from another site, click the **Request Now** button for a remote site on the directory replication connector. There are two update options: updates since the last communication and re-request of all objects. A "re-request all objects" effectively produces a directory replication update message where the starting USN is "1."

Update requests are always sent for the three naming contexts in the table below. Message lengths vary with different naming conventions, and the numbers below are provided as a general guide. The DRA does not have to request or process the contexts in any specific order.

Intersite replication request messages sent on demand

Context	Request length (bytes)
Request site naming context	120
Request configuration naming context	144
Request address book views naming context	120

For the Address book views request only, the local bridgehead server requests updates within the site before sending the request message.

After the remote bridgehead has received the requests, it works out the number of objects that it needs to return and then submits the response messages. If there have been no updates within each context, the response messages are small.

Message lengths vary with different naming conventions, and the numbers below are provided as a general guide.

Intersite replication response message sizes (Exchange level, not network level)

Context	Response length (bytes)
Site naming context	1,400
Configuration naming context	1,320
Address book views naming context	1,176

If there have been updates to the context, the information is bundled up and sent in the response message. The amount of replication traffic caused by modified objects depends on the number of fields populated, so it is not accurately predictable for planning purposes. Allow anywhere between 2 and 5 KB for each replicated object. If necessary, the response message will be compressed.

When the local bridgehead receives updates from another site, it propagates that information (even if the responses indicate no changes) to servers within the local site through normal intrasite replication.

Compression

Exchange servers in the same site normally have good bandwidth, so they do not compress objects that they pass to each other for replication. Between sites, where bandwidth is not always plentiful, bridgehead servers compress replication traffic over 50 Kb. Under this amount it is more efficient to send the information as-is rather than use CPU cycles to compress it. The target bridgehead decompresses information before entering it into the local directory. The compression ratio is roughly 5:1.

Intersite Replication on Startup

Some companies prefer to perform offline backups of their Exchange servers. Although this method is fast and complete, taking down a directory bridgehead and restarting it (either a shutdown or **NET START**) causes a full intersite replication. Five minutes after the directory service makes contact with the MTA process (on the same Exchange server), directory replication request messages are sent to adjacent bridgeheads.

You can stop these directory update messages from being sent using a new registry parameter implemented in Exchange 4.0 SP5, Exchange 5.0 SP2, and Exchange 5.5 SP1.

Directory Replication Registry Parameter Tuning

The registry parameters that control how the directory service process works are found under:

HKEY_LOCAL_MACHINE/System/CurrentControlSet/Services
/MSExchangeDS/Parameters

Value: Replicator Notify Pause After Modification (seconds)

Data type: REG_DWORD

Default: 300

Description: This sets the period that must elapse on the local directory service before it sends notification packets for modifications made in the local directory. These notifications are sent to all of the other servers within the site.

Advice: If you have a large Exchange site spread over a WAN, you may want to increase this value on the servers where you make directory modifications so that directory changes are batched up for more than 300 seconds. Increasing this value increases the time it takes to replicate directory information throughout the site. Generally, a value of 30 minutes (1,800 seconds) is acceptable to most companies.

Value: Replicator Notify Pause Between DSAs (seconds)

Default: 30

Description: This sets the wait time interval between notifying servers in the site that a change has taken place. The wait ensures that the modified directory service is not overloaded with update requests all at once.

Advice: If you have a large Exchange site spread over a WAN, you may want to increase notification time between the servers to 120 seconds, which is acceptable in most situations.

Value: Intrasite Packet Size

Data type: REG_DWORD

Default: 100

Description: This sets the maximum number of updated objects that the local directory service will send in a RPC response when responding to a directory replication update request. If the local directory service has more than this number of objects, it informs the remote directory service (using direct RPC) to request more objects. This acts as a checkpoint and ensures the communication link is still valid.

Advice: Leave this value alone unless you have a specific requirement.

Value: Intersite Packet Size

Data type: REG_DWORD

Default: 512

Description: For a directory service acting as a bridgehead server, this sets the maximum number of directory update objects it will send in one message when responding to a directory replication update request message. If the local directory service has more than this number of objects, it tells the remote directory service (using a message) to request more objects.

Advice: Leave this value alone unless you have a specific requirement.

Value: Replicator Intersite Synchronization at Startup

Data type: REG_DWORD

Default: 1 (not present)

Description: The default means that a full intersite replication occurs when a directory replication bridgehead is restarted. Change this to zero and there is no automatic replication.

Advice: Change this only if you frequently restart directory bridgehead servers.

Public Folder Replication and Status Messages

Public Folder Hierarchy Replication

When public folders are created, modified, or deleted, update information must be sent to all other public information stores within the organization. The information store service is responsible for this action. By default, a thread runs every 15 minutes to check for changes in the public folder hierarchy. If it finds none, it exits without generating data. If it finds changes on the local server, it creates an update messages and submits it to the MTA. Default limits for a single message are 20 new/changed folders and/or 500 deleted folders. The message is sent to all public stores in the organization, propagating changes as if in a mesh relationship. The update message size depends on the number of changes made in the hierarchy.

Hierarchy replication message sizes

Number of changes	Size of message (KB)
1	2
2	3
3	3
4	4

To reduce the frequency of hierarchy change replication, go to the Exchange Administrator program and under *Server* in the public information store object raise the value of the *Replicate always interval (minutes)* parameter. The next time the thread executes it will reread this value and adjust its execution time. You do not need to stop any services for this change to take effect.

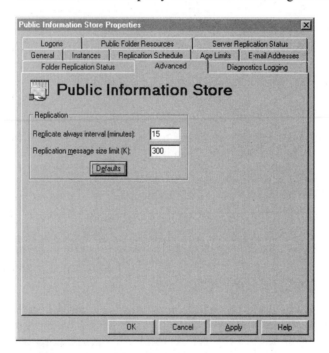

Public Folder Hierarchy Status Messages

Even when public folders are not used for housing information, the existence of a public information store on an Exchange server (default) creates traffic throughout the enterprise. By default, a store thread runs every 12 hours (at 12:15 A.M. and 12:15 P.M. GMT) to determine if a public folder hierarchy status message has been sent out in the last 24 hours. If one has not been sent, one is composed and sent; if one has been sent, no action is taken. The message contains the status of the public folder hierarchy folder, and its size depends on the number of folders in the hierarchy. Note that the thread runs on GMT and is completely independent of the Windows NT locale, time zone, and daylight savings settings.

This mechanism can be troublesome for large environments. First of all, the public folder hierarchy status message is addressed to all other servers that have a public information store. These stores do not see site boundaries, so the message is sent to every public store in the organization. Removing unused public information stores from servers can reduce this traffic. A second problem is the send time of the status message. Depending upon when the information store service is started, it dictates when the status message is sent out, just after midnight or just after midday. The calculation for working out when the status message will be generated is:

Information store startup time + 24 hours + time to next thread execution (every 12 hours)

For example, if the information store is started at 3:00 A.M., Monday morning, the status message will be generated at 12:15 P.M., Tuesday afternoon.

General Public Folder Status Messages

If public folder replication is configured between two or more Exchange servers, the information is truly synchronized between the two systems. If replication messages are somehow lost, the public folder components can recover by identifying inconsistencies and back-filling information. This is a good arrangement, but it generates background status messages.

For efficiency reasons, status messages for each replicated public folder are sent as a single message wherever possible. To reduce the number of status messages flowing through the Exchange network you should:

- Replicate public folders only when you need to.
- Try to establish a common *replication topology.*

Replication topology refers to the number and identity (names) of servers that have an instance of a given public folder. Say you have 200 folders replicated between servers A, B, and C in the same Exchange site. Although each folder must transmit its status, this topology requires only six status messages: A sends one to B and one to C, B sends one to A and one to C, and C sends one to A and one to B. Because all 200 folders are replicated to the same servers, the status information can be bundled into one message.

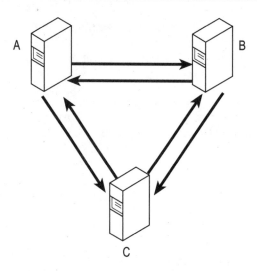

If you create another 50 public folders and replicate them between A, B, and C, you will still have only six status messages, although they will be slightly larger. If you now add another 10 public folders and replicate them only between A and B, *eight* status messages will be generated. Because these 10 folders are not replicated to C, status information cannot be bundled, so separate messages are generated: one from A to B and one from B to A.

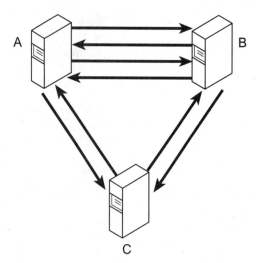

Public Store Registry Parameter Tuning

These parameters control the transmission of status messages by the information store service. By default, none of these parameters exists, and so manual creation is required under the section:

HKEY_LOCAL_MACHINE/System/CurrentControlSet/Services
/MSExchangeIS/ParametersPublic

Store Status

Value: Replication Send Status Timeout
Data Type: DWORD

Default: 84,600 *seconds (24 hours)*

Description: This is the minimum amount of time to wait before sending a public folder status message to the rest of the organization.

Advice: If there are more than 50 sites in the organization with slow links involved, you may want to adjust this parameter on each public store server. Increasing this value lowers the total amount of system traffic generated, although it increases the time required to resolve inconsistencies in the public folder hierarchy.

Value: Replication Send Status Alignment
Data Type: DWORD

Default: 42,300 *seconds (12 hours)*

Description: Minimum period to wait before the public folder status store thread runs.

Advice: Leave this parameter alone.

Value: Replication Send Status Alignment Skew
Data Type: DWORD

Default: 0 *seconds*

Description: This sets an amount of time after 12:15 A.M./P.M. GMT to run the public folder status store thread.

Advice: If the network has to move many system messages during the day, find out when most of the messages are being generated and adjust this parameter to delay generation until quiet times of the day. Some companies adjust this parameter so that all system messages are generated at 6:15 A.M. or 6:15 P.M. local.

Store Startup

When the information store process is started, two status messages are sent to all of the other public stores within the organization to ensure public folder consistency. In environments where Exchange servers are restarted regularly (after nightly offline backups, for instance), this can deluge the hubs with mail. A new registry parameter allows you to prevent status messages on startup. It is recognized only by Exchange 4.0 SP5, Exchange 5.0 SP2, and Exchange 5.5 SP1 or the relative hot fix.

Value: Disable Replication Messages at Startup

Data Type: DWORD

Default: 0

Description: Prevents the information store from sending status messages for public and system folders on startup.

Advice: Adjust this parameter only if public store servers are regularly restarted.

Note Offline backups cause extra administrative burden and do not ensure the integrity of the data within the information store. Use online backups wherever possible.

Intrasite Directory Replication Example

Here is an example that shows the intrasite replication process as it is initiated after creation of a new mailbox on Server 1, one of three Exchange servers in the base configuration:

Server	Current USN
Server 1	1053
Server 2	1060
Server 3	1049

1. The Administrator creates the mailbox directly on Server 1. The new object is stamped with 1054 on all three USN fields. Server 1's **DSA-signature** is written on the object and version 1 is assigned.

2. Exactly 5 minutes after the change is made, a change notification is sent first to Server 2. If these two directory services have not communicated in the last 15 minutes, they authenticate to each other. When authenticated, the push consists of a single 214-byte packet containing the updated naming context. An internal timer now counts down from 30.

3. In response to the push, Server 2 sends to Server 1 an acknowledgment consisting of a single 118-byte packet.

4. Almost immediately, Server 2 requests to synchronize its copy of the naming context with Server 1. It informs Server 1 that it wants to obtain all new objects starting with 1054 and options 3 (normal replication). With "replication" diagnostic logging turned up, this is signified by event 1068 in Server 2's application event log. The request consists of a single 246-byte frame.

5. When Server 1 receives the pull request, it finds all the objects that are stamped with USN 1054 or higher and with its own **DSA-signature.** This process is signified with event 1070 in Server 1's application event log.

6. After Server 1 completes this process, the DSA reports the number of objects found that match the criteria (event 1071) and starts to transmit the information. This will be seen on the network as multiple packets of the maximum frame length for that topology (1,514 bytes for Ethernet, 4,202 bytes for Token Ring).

7. After Server 2 receives all of the information, the DSA sends back a single frame of 60 bytes as an acknowledgment and then reports event 1058 to signify that the replication completed successfully. The new mailbox object is assigned the following USN values in Server 2's directory:

```
USN-Changed: 1061
USN-Created: 1061
USN-Source: 1054
```

8. Even though Server 2's current USN has incremented because of the new object, the DSA knows that it shouldn't replicate this information onward because the object does not have its **DSA-signature.**

9. Server 2 updates its REPS-FROM list on the site naming context for the Server 1 server. This reflects USN 1054.

10. After the timer in step 2 has expired, Server 1 performs this same process for Server 3, although without the timer because there are no other servers in the site to replicate to. After completion, Server 3 assigns the following USN values to the new mailbox object:

```
USN-Changed: 1050
USN-Created: 1050
USN-Source:  1054
```

Tuning Scenario

Based on an actual large Exchange deployment, the example shows the number of system messages generated and how design and deployment mistakes can cause problems.

Configuration Details

Network topology: Data center with 128-Kb/second lines (shared) to each office

Number of Exchange sites: 140 (139 single-server sites)

Messaging topology: Pure hub-and-spoke using X.400 connectors

Directory replication topology: Pure hub-and-spoke

Number of Exchange servers: 141 (all Exchange 5.0)

Problems

- MTAs in the hub site were crashing three times a day.
- MTACHECK would generally run okay, but sometimes an MTAWIPE had to be performed.
- Thousands of system messages (directory service and public store) were in the queues.

Resolution of MTA Stability

The primary issue was MTA instability. There were only two servers in the hub site, each with 70 X.400 connectors and 70 directory replication connectors. Although this is theoretically possible, it cannot be accomplished without manually tuning the 5.0 MTA. Unfortunately, because the MTA kept crashing, more messages would back up in the queues and the sheer number of messages would crash the MTA again, and so on.

Changing MTA registry parameters (doubling the number of threads for the kernel, dispatcher, and TCP/IP) relieved contention on the MTA and reduced crash frequency to every other day.

Although the MTA in Exchange Server 5.5 would have resolved many of these problems, the full release code wasn't ready at the time and so the only way to relieve the pressure was to double the number of hub servers to four. This action stabilized the hubs, although there was still a huge number of messages in the queues.

Working Out Where the System Messages Came From

The next task was to determine why the messages were being generated. A full directory replication cycle was being performed once a day, early in the morning. The hub-and-spoke directory replication connector schedules were staggered appropriately by 3 hours, but a one-hour time block had been set, not 15 minutes.

Hub Directory Replication

When the hub directory replication connector schedule became active at 1:00 A.M., the hub servers would send two directory update request messages to each spoke site. Because a one-hour time block had been set, six additional directory update request messages would be sent to each spoke.

- Total number of request messages generated: 1,112
- Total number of response messages generated: 1,112

Spoke Directory Replication

When each of the spoke directory replication connector schedules became active at 4:00 A.M., each spoke server would send two directory update request messages (addressed to one of the hub servers) for each site obtained through the directory replication connector. Because a one-hour time block was set, six additional directory update request messages would be sent for each site.

- Total number of request messages generated: 154,568
- Total number of response messages generated: 154,568

Hub-to-Spoke Address Book Views Replication

Since address book views are not replicated as per the directory replication connector schedule, every six hours the hub would send each spoke a single update request message.

- Total number of request messages generated in 24 hours: 556
- Total number of response messages generated in 24 hours: 556

Spoke-to-Hub Address Book Views Replication

Every 6 hours each spoke server would send an updated request message for each site gained through the connector. These messages would be processed by one of the hub servers.

- Total number of request messages generated in 24 hours: 77,284
- Total number of response messages generated in 24 hours: 77,284

Public Folder Hierarchy Status Messages

Every 24 hours, each server with a public information store sends out the status of the public folder hierarchy. There must be at least one public information store per site, which means there had to be at least 140 public stores in this organization. In fact there were 141 because both original bridgehead servers also had public stores. Although each of the spoke servers sent only one status message to the hub, this message would get fanned out at the hub because each message was addressed to all public stores in the organization.

- Total number of status messages generated in 24 hours: 19,881

Overall Analysis

This adds up to nearly half a million system messages every 24 hours. Obviously, this is unacceptable and serious tuning was begun. Some obvious errors had been made when installing the directory replication connectors, and these were fairly easy to solve. Most of the other tuning had to be accomplished with registry settings and raw mode of the Exchange directory.

To determine how to go about tuning the system, the consultants asked the system owners three fundamental questions about basic Exchange use:

- How often do you want a full directory replication to occur?
- Do you actively use address book views?
- Do you actively use public folders?

The system owners wanted one full directory replication a day. They did not use address book views or public folders, but wanted to leave the functionality enabled in case they decided to use them.

Active Tuning

Having defined what the company wanted and secured agreement for a general plan of attack, the consultants began tuning.

Directory Replication

The one-hour time block was changed to 15 minutes on each directory replication connector. Activation times were left as they were. Here is how this affected traffic:

Hub to spoke

- Total number of request messages generated: 278
- Total number of response messages generated: 278

Spoke to hub

- Total number of request messages generated: 38,642
- Total number of response messages generated: 38,642

Address Book Views Replication

Because the functionality was left enabled, some sort of replication had to be in place, so the **Period-Rep-Sync-Times** attribute on the hub servers was set to Saturday 10:00 A.M. and on the spoke servers to Saturday 10:00 P.M. Here is how this affected traffic:

Hub to spoke

- Total number of request messages generated in 7 days: 139
- Total number of response messages generated in 7 days: 139

Spoke to hub

- Total number of request messages generated in 7 days: 19,321
- Total number of response messages generated in 7 days: 19,321

Public Folder Hierarchy Status Messages

Public folder functionality was also kept, but to reduce traffic redundant public information stores were deleted. As it was, the only one that could be deleted was at the hub, and this reduced traffic levels insignificantly. Next, the daily automatic status message was changed to weekly, with a registry key. Unlike address book views, the status message cannot be explicitly scheduled for a certain time and day: instead it is sent every *xx* hours. The client company generally took servers down for maintenance only on weekends, so a 7-day schedule fit nicely. For more protection, the consultants implemented a 6-hour time skew so that status would be sent at 6:15 A.M. and 6:15 P.M.—that is, always outside normal working hours. Here is how this affected traffic:

Total number of status messages generated every 7 days: 19,600

The Result

Tuning reduced total system traffic from the original half million to 136,360. The hub servers were eventually upgraded to Exchange Server 5.5 to provide higher throughput on the connections. Although the figures still seem a little high, you must remember that this is a week's total system traffic for all servers. Because Exchange sites can span 128 Kb/second links, the company is redesigning the system to consolidate sites.

Active MTA Registry Parameters

You can find MTA registry parameters under

HKEY_LOCAL_MACHINE\System\CurrentControlSet\Services \MSExchangeMTA\Parameters

Parameter	Description	Tuning tip
Flush results to disk	Has never been used.	
Call-stack diagnostics required	Not used.	
Handle exceptions	Dictates whether the MTA will stop if a critical error occurs. Used in conjunction with *Raise exception on error.*	Leave at "1", unless troubleshooting.
MDB users	Sets the number of directory objects to be cached by the MTA.	Set to one third of the total GAL size for hub servers.
MMI connections	Not used.	

Parameter	Description	Tuning tip
Concurrent MDB/delivery queue clients	Not used.	
MT gateway clients	Number of message transfer gateways to accommodate, including EDK gateways such as the Connector for cc:Mail and Internet Mail Service.	Increase if "insufficient event control blocks" error messages are seen in the Event Log.
Retrieval queue clients	Not used.	
Concurrent connections to LAN-MTAs	Not used.	
Concurrent connections to RAS LAN-MTAs	Not used.	
LAN-MTAs	Not used.	
X.400 gateways	Not used.	
TP4 control blocks	Number of MTA control blocks for TP4 connections.	Increase if more than 4 MTAs are contacted over TP4. The default number of control blocks is 20. Allow for 5 control blocks per MTA connection.
TCP/IP control blocks	Number of MTA control blocks for RFC1006 (X.400) connections over TCP/IP.	Increase if more than 4 MTAs are contacted through X.400 over TCP/IP. The default number of control blocks is 20. Allow for 5 control blocks per MTA connection. Exchange 5.5 allows this value to be a maximum limit of 640, Exchange 5.5 SP1 allows up to 1250 control blocks.
XAPI MA threads	Not used.	
XAPI MT threads	Not used.	
XAPI MA queue threads	Not used.	
XAPI MT queue threads	Not used.	

(continued)

Parameter	Description	Tuning tip
Concurrent XAPI sessions	Number of X/Open sessions to gateways.	Only increase if many (more than 10) gateways are installed on the server.
Submit/deliver threads	Number of threads allocated for Store to MTA interaction.	Increase to 3 for a server with more than 1000 active mailboxes.
Dispatcher threads	Number of threads for MTA core engine.	Increase by 1 or 2 for poorly performing MTAs if they are heavily used.
Transfer threads	Number of threads handling outbound messages destined for gateways and other MTAs.	Increase by 1 or 2 for poorly performing MTAs if they are heavily used.
ds_read cache latency	Minimum amount of time to wait before refreshing directory objects cached by the MTA.	This defaults to 10 minutes. The lowest setting is 5 minutes, but this rarely needs adjusting.
Dispatch remote MTA messages	Dictates whether the MTA can deliver messages (.DAT files) when they have been created by remote MTAs.	Only change this value to 1 in a disaster recovery scenario.
RTS threads	Number of threads allocated for reliable transfer services (OSI stack).	Tune under the direction of Microsoft Technical Support.
Kernel threads	Number of threads allocated for the MTA Kernel (OSI stack).	Increase by 1 or 2 to relieve thread blocking if remote MTAs are located over slow or high-latency RPC links.
Number of RAS LAN-MTAs	Not used.	
Number of remote sites connected over LAN	Not used.	
Number of DLs allowed	Not used.	
DL member cache size	Number of distinguished names (including duplicates in nested lists) that can be cached.	Defaults to 15,000. Increase this value for heavily used dedicated distribution list expansion servers.
Max concurrent XAPI applications	Not used.	

Parameter	Description	Tuning tip
Max RPC calls outstanding	Maximum number of RPC calls that can be simultaneously open without a response.	Do not change.
Min RPC threads	Number of threads allocated for RPC communications.	Do not change.
DB data buffers per object	Not used.	
DB file handles	Not used.	
X.400 Service Event Log	Not used.	
DB file count delete threshold	Not used.	
DB file size delete threshold	Not used.	
Idle state working set size (Kbytes)	Not used.	
Idle state timer	Not used.	
Min. free diskspace : stop work (Mbytes)	Not used.	
Min. free diskspace : restart work (Mbytes)	Not used.	
Diskspace poll interval	Not used.	
Supports 2K TPDU	Dictates whether the MTA forces the sending of 2-KB units to the foreign MTA.	The MTA will normally transfer data in 16-KB units. X.400 standards specify that the maximum allowable unit is 64 KB and should be negotiated on association. Some foreign MTAs such as various ISOCOR products only support 2-KB units and do not negotiate.
Max. RPC delay on LAN (secs)	Not used.	
Max. RPC delay on RAS (secs)	Not used.	
Raise exception on fatal error	Stops the MTA if a critical error occurs (severity level 16).	Use for troubleshooting.

(continued)

Parameter	Description	Tuning tip
Allow fuzzy proxy search	Allows X.400 O/R matching even if the incoming message does not have the correct recipient address. Matching can be accomplished through first name and last name fields within the directory.	Change under the direction of Microsoft Technical Support.
Log proxy resolution	Name of the file to hold fuzzy proxy resolution data.	Useful for troubleshooting fuzzy proxy resolution.
Do not generate bilateral info	Global switch for all connectors as to whether they generate bilateral information. The Exchange MTA uses this to work out if a message is looping or if a message has simply been routed to another country ID and back again.	Change if a connecting foreign MTA has problems interpreting bilateral information.
RFC1006 port number	The TCP port number that the MTA uses for listening to incoming X.400 connections.	The default is 102. This only needs to be changed under specific circumstances such as for routing through a firewall.
Outbound queue alarm on	Number of messages to be present in an outbound queue before an event is logged in the Event Log.	Use for monitoring purposes.
Outbound queue alarm off	Number of messages to be present in an outbound queue before logged events are switched off.	Use for monitoring purposes.
Message timeout (urgent), minutes	Used to override the time period before an urgent message returns non-delivery report through link failure.	Defaults to 2 days. Note: All MTAs in the organization must have the same setting for this to be effective.
Message timeout (normal), minutes	Used to override the time period before a normal priority message returns non-delivery report through link failure.	Defaults to 7 days. Note: All MTAs in the organization must have the same setting for this to be effective.
Message timeout (non-urgent), minutes	Used to override the time period before a low priority message returns non-delivery report through link failure.	Defaults to 10 days. Note: All MTAs in the organization must have the same setting for this to be effective.

Supporting Microsoft Exchange

Based on an extensive project during which Microsoft Consulting Services developed and implemented a 3-tier support structure for a large company, the chapters in Part 2 show how to divide support tasks logically, how to apportion responsibilities, and how to control support issues effectively.

C H A P T E R   5

Establishing 3-Tier Support

Part 2, "Supporting Microsoft Exchange," describes how to organize, staff, and operate a 3-tier support organization that provides helpdesk personnel, operations staff, and systems administrators with guidelines and best practices. Based on Microsoft Consulting Services (MCS) experience with a large telecommunications company that rolled out an Exchange environment built on Microsoft Windows NT Server and Microsoft Systems Management Server, it ranges from high-level processes and procedures for the support organization to high-detail call scripts for helpdesk personnel troubleshooting end-user problems. Although the example is based on Exchange Server 5.5 and the Outlook Client, you can use the principles here to plan your support infrastructure.

This chapter provides an overview of the support organization and the responsibilities of each tier. The remaining chapters focus on the operational and functional details of each tier, including escalation processes, troubleshooting tips for helpdesk, and backup and recovery procedures.

The Existing Support Dilemma

MCS worked with a large telecommunications company that used 10 different e-mail products throughout its organization and wanted to configure one messaging system to improve communications and reduce support costs. MCS recommended Exchange Server and Windows NT Server, and deployed the system with Systems Management Server.

The company used this opportunity to revamp its support organization to better serve its 60,000 users hosted on 300 servers. Originally the helpdesk consisted of a hotline with no escalation procedures. As a result, the staff supporting a number of products had meager resources and the company lacked systematic backup, monitoring, and troubleshooting. MCS recommended a 3-tier structure, relying heavily on a problem management system—a database logging answers and resolutions to end-user questions and server problems. As the database grows, the front-line support group can resolve more end-user problems without having to escalate them to higher levels.

The Proposed Support Solution

Because of the large number of users being served, the support organization divides responsibilities into three levels:

- **Tier 1 Helpdesk**—Handles end-user support, account creation and modification, and system monitoring.
- **Tier 2 Operations**—Performs administration tasks and provides second-level support for end-user problems.
- **Tier 3 Systems Management**—Focuses on capacity planning and other methods of system optimization.

The three-tier support model provides clear guidelines for efficiently supporting a new messaging system and its users. It is based on effective separation of support tasks, a carefully controlled escalation process, and the steady accumulation of support knowledge that prevents "reinventing of the wheel." As the problem management system grows through steady accumulation of resolutions, Tier 1 personnel can solve more and more problems without escalating calls.

Server Categories Supported

The Exchange support organization maintains these categories of servers:

- Windows NT master domain controllers
- Windows NT WINS
- Exchange
- Systems Management Server

Categories not maintained are Windows NT Server resource domains, Windows NT resource domain controllers, application servers, SQL Server, and Web servers.

Support Communications

The Exchange support organization can communicate with end users through public folders, a Web site, e-mail, and telephone. For broad issues affecting the entire group as well as end users, an intranet site:

- Informs end users (production and non-production Exchange users) of system status.
- Distributes on-call schedules and information on group issues to the support organization.
- Automates departmental functions.
- Automates receipt of end-user and administrative requests.

Tier 1: Helpdesk

Tier 1 operates 24 hours a day, 7 days a week (24x7), to support end users and monitor system status. It parses client issues from server or network issues, handling the former and escalating the latter.

Support

Tier 1 personnel understand all aspects of Exchange and Outlook clients, and have a working knowledge of various Microsoft Windows operating systems. Support begins when an end user contacts helpdesk with a client, server, or network issue. The Tier 1 engineers field calls and work with users until problems are resolved, adding solutions to the problem management system database. Problems that can't be resolved are escalated. The call-handling scripts that helpdesk personnel use to investigate and resolve (or escalate) issues are in Chapter 6, "Tier 1 Helpdesk."

Operations

As the only 24x7 group in the organization, Tier 1 tracks the health of the system. If they see alerts displayed on their system status monitors, they escalate the problem to Tier 2, where on-duty or on-call personnel respond immediately.

Administration

Tier 1 support also handles certain limited requests for administrative support:

- Creating Windows NT accounts
- Maintaining Windows NT account groups
- Maintaining Exchange accounts
- Maintaining Exchange distribution lists

Tier 2: Administration

Tier 2 consists of central and remote operations staff. The central operations team performs operations and administrative roles, and provides second-level support for end users. Remote site personnel focus on corporate servers in their location. Tier 2 has available staff 12 hours a day with on-call staff to handle escalations during off hours.

Support

Tier 2 provides support, knowledge, and tools that Tier 1 uses to provide efficient end-user help. To reduce calls to Tier 1 and escalated problems, Tier 2 personnel use the problem management system to detect trends and fix problems before they affect end users. During off hours, Tier 2 on-call personnel have access to the problem management system and can work on problems escalated by Tier 1. They resolve all server operations issues.

Operations

Tier 2 performs:

- System monitoring
- Report generation
- System backup
- Backup tape verification
- Exchange mailbox/folder tape restores
- Server maintenance

Administration

Tier 2 handles all administrative tasks not performed by Tier 1 except for certain domain-level administrative tasks such as maintaining trust relationships. In addition, Tier 2 maintains the support organization's Web site and performs other system administration tasks for its own departmental servers.

Tier 3: System Management

Although team members have expertise in Windows NT, Exchange, and Systems Management Server, some must also function as project manager, programmer, and Web developer. Similar to Tier 2, Tier 3 is a 12-hour operation with off hours covered by on-call team members. Unlike Tier 1 and Tier 2, some Tier 3 tasks fall into categories other than support, maintenance, and administration: system management, departmental infrastructure, Web site, and utility development.

Support

Tier 3 personnel work directly with Tier 2 staff to resolve issues, but do not have direct contact with end users. Tier 3 works to resolve Tier 2 issues, developing solutions that Tier 2 can implement when the same problem recurs. Tier 3 also monitors the problem management system to detect trends and fix them before they affect end users or degrade performance.

Microsoft Technical Support (MTS) is the last level of escalation if Tier 3 cannot resolve a problem. Because the company is allowed only a limited number of support calls to MTS before extra charges apply, Tier 3 reviews, approves, and manages all contacts with MTS.

System Management

Tier 3 is responsible for:

- System analysis
- Capacity planning
- System tuning
- Performance optimization
- System expansion
- Mailbox and public folder recovery
- Pre-production testing

Tier 3 personnel also evaluate and test new system management tools. Each member of the support organization contributes ideas to improve the group's performance. Tier 3 works with a mix of personnel from all tiers to implement approved ideas. Tier 3 also determines departmental hardware requirements, tests new and existing services, and manages the development of required software and databases.

CHAPTER 6

Tier 1 Helpdesk

The chapter continues the 3-tier support organization designed by MCS for a large telecommunications company with 60,000 users hosted on 300 servers. Tier 1 helpdesk provides the initial point of contact between users and support staff and the first line of defense in troubleshooting, resolving end-user problems, identifying server problems, escalating new problems, and keeping the company's problem management system (their knowledge base) current. The chapter describes how to establish a helpdesk and how support personnel should field calls using scripts and procedures.

The helpdesk staff also handles basic administrative tasks and system monitoring, developing troubleshooting tips and basic administration guidelines, intended to resolve more and more recurrent (or similar) problems at the Tier 1 level, reducing reliance on Tiers 2 and 3. The second half of the chapter provides helpdesk personnel with information on how to reset passwords, monitor servers, fix remote access problems, and troubleshoot other issues.

Overview of Helpdesk Roles and Responsibilities

As the first point of contact with support staff, Tier 1 works to resolve problems or escalate calls. Tier 1 helpdesk primarily supports end users with accounts on Exchange, Windows NT Server, and Systems Management Server. Tier 1 personnel perform limited administrative tasks, and do not provide support for legacy systems or to users on Exchange systems installed without company approval (also called rogue systems). Helpdesk duties include:

- Providing support to incoming calls at the workstation and network levels, including logging the incoming calls in the problem management system and escalating as necessary.

- Focusing on issues involving user attempts to log on to the Windows NT accounts domain, Microsoft Outlook startup and configuration, profile setup, sending and receiving mail (including attachments), and using the Outlook calendar.

- Calling users back when issues are resolved.

- Handling remote mail issues.
- Monitoring mail servers, escalating problems to the appropriate tier.

Issues not supported by Tier 1 personnel include:

- Rogue Microsoft Exchange systems.
- MS Mail (refer users to the MS Mail Administrator).
- Share points and domains in the local site resource Windows NT (refer users to the local helpdesk).
- Client installation (refer users to the client deployment group).

All non-supported issues are referred to the appropriate local site administrators. See the section Resources and Contacts for the appropriate contact information.

Helpdesk Personnel Guidelines

Tier 1 personnel need to solve a broad range of problems, but do not require technical expertise in any one area. Tier 1 personnel should understand:

- Outlook.
- Windows NT Workstation (versions 3.51 and 4.0), Windows for Workgroups 3.11, and Windows 95.
- How to set up TCP/IP (configuration and basic troubleshooting).
- How to send mail from Microsoft Office applications (assisting users through menu selections and tasks and diagnosing common problems).
- The responsibilities of each support level so they can route support calls to the correct tier.
- Effective communications, both verbal (for telephone support) and written (on call tickets, documenting problem descriptions and resolutions).

Required Desktop Applications

Tier 1 helpdesk personnel require the following set of applications to resolve client issues while on the phone with users:

Application	Function or task
Windows NT Server Manager	To administer the Windows NT Server domain from Windows NT Workstation
Windows NT User Manager	To administer Windows NT user accounts

Application	Function or task
Microsoft Exchange Administrator	To maintain Exchange mailboxes
Microsoft Outlook	To duplicate caller actions and access Outlook online help to look up "how-do-I" client tasks
Problem management system database	The "Knowledge Base" used to log calls via call tickets. To log calls into and refer to it to find previous, similar problems and the solutions
TCP/IP utilities	To troubleshoot network issues: PING, NET USE
Internet Explorer 4.0	To access the Internet

Other Required Resources

These include:

- **Company directory,** an Intranet Web site containing contact information for all employees and contractors, street addresses for remote offices, and detailed user information for account lookup and verification, including organizational information and titles
- **Microsoft Exchange Server documentation**
- *Microsoft Outlook 97 Administrator's Guide*

Call Handling Procedures

Helpdesk is available Monday through Friday from 8:00 A.M. to 5:00 P.M. local time. Hours of operation can be expanded if necessary. Domestic users contact the helpdesk for support using the telephone. The organization should publish contact phone numbers on the company's intranet site, in the e-mail address book, in in-house publications, and through other avenues. International users should have a separate number.

To handle calls efficiently, the following steps outline how incoming calls are processed.

Note For specific scripting in handling a user call, refer to the Scripts section later in this document.

Identify Problem Area

When the Tier 1 receives a call, the helpdesk engineer should verify whether the problem falls within the support organization's scope. Generally, issues related to client and server infrastructure fall within this scope:

- Outlook
- Exchange Server
- Windows NT Server
- Systems Management Server

If the problem does not fall within the above scope, the helpdesk engineer should refer the user to the appropriate organization:

Infrastructure or system	Contact
Rogue system	Refer users to the rogue system administrator.
Client issues regarding MS Mail	Refer users to the respective MS Mail system administrator.
Local site resource domain issues	Refer users to their respective local helpdesk.
Client installation-related issues	Refer users to client deployment.
Forms and public folder application issues	Refer users to development support.

Obtain Information from the User

- User's name, phone number, location, times available, and best method of contact.
- Product being used when the problem occurred.
- Operating system and hardware environment.
- Description of the problem.
- Resolution expected by the user.
- Time frame in which the user expects the problem to be resolved.

Use relevant questions from the list below, from *Microsoft Sourcebook for the Helpdesk,* to elicit detailed and specific information about the problem.

1. A complete problem description.
2. Whether the problem is reproducible.

3. The steps to follow to reproduce the problem.

4. The exact text of the error message resulting from the problem, including numbers.

5. The symptoms of the problem.

6. When the problem started.

7. How long the problem has been occurring.

8. What specifically is being done when the problem occurs.

9. Whether it ever worked and, if so, when and for how long.

10. Specifically what software or hardware has changed and what is different now from the time when it did work.

11. What steps the user has taken to solve the problem.

12. The factors that have been eliminated as unrelated to the problem.

13. The severity of the problem—that is, the impact on the users', department's, and company's business.

14. Whether other applications are involved.

15. The operating system and version numbers.

16. What patches have been applied.

17. Hardware configuration.

18. Software configuration.

19. Network configuration.

20. Contents of important system files.

21. Contents of audit, event, or error log.

22. When the user last backed up the data

23. Additional data that should be in the call history.

24. Whether there a possible workaround to the problem to use while the problem is researched.

25. What known problem and its resolutions this issue could be related to.

26. How quickly the user needs a resolution.

27. Who has worked on the problem in the past.

Assign a Priority to the Problem

Priorities are assigned based on the problem's severity; the higher the priority, the more quickly Tier 1 personnel should begin working on it. Use the table below as a guideline in assigning priorities.

Severity level	Definition	Response times
Server Down	Windows NT Server or Exchange Server is not functioning, or there is a network outage.	Immediate escalation
1—Emergency	The issue is critical and affects many users.	Less than 1 hour
	Users cannot work or are severely impacted, including connector and gateway issues where message flow is affected.	
2—Immediate	Users can perform work, but a specific application is not available or is not working at all.	Less than 2 hours
	Users are significantly impaired or there is significant customer concern.	
3—Moderate	A function is not working.	Less than 4 hours
	The issue is important but has no significant impact on current productivity.	
4—Normal	The user has requested an information update or installation but is able to work normally.	Less than 24 hours
5—Informational	The user has requested information only.	Less than 24 hours

Note These are maximum response times. Approaching the maximum is considered the exception, not the norm.

Enter Problem into Problem Management System

Enter the information gathered from the user and the priority into the call ticket. The problem management system places calls in priority order in each support engineer's call queue.

Categorizing Incoming Calls

Generally, the incoming calls can be categorized as:

- Mail access problems
- Mail failures
- Account issues

Detailed handling procedures for each of these areas are listed in the following sections.

Mail Access Problems

What to do when a user cannot connect to the e-mail system.

1. Determine which e-mail package the user is using:
   - **MS Mail:** For issues relating to MS Mail, send the call ticket to the local site desktop support (messaging) with the relevant user information and problem description.
   - **Outlook:** These issues are the responsibility of the Tier 1 group. Obtain more information about the problem.
2. Find out the user's location. This information will help you direct the problem to the appropriate resource at the user's site.
3. Determine which domain the user is trying to log on by asking the user. If the user doesn't know, you can look up the information in user's mailbox in the Microsoft Exchange Administrator program.
4. Look up the user's Exchange logon server and ID to make sure the user actually has an account and to verify that the account information is correct.
5. Verify that the user's information matches the information about the user in the directory. If information in the directory is incorrect, update the user's mailbox with the correct information.
6. Check if the user is validated on the domain.

   If **yes** and there was an error message, record the error message. Refer to the Troubleshooting section in the second half of this chapter for specific errors on Windows NT Logon Problems. If the issue cannot be resolved, route the call ticket to Tier 2.

If **no,** determine which domain the user is attempting to log on to:

- **Production domain:** Refer to the Troubleshooting section, Domain Issues and Password Issues, for resolution. If the issue cannot be resolved, route the call ticket to Tier 2.

- **Rogue domain:** This is not supported. Route the call to the rogue system administrator.

- **Other domains:** If the name of the domain administrator is available, contact the administrator of the domain the user is trying to log on to and discuss the issue.

7. Record as much detail as possible about the issue and forward the ticket to Tier 2 for resolution.

Mail Failures

What to do when the user's e-mail fails.

1. Determine which e-mail package the user is using:

- **MS Mail:** For issues relating to MS Mail, send the call ticket to the local site desktop support (messaging) with the relevant user information and problem description.

- **Outlook:** These issues are responsibilities of the Tier 1 group. Obtain more information about the problem.

2. Find out the user's location. This information will help you direct the problem to the appropriate resource at the user's site.

3. Determine which domain the user is trying to log on to. You can ask the user, or look up the information in the user's mailbox in the Exchange Administrator program.

4. Determine the address the user was trying to send to. Look up the address in the global address list (GAL) and make sure it exists.

5. Record the exact error message the user received.

6. Refer to the Troubleshooting section, Mail Sending/Receiving, for possible resolutions.

7. If the issue cannot be resolved, record as much detail as possible and route the call ticket to Tier 2.

Account Issues

These include new accounts, client usability, and other client issues.

New Accounts

1. Set up a new Windows NT user account on domain PRODUCTION.
2. Create an Exchange mailbox for the user.
3. Determine if the user had a previous mail account and if the user needs the old mail forwarded.

   If **yes,** obtain the administrator's name for the old account (if possible) and record in the call ticket. Set up mail forwarding, based on the following information, or forward the ticket to Tier 2 to set up mail forwarding:

Old mail system	Forwarding (yes/no)
UNIX	Set up mail forwarding
MS Mail	Migrate to production Exchange, then delete old account (no forwarding)
Microsoft Exchange	Migrate to production Exchange and delete old (including rogue) mailboxes (no forwarding)

5. Provide the user with Windows NT logon information: account name, password, and logon domain.

Client Usability

For client features and usability (questions on 'How-do-I...?') issues, refer to the Outlook online help, the *Outlook User Manual*, and the online tutorial folder.

Other Client Issues

For other issues, refer to the list below to determine if it is covered in the Troubleshooting section in the second half of this chapter. The list contains typical problems users may encounter. Problems not listed here are generally escalated to Tier 2.

Windows NT Logon Problems

- Unavailable domain controller
- Account issues
- Domain issues
- Password issues
- Logon script issues

Exchange Problems

- Inability to connect to a server
- Addressing
    - A recipient could not be found in the global address list.
    - A non-delivery report indicates an invalid address.
    - A personal address book (PAB) entry is invalid for a recipient in a different site.
    - A PAB entry is invalid for a recipient in a same site.
    - A recipient could not be found.
- Mail sending/receiving
    - Inbound mail is late or doesn't arrive.
    - Outbound mail is late or doesn't arrive.
    - User can't send to recipient in a different site.
    - User can't send to a user in the same site.
    - User can't send to a user on the Internet.
    - User can't send to a user on the same server.
- Profile problems
    - There is no personal folder file.
    - User can't create, modify or delete a profile.
    - The Microsoft Exchange Server information service isn't listed in profiles.
    - The **Choose Profile** box has a **Password** box.
    - The personal address book (PAB) isn't accessible.
    - The profile is gone after updating the operating system.

- Calendar problems
    - User can't synchronize offline schedule.
    - User can't access another user's schedule.
- Public folders
    - User requests a new public folder be created.
    - User can't access a public folder.
    - User can't view a public folder in the hierarchy.
    - User can't send mail to a public folder.
    - Public folder replication isn't working.
- Distribution lists
    - User requests a new distribution list be created.
    - User can't send to a distribution list.
    - A distribution list is missing members.
- Problems with attachments
    - Mail sent from Microsoft Exchange is received with garbled text or extra attachments.
    - User cannot open attachments in Microsoft Exchange.
    - Attachment sent to SMTP host is not received.
- Sending mail from Microsoft Word
    - User can't access Microsoft Exchange from Word **Send** option.
- Remote access problems
    - A modem isn't working.
    - A modem doesn't connect at the highest possible speed.
    - There are no options for remote use with a Windows client.
- Hot links
- Outlook preview pane option
- Outlook printing incorrectly

Helpdesk Call Scripts

This section provides scripts for handling helpdesk calls.

Qualifying Scripts for Helpdesk Personnel

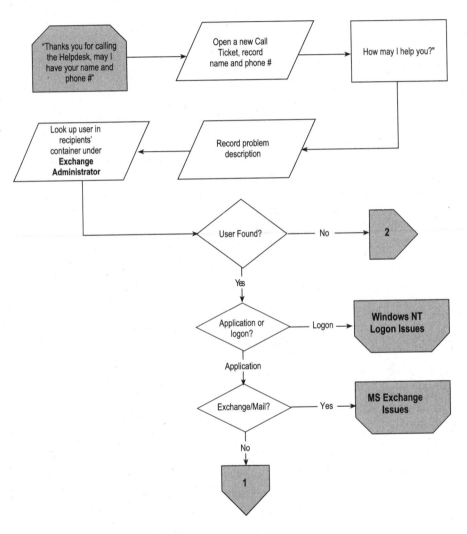

First half of qualifying script for Tier 1 support

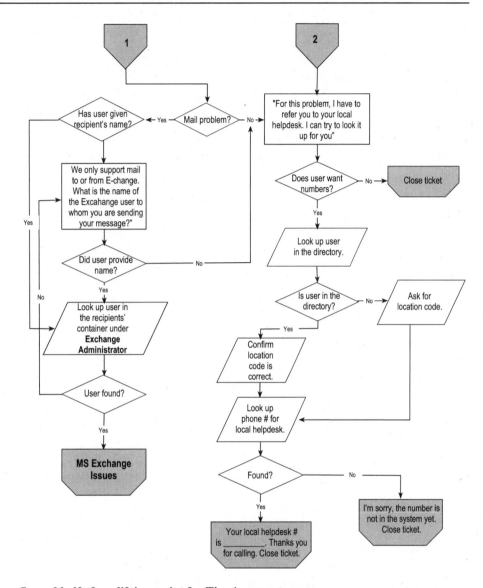

Second half of qualifying script for Tier 1 support

Windows NT Logon Issues Script

Follow this flowchart when handling Windows NT logon issues. Numbered issues correspond to the Troubleshooting Windows NT Logon Problems section in the second half of this chapter.

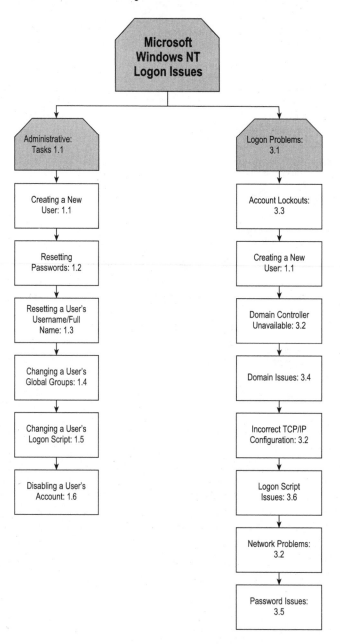

Script for handling Windows NT logon issues

Microsoft Exchange Issues Script

Use this flowchart when handling Exchange issues. Numbered issues correspond to sections in the Troubleshooting Exchange Problems section later in this chapter.

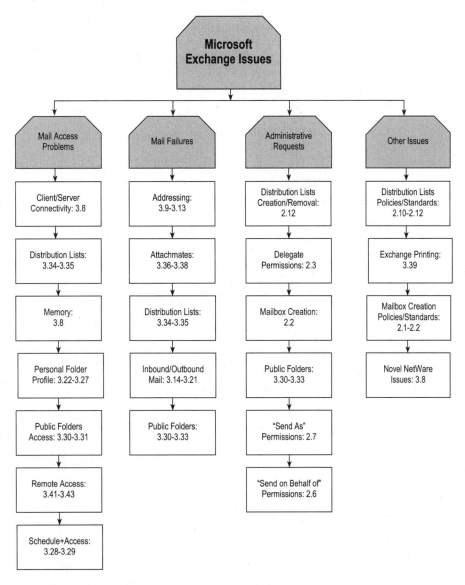

Script for handling Microsoft Exchange issues

Escalation Procedures

Help calls are escalated only after the call-handler has exhausted all Tier 1 resources. When client-related issues must be escalated to Tier 2, the resolution is entered into the problem management system so it is available to Tier 1 personnel the next time a similar problem is reported.

Server-related calls, such as "server is down," are immediately escalated through the Tier 1 team lead, who in turn escalates the problem to the Tier 2 team lead by telephone or e-mail. Tier 1 helpdesk engineers must escalate problems through the Tier 1 team lead, never directly to Tier 2.

Some client-related calls can be escalated to "emergency," taking priority over other calls in the system. Use these criteria:

- Severity level of call: emergency status or inability to work
- Level of user in organization
- Length of time the user has been out of commission with this problem

Under these circumstances, the helpdesk engineer consults the Tier 1 team lead, who reviews the emergency rating and, if appropriate, escalates the call to the Tier 2 team lead or, if desktop-related, to the local site desktop support coordinator. Emergency issues should be referred by telephone. The helpdesk engineer then informs the user by phone of the escalation and contacts the user again when the problem is resolved.

Interface to Other Support Organizations

Tier 1 personnel can field support calls in areas outside of the scope of Tier 1 responsibilities. In such cases, the helpdesk engineer should refer the user to the group best able to assist, such as the user's local desktop support organization. To determine a user's desktop support organization:

1. From the Microsoft Exchange Administrator program or from the directory system, determine the office location from which the user is calling.

2. If unable to look up the user's location, find out whether the user knows who it is and how to contact that person or group. (If it is a location not listed in the Resources and Contacts section below or the information is incorrect, post the information in the appropriate shared folder.)

3. Refer to the section Resources and Contacts in this document to contact the desktop support organization for that location.

4. Explain the caller's problem to the support person and relay any helpful ideas you may have on the source or solution. Ask the caller if what you described is accurate and complete. Stay with the caller and the local support person until the case is taken. Give the local support organization your ticket number and ask for their ticket number. Place their ticket number into the note field of the call ticket and use the number when you ask the support organization for updates.

This is only for problems outside Tier 1 engineers' responsibilities. For other problems, contact Tier 1 escalation for support.

Resources and Contacts

Keep the following list of phone numbers and contacts current and publish it in an easily accessible location for use by Tier 1 personnel.

Escalation Phone Numbers

- Site-specific helpdesks: locations and phone numbers.
- Rogue Exchange system administrators: locations, names, and phone numbers.
- Microsoft Mail system administrators: locations, names, and phone numbers.
- Other mail systems administrators: locations, names, and phone numbers.

Microsoft Exchange Servers and Sites

- Locations, site names, server names, and number of users.

Public Folder Owners

- Folder names, owners' names, and phone numbers

Windows NT Administration Tasks

The following Windows NT account creation and administration tasks require Windows NT Server domain administrator privileges to be performed. Not all Tier 1 personnel will by default have the required privileges to perform these tasks.

Note Numbers next to subheads below correspond to issues highlighted in the call scripts provided in the section Helpdesk Call Scripts (see figures above).

Resetting a Password (1.2)

When users forget their passwords, there is no way to look the old ones up—the helpdesk engineer must assign new ones. To do this, first confirm the user's identity and then follow these steps:

1. From the **Administrative Tools** group, start **User Manager for Domains**.

2. In the **Username** column, select the user account by double clicking on it.

3. In the **Password** box, enter the default password. Reenter the same password in the **Confirm Password** box. The default password is *welcome*.

4. Make sure **User Must Change Password at Next Logon** checkbox is selected.

5. Click **OK**.

6. Inform the user of the new password and explain that a new one must be chosen immediately after logging on.

7. Close **User Manager**.

Creating a New User Account (1.1)

1. From the **Administrative Tools** group, start **User Manager for Domains**.

2. You will see the users of the domain to which you log on. If you need to add a user to a different domain, from the **User** menu, click **Domain** and choose the domain.

3. From the **User** menu, click **New User**.

4. Obtain the user information from the directory system. Enter the following information:

   - **Username:** The user's directory handle.

   - **Full Name:** The user's full name, as it appears in directory.

   - **Password:** Enter the default logon password. This is the user's directory handle.

   - **Confirm Password:** Reenter the default logon password. This is the user's directory handle.

   - **Checkbox:** Make sure **User Must Change Password at Next Logon** checkbox is selected.

5. Click the **Groups** button. Make the user a member of the site global group (that is, if adding the user to the production site, add the production group to the **Member of** box). Click **OK**.

6. Click the **Profile** button. In the **Logon Script Name:** box, type **LOGIN.BAT**. Click **OK**.

7. Click the **Add** button.

8. Add the Exchange mailbox at the same time the Windows NT account is created. You are prompted to enter the Microsoft Exchange information; refer to the Microsoft Exchange Administration Tasks: Mailbox Creation section to complete the setup.

   (You can refer to Chapter 17, "Deploying Specialized Directories with ADSI," in the companion book *Deploying Microsoft Exchange Server 5.5* for a description and sample code for creating an Exchange mailbox and a Windows NT account and associating the two using a Web page.)

9. When done adding users, click **Cancel** to exit. Close **User Manager**.

Resetting a User Account's Username and Full Name (1.3)

1. Confirm the user's identity to make sure the caller is the owner of the Windows NT account requiring a reset name.

2. From the **Administrative Tools** group, start **User Manager for Domains**.

3. If the user's handle has changed, from the **User** menu, click **Rename**. In the **Change to:** box, enter the user's directory handle. Click **OK**.

4. If the user's full name has changed, in the **Username** column, select the user account by double-clicking on it. Use the **Change the Full Name:** option to match the user's directory full name. Click **OK**.

5. Close **User Manager**.

Changing a User's Global Groups (1.4)

1. Confirm the user's identity, to make sure the caller is the owner of the Windows NT account requiring the changes.

2. From the **Administrative Tools** group, start **User Manager for Domains**.

3. In the **Username** column, select the user account by double-clicking on it.

4. Click the **Groups** button. Add or remove the desired groups from the **Members of:** box. When done, click **OK**.

5. Close **User Manager**.

Changing a User's Logon Script (1.5)

1. Confirm the user's identity.
2. From the **Administrative Tools** group, start **User Manager for Domains**.
3. In the **Username** column, select the user account by double-clicking on it.
4. Click the **Profile** button. In the **Logon Script Name:** box, enter the name of the new logon file (for example, **LOGIN.BAT**).
5. Click **OK**
6. Close **User Manager**.

Disabling a User Account (1.6)

Disable user accounts that are no longer needed rather than deleting them: this preserves the unique SID (security identifier) for the accounts and allows you to reassign the accounts to those users if necessary.

1. Confirm the user's identity, or check with the supervisor to make sure the account is to be disabled.
2. From the **Administrative Tools** group, start **User Manager for Domains**.
3. In the **Username** column, select the user account by double-clicking on it.
4. Select the **Account Disabled** checkbox. Click **OK**.
5. Close **User Manager**.

Microsoft Exchange Administration Tasks

This section describes Exchange mailbox administration. Performing these tasks requires certain privileges that not all helpdesk engineers will have.

Administration tasks that fall under the scope of Tier 1 administration:

- **Mailboxes**—Creating and setting permissions.
- **Public folders**—Establishing and adding users.
- **Distribution lists**—Creating and removing.

Note Numbers next to subheads below correspond to issues highlighted in the call scripts provided in the section Helpdesk Call Scripts.

Mailbox Policies and Standards (2.1)

An Exchange mailbox receives electronic messages sent from other users. Every user on Exchange has a mailbox and appears in the global address list (GAL). The following standards are required when creating a mailbox:

- All entries in the **General** properties page of the user's mailbox are to be made in upper/lower case to ensure a uniform appearance of the GAL.
- The Exchange alias must match the user's account name.
- Mailbox proxy addresses should adhere to the following conventions:

  COMPANYNAME / *site* / *alias*

  SMTP *alias@companyname.com*

  X400 c=US;a=p=*companyname*;o=*site*;s=*LastName*;g=*FirstName*;i=*Initial*.

  The primary SMTP reply address is to be set to alias@companyname.com. Other (secondary) SMTP proxies can be maintained, so that the user will continue to receive any mail addressed to the old SMTP address.

Generally, there is only one associated Windows NT account per mailbox.

Mailbox Creation (2.2)

This section describes how to set up a mailbox for a new Exchange user with a valid Windows NT logon ID already defined. If no logon ID is defined, refer to the Windows NT Administration Tasks section before creating the Microsoft Exchange mailbox for the user. For more information about creating mailboxes, see the topic on setting up recipients in the *Microsoft Exchange Server Getting Started Guide.*

Refer to Chapter 17, "Deploying Specialized Directories with ADSI," in the companion book *Deploying Microsoft Exchange Server 5.5* for a description and sample code for creating an Exchange mailbox and a Windows NT account and associating the two using a Web page.

To create an Exchange mailbox, start the Exchange Server Administrator program and connect to the server on which the mailbox is to be created (for example: Production).

1. In the **Administrator** window, choose **Recipients**.
2. From the **File** menu, choose **New Mailbox** to open the **Mailbox** dialog box.
3. When the **Microsoft Exchange Properties** dialog box appears, enter all the pertinent new user information including:
   - **First Name:** User's first name (in upper/lower case).
   - **Initials:** The user's middle initial in upper case (blank if the user has no middle initial).

- **Last Name:** User's last name (in upper/lower case).
- **Display:** User's name as it will appear in the directory (in upper/lower case).
- **Alias:** A unique short name based on the user's directory handle.
- **Title:** User's title.
- **Company:** User's company or business unit.
- **Department:** The department for which the user works.
- **Office:** User's office or room number.
- **Other Properties:** Any other relevant user information.

4. Click the **Primary Windows NT Account** button.

- Click **Select an existing Windows NT account**.
- Select the domain the user's account resides in from the domains shown in **List Names From:**.
- Locate and highlight the user's name in the **Names:** list, then click **Add**.
- Click **OK**. You have linked the Exchange account with the user's Windows NT logon account, giving the user access to the Exchange mailbox.

5. Select the **E-mail Addresses** tab.

- Verify that the user's proxy addresses have been created correctly. Correct any wrong entries

  USER NAME / *site* / *alias.*

  SMTP *alias@companyname.com*

  X400
  c=US;a=;p=*COMPANYNAME*;o=*site*;s=*LastName*;g=*FirstName*;i=*Initial.*

- If needed, you can add a (new) secondary SMTP address: *alias@companyname.com*.
- You can also set this secondary SMTP address as the primary reply address:

  Highlight the SMTP address and click **Set as Reply Address**.

6. Select the **Distribution Lists** tab.

- All users by default should be added to their Location Code distribution list, which is referenced in the directory.
- Add the user to all other appropriate distribution lists by selecting **Modify**.
- Click **OK**.

7. Click **OK** to close the **Microsoft Exchange** properties dialog box.

Delegate Permissions (2.3)

Microsoft Outlook users who want an assistant to handle some e-mail and scheduling tasks for them can assign others to act as delegates. A delegate can perform various actions on the original owner's mailbox or schedule depending on the permissions granted by the owner.

To give a user access to a mailbox folder, first provide access to the mailbox and then grant a minimum of Read permission to one or more folders. Because the default permission in each mailbox folder is None, the user can open only those folders for which the permission has been changed. See the instructions below on how to set up the various types of delegate permissions.

Delegating a User (2.4)

To make a user a delegate of a mailbox:

1. Log on to the client as the owner of the mailbox and select the Mailbox top-level folder on the left side: Mailbox - *<username>*
2. From the **Tools** menu, choose **Options**, and then select the **Delegates** tab.
3. Choose **Add** to add a name to the **Name/Role** box.
4. Under **Type Name or Select From List**, type or select the name, click **Add** and then click **OK**.
5. Choose the **Inbox** and give the user the proper role.
6. Click **OK**.

The delegate now can open the mailbox and view messages in the Inbox.

Opening Another User's Mailbox as a Delegate (2.5)

The user acting as a delegate for another user's mailbox must complete the following steps:

1. From the **Tools** menu in the client, choose **Services**.
2. Select **Microsoft Exchange Server**, choose **Properties**, and then select the **Advanced** tab.
3. Click **Add** to add a name under **Open these additional mailboxes**.
4. Type the mailbox for which you have been made a delegate.
5. Click **OK**.

The additional mailbox appears in the folder list of the viewer along with your mailbox.

Sending on Behalf Of (2.6)

To send mail so that another user's name appears in the **From** box, "Send on Behalf of" permissions must be established. When this permission is granted, any mail sent by the delegate for the user will display the following text in the **From** box: *User 1 sent on behalf of User 2*

Setting Up a Mailbox to "Send on Behalf of" Another Mailbox

To grant "Send on Behalf of" permissions from the client:

1. Log on to the client as the owner of the mailbox and select the Mailbox top-level folder on the left side: Mailbox - *<username>*
2. From the **Tools** menu, choose **Options**, and then select the **Delegates** tab.
3. Click **Add** to add a name to the **Name/Role** box.
4. Under **Type Name or Select From List**, type or select the name, choose **Add**, and then click **OK**.
5. Choose the Inbox and give the user the proper role.
6. Click **OK**.

Removing the Additional Mailbox from the User's Profile

When a user acting as a delegate needs to remove the additional mailbox from the user profile:

1. From the **Tools** menu, click **Services**.
2. In **The following information services are set up in this profile** box, click **Microsoft Exchange Server** and then click **Properties**.
3. Click the **Advanced** tab.
4. In the **Open these additional mailboxes** box, select the mailbox name you want to remove, and then click **Remove**.
5. To confirm that you want to remove the mailbox, click **Yes**.
6. Click **OK** until all open dialog boxes are closed.

Granting "Send on Behalf of" Permissions from the Administrator Program

1. Double-click the mailbox, and then click the **Delivery Options** tab.
2. Under **Give Send On Behalf Of permissions to**, click **Modify**.
3. Double-click the mailbox you're granting these permissions to, and click **OK**.

Sending Mail on Behalf of Another Mailbox

1. Click the **New Message** button.

2. From the **View** menu, click the **From** box.

3. Click **From** and select the person for whom you're sending mail.

Sending As (2.7)

This section describes how to set up a mailbox to "Send As" another mailbox. Unlike "Send on Behalf Of," this allows users to address a message from another user with no indication to readers that the message was sent by a delegate. Send As permissions can be granted only from the Exchange Administrator program and through a Windows NT account rather than an Exchange mailbox.

Note   Send As permissions override Send on Behalf of permissions. If a user grants a delegate both Send As and Send on Behalf of permissions, the Send As permissions take precedence and message recipients will not know the message was sent by a delegate.

Granting "Send As" Permissions

1. In the **Exchange Administrator** program, double-click the mailbox, and then click the **Permissions** tab. If you don't see the Permissions tab, click **Options** from the **Tools** menu, select the **Permissions** tab and select the **Show Permissions page** for all objects and **Display rights** for roles on **Permissions** page checkboxes.

2. Select the Windows NT account you're granting these permissions to or click **Add** to add an additional account.

3. Select **Send As**.

4. Click **OK**.

Sending Mail as Another Mailbox

1. Choose the **New Message** button.

2. From the **View** menu, click **From Box**.

3. Click **From** and select the person for whom you're sending mail.

Granting Access to Your Calendar (2.8)

All users can see other users' free and busy times for planning meetings. However, unless a user explicitly grants you permissions, you cannot open or view that user's appointment book.

Setting Up Access to Your Calendar

1. From the **Tools** menu in Outlook, choose **Options**.

2. Choose **Delegates** then **Add**, select the delegate, and click **OK**.

3. Give the user to proper permissions to the calendar and choose **OK**.

Viewing Someone Else's Calendar

Items marked as Private can only be viewed by someone else when the user adds that person as an owner or delegate owner.

1. From the **File** menu in Outlook choose, choose **Open** and then click **Other Users Folder...**.

2. Select a user, change the folder to **Calendar** and click **OK**.

You can also view schedule details in the **Planner** view by double-clicking a time period and then clicking the user's name in the pop-up that appears.

Public Folders (2.9)

Tier 1 personnel should understand the public folder structure and how to look up the owner of any public folder. However, Tier 1 personnel cannot create new public folders and if they receive a request for a new public folder, they should create a ticket and escalate it to Tier 2.

If a user requests to be added to an existing public folder, look up the owner of the folder and have the user contact the owner. For certain privileged folders, it may not be possible for Tier 1 personnel to look up the owner. In this case, create a call ticket and escalate to Tier 2. Likewise, if a public folder is to be removed, create a call ticket and escalate to Tier 2.

Distribution Lists (2.10)

A distribution list groups a number of recipients under a common, easy-to-remember name, making it easy to send information to all members of the distribution list. Distribution lists appear in the global address list (GAL) in bold type and recipient names are sorted alphabetically. All users are automatically made members of their Location Code distribution list when the mailbox is first created. If a user requests to be added to other distribution lists, create a call ticket and escalate to Tier 2, which has the authority to add users.

For more information about distribution lists, look for the topic on setting up recipients in the *Microsoft Exchange Server Getting Started Guide.*

Policies and Standards (2.11)

Tier 2 personnel create distribution lists and assign ownership to individual users, who then maintain the list. Any modifications to the distribution lists are to be referred to the owner of the list. There are two standards to follow when creating lists:

1. Distribution lists are created for groups of 10 or more recipients only.
2. Distribution lists are visible in the GAL on every client desktop. There may be hundreds or even thousands of lists, so it is important to choose a meaningful and descriptive name.

Creation and Removal (2.12)

To create a distribution list, start the Exchange Administrator program, connect to the server on which the list is to be created, and follow the below steps.

1. In the **Administrator** window, click **Recipients**.
2. From the **File** menu, choose **New Distribution List**.
3. Name the list, giving it meaningful and descriptive Display and Alias names.
4. Click **Modify** and add the appropriate recipients to the **Members** list.
5. Optionally, a user can be granted ownership of the list by clicking **Modify** under Owner and selecting a user. This will allow the user to control the list, adding and deleting recipients.
6. Click **OK**.

The new distribution list will appear in the GAL and will be replicated to all other Exchange servers.

Monitoring

Tier 1 monitors the overall health of the system by observing the system monitors and receiving any automated alerts, which are escalated to Tier 2. Tier 1 personnel do not resolve alert issues because they do not have the resources or authority to take actions at the server level.

Windows NT Monitoring

Tier 1 uses Server Manager to monitor the Windows NT environment, but only the production domain. The account domains are not monitored because multiple domain controllers provide authentication redundancy, so a single server failure does not prevent user authentication.

Server Manager displays active servers in the domain with a normal-appearing icon, whereas the icon for unavailable servers appears grayed-out . By selecting an individual server, then choosing **Computer**, then **Services**, you can display the individual services on that server and check their status (Started or Stopped). If a server is unavailable, Tier 1 should immediately escalate the issue to Tier 2, which will investigate and resolve the problem.

Exchange Monitoring

To monitor system performance, helpdesk engineers should be able to see a monitor PC that displays the status of all Exchange servers and their connectors. If a monitor shows an alert status, helpdesk personnel will know before users start to call and can escalate the outage to Tier 2.

Location of Monitor PC

Place the monitor where the helpdesk engineers can see it constantly. They must be able to determine at a glance if any condition becomes an alert (turns red).

Interpreting the Exchange Monitor Screen

The monitor screen shows:

- The server monitor for all Exchange servers.
- The link monitor for all Exchange site links.

Next to each monitored item (server and link) a status arrow indicates its status. An item can be in any of four states:

Indicator	Status
Green up arrow	Status is OK.
Yellow sideways arrow	Possibly a problem is developing or probes are tardy.
Red down arrow	Status is Alert, indicating a problem with the device and requiring action.
Blue question mark	Status is Unknown because not enough time has elapsed to determine the state. Give it some time, and it will change to one of the arrows.

Under normal operating conditions, the monitor displays a green up arrow for each running server or site link. An engineer can verify all-green status with a quick glance.

Yellow Monitor

A yellow sideways arrow often displays only with link monitors and indicates that a problem is developing with a site connector or that mail message probes are being delayed because of high traffic on the link. A yellow condition is not yet cause for alarm—it can clear up on its own.

Red Monitor

A red monitor indicates that a problem has developed and Tier 2 should be notified immediately of the device in the alert condition. Tier 2 investigates the cause. Tier 2 should keep Tier 1 informed with progress reports, estimates of how long before the problem is resolved, the number of affected users/services, and the time that the problem was finally resolved.

Server and Link Monitors

A red server indicates that one or more Exchange services running on that server are stopped. This condition must be escalated to Tier 2 support personnel, who determine the cause of the problem and attempt to fix it.

A red link indicates that message exchange is no longer taking place over the connector and could mean a network problem with the physical link or a message transfer agent (MTA) service problem on either server serviced by the link. Because Exchange cannot transfer mail over a failed link, this condition must immediately be escalated to Tier 2 support personnel, who determine the cause of the interruption and attempt to fix it.

Troubleshooting Windows NT Logon Problems

This section covers some typical problems that may be encountered with Windows NT and Exchange. The information in this section is maintained, updated, and expanded by the Tier 1 personnel as new problems are encountered and solutions found. It should act as an up-to-date reference.

Note Numbers next to subheads below correspond to issues highlighted in the call scripts provided in the section Helpdesk Call Scripts.

Windows NT Logon Problems (3.1)

The following tables describe actions to be taken when problems arise in the areas of domain controllers, domains, logons, and passwords.

Domain Controller Unavailable (3.2)

Reasons	Actions
No domain controller is accessible to validate logon.	Network problems could be preventing authentication. Escalate the issue to the local network support.
Authentication fails.	Check that the domain name, user name, and password are correct. Passwords are case sensitive.
	In Windows 95, check that the Client for Microsoft Networks (in the **Control Panel**, **Network** property sheet) has the correct Windows NT Server domain.
TCP/IP configuration is incomplete or incorrect.	Check the TCP/IP setup for correct gateway and WINS configuration.
	Verify TCP/IP by PINGing the loopback address (127.0.0.1) and known remote address.
Using RAS, the authentication fails.	Attempt to log on again. The client may have a bad connection and be timing out.
	Disconnect and redial to reestablish the connection.
The network may be down.	Escalate the issue to the local network support.

Account Issues (3.3)

Reasons	Actions
Account has been disabled.	In User Manager for Domains, reenable the account.
Account has expired.	In User Manager for Domains, reenable the account.
Account has been locked out because of too many logon failures.	In User Manager for Domains, reenable the account.

Domain Issues (3.4)

Reasons	Actions
User is selecting the wrong domain.	User account is in another domain (account has been relocated). Verify the correct domain for the user.
Domain trust relationships are incorrect.	Verify proper trust relationships exist.

Password Issues (3.5)

Reasons	Actions
User is typing in the correct password, but can't log on.	Passwords are case-sensitive. Verify the user is typing in the correct case. Make sure CAPS LOCK is not on.
User forgot password.	There is no way to determine the old password. In User Manager for Domains, give the user a new password.
The user's password has expired.	Have the user enter a new password or assign the user a new password in User Manager for Domains.
User cannot change password.	The Windows NT account may be locked out or disabled because of too many logon failures. In User Manager for Domains, reenable the account.
	The user entered a new password that is less than the minimum length set for the account.
	The user is trying to reuse a password that was previously used. The account policies may restrict the reuse of passwords.

Logon Script Issues (3.6)

Reasons	Actions
The logon script does not execute.	Verify the account has a valid logon script. Re-create from a similar account if none exists.
	Verify the logon script does not contain an error. Execution will stop when an error is encountered.
The authenticating BDC does not have a replica of the logon script.	Issues with Windows NT replication. Escalate to Tier 2.

Troubleshooting Exchange Problems (3.7)

The following tables describe actions to be taken when problems arise in the areas of connectivity, addresses, undelivered mail, profiles, scheduling, public folders, distribution lists, printing, attachments, and remote access.

Note Numbers next to subheads below correspond to issues highlighted in the call scripts provided in the section Helpdesk Call Scripts.

Inability To Connect to a Server (3.8)

Reasons	Actions
The profile is not correctly configured.	From the Outlook **Tools** menu, click **Services**, and check the server and mailbox name. You can also direct the user to go to the **Control Panel** and then open the **Mail and Fax** application.
You did not log on to a Windows NT security account that has Send Mail permissions for this mailbox.	Use the Exchange Administrator program to determine which account has permissions for this mailbox. Log on again.
The server is unavailable.	Use the Windows NT Server Manager, Exchange Server Monitor, or the NET USE command to verify that the server is down.
	If it is an Exchange Server, use a link monitor or server monitor to check the service.
	If not, at the Windows NT command prompt, use the **Net View \\\servername** command to determine if the server is running or use the RPC ping utility to test for network connectivity to the server. If server is running but this test fails, there is a network problem.
The server is using a different network protocol.	At the Windows NT command prompt, use RPING to determine RPC connectivity. If necessary, update the server or all affected clients with matching network protocols.
The common network protocol being used is not routed between LAN segments.	Move the client or server computers to the same LAN segment, modify the router or bridge to route the network protocol, and update the client and server to use a commonly routed network protocol.
You do not have User permissions for the mailbox.	Check the mailbox **Permissions** property page and modify if necessary.
The required services (directory service or information store) are not running on the server or they are busy.	First determine whether these services are running, using Windows NT Server Manager or Exchange Server Monitor. If either service is not running, use the Windows NT Server Manager to restart it.
	If the services are running, determine whether they are too busy to accept a connection, using performance monitor.

Reasons	Actions
The bind parameter is missing or incorrect (Windows 3.*x* and Windows for Workgroups, or Windows 95, Windows NT Server and Windows NT Workstation).	For Windows 3.*x* and Windows for Workgroups, add the missing protocol sequence. In the [Exchange Provider] section of EXCHNG.INI, the RPC_Binding_Order must include an entry for the protocol you use. Add **ncacn_np** for named pipes, **ncacn_spx** for SPX, or **ncacn_ip_tcp** for TCP/IP. For Windows 95, Windows NT Server and Windows NT Workstation, use the Registry Editor to modify the binding order in HKEY_LOCAL_MACHINE\Microsoft\Exchange\Exchange Provider. For example, to establish SPX, TCP/IP, and NetBIOS connections in that order, use: RPC_Binding_Order=ncacn_spx,ncacn_ip_tcp, netbios
An IPX/SPX parameter is missing from a Windows for Workgroups initialization file. (This applies only to Windows for Workgroups using IPX/SPX Transport.)	Add **DirectHost=OFF** to the Network section of SYSTEM.INI.
You're running out of memory.	Try increasing conventional memory by removing unnecessary drivers or loading drivers high. Novell NetWare users can reduce the IPX packet size. In the **Protocol IPX** section of NET.CFG, add **IPX PACKET SIZE LIMIT 1496**.
The Windows NT Server running Exchange Server is not configured to support Novell NetWare clients.	Make sure the server is running the Gateway Services for NetWare and that the NWLink IPX/SPX transport is configured correctly using the **Network** option in **Control Panel**.
Novell NetWare client and server computers have different frame type versions.	On the client computer, the frame type is in the **Link Driver** section of the NET.CFG file. On the server, the frame type is in the configuration of the NWLink IPX/SPX-compatible transport object in the **Network** option of **Control Panel**. If the server computer supports more than one frame type, make sure that the internal network number is unique and that **Auto Frame type detection** is not selected.
A Novell NetWare client computer is missing required libraries.	Verify that NWIPXSPX.DLL and NWCALLS.DLL are in the system directory. If not, contact Novell for a WINUP9 upgrade.

(continued)

Reasons	Actions
There is no SAP agent computer accessible to both of the computers running Exchange Client and Exchange Server.	Make sure that both the client and server computers can log on to a SAP agent computer. The SAP agent can run on an Exchange Server computer or on a NetWare server.
	Verify that the client and server are on the same network segment and that the router between the segments is configured to transport SAP-type 0x640 messages.
An RPC runtime parameter is invalid. Novell NetWare networks in which both Windows NT and Exchange Server are shared require this parameter.	In the RPC runtime preferences section of WIN.INI, point the RPC_REG_DATA_FILE parameter to the full path of a valid RPCREG.DAT file. You must be able to write to that directory.

Recipient Not in Global Address List (3.9)

Reasons	Actions
The recipient is in a different site in your organization or in a foreign system and the directory has not been replicated.	Use the Exchange Administrator program to see the directory replication schedule. Replication messages can be traced in the message-tracking log.
	Use the Windows NT application event log to determine if there are errors in directory replication.
The recipient has been removed from this site or another site in the network.	Use the Exchange Administrator program to confirm that the recipient was removed.
The recipient is hidden from the Address Book.	From the **View** menu in the **Administrator** window, click **Hidden Recipients.** The recipient should appear. All public folders are hidden recipients.
There are two entries for a mailbox in the GAL.	This usually happens with custom recipients. The account for the user has accidentally been created twice. Verify which account has the latest access date and remove the extra account. You may have to work with the server administrators to combine the accounts.

Non-Delivery Report Indicates Invalid Address (3.10)

Reasons	Actions
The recipient's address is incorrect.	Confirm the recipient's address and update the user's personal address book (PAB) and the global address list (GAL).
The recipient was removed from another site or foreign system and the directory has not been replicated or synchronized.	Confirm that the recipient was removed. Make sure the update is included in the next directory replication.
There is a routing problem.	Trace the message in the message-tracking log. Confirm that the address space is configured correctly.

Personal Address Book (PAB) Entry Invalid for Recipient in Different Site (3.11)

Reasons	Actions
The address entry is incorrect.	Verify the recipient's address in the GAL. Copy from the global address list to the personal address book. Use the Exchange Administrator program to check the address space.
The recipient has been removed.	Verify the entry in the global address list. If it is there, wait for the next directory replication and check again.
The address space for entries is not mapped to a gateway or connector.	Update the **Address Space** property page for the connector or gateway.

Personal Address Book (PAB) Entry Invalid for Recipient in Same Site (3.12)

Reasons	Actions
The recipient has been removed.	Verify the entry in the GAL.
The recipient was moved to a different recipient container.	Check the GAL to see if recipient has been moved.

Recipient Not Found (3.13)

Reasons	Actions
There is no such address in the network or in the domain of the gateway host.	Verify the address and the mapping of the address to a host.
The address was not unique.	Verify the address. Make sure that all addresses in your network are unique.
The address was a phrase in several addresses but not an entire address of any mailbox.	Have users press CTRL+K to verify the address before sending.

Inbound Mail Not Reaching Recipient's Inbox (3.14)

Reasons	Actions
The profile is configured to deliver to a server mailbox.	In **Control Panel**, click the **Mail and Fax** icon. Click **Show Profiles**. Select a profile and choose **Properties**. Click the **Delivery** tab. Also, modify the server's access to deliver messages to the default information store.
A client rule is moving all new mail to another folder.	From the Microsoft Exchange Client **Tools** menu, click **Inbox Assistant** and delete the rule.
Mail cannot be received from foreign system.	Verify that the gateways are working. Work with Tier 2 to verify that the gateways are configured correctly.
	The sending foreign system may be experiencing delivery problems. This issue must be resolved on the foreign system.

No Mail Received after Migration to Microsoft Exchange (3.15)

Reason	Actions
Users on old system (for example, MS Mail) are still sending to the old address.	User needs to inform correspondents to update their PAL with the new address.
	All migrated users should have a custom recipient set up to auto-forward mail to the new Exchange mailbox.

Outbound Mail Sent to a User Never Arrives (3.16)

Reasons	Actions
There is a problem on a foreign system.	Use the message-tracking log to trace the path of the message to the gateway. Look for the message in the message queues of the connector. Check the Windows NT application event log for errors. If it is an Internet message, use diagnostics logging to create an SMTP protocol log and resend the message.
The message is still in the Outbox because the information store or MTA is not running.	Make sure that the originator can send to other Exchange Server mailboxes or check the service with performance monitor or a server monitor.
The message stopped at an intermediate server or system.	Use message tracking to find the problem server. For more information, see the *Microsoft Exchange Server Maintenance and Troubleshooting Guide.*
A message sent to foreign system never arrives.	Instruct the user to resend the message if no apparent cause for the failure is determined. Some gateways fail on messages and return other messages being processed in the same batch.

Inability to Send to Recipient in Different Site (3.17)

Reasons	Actions
The connection between sites is down.	Use link monitor logs to determine when the connection was last working. Use server monitor to determine if all the services at both computers are working. Use the Exchange Administrator program or performance monitor to check the message queue lengths.
There is an error in the personal address book.	Use your client global address list to address mail. Remove or modify the personal address book entries as necessary.
The message-tracking log on one of the servers has run out of disk space.	Use performance monitor to determine if the MTA is running. If not, check the available space on disk where the tracking log is stored.
The private information store on one of the servers is not working.	Use Performance Monitor or server monitor to determine if the service is running. If it's down, restart the private information store from the **Services** applet in **Control Panel**.
The recipient address is no longer valid because the recipient has moved to another recipient container or site.	Connect to a server in the other site and verify that the recipient still exists. Check for directory replication problems if this recipient modification is not a recent change.

Inability to Send to User in Same Site (3.18)

Reasons	Actions
There is an error in the personal address book.	Use your client GAL to address mail.
The message-tracking log on one of the servers has run out of disk space.	Check to see if MTA is running on both servers. If not, check available disk space where the tracking log is stored.
The network connection between servers is down.	Use link monitor to determine when the connection was last working. Use server monitor to determine if all the services at both computers are working. Use the Exchange Administrator program or Performance Monitor to check queue lengths.
The private information store, MTA, or directory on one of the servers is not working.	Use Performance Monitor or server monitor to determine if the services are running.

Inability to Send to User on the Internet (3.19)

Reasons	Actions
Mail does not arrive at its destination because either a server or Internet Mail Service is down.	Use the Exchange Administrator program message tracking facility to locate the problem.
Mail is returned because the sender's address contains delivery restrictions that exclude the sender from using Internet.	Change the delivery restrictions in the Internet Mail Service.
There is an error in the personal address book.	Use the client GAL to address mail.

Inability to Send to User on Same Server (3.20)

Reasons	Actions
There is an error in the personal address book.	Use the client GAL to address mail.
The message-tracking log has run out of disk space.	Determine if the MTA is running. If not, check the available space on the disk where the tracking log is stored. **Note:** The MTA is not needed for local delivery (unless the recipient is a distribution list). The Internet Mail Service will continue to send a message if message tracking fails.
The private information store or directory is not running.	Use server monitor or Performance Monitor to determine if the services are running.

Late or Lost Mail (3.21)

Reasons	Actions
The intermediate server or a component is down.	Track the message to its current location and troubleshoot from there. If the route taken seems unusual, there may be a problem along the usual route.
The connection between sites is too slow for traffic.	Use the Exchange Administrator program to check the queue size. Use Performance Monitor to compare that with the messages per second processed for that MTA.

No Personal Folder File Found (3.22)

Reasons	Actions
The file was moved to a different location or is on an unavailable network share.	Relocate the personal folder file (.PST) or reconfigure the personal folder file information service. An interim solution is to create a new personal folder file.
The personal folder file information service was not added to the profile.	From the Outlook client **Tools** menu, click **Services**, and add Microsoft Exchange Server.

Inability to Create, Modify, or Delete a Profile (3.23)

Reason	Action
The profile is stored on the network in a directory where the user has Read-only permissions.	Change the permissions for the directory.

Microsoft Exchange Server Information Service Not Listed in Profiles (3.24)

Reasons	Actions
An error was made when customizing Setup.	Customize Setup or change the customized Setup so that the Exchange service is added to the default list of services.
The option was chosen to be installed when Outlook was set up.	Rerun the Outlook setup and select **Add the Exchange Service** component.
The user created a new profile and didn't add the correct information services.	From the Outlook client **Tools** menu, click **Services** and add the correct information service.

Choose Profile Box Has a Password Box (3.25)

Reason	Action
The workstation is configured for multiple profiles.	When the **Choose Profile** dialog box appears at startup, the user is prompted to choose a profile. In Windows 3.1, this box contains a **Password** field. Users will usually attempt to enter their Windows NT logon password here. This is incorrect—this password is for accessing secured profiles (set up in Exchange Services) and is to be left **blank**. The Windows NT logon dialog box will appear *after* the profile is chosen.

Personal Address Book (PAB) Not Accessible (3.26)

Reasons	Actions
The password for the PAB was lost.	Create a new PAB.
The PAB is not available on the network or on a local drive on this computer.	Create a new PAB or reconfigure the PAB service to point to an existing PAB.

Profile Gone after Updating Operating System (3.27)

Reason	Action
You upgraded MS-DOS to Windows or Windows 3.x to Windows 95 or Windows NT.	Create a new profile.

Inability to Synchronize Offline Schedule (3.28)

Reason	Action
Network connectivity to the Exchange server is preventing schedule synchronization	Verify connectivity to the server. Refer to the Client/Server connectivity section.

Inability to Access Another User's Schedule (3.29)

Reason	Action
Other user has not granted permissions.	By default, no one can view your schedule. Ask the other user if he/she has given default Read access to his/her schedule or to specifically grant you access.

Inability to Access a Public Folder (3.30)

Reasons	Actions
The server with the replica of the public folder is not running.	Determine the home server for the public folder and verify that the server is running.
A replica of the public folder is on a server in a site that can't be reached by the client network protocol.	Determine what router, bridge, or gateway prevents the passage of the user's network protocol. Add the missing network protocol to the router or add an acceptable network protocol to the user's computer.
A replica of the public folder is on a server in a site where affinities have not been established.	Use the information store site configuration **Public Folder Affinity** property page to establish affinities.
You do not have permissions to access the folder.	Use Outlook to grant permissions to access the public folder.
You lost the connection to the server.	Restart the client.

Inability to View Public Folder in the Hierarchy (3.31)

Reasons	Actions
The public folder does not exist in your site or has not been replicated to your site.	Use the public information store **Instances** property page to add the public folder to the list to be replicated to this server.
No affinities were assigned to the public folder.	Use the information store site configuration **Public Folder Affinity** property page to establish affinities.
The public folder is replicated in the site, but directory replication has not occurred.	If the folder was just added to the site, check the public information store **Replication Schedule** property page for the next scheduled replication. If the folder is still not visible after replication, increase the diagnostics logging level of the **Replication** category group, and then check the Windows NT application event log for public folder replication errors.
The folder is set to not be visible.	With the Outlook client, change the options of the folder so it is visible to the proper users.

Inability to Send Mail to a Public Folder (3.32)

Reasons	Actions
The public folder is hidden from the Address Book.	Use the Administrator program to check the **Hide From Address Book** attribute in the public folder's **Advanced** property page.
The public folder does not have permission to create mail messages.	In the **General** property page of the public folder, click the **Client Permissions** button, and then select **Create Items.**
Mail is returned because this user is excluded from sending to public folders.	Use the Exchange Administrator program to check the **Reject Messages From** attribute in the **Delivery Restrictions** property page.

Public Folder Replication Not Working (3.33)

Reasons	Actions
Mail between sites is not scheduled for this time.	Check the connection schedule. Send a test message to a mailbox or configure a link monitor.
Mail is not flowing between sites.	Treat this as a mail problem between sites. Check link monitors and queues. If necessary, track public folder replication messages.
Public folder replication is not scheduled for this time.	Check the public folder replication schedule.
The public information store or MTA on the source or destination server is not working.	Use link monitor to check the MTA and the server; use Performance Monitor to check the public information store.

Inability to Send to a Distribution List (3.34)

Reasons	Actions
User does not have the necessary permission to send to the list.	This is probably by design. Verify with Tier 2 if the user is supposed to have access to this list.
Migrated user is no longer receiving mail from legacy distribution lists.	Update legacy distribution list with user's new Exchange mailbox. User needs to contact the owner of the group distribution list and have owner delete old mailbox and add new one from GAL.

Distribution List Missing Members (3.35)

Reasons	Actions
List is incomplete.	Add the missing names to the list.
Replication has not yet completed.	Work with Tier 2 to verify that directory replication is working properly.

Mail Received with Garbled Text or Extra Attachments (3.36)

Reason	Actions
The message was formatted with rich text and could not be resolved by the receiving system.	Remove the instruction to send the message in rich text format. The rich text format option is found in three places: ■ In the sender's personal address book, double-click the recipient's name, and then click the Address tab. Make sure Always send to this recipient in Microsoft Exchange rich-text format is not selected. ■ In the custom recipient's Advanced property page, make sure Allow rich text in messages is not selected. ■ In the Internet Mail Service Internet Mail property page, click the Interoperability button. Make sure Send Microsoft Exchange rich text formatting is not selected.
There are uuencode versus MIME issues.	Exchange sends attachments in MIME format (default) and will receive and decode both uuencoded and MIME attachments automatically. However, MS Mail and UNIX cannot read MIME. When sending to MS Mail or UNIX recipients, the user must specify uuencode for messages containing attachments. In a **New Message** window, Click **File**, **New Message**, **Properties**, and **Send Options**. Under **Internet**, select **uuencode**. This must be done on a per-message basis.

Inability to Open Attachments in Microsoft Exchange (3.37)

Reasons	Actions
Missing **SET TEMP=** parameter in AUTOEXEC.BAT.	Add the **SET TEMP=** parameter in the user's autoexec file.
There is insufficient disk space for temporary files.	Free up local hard disk space.
This error is received: No association can be made with the attachment.	This error can sometimes be resolved by shutting down and restarting Windows.

Attachment Sent to SMTP Host Not Received (3.38)

Reason	Action
The message was sent using MIME encoding, which the SMTP host cannot read.	Resend the message using uuencode.

Microsoft Exchange Prints Incorrectly or Not At All (3.39)

Reasons	Actions
A variety of errors can occur when printing messages from within Outlook, ranging from error to printing blank pages, incomplete text, or just garbage.	This is caused by the Windows print driver. Changing the driver to a more generic driver, such as HP LaserJet, resolves these issues.
Printing to a black-and-white printer with a color printer driver causes random symbols to be printed.	Color formatting Outlook causes this problem when printing to a standard black-and-white printer. Have user print to the color printer or not use color formatting.

Inability to Access Microsoft Exchange after Workstation Upgrade (3.40)

Reason	Actions
A workstation operating system upgrade (to Windows NT 4.0, for example) may wipe out the Outlook client configuration.	Verify that the user has a proper Windows NT Server domain account, proper computer name (must follow naming convention), and domain membership. Create, if necessary.
	Uninstall Outlook, connect to the share point, and reinstall Outlook. You will need to create a new profile.

Modem Not Working (3.41)

Reasons	Actions
The modem or modem cable is defective.	Test with any other communications software.
The remote network software is configured incorrectly.	Use the appropriate software to check the phone number, baud rate, communications ports, and settings.
You connected a PCMCIA modem to digital phone line and destroyed the modem.	Contact the modem manufacturer for information.

Modem Not Connecting at Highest Possible Speed (3.42)

Reasons	Actions
The modem at other end is not as fast or uses different compression protocols.	Upgrade the other modem.
The phone line cannot handle a high-speed connection.	Try connecting from a different phone line.

No Remote Use Options with Windows Client (3.43)

Reason	Action
You are using the wrong profile or information service.	Add the Exchange remote information service to a new profile.

Closing Remarks

Tier 1 helpdesk personnel are able to shoulder more of the load as the support organization's problem management system (knowledge base) grows more comprehensive. As issues are resolved and descriptions of their solutions are added to the problem management system, it becomes an increasingly useful resource. Consider building one for your organization's support infrastructure. It can be made available to end users who want to diagnose and solve their own problems. The capture and resolution of more issues at Tier 1 leaves personnel in Tiers 2 and 3 free to focus on evaluating new products and technologies to make the organization run more efficiently.

C H A P T E R   7

Tier 2 Administration

This chapter describes the second support tier: how it solves end-user issues escalated by Tier 1, schedules routine maintenance, performs Windows NT and Exchange administrative tasks, and escalates tough problems to Tier 3. The second half of the chapter includes tips and procedures for troubleshooting and server recovery.

This and the other chapters detailing the 3-tier support organization are based on the example of a large telecommunications company deploying a messaging infrastructure supporting 60,000 users and based on Windows NT Server, Exchange Server, and Systems Management Server. Product versions and names are supplied to give context to the discussion and to demonstrate how the various versions fit together. To apply the material here to your own organization, you can extrapolate user environment particulars.

Roles and Responsibilities

Tier 2 personnel primarily administer the Windows NT server infrastructure and support Tier 1 helpdesk engineers in solving end-user problems. Tier 2 responsibilities are to:

- Provide second-level support for Tier 1.
- Assign advanced mailbox permissions, create and maintain public folders, maintain distribution lists, and assist Tier 1 personnel with mailbox creation where necessary.
- Perform scheduled maintenance on Windows NT servers.
- Maintain messaging transport components (queues and connectors).
- Troubleshoot mail transport problems, escalating to Tier 3 if necessary.
- Troubleshoot problems at the server and network level, escalating to Tier 3 if necessary.
- Maintain messaging interface to other mail systems (primarily UNIX).
- Perform and validate nightly backups.

- Restore servers in case of data loss.
- Monitor servers and connectors and resolve any problems.

Personnel Guidelines

To be effective, Tier 2 personnel should understand:

- Windows NT Server versions 3.51 and 4.0.
- Microsoft Visual Basic, HTML, and Microsoft SQL Server.
- How to support desktop operating systems: MS-DOS, Windows 3.1, Windows 95, and Windows NT Workstation versions 3.51 and 4.0.
- How to configure and troubleshoot TCP/IP.
- How to support and troubleshoot LAN and WAN environments.
- How to administer Exchange Server, Systems Management Server, and Windows NT Server.
- How to communicate verbally (for telephone support) and in writing (on call tickets, documenting problem descriptions and resolutions).

Tier 2 personnel need these resources:

Troubleshooting resource	Use
Windows NT Server Manager	To administer the Windows NT Server domain from Windows NT Workstation.
Windows NT User Manager	To administer Windows NT user accounts.
Microsoft Exchange Administrator	To maintain Exchange mailboxes.
Microsoft Outlook	To duplicate caller actions, access Microsoft online help, and look up "how-do-I..." client tasks.
Problem Management System	The Knowledge Base used to log calls using call tickets. As this grows, it becomes more useful to support staff seeking previously developed solutions and information.
TCP/IP utilities	To troubleshoot network: PING and NET USE.
Internet Explorer 4.0	To access the web.
The Directory (Web site)	To look up user information and verify accounts.
Microsoft Exchange Server Maintenance and Troubleshooting Guide	

How Tier 2 Is Contacted

Tier 2 personnel learn of problems through the problem management system, from contacts with Tier 1 helpdesk engineers, and by escalation from Tier 1 engineers in the case of serious issues (service outages). Users do not contact Tier 2 directly.

Tier 2 provides support 12 hours a day, 5 days a week. During off hours, personnel are available on call and should respond within 30 minutes to server-level outages reported by phone or pager. They communicate solutions and resolutions back to Tier 1, which records them in the problem management system for future reference by all support tiers.

Scheduled Operations

To maintain the Windows NT Server infrastructure, Tier 2 performs most tasks at scheduled intervals. (Tasks are described later in this chapter.)

Frequency	Product	Tasks
Daily	Windows NT	Examine Windows NT event logs.
Daily	Windows NT	Examine backup logs.
Daily	Windows NT	Rotate backup tapes.
Daily	Windows NT	Perform full online backup.
Daily	Exchange	Examine server and link monitors.
Daily	Exchange	Examine performance monitor counters.
Daily	Exchange	Examine MTA queues.
Weekly	Windows NT	Check available physical memory.
Weekly	Windows NT	Check available disk space.
Weekly	Exchange	Examine message tracking log buildup.
Weekly	Exchange	Verify public folder replication status.
Monthly	Windows NT	Verify system resources.
Monthly	Windows NT	Purge disk array.
Monthly	Exchange	Validate backup.
Quarterly	Exchange	Send size limit notices to public folder owners.
Semi-annually	Exchange	Remove unused Exchange accounts.
Annual	Windows NT	Archive log files and store.
As required	Exchange	Maintain information stores.
As required	Exchange	Perform offline defragmentation.
As required	Exchange	Check mailbox and public folder usage.
As required	Exchange	Check storage limits.

Daily Windows NT Tasks

Examining Windows NT Event Logs

Check servers using the application event log in the Windows NT event viewer for recent error events (shown with red stop signs) and warning events (yellow exclamation points). Both require immediate resolution. Recent events (blue information symbols) indicate no server problems.

Clear the Windows NT application event log if it is too large or contains old information, but only after retrieving anything needed for troubleshooting because clearing the log permanently erases all entries.

Examining Backup Logs

Verify that the daily differential backup has completed successfully with no errors. For an Exchange server, monitor the EDB*.LOG files in the DSADATA and MDBDATA directories to see if there's an accumulation of transaction log files that would indicate faulty backups. Transaction files should be purged using full or differential online backups available with the Exchange Server functionality of Windows NT Backup.

Warning Do not delete the EDB*.LOG files manually. To remove, perform a full or differential backup.

Online Backups

An automatic, scheduled nightly backup does not interrupt mail service because it is scheduled during off hours to minimize performance degradation. After verifying a successful backup by viewing the backup log files, remove and store the tapes. Replace with new backup tapes.

Daily Exchange Server Tasks

- **Examine server and link monitors**—Server monitor checks services required on Exchange servers; link monitors verify message flow between sites and to foreign connectors. On monitor displays, a green status indicates that all services and links are operating and red indicates a service interruption and must be investigated immediately.

- **Examine performance monitor counters**—Look for Exchange performance monitor and Windows NT performance monitor values that are excessively high or low, particularly on these counters:
  - **CPU utilization**—Should be less than 60 percent.
  - **Disk space available**—Sufficient free space is required.
  - **Queue length**—An excessive number of messages should not be undelivered.
  - **Messages per hour**—A normal amount of messages should be processed.
- **Examine MTA queues**—Each Exchange server has different queues for undelivered MTA messages on site servers and any installed gateways and connectors. An excessive number of messages in any one queue indicates problems with the MTA, the routing tables, or network connectivity between servers. Follow these steps to investigate:
  1. In the Microsoft Exchange Administrator program, open the site in question.
  2. Under each server, select **Message Transfer Agent.**
  3. Use the **MTA Queues** property to display and verify that each queue is delivering messages.

Weekly Windows NT Tasks

- **Physical memory availability**—To make sure error correcting code on the server hasn't corrupted memory, check the amount of physical system memory against specifications.
- **Disk space availability**—If a check of the drive arrays on each server reveals a nearly full disk, increase the size of the disk array or remove old files after checking with the Tier 2 team leader.

Weekly Exchange Tasks

- **Message tracking log buildup**—If message tracking is enabled, monitor the *.LOG files in the TRACKING.LOG directory to ensure they don't fill the disk. Each day a new log file is generated and named by the date. Some of these files can be quite large, depending on message throughput. If disk space is low, you can delete them manually.

You can also configure the server to delete the message tracking log files automatically:

1. Double-click **System Attendant** and click the **General Properties** page.

2. Select the **Remove Older Than __ Days** checkbox and type the number of days after which you want the message tracking log files to be deleted. The standard is 7 days but set it in relation to the backup schedule.

- **Public folder replication status**—To check the replication status on either a public folder or public information store, check the:

  - Folder replication status for the status either of servers on which a public folder is replicated or of all public folder replicas on the server.

  - Server replication status for status of servers with which the server replicates.

Other Scheduled Windows NT Tasks

- **Verify system resources**—Every month check that the server has adequate memory resources. Verify that the swap file is at least equal to the system memory installed plus 20 MB.

- **Purge disk array**—Remove any unneeded or obsolete applications from the disks every month. Check for any obsolete directories or temporary files left behind, possibly from a troubleshooting session, and remove them.

- **Archive log files to storage**—Once a year archive the year's log files to storage media.

Other Scheduled Exchange Tasks

- **Validate the backup**—At least once a month validate information store backups by restoring them to a server that is not part of the production system organization. Regular validation ensures that good tapes are available in the event of a disaster.

- **Issue public folder storage size warnings**—Every three months, remind owners of large workgroup folders to remove outdated materials.

- **Verify unused mailboxes**—Every six months, view the last access date for mailboxes from the Exchange Administrator program's private information store Mailbox resources. Contact the owners of mailboxes that show no activity to determine if the mailbox can be deleted.

- **Information store maintenance**—As needed, check the information store **Maintenance** property page in the server object directory to ensure that maintenance routines run at least once a day during off-peak hours.

- **Perform offline defragmentation**—Take the server offline when a large amount of data has been deleted from the information and directory stores and use ESEUTIL to defragment the databases. Exchange Server performs constant online compaction, but running ESEUTIL shrinks the size of the *.EDB database files.

  Offline defragmentation interrupts service to end users and should be performed only during scheduled server downtime. Also, the server must have as much disk space available as the size of the database to be defragmented. To perform offline defragmentation, refer to the second half of this chapter or to the *Microsoft Exchange Server Maintenance and Troubleshooting Guide*.

- **Monitor mailbox and public folder use**—Periodically monitor active mailboxes and public folders by checking the **Logons** property pages in the private and public information store. Check the **Mailbox Resources** and **Public Folder Resources** property pages to see how individual users and public folders are using storage space.

- **Monitor storage limits**—Monitor storage limit settings on mailboxes and public folders and adjust periodically for certain users or public folders.

Monitoring

The objective of monitoring is to fix problems before they affect users. This section focuses on types of monitoring tools available for Windows NT and Exchange.

Windows NT Monitoring

Domain servers send updated information every 15 minutes to Windows NT Server Manager. Active servers are displayed on the monitor's screen with normal-appearing icons and the icons of unavailable servers appear shaded. To view the status (started or stopped) of individual services on a server, click **Computer** and then **Services.** A status of started only means the service is running, not that it is operating properly.

Exchange Server displays stopped server services by displaying a red "down" icon next to a server. Click on the icon to identify which service is not functioning.

Performance Monitor

Configure Windows NT Performance Monitor to automatically generate e-mail alerts if Windows NT Server processes exceed thresholds on these parameters:

Object	Counter	Alert threshold
LogicalDisk	% Disk Time	Greater than 80%
Memory paging	Pages/sec	Average more than 4 pages/sec
Processor	% Processor Time	Greater than 80%
Redirector	Bytes Total/sec	Depends on NIC throughput
Redirector	Network Errors/sec	Greater than 0

The thresholds monitored are derived from a production server baseline and should be revised when the system load changes.

Event Log

Windows NT event logs, maintained on each server, record all significant events. If alerts are received or the server is not performing properly, check the event log details for the errors. The configuration of the Windows NT event logs is:

- Event log size: 512 KB
- Keep events for 10 days, overwrite as needed

Exchange Monitoring

Server monitor (which verifies that selected Windows NT services are operating) and link monitor (which sends test messages to verify message flow) are used to monitor Exchange. These monitors can be configured automatically to notify administrators (through e-mail or pager), reset services, or even reboot servers, but this is *not* recommended for several reasons:

- If multiple monitor computers are running, the actions may interfere with each other.
- After services are stopped, automatic restarts could interfere with backups, troubleshooting, upgrades, and so on.
- Tier 2 personnel familiar with the system layout should decide when to restart services or reboot servers.

On an Exchange server, these processes are monitored constantly:

- MTA queue lengths
- Available disk space
- Messages per hour on hub servers and gateways
- Server CPU usage
- Number of Exchange users per server

Monitors check Exchange servers in hub sites and larger sites with clusters of 5,000 or more users. The Internet Mail Service, X.400 Connectors, and queue lengths of the bridgehead servers are also monitored. One central monitor displays:

- Messaging servers
- Intersite links
- Internet connectors
- Performance monitor

The following describes the Exchange monitor screens. For more detailed information on how to set up monitors, refer to "Monitoring Your Organization" in the *Microsoft Exchange Server Maintenance and Troubleshooting Guide* (part of the Exchange Server 5.5 Online Books).

Server Monitor

Each Exchange Server is on the list of monitored servers, and those in an alert state are displayed first to avoid scrolling. The **Services Property** page on each server indicates which services are monitored. If no services are selected, the default services monitored are:

- Microsoft Exchange directory
- Microsoft Exchange information store
- Microsoft Exchange message transfer agent

A red icon indicates one or more server services are down. Take these steps to investigate.

1. Double-click on the server displaying an alert condition.
2. Click the **Services** tab to display the individual services and the status (active or stopped) of each.
3. If a service is stopped, refer to the second half of this chapter.

Link Monitor

Link monitors test message speed by sending ping messages between sites or to gateways. The link monitor lists, in alphabetical order, all messaging links between sites and to each foreign connector (for example, SMTP or a connector to UNIX). Each connector has a log file to help troubleshoot connection problems. The polling interval or time it takes a test message to make one round trip depends on link speed and may need to be reset so the monitor remains green under normal operations.

Foreign link monitors check each Internet Mail Service or other gateway implemented. Send a poll to a fictitious SMTP address (for example, bounce@companyname.com) to check speed across the gateway. Create a custom recipient for this purpose and hide it from the address book so users don't send mail to it. A link monitor that displays red indicates that a link is down and must be investigated immediately.

MTA Queues

MTA queue lengths and the number of messages per hour are monitored in a Windows NT performance monitor screen. The objects to be monitored for the MTA are:

Object	Counter	Alert threshold
MSExchangeMTA	Work Queue Length	Varies; currently about 200
MSExchangeMTA	Messages per second	0

A steady, rapid increase of MTA queue lengths indicates that a queue or queues are not emptying and could mean either a link is malfunctioning (link monitor is red) or a server MTA process is not running (server monitor is red). The number of messages per hour depend on the time of day and usage level; if it drops to zero during a busy period, check the link and server monitors for problems.

Windows NT Administration

At times, Tier 2 personnel help Tier 1 perform Windows NT administrative tasks, including account creation, maintenance, group memberships assignments, and file system permissions. Other tasks are described in this section.

Clear the Event Logs

The Windows NT event logs for system, security, and application should be saved and cleared at regular intervals. These logs contain troubleshooting and system analysis information and must be kept for one year for security purposes. The standard command used for dumping the event log from the registry into a file is DUMPEL.EXE:

```
dumpel -l system -f  sys.out -t -s ltopsfps01
```

This command dumps the system event log for the server LTOPSFPS01 in a tab delimited file (-t) into a file called SYS.OUT, which is saved in a central location.

Create Global Groups

After receiving approval from the Tier 2 team leader or a member of Tier 3, Tier 2 administrators create new global groups required in the account domains. Name the group something indicative of its purpose, include the group owner in the description, and add the members to the group membership list.

Create a Logon Script

Logon script is created and proliferated on the domain controllers and replicated to the backup domain controllers. All logon scripts include the scare screen or warning program, WARN.EXE.

Exchange Administration

The Exchange Server Administrator program is used to administer services and systems components, view and manipulate the organizational structure, and perform other functions. Exchange Administrator program can be installed on the Exchange server itself or on the administrator's Windows NT Workstation (Windows NT 3.51 with Service Pack 4 or later) for desktop administration of the entire Exchange topology.

Mailbox Administration

Mailboxes are the containers for receiving and sending mail. Usually, each user has one mailbox, but there may also be special mailboxes shared by a group of users such as a common helpdesk mailbox.

Policies and Standards

To have easily identifiable mailbox names, base them on existing standards for phone and address books. Names for directory and alias are entered when creating accounts. The rest of the directory information is provided automatically by an update from the directory. The Mailbox Alias Name is the user's alias. The format of the user's Display Name is *<last name>*, *<first name>* *<initials>* (*<preferred name>*). The user's proxy addresses include the following SMTP proxies:

- *<handle>*@**companyname.com.** Set as the default reply address.
- *<handle>*@*<local IMC name>*.**companyname.com.** To match the user's e-mail address in the directory.

Mailbox Creation

Mailboxes are created when the user's Windows NT account is started. For users with Windows NT accounts, Exchange mailboxes can be created with the Exchange Administrator program. Look up the user in the directory and create the account based on that information.

Mailbox Removal

If an Exchange mailbox shows no activity for a long time, the mailbox owner should be asked if the mailbox should be retained. If the owner is unavailable, contact the user's supervisor. The last access date for a mailbox is displayed in Private Information Store Mailbox resources from the Exchange Administrator program.

Normally, a mailbox is declared inactive after 12 months. To remove an inactive mailbox, click **Recipients** in the **Administrator** window, highlight the mailbox to be removed, and press DEL.

Mailbox Maintenance

Simple mailbox maintenance—such as name changes, additions to distribution lists, or corrections of proxy addresses—is handled by Tier 1 staff. Tier 2 administrators perform more complex maintenance, including alias and proxy address changes, changing the storage limit available to the user, changing the server housing the mailbox, and relocating mailboxes to other sites.

Mailbox Cleaning

User mailboxes do not require administrator maintenance; however, the user should keep the mailbox clean by deleting unnecessary messages (especially those with large attachments) and messages in the Sent and Deleted Items folders.

If a mailbox needs to be cleaned to recover space in the private information store, the task can be done from the Exchange Server Administrator. Single or multiple mailboxes can be selected, and the cleaning can be performed while users are logged on.

1. In the Administrator window, click Recipients, then Mailboxes.

2. From the Tools menu, click Clean Mailbox.

3. Set the desired options and click OK to start the cleaning process.

Note   You can set these options so that all the user's mail is deleted. Make sure you do not do this inadvertently.

Storage Limits

Users exceeding the allocated storage limit are barred from sending mail (although they continue to receive mail) and must clean out their mailbox first to restore the send capability. Those wanting to increase online storage must demonstrate a legitimate business reason approved by the Tier 2 team leader.

Advanced User Permissions

Users can be granted permissions to mailboxes other than their own, allowing them to access that mailbox as if they owned it. This access may be required if users share a common mailbox or are absent. Permissions are assigned from the mailbox **Permissions** property page.

Assigning or Changing Proxy Addresses

At times, a user may request a nickname SMTP proxy address or a change to a proxy address. Both changes require exception handling of proxy addresses and should be evaluated for their impact on external organizations trying to reach that user.

Mailbox Relocation

To balance load, you may want to relocate a mailbox to another server. There are two ways to do this:

- **Relocation within the same site**—Changing the **Home Server** field in the **Advanced User** property page to the new server automatically moves the mailbox to the server specified. No other action is required.

- **Relocation to a different site**—Moving a mailbox to a different site for a user who is relocating cannot be accomplished by changing the home server. Instead, follow these steps:

1. From the **Administrator** window, select the mailbox and select **Hide from the Address Book.**
2. Copy the online mailbox to a .PST file. This file contains all the user's mail.
3. Save the .PST file.
4. Delete the mailbox from the site.
5. Create a new mailbox on a server in the new site.
6. Copy the .PST data from the saved file into the new online mailbox.

Public Folders

Policies and Standards

New top-level folder requests should be submitted to Tier 3 for consideration. Workgroup folder requests are directed to the top-level folder's owner, who can create the folder and assign appropriate permissions. These folders reside on the same server as the users requiring access and are not commonly replicated.

The display name of the folder appearing in the GAL should be meaningful and contain a concise description of the folder's contents. The folder name should not begin with a special character (such as a tilde "~") and should be in upper/lower case. The folder description field describes the folder's purpose and contents, information also contained in the Read Me file posted in every folder.

Replication

If a site does not have a dedicated public folder server, workgroup folders are created on the server where the majority of their users are located. Workgroup folders are not replicated elsewhere. However, users on other sites who require access to the folders can be accommodated through folder affinity, which allows geographically dispersed workgroups to share information.

Public Folder Maintenance

To prevent public folders from growing too large, the content should be reviewed periodically and any outdated material deleted from the folder. Public folder owners should assign folder size and time limits within which the contents should be deleted. Owners of large workgroup folders should be contacted periodically and reminded to remove outdated materials from their folders.

Distribution Lists

All distribution lists (DLs) created are visible in the GAL. To prevent the creation of duplicate names, DLs are created and maintained in a central container. Ownership of DLs is assigned to users, who add or delete members as requested by other users.

Maintaining Exchange Server

The entire messaging system is administered centrally by Tier 2 personnel. Exchange automatically performs housekeeping and maintenance functions in the background, without interrupting message service. However, manually performing these functions is a good idea after a significant change to the system or to resynchronize a server directory after a long server absence.

This section describes specific, nonscheduled procedures to maintain Exchange Server stores (information store and directory service) and the message transfer agent (MTA). These procedures are used when trouble develops and contain recovery steps to return a damaged store to normal operation. Scheduled Exchange Server maintenance consists of periodically verifying:

- Correct messages transferred by the MTA, connectors, and gateways.
- Adequate information store performance and resources.
- Proper directory functionality and correct information sharing by directory replication and synchronization.
- Current backups for each server's directory and information store.
- Correct mailbox administration.

For more information about Exchange maintenance, refer to "Maintaining your Organization" in the *Microsoft Exchange Server Maintenance and Troubleshooting Guide*.

MTA Maintenance

One MTA in each Microsoft Exchange Server delivers messages from the MTA queue to other servers. If the MTA is not performing properly, use these procedures.

Rebuilding Routing Tables

The MTA routing table is rebuilt automatically once a day or when changes are made to the address space on a connector. Changes are replicated to the routing table of all other Exchange servers. If a routing table does not reflect a recent change, it can be rebuilt manually by:

1. Clicking **Servers** and selecting the correct one in the **Administrator** window.
2. Double-clicking on the **MTA**.
3. Clicking **Recalculate Routing**. This updates the servers' MTA routing table and replicates the change to other servers in the site.

Checking MTA Queues

Each server creates different queues for all messages awaiting delivery by the MTA. You can view these by:

1. Selecting the **Queues** tab.

2. Double-clicking on the specific queue. To delete or return individual messages, change the message priority or view detailed message information, double-click on the message.

MTA Diagnostic Logging

Increasing the diagnostic level of the MTA is useful in troubleshooting MTA problems.

1. View the server's event log to see MTA error messages. If there are problems with the server's MTA, raise the diagnostics logging level of the MTA.

2. Use the **Diagnostics Logging** property page to change the level of diagnostics recorded in the server's application event log.

Information Store Maintenance

The information store contains all mailboxes and mail data for users with the Exchange Server set as their home server (private information store) and for public folders (public information store) housed on that server.

Viewing Private Information Store Statistics

Private information store statistics show how much space mailboxes are using and whether present disk resources are sufficient. To view the mailbox resource property page:

1. Click **Servers** and select one in the **Administrator** window.

2. Double-click on **Private Information Store**.

3. Select the **Mailbox Resource** tab to display such mailbox details as:

    - Mailbox name
    - Associated Windows NT account
    - Total kilobytes used by the mailbox
    - Total number of messages in the mailbox
    - The storage limits set on the mailbox
    - The last time the mailbox was accessed

Statistics for the Public Information Store

The public information store contains names and resources used by public folders. To view the **Public Folder Resource** property page:

1. Click **Servers** and select a server in the **Administrator** window.
2. Double-click on **Public Information Store**.
3. Click the **Public Folder Resource** tab to display the following details:
   - Folder display name
   - Total kilobytes used by the folder
   - Total number of messages in the folder
   - Last time the folder was accessed
   - Number of folder owners
   - Number of folder contacts

Maintenance Schedule for the Information Store

Exchange Server needs to perform periodic information store maintenance, including defragmentation and compacting of public and private information stores. There are two maintenance modes.

- **Online maintenance**—Scheduled nightly, online maintenance slows the server and should be scheduled during periods of low server activity, usually between 1:00 and 6:00 A.M. Do not schedule online maintenance during online backups if possible. To change the maintenance schedule:
  1. Click **Servers** and select a server in the **Administrator** window.
  2. Click **Properties** from the **File** menu.
  3. Click the **IS Maintenance** tab.
  4. Assign specific times in the schedule grid. *Do not* select **Always!**
- **Offline maintenance**—Requiring information store shutdown, offline maintenance is a manual process that produces better results and recovers freed space. Database records are compressed into a temporary file (*.BAK), which is initially the same size as the *.EDB file being compressed. To compress, the free disk space in Exchange Server must equal the size of the *.EDB file. To compact the information store:
  1. In **Control Panel**, stop the Exchange information store service to disconnect users.
  2. From the **File** menu, click **Run**.

3. In the **Command Line** box, type **eseutil /d d:\exchsrvr\mdbdata\priv.edb /bpriv.bak**, where d is the drive letter of the Exchange private information store location. Click **OK** to compact the private information store. The time required depends on the size of the information store and the speed of the system.

4. In the **Command Line** box, type **eseutil /d d:\exchsrvr\mdbdata\pub.edb /bpub.bak**, where d is the drive letter of the Exchange public information store location. Click **OK** to compact the public information store.

5. In the **Command Line** box, type **eseutil /d d:\exchsrvr\dsadata\dir.edb /bds.bak**. Click **OK** to compact the directory information (GAL).

6. When compacting is complete, restart the Exchange information store service.

7. Verify that users can log on again. Use any Outlook client to verify that the folders and information in the public or private information store are uncorrupted before removing the backup (temporary *.BAK) files.

Running the ESEUTIL Database Repair Utility

The command line parameters for running ESEUTIL.EXE—used to repair three types of databases in case of corruption—are:

- **Directory database**—\EXCHSRVR\DSADATA\DIR.EDB
- **Private folders database**—\EXCHSRVR\MDBDATA\PRIV.EDB
- **Public folders database**—\EXCHSRVR\MDBDATA\PUB.EDB

In each of the above, "\EXCHSRVR" indicates the directory where the Exchange Server was installed.

Note Because of possible data loss, this utility should be run by experienced Exchange administrators in the event of database corruption and only as a last resort. *Do not* use it as a regular maintenance tool.

To see the command line options for Exchange Server database utilities, open an MS-DOS command prompt on the Exchange Server computer and change to the \WINNT\SYSTEM32 directory. Then type **ESEUTIL.EXE /?**. You will see:

```
Microsoft(R) Exchange Server Database Utilities
Version 5.5
Copyright (C) Microsoft Corporation 1991-1997. All Rights Reserved.

DESCRIPTION: Maintenance utilities for Microsoft(R) Exchange Server
databases.
```

```
MODES OF OPERATION:
Defragmentation:   ESEUTIL /d <database name> [options]
       Recovery:   ESEUTIL /r [options]
      Integrity:   ESEUTIL /g <database name> [options]
        Upgrade:   ESEUTIL /u <database name> /d<previous .DLL>
                   [options]
      File Dump:   ESEUTIL /m[mode-modifier] <filename>
         Repair:   ESEUTIL /p <database name> [options]
```

```
   Note log file path must be specified explicitly unless using /IS or
   /DS options.
```

```
<<<<<  Press a key for more help  >>>>>
D=Defragmentation, R=Recovery, G=Integrity, U=Upgrade, M=File Dump,
   P=Repair
```

- Selecting D displays defragmentation options:

```
DEFRAGMENTATION/COMPACTION:
   DESCRIPTION:  Performs off-line compaction of a database.
        SYNTAX:  ESEUTIL /d <database name> [options]
    PARAMETERS:  <database name> - filename of database to compact, or
                                   one of /ispriv, /ispub, or /ds (see
                                   NOTES below)
       OPTIONS:  zero or more of the following switches, separated by a
                    space:
                 /l<path> - location of log files (default: current
                               directory)
                 /s<path> - location of system files (eg. checkpoint
                               file)
                            (default: current directory)
                 /b<db>   - make backup copy under the specified name
                 /t<db>   - set temp. database name (default:
                               TEMPDFRG.EDB)
                 /p       - preserve temporary database (ie. don't
                               instate)
                 /o       - suppress logo
         NOTES:  1) The switches /ispriv, /ispub, and /ds use the
                    Registry to automatically set the database name,
                    log file path, and system file path for the
                    appropriate Exchange s tore.
                 2) Before defragmentation begins, soft recovery is
                    always performed to ensure the database is in a
                    consistent state.
                 3) If instating is disabled (ie. /p), the original
                    database is preserved uncompacted, and the
                    temporary database will contain the defragmented
                    version of the database.
```

- Selecting R displays recovery options:

```
RECOVERY:
     DESCRIPTION:  Performs recovery, bringing all databases to a
                   consistent state.
          SYNTAX:  ESEUTIL /r [options]
         OPTIONS:  zero or more of the following switches, separated by a
                   space:
                   /is or /ds - see NOTES below
                   /l<path>   - location of log files
                                  (default: current directory)
                   /s<path>   - location of system files (eg. checkpoint
                                  file)
                                  (default: current directory)
                   /o         - suppress logo
           NOTES:  1) The special switches /is and /ds use the Registry
                      to automatically set the log file path and system
                      file path for recovery of the appropriate Exchange
                      store(s).
```

- Selecting G displays integrity options:

```
INTEGRITY:
     DESCRIPTION:  Verifies integrity of a database.
          SYNTAX:  ESEUTIL /g <database name> [options]
      PARAMETERS:  <database name> - filename of database to verify, or
                                     one of /ispriv, /ispub, or /ds (see
                                     NOTES below)
         OPTIONS:  zero or more of the following switches, separated by a
                   space:
                   /t<db>     - set temp. database name (default:
                                  INTEG.EDB)
                   /v         - verbose
                   /x         - give detailed error messages
                   /o         - suppress logo
           NOTES:  1) The consistency-checker performs no recovery and
                      always assumes that the database is in a consistent
                      state, returning an error if this is not the case.
                   2) The special switches /ispriv, /ispub, and /ds use
                      the Registry to automatically set the database name
                      for the appropriate Exchange store.
```

- Selecting U displays upgrade options:

```
UPGRADE:
    DESCRIPTION:  Upgrades a database (created using a previous release
                  of Microsoft(R) Exchange Server) to the current
                  version.
         SYNTAX:  ESEUTIL /u <database name> /d<previous .DLL> [options]
     PARAMETERS:  <database name>    - filename of the database to
                                       upgrade.
                  /d<previous .DLL> - pathed filename of the .DLL that
                                       came with the release of
                                       Microsoft(R) Exchange Server from
                                       which you're upgrading.
        OPTIONS:  zero or more of the following switches, separated by a
                  space:
                  /b<db> - make backup copy under the specified name
                  /t<db> - set temporary database name (default:
                           TEMPUPGD.EDB)
                  /p     - preserve temporary database (ie. don't
                           instate)
                  /o     - suppress logo
          NOTES:  1) This utility should only be used to upgrade a
                     database after an internal database format change
                     has taken place. If necessary, this will usually
                     only coincide with the release of a major, new
                     revision of Microsoft(R) Exchange Server.
                  2) Before upgrading, the database should be in a
                     consistent state. An error will be returned if
                     otherwise.
                  3) If instating is disabled (ie. /p), the original
                     database is preserved unchanged, and the temporary
                     database will contain the upgraded version of the
                     database.
```

- Selecting M displays file dump options:

```
FILE DUMP:
    DESCRIPTION:  Generates formatted output of various database file
                  types.
         SYNTAX:  ESEUTIL /m[mode-modifier] <filename> [options]
     PARAMETERS:  [mode-modifier] - an optional letter designating the
                  type of file dump to perform. Valid values are:
                               h - dump database header (default)
                               k - dump checkpoint file
                  <filename>      - name of file to dump. The type of
                                    the specified file should match the
                                    dump type being requested (eg. if
                                    using /mh, then <filename> must be
                                    the name of a database).
```

- Selecting P displays repair options:

```
REPAIR:
      DESCRIPTION:  Repairs a corrupted or damaged database.
           SYNTAX:  ESEUTIL /p <database name> [options]
       PARAMETERS:  <database name> - filename of database to compact, or
                    one of /ispriv, /ispub, or /ds (see NOTES below)
          OPTIONS:  zero or more of the following switches, separated by a
                    space:
                    /t<db>          - set temp. database name (default:
                                      REPAIR.EDB)
                    /d              - don't repair the database, just scan
                                      for errors

                    /v              - verbose output
                    /x              - give detailed error messages
                    /o              - suppress logo
            NOTES:  1) The switches /ispriv, /ispub, and /ds use the
                       Registry to automatically set the database name for
                       the appropriate Exchange store.
                    2) Recovery will not be run
```

Directory Maintenance

The directory stores all available information (mailboxes, servers, folders, and others) about an organization's resources and users. Maintain the directory on each Exchange server by periodically verifying that the replicated directory information is correct.

Directory Consistency and Replication

Restart the directory replication cycle if the process is interrupted or to check that directory synchronization has incorporated the most current information. Normally, directory replication between servers in the same site is a constant, automatic process occurring in the background. Replication between sites is a scheduled process using the directory replication connector.

Initiating Knowledge Consistency Check (KCC)

The administrator can initiate a knowledge consistency check of all directories in the organization if a site or server has an incomplete directory that doesn't list all servers in the organization or if an error occurred during directory replication.

1. In the Administrator window, click Servers and select a server.

2. Double-click on Directory Service.

3. Click the General tab.

4. Select either:

- **Update now**—Requests updates from other servers within this site, resynchronizing the server directory with the site.
- **Check now**—Initiates the knowledge consistency check of all directories in the organization.

Note   This process can take a long time for large organizations.

Directory Replication

The directory is the standard source for directory information storing all user information. If the replication with the directory system is suspected to be faulty, escalate the issue to Tier 3.

Escalation Procedures

Unresolved issues are escalated to Tier 3 or transferred to the appropriate group, such as the local desktop support, at the user's location. If such an outside group is required for resolution, Tier 2 identifies the user's location, contacts the appropriate group, and enters that group's ticket number in the problem management system.

Reports

Reports on the messaging and server systems are created by tools such as Crystal Reports (installed from the Exchange Resource Kit CD-ROM), which allow administrators to track traffic analysis, load balancing, and usage measurement. A number of these ready-to-run reports are included.

Reports generated by Tier 2

Report title	Description	Publishing frequency
Server Disk Usage	Disk usage on all servers	Weekly
Server Backup Status	Status of backups performed, including bytes backed up and bytes restored, broken down by site and server	Weekly
Server Outages	Downtime by site, server, and service; number of reboots	Weekly
Exchange Information Store Sizes	Disk space used by all Exchange public and private information stores	Weekly
Exchange Message Statistics	Throughput by link	Weekly

(continued)

Reports generated by Tier 2   *(continued)*

Report title	Description	Publishing frequency
Exchange Client Population	Number of users added each week and a graph of the total population	Weekly
Web Server Activity	Hit rates	Weekly
Tier 1 Activity	Password resets; account changes; account lockouts	Weekly
SMS Activity	Number of packages distributed by site; systems surveyed by site	Weekly

Web Site Updates

Tier 2 personnel maintain the support organization's Web site, including information about outages and scheduled maintenance periods that cannot be distributed by Exchange in server-down scenarios. Distribution of information should be balanced between Exchange public folders and the Web site. The Web site also distributes information to non-Exchange users and users not yet migrated to the production Exchange environment. The information maintained by Tier 2 includes:

- **Event log**—Problems that affect service levels must be published to inform users and others trying to communicate with users.

- **Frequently Asked Questions (FAQs)**—Typical questions asked by users and other support personnel.

- **Status reports**—Generated by Tier 2, these reports are required for proper system analysis and capacity planning. In addition, some special reports are generated on the fly in response to user problems or requests.

- **Other support avenues**—To help reduce the support load, contact information and instructions on when to contact the other support organizations are available.

Backup

Tier 2 staff are responsible for tape backup, recovery, and server and mailbox troubleshooting. The rest of this chapter includes tips and procedures for troubleshooting and for server recovery.

Exchange uses the Windows NT security model for authentication, so backup and restore procedures for both products must be followed. Because of this relationship, similar disaster recovery methods are used for Exchange and Windows NT.

Online Versus Offline Backup

Offline backup is file based, and all files are closed so users can't access the server while the backup is in progress. Because all Exchange services must be stopped, offline backups are performed only at scheduled times when servers are down. They allow the administrator to take a snapshot of a server, while the server is offline.

Online backup, which does not disrupt messaging, happens every night and requires that the respective service (information store and directory) is running. The backup also captures Windows NT registry and open files.

Local Versus Remote Backup and Restore

Not all servers have tape drives installed. Servers without tape drives are backed up remotely from a server with a tape drive. The procedure differs slightly for local and remote data:

- Local backup and restore means the backup occurs with a tape drive physically installed on the server being backed up.

- Remote backup and restore is performed over the network and backs up a server with the tape drive physically installed in another server.

Location of Data Files

There are two types of Exchange data: user data and configuration data. User data is stored in the information store (PUB.EDB and PRIV.EDB), personal folders (.PST), offline folders (.OST), personal address book (.PAB), and transaction logs. Configuration data is stored in the Exchange Directory (DIR.EDB), the Windows NT registry, various subdirectories under the Exchange Server installation path, and any paths created after running the Exchange Performance Optimizer.

Exchange database files are located in the directories listed below. Users can change the default path of \Exchsrvr during installation. Transaction logs can be placed on a separate physical disk from the information store and directory files through the Exchange Performance Optimizer. In addition, paths for all the database files can be reconfigured using the **Database Paths** page on the server object.

- Information store

    Private: \Exchsrvr\mdbdata\PRIV.EDB

    Public: \Exchsrvr\mdbdata\PUB.EDB

- Directory

  \Exchsrvr\dsadata\DIR.EDB
- Transaction logs

  Information Store: \Exchsrvr\mdbdata*.LOG

  Directory: \Exchsrvr\dsadata*.LOG

Backup Software

Arcada Backup Exec allows a full online backup of the entire server without stopping any services. It is installed into a common group called Backup Exec on the server housing the tape drive. The example below uses Backup Exec, chosen by the telecommunications company. If you do use a third-party tool, use an Exchange-aware online backup solution. For more information about backup, see the *Microsoft Exchange Server Maintenance and Troubleshooting Guide*.

Performing Online Backup

To ensure full recovery of a server in case of a disaster, the daily backup process is a full online backup and includes the Windows NT registry and any open files. Online backup is scheduled during a period of low user activity (preferably at night) and backs up the entire server, including the Exchange data stores.

After a backup job has been created, it runs every day of the week. Tier 2 staff monitors it for successful completion, changes the tapes (daily), and stores the tapes offsite (weekly). Tapes are rotated between six sets of five or six tapes each.

Creating the Daily Backup Job

1. Select the resources to be backed up for the job, including physical drives (C$ and D$), shares, SQL databases, Exchange information stores, etc. The backup uses these selections when it executes.

   - From the Backup Exec common group, start Backup Exec.
   - Open the **Backup Selections** window.
   - Select **Network Microsoft Windows Network** and the name of the domain your server belongs to.
   - Locate the server you want to back up and select the C$ and D$ drives and the Exchange stores. For example:

     EXSERVER

     [√] *server_name*\C$

     [√] \\ *server_name* \D$

[√] \\ *server_name*\Microsoft Exchange Directory

[√] \\ *server_name*\Microsoft Exchange Information Store

- From the **Select** menu, click **Save Selections**. In the **Selection List** box, enter "**Select-Standard-Nightly**" and click **Save**. This saves the backup options.

2. Create the Backup Job.

- From the **Jobs** menu, click **Setup**, then **Full Backup**, then **Create**.

- In the **Job Name:** box, enter the job name. For a daily on-line full backup, enter *server_name*-STD-FULL.

- Verify that Operation is set to BACKUP.

- Set the **Selection List:** to **Select-Standard-Nightly** (backup options created in Step 1).

- Click the **Options** button and select the **Overwrite the media** checkbox.

- Verify the backup Methods are set to **Files: NORMAL-Back up all files** and **Exchange Servers: FULL-Database & Logs**.

- Click the **Advanced** button. Check that:

  - "Verify After Backup Completes" is selected.

  - Compression is set to Hardware.

  - Backup Open Files is set to Yes (*do not* select Wait).

  - "Include Catalogs" is selected.

  - Catalog is set to Full.

- Click **OK**. Return to the **Jobs-Setup** box by clicking **OK** twice more.

3. Schedule the job.

- In the **Jobs/Setup** dialog box, click **Schedule a Job**.

- Click **Add**. In the **Job:** list, select the backup job you wish to schedule (*server_name*-STD-FULL, created is Step 2).

- Select the times you want this job to run. For a **Daily On-line Backup**, select **Monday through Friday** for **Days of the Week**. For **Start Date/Time**, select **Today's date** and set the time for the backup job.

- Click **OK**.

- Click **Close** to exit the **Schedule a Job** dialog box. Click **Close** again.

4. Exit Backup Exec. Verify that the jobs execute by checking the backup logs on a daily basis.

Full Server Recovery

A full server recovery re-creates a server from scratch after a hard disk failure and requires administrators to reinstall the operating system and recover the server configuration from tape.

Exchange Issues

Restoring an Exchange Server to a different physical computer requires that you reinstall Windows NT and create a new registry. A new Windows NT SID (security identifier) is required for the recovery computer in the domain. You can, however, restore a Windows NT registry to the same physical computer (by, for example, replacing a hard disk on a computer), allowing the computer to maintain its unique SID.

A full server recovery restores an original production server with all Windows NT security and configuration information and, when completed, allows users to log into their mailboxes using their current passwords. A full server recovery requires that:

- The server's C: and D: drives are restored first.
- The server is restarted and the Exchange system attendant is running.
- The server's information store and directory are restored.

Exchange relies on Windows NT security for providing access to mailbox data. Exchange uses Windows NT account SID information in object properties in the Exchange directory. For a successful directory service restore, there are two key conditions:

- The directory service must be restored to a Windows NT–based computer that has the same site, organization, and server name as the production server. To do this, restore the server's C: and D: drives.
- The recovery server must have access from the domain in which Exchange Server was originally installed, so the server must be on the network with access to the PDC (or BDC).

The following sections illustrate a single server site recovery using a full online backup tape of an information store from a production server. The backup type was set to **Full Backup**, which performs a full online backup of the server, the information store, and the directory.

Requirements

A full server recovery requires:

- A full backup of the server drives (C, D), the information store, and the directory.
- A replacement computer with the same hardware capacity as the production server.
- Access to the original Windows NT SAM (access to PDC/BDC).
- A production server configuration sheet.
- Windows NT Server and Windows NT Service Pack installation software (CD-ROM).
- Exchange installation software (CD-ROM) and applicable service pack.
- Exchange production server configuration sheet.

Prepare Recovery Computer

Install Windows NT to a computer with the same name as the crashed server. The recovery server should have the same Windows NT service pack installed to match the production server's configuration. Make sure there is enough disk space for restoring the entire information store and directory from the backup tape and that the tape drive is compatible with tape drives deployed on production servers. If the restore is being performed remotely, the recovery server does not need a tape drive.

To expedite the restore process, keep a copy of the Windows NT installation code and service pack available on a network share and refer to the production Windows NT Server configuration sheet for pertinent settings, including protocol addresses, partitioning information, protocols, options, tuning, and so on.

Reinstall Windows NT

1. Start the Windows NT installation process using the most convenient method (CD-ROM, network share, or others). Follow the Windows NT installation instructions.
2. Set up the drive array for a 2-GB (2,048-MB) C: partition formatted for NTFS and install Windows NT.
3. Set up the TCP/IP configuration with the correct TCP/IP parameters from the server setup sheet.

4. After setup is complete, log on with the Administrator account. In **Administrative Tools**, use **Disk Administrator** to change the CD-ROM drive letter to E:, set up the remaining free space as drive D:, save the changes, and then format D: for NTFS.

5. If the backup software was lost, reinstall Arcada Backup Exec on the local server before completing restore.

Run the Online Restore

Before performing restore, reinstall Windows NT, make sure the server is on the network, and partition and format drive D: for NTFS. Then follow these steps:

1. Insert the last online backup tape.

2. From the Backup Exec common group, start **Backup Exec**.

3. Open the storage media window and select the current tape (in the left windowpane). The list shows all volume names and server objects on the tape.

Note Several cataloged backup jobs may be listed in the window. Select the highlighted icon (the one with the tape symbol in bold type), which is the backup tape currently in the drive.

---

4. Choose the C: and D: drives. (If restoring a Exchange server, *do not* select the Exchange directory service and Exchange information store; they can be restored *only* after starting the Exchange system attendant.) Check marks below indicate the selections (server_name is the name of the server being restored):

   server-name

   [√] \\server_name\C$

   [√] \\server_name\D$

   [ ] \\server_name\Microsoft Exchange Directory (*Do not* select)

   [ ] \\server_name\Microsoft Exchange Information Store (*Do not* select)

5. Click the **Restore** button.

6. When the **Restore Job** dialog box appears:

   - Under Options, click Restore Registry, Restore Security, and Preserve Tree.

   - Click Advanced. Make sure Restore over existing Files is selected. Click OK.

7. Click **Run Now**.

8. When the message "The active files restored will not become usable until the computer is restarted" appears, click **OK**.

9. Shut down and restart the server to which you are restoring. (If restoring remotely, this is *not* the server from which you are running the restore.)

10. When the server has restarted, log on as Administrator. Warning text reading At least one service or driver failed during system startup is normal because the Exchange stores need to be restored. Click **OK**.

11. In **Control Panel**, make sure the Exchange system attendant service has started. If not, click the **Start** button: this service must be running for a successful information store and directory service restore. Close **Control Panel**.

12. From the server containing Arcada Backup Exec, start **Backup Exec**.

13. Open the **Storage Media** window and select the current tape (in the left windowpane).

14. Select the Exchange stores: Directory Service and Information Store.

    server-name

    [ ] \\server_name\C$ (do **not** select)

    [ ] \\server_name\D$ (do **not** select)

    [√] \\server_name\Microsoft Exchange Directory

    [√] \\server_name\Microsoft Exchange Information Store

15. Click the **Restore** button.

16. When the **Restore Job** dialog box appears:

    - Click **Advanced** and make sure these Exchange Server options are checked:

      [√] No Loss Restore (Don't delete existing log files)

      [√] Restore Public Folders

      [√] Restore Private Mailboxes

    - Click **OK**.

17. Click **Run Now**.

18. When the restore job finishes, click **OK**.

19. Exit Arcada Backup Exec.

20. Shut down and restart the remote server (the one just restored to—*do not* restart the server from which the restore is running.). Instead of rebooting, go to **Control Panel** to start the Exchange services in this order:

    - Exchange directory

    - Exchange information store

    - Exchange message transfer agent

    - All remaining Exchange services active on the server

Post-Restore Steps for Exchange Servers

Restart all Exchange services and verify they are set to **Automatic startup**.

Run the DS/IS Consistency Adjuster

Check the directory against the information store to make sure they are synchronized. Make sure both the directory and the information store have been restored before executing this procedure, which adjusts the inconsistencies between the information stores and the directory.

1. Run the Exchange Administrator program and select the desired server.
2. Click **File**, **Properties**, **Advanced** tab.
3. Choose the **Consistency Adjuster** button.
4. Select **All inconsistencies** and choose **OK**.
5. Click **OK** on the **DS/IS** message.
6. Click **OK** on the server **Properties** screen.

Review Mailboxes for Windows NT Account Association

1. Highlight the **Recipients** container under the site.
2. Double-click on any user.
3. Review the **Primary Windows NT Account** field to see if the Windows NT account matches the mailbox.
4. Repeat this procedure for several users to ensure that the mailboxes will be linked to the proper Windows NT logon accounts.

Test User Logon from Client Workstations

1. Run the Exchange client.
2. Verify that the user's password works.
3. Repeat this from several workstations, to make sure the server is available to users.

Single Mailbox Recovery

If you need to recover a single Exchange mailbox (because the mailbox or some of its data were deleted), perform the procedure below. Note that you must restore the *entire* information store before you can retrieve data from a specific mailbox. Restoring the information store to the production server resets the entire server to the point when the last backup was taken and wipes out all user mail received since then.

The sections below detail the procedures, which require administrator and backup operator privileges and involve:

- Preparing a new server running Windows NT Server.
- Installing Exchange with the same site and organization name to which the mailbox to be restored resided.
- Restoring the information store from a backup tape.
- Logging on with Exchange administrative privileges.
- Assigning the Windows NT administrator ID access to the desired mailbox.
- Restoring mailbox data to a .PST file and attaching the .PST to the desired user profile.

You can maintain the single mailbox recovery server online with production servers because its name need not be the same as the production server running Exchange. You should not use this server, however, for directory replication with the production servers. The following are required:

- A dedicated server with enough capacity to restore the entire private information store database.
- A backup of the private information store database.
- Outlook and Exchange Server installation code.
- Windows NT and Windows NT service pack installation code.

Note   You can also use the Deleted Items Retention feature to retrieve deleted items. In Outlook, users can find this feature in the **Tools** menu under **Recover Deleted Items**.

Prepare Recovery Computer

For quick recovery, the recovery computer should be available at all times and have the proper Windows NT service pack installed. Make sure there is enough disk space to restore the *entire* information store from the backup tape. If you are not restoring remotely from a server with a tape drive installed, make sure the recovery computer is equipped with a tape drive compatible with the drives on the production servers.

1. If needed, prepare the recovery server with the same drive configuration as the production Exchange server: two NTFS partitions (C: 2 GB, remaining space is D:).

   The server name of the restore computer can be different for the single mailbox restore procedure.

2. This server should have the respective Windows NT service pack installed. If not, install it and restart the server.

3. Log on with Administrator privileges to the recovery server. Your own account should have administrative privileges; if not, use the Domain Administrator account.

4. Install Exchange, from the Exchange Server CD-ROM.

   - Select the **Complete/Custom** installation option.

   - Select **Create a New Site**. Use the same organization name and site name used on the server from which you are restoring the mailbox.

   - For the site service account, enter the same account and password you used to log on. This installs Exchange server.

   - Run Performance Optimizer to configure the recovery server to match the production server by placing the information and directory service stores on the D: drive because there will not be enough free disk space to restore the information store to the default location (C:). For the system parameters, use the default settings requested by Optimizer. The location of the Exchange files should come up as:

     - Private information store—D:\exchsrvr\MDBDATA
     - Public information store—D:\exchsrvr\MDBDATA
     - Information store logs—C:\exchsrvr\MDBDATA
     - Directory services—D:\exchsrvr\DSADATA
     - Directory services logs—C:\exchsrvr\DSADATA
     - Message transfer agent—D:\exchsrvr\MTADATA

   - Let Optimizer move the files automatically to the above locations.

   - Start all services by clicking **Finish**. In **Control Panel**, verify that all Exchange services have started without error.

5. Access a mailbox from a workstation with the client installed and with access to the recovery server. If necessary, install the Outlook on the recovery server.

Restoring the Information Store from Tape

1. On the recovery server, from **Control Panel**, stop the Exchange information store service.

2. Log on to the server from which you will be running the restore operation. You must log on with an account that has privileges to run a restore operation (Administrator, or an account that is a member of the backup operators group).

3. Restore the information store to the recovery server. Note that you will be restoring to a different server than the one from which the backup came.

   - Refer to the Run the Online Restore section listed above to restore the Information store but use the instructions below instead of Step 4.

- In Step 4, select only the Exchange information store (do not restore all drives or the Exchange directory), which will display as: [X] \\Server_name\Microsoft Exchange Information Store.

- Redirect the restore job to a different server. In the **Restore Job** window, set **Types of Jobs to Redirect** to **Exchange Sets**.

- In the **Exchange Database Set Destination** in the **Restore To** box, type: \\Recovery_server_name. The recovery_server_name is the Windows NT computer name of the server to which you are restoring (not the name of the server from which the backup set came).

- Click **Advanced**. Under **Exchange Server**, clear the other options and select only **Restore Private Mailboxes:**

  [ ] No Loss Restore (Don't delete existing log files)

  [ ] Restore Public Folders

  [√] Restore Private Mailboxes

- Click **Run Now** to restore the information store.

4. From **Control Panel**, restart the recovery server's Exchange information store service.

Recover User Mailbox

1. Log on to the recovery server using the Windows NT account with which you installed Exchange.

2. Run the Exchange Administrator program.

3. Select the **Recipients** container and double-click on mailbox you want to recover.

4. From the **General** tab, click **Primary Windows NT Account**.

5. From the **Primary Windows NT Account** dialogue box click **Select an Existing Windows NT Account**. Click **OK**.

6. From the **Add User or Group** screen, click **Administrator** (or your own account, if you logged on with it), then click **Add**. Click **OK**.

7. Click **OK** on the **User Property** screen.

8. From the Exchange client program group (on the server if you installed the Exchange client or from your own workstation), run Exchange services.

9. Configure a profile for the desired user.

10. Start Outlook, and select the profile you just created.

11. Click **Tools** and **Services,** and add a Personal Folder file to the profile.

12. Copy the needed information to the .PST file. Return recovered mail to user.

When the deleted mail has been recovered, you should return the messages to the user's production mailbox. To do this, you temporarily take ownership of the user's mailbox.

1. From the Exchange Administrator program, connect to the production Exchange server on which the user's mailbox is located.

2. Select the **Recipients** container and double-click on the user's mailbox name.

3. From the **General** tab, click **Primary Windows NT Account**.

4. From the **Primary Windows NT Account** dialogue box choose **Select an Existing Windows NT Account**. Click **OK**.

5. From the **Add User or Group** screen, click **Administrator** (or your own account if you logged on with it), then click **Add**. Click **OK**.

6. Click **OK** on the **User** property screen.

7. From **Control Panel,** click **Mail & Fax**.

8. Configure a new profile for the desired user, using the production server name. (*Do not* use the profile created in the Recover User Mailbox section because it will point to the recovery server.)

9. Start Outlook and select the profile you just created.

10. Add a personal folder file to the profile. Use the .PST file created in Step 11, in the Recover User Mailbox section.

11. Drag-and-drop the messages you want recovered from the personal folder to the mailbox-*username*.

12. Under **Tools Services**, remove the personal folder service you created for the recovery operation.

13. Remove your account from the Primary NT Logon Account on the user's mailbox. From the Exchange Administrator program, connect to the production Exchange server on which the user's mailbox is located.

14. Select the **Recipients** container and double-click on the user's mailbox name.

15. From the **General** tab, click **Primary Windows NT Account**.

16. From the **Primary Windows NT Account** dialogue box, select **Select an Existing Windows NT Account**. Click **OK**.

17. From the **Add User or Group** screen, select the user's Windows NT logon account.

18. Click **OK** on the **User Property** screen to return the mailbox to the user.

.PST, .OST, and .PAB Recovery

.PST

If users store .PSTs on local drives that are not being backed up, there is no way to recover the .PSTs. If users store .PSTs on file servers (home directories), they are backed up with the nightly server backup and recovery is simply a matter of restoring the .PST and adding it to an existing user profile.

Unfortunately, online users all too often store their messages online in the Exchange information store and never use a .PST file. If a user password protects the .PST then forgets the password, the password and data are gone forever. Make sure users are aware of this.

.OST

.OST data is at risk when changes made to the local .OST file have not been replicated up to the server-based store. If a user computer crashes, a new .OST can be created on the replacement computer and all server based-information can be sent to the .OST file during synchronization.

.PAB

Personal address book files can be stored on a server directory, which is backed up nightly, or locally, which cannot be recovered if users don't back up their own.

General Troubleshooting

Troubleshoot a server by isolating each stage to narrow the problem down and keep the investigation as simple as possible. Start by answering these questions:

- Has it ever worked?
- Have the release notes, documentation, and online help been studied?
- Can the problem be readily reproduced?
- Is any beta software installed on this workstation?
- Have variables such as workstations, profiles, user accounts, public folders, personal folders, and attachments been isolated?

Troubleshooting can be divided into two approaches: *active* and *reactive*. *Active* tools detect problems before they occur. These include the monitoring and other procedures described in the first half of this chapter.

Reactive tools find the causes of problems after they occur. Some tools are used both to monitor system condition and troubleshoot problems after the fact. This section discusses reactive troubleshooting techniques and tools, including:

- **Windows NT Event Viewer**—Filters and sorts out logged events, including successful and failed events, logon attempts, and directory and security alerts.
- **Windows NT Server Manager**—Configures services and server shares on all visible Windows NT–based computers.
- **Windows NT Performance Monitor**—Monitors:
  - PVIEWER.EXE, which manages processes on a Windows NT–based computer
  - PING, which checks TCP/IP connectivity

Other reactive tools commonly used to troubleshoot Windows NT servers include Windows NT Control Panel, Dr. Watson, Network Analyzer, and Windows NT diagnostics

Windows NT Event Viewer

Event Viewer allows you to administer, track, and filter all Windows NT events on a server from a single place. It is the first place to look for evidence of configuration flaws or problems.

Events are recorded in three types of logs: system, security (audit), and application. All users can view system and application logs, but only administrators can view security logs. Services write to security logs only when there is a security breach.

Windows NT Server Manager

Server Manager allows administrators to access the services and control panel options of any Exchange server remotely. It can also be used to promote a server to PDC or synchronize Windows NT information in a domain if there is a problem with the PDC.

This tool validates whether the RPC and services related to Windows NT Server are still running in a given server. Administrators can use this tool to send network alerts to users when stopping services, stopping file sharing, or restarting the computer.

Performance Monitor

The Windows NT Performance Monitor tracks the real-time operation of all Windows NT Server components, gathers statistical information to determine the normal range of system and network operating conditions, detects bottlenecks, monitors queues and configuration parameters, and tunes performance.

PVIEWER

PVIEWER.EXE, a utility included in the *Windows NT Resource Kit,* allows you to view and stop any process running on the Windows NT–based computer and to find statistics on memory usage and process usage.

Typically, PVIEWER is used to stop processes that have terminated abnormally, leaving remaining program stubs in memory or processes without a user interface and not displayed in the Task List, such as the MAPI spooler: MAPISPL32.

PVIEWER also displays and terminates services that are considered runaways. For example, sometimes a nightly backup does not unload cleanly and leaves a runaway program, the symptoms of which are that server usage is 100 percent even though no changes have been made on the server. PVIEWER.EXE allows the administrator to find and terminate the process without taking the server down.

Windows NT Troubleshooting

If the Windows NT operating system doesn't boot up or there is an error during the boot procedure, the problem must be resolved before any potential issues with the application(s) on that server can be addressed.

Windows NT troubleshooting tools are:

The boot screen on the server console

Windows NT Event Viewer

Windows NT Administrator

Windows NT Control Panel

Dr. Watson log files

The following sections address Windows NT troubleshooting scenarios.

Server Does Not Power Up

If the server does not turn on, verify that it is plugged in and that the circuit has power. If other servers on the same circuit are operational, check the power supply of the affected server, then verify that the server passes its power-on self-test and that all devices initialize properly. If there are CMOS errors, correct them by using the server setup sheet. If there are hardware faults and the server does not start executing the Windows NT loader, refer to the Server Hardware Issues section later in this chapter.

Server Does Not Boot

On the server console, verify that there are no messages indicating missing or corrupt boot files. If files are indicated missing or corrupt, use the Emergency Repair Disk or the Last Known Good configuration to recover the Window NT operating system.

If the server hangs at the blue screen and displays a STOP error on the first two lines on the screen, look up the error message in TechNet for suggested resolutions. If no resolution can be found, boot the server using the Last Known Good configuration. If that fails, attempt to repair the installation with Windows NT boot diskettes, CD-ROM, and the Emergency Repair disk for that computer. If this fails, restore the servers C: drive, as described in the Restoring the Operating System section below.

Windows NT Services Fail on Startup

At this stage, the server should boot and you should be able to log on to the server console using the administrator password. When a message comes up reading **One or more services failed on startup,** check the event log for failed services and the reason for failure.

Stop as many services as possible and restart them one by one. Keep checking the event log for specific errors to isolate the faulty service. Refer to TechNet for more information on specific errors displayed in the event log and their resolution.

Hard Disk Errors

Check the hard drives for errors using CHKDSK.EXE. If there are errors, reinstall Windows NT with the upgrade option. If the drive has so many errors that a reinstall is not possible, you may have to reformat and restore the C: drive, as described in the next section.

Restoring the Operating System

If attempts to recover the operating system fail, restore the C: drive from the last backup. First bring the server back on the network so a restore can be performed.

Reinstall Windows NT from the installation CD-ROM by referring to the steps in the Reinstall Windows NT section above. Restore the server's C: drive from the pervious night's backup and restart the server, verifying that it starts with no errors.

Exchange Troubleshooting

Tools used in Exchange troubleshooting include:

- Windows NT Event Viewer
- Microsoft Exchange Administrator program
- Microsoft Exchange message tracking

Windows NT Event Viewer

Event Viewer is used by all Exchange services to store errors and events and is the first place to look for configuration flaws or problems with any component on an Exchange server. All Exchange services write to the application log.

Exchange components include system attendant, MTA, directory, public information store, private information store, the administrator program, directory import, directory synchronization, Microsoft Mail connector interchange, and Internet Mail Service interchange.

Each major Exchange component also logs events to its own log file for easy access and backup. Four levels of logging can be configured through the Exchange Administrator program:

- No logging
- Low-level logging—fatal conditions only
- Medium-level logging—near-fatal conditions only
- High-level logging—all events and conditions

Generally, setting the logging to low or medium provides all the detail you need and takes up less space. If you select high-level logging to track all events and conditions, back up and remove the log files more often to avoid consuming hard disk space. In addition, extensive logging impacts process and hard drive performance.

Exchange Administrator Program

Functions available in Exchange Administrator include:

- **MTA queues**—A property sheet can be used to obtain a snapshot of the messages waiting to be processed by an MTA. Exchange creates different queues for each server in a site and gateways. Information captured includes priority of individual messages and detailed message information.

- **Directory knowledge consistency**—These functions allow manual synchronization of inconsistencies between Exchange servers.

  - **Synchronize Now** requests directory updates from all other Exchange servers within the site.

  - **Check Knowledge Consistency** requests the complete list of servers in the site and other known sites and is typically used to bring a server up to date if it has been down or off the network.

- **Rebuild routing table now**—The routing table is manually re-created by forcing the MTA to reread all information on connections and address space.

- **Information consistency adjustment**—Inconsistencies between the information store and the directory are resolved. Use this only *after* the **Synchronize Now** function.

Message Tracking

Message tracking allows administrators to view, sort, and filter a wealth of information collected by individual servers or the messages sent, received, and delivered by the server.

Types of information captured are originator, originating server, and date and time of message sent. Reported events include message submitted, distribution list expansion, message transferred, message received, message delivered, log file not available, report generation (NDR), report transfer out, report transfer in, X.400 event #10 (NDR delivered to the originator), X.400 event #28 (message redirect from mailbox to alternate recipient), and message delivered locally.

Message tracking pinpoints messages up to the point where forwarding stops and determines Exchange quality of service in areas such as performance, round trips between two servers, alternate route setup, and usage and reliability issues such as lost mail.

Exchange Troubleshooting Tips

If problems occur with the Exchange system, follow these suggestions:

- Ensure that the user's name, as well as the Exchange Server computer name, is spelled correctly.

- Ensure that the Exchange directory service is running on the Exchange Server computer.

- Ensure that the user's workstation can see the Windows NT Server computer.

- Run the RPC Ping utility from the Support directory of the Exchange Server CD-ROM. Ping the Exchange Server computer with RPC Ping as the endpoint.

- Run Outlook on the Exchange Server computer or from another workstation. If it doesn't work, the problem is a server issue.

- Try logging on from another workstation as the same user who is encountering the problem.

- Network auto-detect on the Windows NT Server. If there's only one network, turn it off and specify the network type.

- Test with computers on the same network segment.

Examine alert details sent by server or link monitors that may indicate a service is not responding or a link is not sending messages. Link alerts could indicate problems with the MTA or at the network level, preventing servers from communicating. Also examine the Windows NT application event log, which records critical events as they occur. If you suspect an Exchange service, choose a higher diagnostic logging level for that component and check the messages for clues.

Troubleshooting scenarios are of three categories:

- Security
- Exchange services faults
- Configuration and management control

Troubleshooting Security Issues

Security failures usually indicate that access control is not set up correctly because the Exchange service account:

- Does not have administrator privilege.
- Has an incorrect password.
- Does not have Logon as service privilege.

Use Windows NT user manager and the control panel to diagnose these problems.

The Exchange service account validates both the directory service and the MTA as they connect to their remote server counterpart. Make sure the account has the proper administrator privileges and is configured to log on as a service. Also verify that the account password is correct. If different accounts are used to connect sites, trust relationships between the account domains must exist for the service accounts to be able to log on.

Troubleshooting Exchange Services Faults

Software failures because of server or server services not running indicate problems with:

- MTA service
- Information store
- Directory service
- Other dependency services

To diagnose the problem, use Exchange server manager, Exchange server monitor, Windows NT server manager, and Windows NT Performance Monitor.

MTA Service Not Running

There are three reasons the Exchange MTA can fail to start:

1. Insufficient available hard disk space. When the Exchange MTA database disk has less than 10 megabytes (MB) remaining, the MTA shuts down and a Field Engineering Event 9411 is added to the event log. You can solve this problem by:

    - Stopping all Exchange Server services and freeing disk space on the hard disk used by the Exchange MTA by deleting other files or moving them to another location. Restart the Exchange Server services afterwards.

    - Moving the Exchange MTA database to a location with more disk space by using the Exchange Performance Optimizer (run it with the **-v** option to skip the step of analyzing the hard disks).

       After restarting, monitor the Exchange MTA work queue, which should go down. If it doesn't, use either the Exchange Administrator program or Performance Monitor to find out which queue is backing up then correct it.

2. Both the Exchange directory service and the Exchange system attendant service must run for the Exchange MTA to start. If one service does not start, follow the troubleshooting steps to fix it.

3. Corruption in the Exchange MTA database can prevent the Exchange MTA service from starting. When this happens, a fatal event is logged in the Windows NT event log. To fix the corruption, use the MTACHECK.EXE utility in the \EXHSRVR\BIN subdirectory. To run the utility, refer to the Utilities for Troubleshooting section of *Microsoft Maintenance & Troubleshooting* in the Exchange Server 5.5 Online Books or the online help in the Exchange Administrator program.

Information Store Not Running

The information store can fail to start because of a sudden loss of power to an Exchange Server or faulty hardware that incorrectly wrote information to a disk. This section outlines how to fix this.

The steps work best if circular logging is turned off and regular backup procedures are in place. If circular logging is turned on (the setup default), steps 1, 2, and 6 through 9 are valid because circular logging automatically writes over transaction logs files after the data they contain has been committed to the database. If a backup is unavailable, then steps 1, 2, 8, and 9 are valid.

Each of the below steps preserves as much data as possible, so it may not be necessary to follow all of them to recover an information store.

1. Check the Windows NT event viewer application log for EDB, MSExchangeIS, MSExchangePriv, and MSExchangePub error messages. Two of the most common error messages reported to the Application log are:

   - **Reclaiming Disk Space for the Information Store**—To free up disk space, perform offline compacting by following the procedure outlined in the Maintenance Schedule for the Information Store section earlier in this chapter.

   - **Error -1011: Isinteg -patch needs to be run**—This error occurs because globally unique identifiers (GUIDs) used by the restored information store match old ones and must be replaced by unique GUIDs. Run **Isinteg -patch** against the entire information store (both the PUB.EDB and PRIV.EDB files) to generate new GUIDs and prevent incorrect backfilling of replication information.

     To run **isinteg –patch**, first ensure that the directory and system attendant services are running. (If either is not running, **isinteg** fails with a DS_COMMUNICATIONS_ERROR message.) Then change to the Exchsrvr\Bin directory and type **isinteg –patch**. After **isinteg** reports that the information store has been updated successfully, restart the information store service.

2. Shut down all Exchange services and reboot the Exchange server. When the information store restarts, it automatically tries to recover and return the database to a consistent state.

3. Make a full offline backup of the information store by stopping all Exchange services. This back should include all .EDB and .LOG files, which can be stored on different physical drives. To determine where they are located, look in the registry under the HKEY_LOCAL_MACHINE subtree in the \SYSTEM\CurrentControlSet\Services\MSExchangeIS\ParametersSystem subkey.

Note As a precautionary measure, look at the DB Log Path parameter to capture the existing state of the Exchange Server before proceeding. This step will be necessary if or when you reach steps 8 or 9 of this procedure.

---

4. Restore the last full online backup, but do *not* select the **Start Services after Restore** checkbox. Next restore any differential (from the time of the last full online up to the day before the crash) online backups of the information store. Select the box **Start Service after Restore** only when the *last* differential backup is restored. *Do not* check the box to erase all existing data!

5. If Step 4 still does not start the information store, go into the Event Viewer application log and review the logged messages for the source EDB. There will be one message per log file replayed during the restore in step 4. If a message indicates problems replaying a particular log file, remove the corrupted log file and all files greater in number from the Mdbdata directory and try restarting the information store. If successful, this results in the loss of only the data stored in the removed log files.

6. If Step 5 fails, restore the last full online backup of the information store. Select the boxes to **Start Service After Restore and Erase** all existing data. Next run the **DS/IS consistency adjuster** on the **Advanced** tab of the **Server Object** properties page in the Exchange Administrator program.

7. If Step 6 fails, repeat it using the previous version of either a full offline or full online backup.

8. If Step 7 fails, delete all .EDB and .LOG files from the Mdbdata directory and restore a copy of the PRIV.EDB and PUB.EDB from the backup of the database when the problem started (Step 3). Then go into the Exchsrvr\bin directory and run **Eseutil /d** *<path to database>* **/ispri** followed by **Eseutil /d** *<path to database>* **/r /ispub**. This defragments the private and public information stores and fixes any database errors it encounters. Once ESEUTIL.EXE has finished successfully, try restarting the information store. If it starts, run **isinteg -fix** against both the private and public information stores to clean up any inconsistencies created by ESEUTIL.EXE.

9. If all of these steps fail, the last resort is to clear the information store. To determine if the problem exists in the public or the private information store, wipe them one at a time starting with the public store.

Warning This process deletes all user mail messages, all user folders (wiping the private store, PRIV.EDB), and all public folders (wiping the public store, PUB.EDB).

To wipe the public information store:

- Ensure that you have completed Step 3 (full backup) or copy the Exchsrvr\Mdbdata directory to another location on the hard drive.

- Delete all EDB*.LOG files, RES*.LOG files, EDB.CHK, and PUB.EDB in the Exchsrvr\Mdbdata directory.

- Restart the information store service. If it starts, all public folder information (a new PUB.EDB, RES*.LOG and EDB.CHK will be created automatically) and all log file information have been lost. However, you retain all user mail messages and folders stored in the private information store (PRIV.EDB).

If wiping the public information store fails:

- Remove all information in the Mdbdata directory.

- Bring back a copy of the PUB.EDB from tape or alternate location.

- Restart the information store. If the service starts, the public folder information will be intact, but all user mail messages, folders, and information in the logs will be lost. The users' mailboxes will be recreated the next time users log in.

If the above steps fail, remove all information from the Exchsrvr\Mdbdata and restart the information store service, which returns it with installation defaults. Then run the **DS/IS consistency adjuster** (**Advanced** tab of server object) to clear up any directory/information store inconsistencies.

Directory Service Not Running

The directory service manages the transfer of all organizational information between servers within a site and with the MTA service. Directory replication problems between sites are usually caused by connection or configuration errors. The steps below cover most of them.

Directory Information Not the Same on Servers Within a Site

- Check the Windows NT application event log for replication failure messages.
- Check for network connectivity between the servers (**PING, NET USE**) to see if the servers can communicate with each other.

Directory Information Not the Same Between Servers in Different Sites

- Check the Windows NT application event log for replication failure messages.
- Check for network connectivity between servers.
- Check the directory replication schedule and force an update by clicking the **Request Updates Now** button.
- Increase the diagnostics logging level and check for errors in the Windows NT application event log.
- Check for directory consistency within the site.
- Check the MTA queues for directory replication messages. If long queues are present, check the MTA configuration and status. If the MTA is delivering directory replication messages, use message tracking to examine the process.

Other Related Services Not Running

The main Exchange service will not start if a dependent service is not running, and the event will be recorded in the Windows NT application event log. Verify all needed dependency services start correctly by referring to the below list, which names the services used by Exchange Server, the files executed when the service starts, and the service dependencies:

- **MSExchangeSA**—Exchange system attendant.

  File: EXCHSRVR\BIN\MAD.EXE

  Depends on:
  - EventLog
  - OLE (%windir%\system32\scm.exe)
  - NtLmSsp (NT LM Security Support Provider-Services.exe)
  - RPCLocator (%windir%\system32\locator.exe)
  - RPCSS (RPC Server Service-%windir%\system32\rpcss.exe)
  - LanmanWorkstation
  - LanmanServer

- **MSExchangeDS**—Exchange directory service.

  File: EXCHSRVR\BIN\DSAMAIN.EXE

  Depends on: MSExchangeSA

- **MSExchangeIS**—Exchange information store.

  File: EXCHSRVR\BIN\STORE.EXE

  Depends on: MSExchangeDS

- **MSExchangeMTA**—Exchange message transfer agent.

  File: EXCHSRVR\BIN\EMSMTA.EXE

  Depends on: MSExchangeDS

- **MSExchangeDX**—Exchange directory synchronization.

  File: EXCHSRVR\BIN\DXA.EXE

  Depends on: MSExchangeMTA

- **MSExchangeFB**—Exchange Schedule+ free/busy connector.

  File: EXCHSRVR\CONNECT\MSFBCONN\MSFBCONN.EXE

  Depends on:
  - MSExchangeDS
  - MSExchangeIS
  - EventLog

- **MSExchangeIMC**—Exchange Internet Mail Service.

  File: EXCHSRVR\CONNECT\MSEXCIMC\MSEXCIMC.EXE

  Depends on:
  - MSExchangeIS
  - MSExchangeMTA
  - TCPIP (%windir%\system32\drivers\tcpip.sys)

- **MSExchangeMSMI**—Exchange Mail Connector interchange.

  File: EXCHSRVR\CONNECT\MSMCON\BIN\MT.EXE

  Depends on:
  - MSExchangeDS
  - EventLog

- **MSExchangeKMS**—Exchange Key Management server.

  File: SECURITY\BIN\KMSERVER.EXE

  Depends on: MSExchangeDS

- **MSExchangeATMTA**—Exchange Mail Connector (Apple Talk) MTA.
  File: EXCHSRVR\CONNECT\MSMCON\BIN\MACGATE.EXE
  Depends on:
  - EventLog
  - MSExchangeMSMI
  - LanmanServer

Troubleshooting Configuration Management and Control Issues

Configuration mistakes and improper setup are indicated by:

- Undeliverable messages
- Queues growing with messages awaiting delivery
- Routing table errors
- Address errors
- Link configuration errors
- Profile errors

Use the Exchange Administrator program and Outlook to verify configurations and proper setup. Verify the setup against the server configuration sheets and Exchange installation documents.

Server Hardware Issues

If servers fail because of bad disk drives, bad memory, bad adapter cards, or other hardware problems, install replacements quickly to get the server operational again. Replacement parts policies and procedures for server hardware are described below. To guarantee service levels, Tier 2 and certain remote server sites should stock items for quick replacement. In some cases, it may be quicker to buy the part at a local computer store than to wait for delivery, although anyone contemplating this should first get authorization from the Tier 2 team leader.

Disk Drives

- **S40: Single-drive failure**—All S40s are configured with RAID5 and should continue operating normally in the event of a single drive failure, although redundancy is lost and the system is exposed until a new drive is installed. When a new disk is acquired, wait for off-peak hours if possible and swap the new disk in. The RAID should recover automatically as long as the Mylex Autorebuild utility is running. This rebuild process takes several hours and significantly affect server performance.

- **S40: Multiple-drive failure**—See the Disaster Recovery section of the next chapter.

- **3416**—Server is not operational until repairs are made. When the new disk arrives, swap it in and recreate the server by following the server installation instructions.

- **Site spares**—One S40 Hot Swap drive per site.

- **Central spares**—Twenty S40 Hot Swap drives and ten 3416 hard drives (not Hot-Swap).

Memory

- **S40**—The S40s contain error correcting code (ECC) memory and can survive some memory failures. When errors start occurring, new memory should be installed during off-peak hours. Memory errors should be detected by monitoring the amount of physical memory reported by the server.

- **3416**—Server is not operational until repairs are made. Install a replacement part.

Network Card

- **S40**—Server is not operational until repairs are made. If there are two network cards in the S40 and the second card is not configured in Windows NT, remove the card and add the configuration for the second card. Install a replacement for the broken part.

- **3416**—Server is not operational until repairs are made. Install a replacement part.

CHAPTER 8

Tier 3 Systems Management Procedures and Disaster Recovery

This chapter describes the third support tier, the *last line of support*. Tier 3 provides around-the-clock support for Tier 2 and takes whatever steps are necessary to restore messaging service. Key responsibilities are systems management, analysis, and optimization, pre-production testing, and disaster recovery. Tier 3 support is vital to the messaging system's short-term health and long-term performance. Through its focus on the deployment, monitoring, and troubleshooting procedures of the entire support organization, Tier 3 provides continual improvement in end-user and server support and maintenance.

To round out the discussion of the 3-tier model and provide a clear picture of Tier 3 responsibilities, this chapter discusses, among other things, testing and disaster recovery. These topics are covered much more thoroughly in chapters devoted to them in, respectively, *Deploying Microsoft Exchange Server 5.5* (Chapter 3) and in Chapters 9, 10, and 11 of this book (Part 3 "Disaster and Recovery Planning").

This and the preceding chapters detailing the 3-tier support organization are based on the example of a large telecommunications company deploying a messaging infrastructure supporting 60,000 users and based on Microsoft Windows NT Server, Exchange Server, and Systems Management Server. Product versions and names are supplied to give context to the discussion and to demonstrate how the various versions fit together. You can apply the material here to your own organization.

Roles and Responsibilities

Unlike Tiers 1 and 2, Tier 3 tasks are not divided into support, operations, and administration but instead fall into support and non-support categories such as system management, departmental infrastructure, and Web site and utility development. Tier 3 also provides:

- System management functions, including system monitoring, reporting, analysis, tuning and performance optimization, expansion and upgrade.

- Capacity planning.
- Disaster recovery.
- Pre-production testing.
- Abnormal situation management.
- Knowledge transfer to Tier 2.
- Development of procedures for Tiers 1 and 2.
- Escalation authority to Microsoft Product Support Services, an outside source of support for the corporation.

Personnel Guidelines and Resources

Tier 3 personnel should be:

- Proficient in all aspects of three products (Windows NT, Exchange, and Systems Management Server)
- A technical expert in at least one of the above products
- Certified through a Microsoft Windows NT Certification Test
- Ready to become a Microsoft Certified Product Specialist on Exchange or Systems Management Server within 30 days of hire
- On a path to becoming a Microsoft Certified System Engineer within 6 months
- Proficient in TCP/IP LAN/WAN infrastructure
- Committed to working whatever hours are required to restore service levels
- Strong system analysts
- Excellent communicators
- Able to manage small teams and travel when required
- Proficient in client and server hardware

Tier 3 should have access to these resources:

- **Microsoft Technical Support (MTS)**—Even though Tier 3 contains the most technically knowledgeable people in the support organization, some issues require the assistance of MTS.
- **Corporate enterprise architecture group**—Tier 3 works closely with the company's architecture group to develop new and existing services and solve potential architecture and engineering problems.

How to Contact Tier 3

Only qualified Tier 2 personnel and these three organizations contact Tier 3:

- Enterprise architecture group
- Enterprise security organization
- End-user computing services (non-messaging issues)

Like Tier 2, Tier 3 is staffed onsite 12 hours a day. Other hours are covered by on-call staff who can be reached by telephone and pager. They must respond within 15 minutes and be less than one hour away from the site for which they are responsible.

System Management

System management and analysis are key components of Tier 3's focus on maintaining service levels and managing system capacity through analyzing trends in system load and usage. Tier 3 looks for deviations from established baseline parameters and fixes them by tuning, optimizing, or expanding the system.

System Analysis Overview

Tier 2 personnel monitor the system for deviations from baseline ranges for Windows NT and Exchange Servers and correct any problems before trouble or bottlenecks occur. Tier 3 complements this effort by looking for trends and other incidents that, over long periods of time, will degrade performance. Steps involved in Tier 3's systems analysis are to:

- Identify performance parameters to be monitored.
- Collect and record these parameters over time.
- Analyze the recorded data.
- Correct problems.

Data Collection

This section describes the tools and techniques Tier 3 staff use to collect and manage data.

Performance Monitor

Windows NT Performance Monitor provides a graphical interface for viewing statistics on various system components such as processor, memory, network, queues, and so on. Windows NT defines various objects and counters in the hardware and operating system, and Exchange defines them for messaging. (The list of counters is long, so it has been moved to the section called Performance Monitor Counters at the end of this chapter.)

Performance Monitor captures the values of both sets of counters using one of four methods:

- Logging the counters to a file
- Sending alerts when counters reaches a triggerpoint
- Graphing counter values over time
- Displaying a snapshot of counter values in reports

Data Logging Service and Workloads

To provide unattended logging of counters, the data logging service is available on every server. Instructions for installing the data logging service can be found in the Performance Monitor Counters section at the end of this chapter.

The Windows NT Server network counter are logged for real workloads (end-users' network messaging demands) and synthetic ones (created for test purposes).

Synthetic workloads allow characterization of the system behavior under various stress conditions such as trying to determine the system's limits. The Response Probe utility in the *Microsoft Windows NT Resource Kit* can generate synthetic workloads for Windows NT.

Data Access and Archival Techniques

Monitoring the performance counters generates about 10 KB of data for each snapshot (100 data points at 100 bytes/data point). Logging this information at the recommended logging interval of 15 minutes yields 40 KB of data per hour, 1 MB of data per server per day. To manage the data, "staged data reduction" techniques described below are used:

1. Snapshots are recorded in a local log file for each server.
2. At the end of the day, the entire local log file is compressed and archived to a central server so the daily log can be reused the next day.
3. Every week the archived data is reduced further to facilitate trend analysis and report generation.

4. At the end of the month, the archive is burned onto a CD-ROM for archiving and rapid retrieval and analysis.

5. At the end of the year, tapes are cut for long-term storage.

At the end of each day, the data (1 MB/server) is compressed, moved to a central server, expanded, and stored. The central log processing server then:

1. Converts the log file to ASCII.

2. Inserts data into a SQL Server database.

3. Generates detailed daily and weekly activity reports.

4. Reduces the data for storage to CD-ROM (weekly, monthly, quarterly, or yearly as decided by system management).

5. Produces exception and threshold-warning reports.

Note The 15-minute logging interval may not be suitable for analyzing some server bottlenecks. Shorter-lived bottlenecks may be missed if a counter value is not an average measurement.

Performance Monitor Data Points

The Performance Monitor counters relevant to Exchange fall into these categories:

- Windows NT general performance counters
- Exchange message transfer agent
- Exchange directory
- Exchange information store

Refer to the end of this chapter for a list of general Performance Monitor counters and data points to be monitored for a given server type (Exchange, Systems Management Server, PDC, WINS, and so on).

Capacity Planning

This section briefly describes general capacity planning concepts, which are described more fully in later sections. Periodic load reviews on Windows NT Server systems identify areas that need upgrading. Capacity planning involves sizing different aspects of the Windows NT Server network and is developed after each Windows NT Server and some application Windows NT servers are examined. Sizing is performed in the following areas:

- Windows NT Server hardware configuration, such as memory, CPU, disk throughput, disk capacity, and LAN card speed

- Server room configurations, such as server room LAN bandwidth and WAN connection bandwidth
- Exchange site configuration
- Systems Management Server site configuration

Observed parameters

System parameter	Exchange	PDC/ BDC	WINS	File/ Print*	Web*	SQL*
Average CPU usage	X	X	X	X	X	X
System memory	X	X	X	X	X	X
LAN card usage	X	X	X	X	X	X
Disk throughput	X	X	X	X	X	X
Available disk space	X			X	X	X
Response time	X	X	X	X	X	X
Number of users	X	X				
Information store sizes	X					
Connector throughput	X					

* Items marked with an asterisk are departmental servers in the support organization.

Windows NT Server Hardware Configuration

Windows NT Server hardware configuration can affect performance if server load increases beyond the configuration's capacity. Server configuration items that affect capacity include:

- **CPU usage**—Monitor the average CPU usage and compare it to the previous review. If there's a significant increase, install faster CPUs or use more CPUs per server.
- **System memory**—Verify the server is not excessively swapping to disk and check that the installed system memory is adequate for the swap files. Add more memory if needed.
- **Disk throughput**—Verify that peak and average disk throughput are not bottlenecking. If they are, try different spindle combinations of the RAID drives or install additional or higher speed drives.
- **LAN card usage**—Verify that LAN card usage is not a bottleneck during peak times, and install faster LAN cards (see Server Room Configuration section) if it is.
- **Disk space**—Compare available disk space to the space available in the previous review. If there's a problem, install higher density drives, increase the number of drives in RAID, or add a server.

Server Room Configuration

- **LAN hub speed**—Compare the LAN card usage of all servers to the usage displayed in the previous review and upgrade from 10 MB to 100 MB or from 100 MB to asynchronous transfer mode (ATM).

- **WAN router speed**—Compare the WAN link usage during peak network load periods and monitor response times over the WAN. If there are discrepancies, adjust replication schedules (if applicable) or discuss concerns with the group in charge of system architecture.

Exchange Site Configuration

- **Number of users**—Monitor the growth of the user population and add more servers if the maximum number of users exceeds 350 to 500 per server depending on the usage (light, medium, or heavy).

- **Information store sizes (Exchange)**—Both public and private information stores must be tracked and trends monitored. Add more disks as needed.

- **Connector throughput (Exchange)**—Because only a few sites have Internet Mail Service and every site has an X.400 connector to a parent site, monitor throughput on both connectors. If throughput hits a maximum hardware limitation, increase the number of connectors at the hub sites or adjust replication schedules.

- **Response time**—Verify that perceived response time is within acceptable parameters. If not, check the options in the Windows NT Server Hardware Configuration and Server Room Configuration sections immediately above.

System Baseline Establishment and Maintenance

Baselines for normally operating Windows NT Servers are established by running various tools against the servers. Comparing current server parameters against known, normal operating parameters helps determine if server performance is deteriorating over time so that measures can be taken before the system is affected. For information on what kinds of measures to take, see the Capacity Planning section above.

Establishing a System Baseline

Before going into full production, create a baseline performance document that defines monitored parameters and their high- and low-end value tolerances. In production, this serves as a troubleshooting reference and helps identify parameter that approach or violate limits.

Maintaining the System Baseline

The baseline performance document should be updated when changes are made to:

- Server hardware specifications
- New server platforms
- Tools for measuring baseline information
- Improve the knowledge about Microsoft BackOffice Windows NT Server operation
- Versions of Microsoft BackOffice software

Exchange System Tuning

Exchange servers can be tuned for maximum performance with the Performance Optimizer (PERFWIZ.EXE). It analyzes local hard disks, makes recommendations on where to place Exchange components on different drives, and modifies registry settings to improve server performance.

System Monitoring and Reporting

This section describes items monitored, system parameters, and data reported for proper systems management. By editing the Winlogon registry, administrators can set up monitor computers to log on and restart all monitor processes without operator intervention in the event of a power outage or accidental reset. System reports, tied to system monitors in most cases, are used to perform the systems analysis discussed in the previous section.

Other than for short-term problem resolution efforts, Performance Monitor should not constantly monitor and graph server parameters collected over the WAN. Instead, run Performance Monitor on local server monitors to reduce the network impact. Windows NT parameters are collected using Performance Monitor logging described in the Performance Monitor Counters section at the end of this chapter.

Exchange Monitors

Link Monitor

A link monitor checks the status of every connector in the messaging system by sending test messages at regular polling intervals over all configured connectors (X.400, Site, Internet Mail Service). Link status (active, down, or unknown) is displayed, and log files for each connector are made accessible from anywhere on the network with a UNC in the format: *Server_name*\C$*log_file*.LOG.

Red arrow alerts indicate a *down* link over which no traffic is flowing.

Server Monitor

Server monitors check the Exchange services on every Exchange server in the system and notify administrators of alert states using pager, e-mail, or network alert. Default services monitored are the directory, information store, and MTA. If you want to monitor other services (Internet Mail Service, gateways, replication, or others), specify them for each server under the **Services** property page.

To configure a server monitor to take specific actions (such as restarting a service or rebooting a server) based on an alert condition, modify the **Action** property page.

Caution   Allowing a monitor to reboot a server automatically can have serious impact on non-Exchange services and the user community.

Performance Monitor

Performance Monitor checks vital server parameters and generates an alert if the counters fall outside of tolerances. On Exchange servers it monitors:

- MTA work queue lengths
- Logical disk free megabytes
- Messages per hour on hub servers and gateways
- Process, percent processor time (CPU usage)
- Number of users per server

System Expansion and Upgrade

A lab environment is used prior to production to test new products, upgrades, and expansions required by capacity planning. The following areas may change as a result of the testing process:

- Capacity planning techniques
- Baseline measurements
- Reports and monitoring techniques
- New rollout and support procedures
- User education

Implementing Production Changes

The following sequence of pre-production testing and rollout provides Tier 3 with invaluable experience in deploying system upgrades and expansion. This knowledge is added to procedures and documentation for the benefit of the entire support organization.

Pre-production Validation Testing

New configurations are set up in a lab of simulated users to test:

- Compatibility with existing infrastructure
- Load limits and balancing
- Performance baselines, adjusted as appropriate
- Installation and upgrade procedures and documentation
- Deployment using Systems Management Server

The support organization conducts its own small test site of 50 users so problems can be found and resolved quickly before new systems are deployed to end users. The focus is to:

- Perform real-world daily testing
- Test while running a load simulator against the system
- Mitigate problems with production sites running different configuration levels

Changes to deployment procedures made during the above small site testing are tested in a lab configured to match the site used for a large site test of 500 users.

Production Rollout

- **Large site (500 users)**—Before end users use the new system for the first time, Tier 3 personnel should know all subtleties and compatibility issues of the new features. Because the small site lab test probably resulted in procedural changes to the upgrade/expansion process, the large site test is an important milestone.

- **Multiple sites (2 or 3 sites)**—This phase is used if there are concerns about replication or communication between two sites with the new configuration level. Tests of two sites of different configuration levels are performed during the small site and large site deployment phases.

- **Full scale deployment (entire enterprise)**—Full-scale deployment is used to upgrade/expand all affected sites.

Pre-Production Configuration and Test Lab

Test Lab

A production and configuration test lab tries out new software to be deployed and proposed hardware and software configurations. The messaging environment is a mix of servers, the exact configuration of which is described in the Windows NT engineering documents produced by the architecture group and maintained by Tier 3. The lab duplicates and tests these configurations, simulates the site configuration for each deployed product, and tests how the servers perform while interacting with the LAN and WAN infrastructure.

The numbers listed below are estimates of the servers required for the test lab. Remember that lab servers are often in disaster recovery. If you configure the lab with the minimum necessary servers, however, you may have to put projects and baseline testing on hold if there is a conflict of need.

Pre-production Configurations

Windows NT

The Windows NT environment consists of primary and backup domain controllers, WINS servers, and master directory replication servers. The lab configuration consists of:

- 2 primary domain controllers
- 2 backup domain controllers
- 2 WINS servers
- 2 directory replication servers

Exchange

The Exchange environment consists of multiple sites, each of which has multiple servers that are either grouped in server farms or are geographically dispersed and connected with high-speed links. Some locations with a small number of users have access over a WAN link to an Exchange server at a larger facility.

The lab can test two medium-size site configurations or (using the same hardware) one large site. A lab configuration to simulate a medium-size site consists of:

- 1 bridgehead server
- 1 public information store server
- 1 private information store server
- 10 clients of various operating systems

- 3 hot spare servers (see Disaster Recovery section)
- 1 directory import server

System Management Server

The production Systems Management Server environment consists of a central site, over 30 primary sites, and over 100 secondary sites. The lab configuration consists of:

- 1 central site server
- 2 primary site servers
- 4 secondary site servers
- 10 clients of various operating systems

Abnormal Situation Management

Abnormal situations are events such as server crashes that are outside normal day-to-day support and cannot be resolved through documented procedures. Tier 3 is on call to handle such issues when escalated by Tier 2.

Base Information

Before beginning a recovery effort, Tier 3 needs the following information:

- Computer type and location
- Problem severity
- Problem description and symptoms
- Process used to diagnose

Procedure

1. Inform the users and management through system log and Web.
2. Isolate the computer to determine if the network is the problem.
3. Verify that the computer is configured correctly.
4. Isolate the services to determine if the operating system runs without them.
5. Consult these sources (in this order):
   - Green Book (see Document Maintenance below for a description) or the internal problem tracking and resolution database
   - Microsoft TechNet
   - Internal experts
   - Microsoft Technical Support (MTS)

Disaster Recovery

This section describes disaster scenarios and steps to fix them. It is adapted to the three-tier model under discussion and represents only basic relevant procedures and concerns. For a full discussion of planning and disaster recovery, see Chapters 9 through 11 in Part 3.

Windows NT Disaster Recovery

Losing a BDC

When a backup domain controller is down because of a hardware failure, the other domain controllers continue to allow the clients access to the network. After fixing the hardware or acquiring a new computer, reinstall Windows NT according to the original configuration and engineering document.

Losing a PDC

When a primary domain controller is down because of hardware or software failure, get a backup domain controller online as soon as possible to keep the system structure and architecture intact. In the event of a software problem, reinstall the computer as a backup domain controller and promote it to the primary domain controller. After repairing or replacing server hardware, reinstall Windows NT according to the original configuration and engineering document and promote it to the primary domain controller.

Losing a Master Directory Replication Server

If a master directory replication server (usually a domain controller) goes down, install a backup of the export directory on a server at the hub site and export it to the domains. After fixing the original server, restore the directory.

Losing a WINS Server

If a WINS server is lost, install a new server with the current configuration, enable WINS, and restore the most recent backups. Replicate the WINS server and initiate a scavenging of the database to eliminate old records.

Losing a Hub Site Server Room

Losing a hub site server room means losing all the equipment at a particular site. If hardware fails because of a room integrity failure, the PDC and master directory replication server are enabled at another hub site. If there's still network connectivity at the hub, enable the servers at the hub site as soon as space becomes available. When space is available for the former server room, reinstall all servers as backup domain controllers and promote one to primary.

Exchange Disaster Recovery

Losing a Server

If server hardware fails, build a new server from the pool of hot standby servers and restore it according to the Exchange restore procedures. Hot spares must be available at each domestic hub site.

Losing a Site or Hub Site

The loss of a site may require many replacement servers. The production lab equipment can serve as emergency replacements until the damaged servers are repaired or replaced.

Microsoft Systems Management Server and SQL Server Disaster Recovery

Restore sites from the most configuration tape, made when services are offline. Other backup tapes are for SQL Server data. Restore the central site using production test lab equipment if the server will be down for any length of time.

Departmental Infrastructure

Each member should contribute ideas for improving the organization and server maintenance. Tier 3 personnel should manage a team of representatives from all three tiers to implement the best ideas. Tier 3 also defines the computers, software, and databases needed to run the support organization.

A list of pre-production lab servers is in the System Expansion and Upgrade section above. This section also describes a small production site for pre-rollout testing of upgrade procedures. A partial list of servers needed for this site includes:

- 1 bridgehead/public information store server
- 1 private information store server
- 1 Systems Management Server secondary site server
- 1 WINS server
- 1 BDC
- 3 clients of various operating systems

Departmental servers that are part of the support organization's resource domain include:

- 1 file and print server (BDC)
- 1 SQL server (BDC)
- 1 helpdesk system server (BDC)
- 1 Web server
- 1 log file processing server (BDC)
- 1 domain controller (BDC)

Client workstations in the organization have these hardware specifications:

- P90+ (Tier 1) and P6 (Tier 2, Tier 3)
- 64-MB RAM, 2-GB hard disk, and 17-inch monitor (21-inch option for Tier 3)
- CD-ROM and multimedia system

Document Maintenance

Body of Knowledge (BOK)

The support organization should develop a Body of Knowledge containing documents, electronic files, and CD-ROMs needed by all three tiers. Tier 3 should maintain subscriptions to Microsoft TechNet and the Microsoft Developer Network (MSDN) and make this information available to the rest of the team:

Green Book

The support organization should also make a Green Book. This is a subset of the BOK used with the problem management system to troubleshoot problems. In both printed pages and CD-ROM formats, the Green Book contains:

- Architecture and engineering documents
- Server operations manuals
- Knowledge Base public folders

System Baseline Statistics

Tier 3 is responsible for establishing and maintaining the baseline statistics described in the Systems Management section above.

Performance Monitor Counters

This section describes the Performance Monitor counters recorded and used for systems analysis and troubleshooting. To allow unattended logging of these counters, set up Performance Monitor as a service by following the steps below. A description of how specific counters are used can be found in the Systems Management section. You can also refer to the *Microsoft Exchange Server 5.5 Resource Guide*.

Configuring the Data Logging Service

The data logging service is a Windows NT service that facilitates data collection on local servers and transmits it to a central server for analysis. You have to set it up only once.

▶ **To set up the data logging service**

1. Create a settings file, *serverrole***.PMW** (for example: MICROSOFT EXCHANGE.PMW) using Performance Monitor.

   - Select View Log.

   - From the Performance Monitor object list for the type of server being configured, add the objects listed. The granularity for logging is an entire object, not individual counters.

   - Specify the logging interval (900-second) but do not start logging.

   - Save the settings (using Save Workspace) in serverrole.PMW in the %SystemRoot%\System32 directory.

2. Copy DATALOG.EXE from the *Windows NT Resource Kit* to the %SystemRoot%\System32 directory. Note that MONITOR.EXE is installed when the *Windows NT Resource Kit* is installed.

3. Open a command prompt window.

4. Type **monitor setup** to install the Performance Monitor service. This command sets up the Performance Monitor service registry variables and installs the service in the service controller.

5. Type **monitor** *serverrole***.pmw** to establish the current workspace settings file.

6. Start the data logging service by typing: **monitor start**.

7. Configure the data logging service to start automatically by typing: **monitor automatic**.

8. In **Control Panel**, configure the **Scheduler** service for **Automatic** startup so it monitors in the background when no one is logged on.

9. Schedule an AT job to run at midnight each day and stop the service, compress the log, start the service, and transmit the log to the central log server.

Data Logging Service Performance Monitor Counters

Objects monitored by the data logging service are listed below. Note that objects associated with the network monitoring agent are noted by the initials (NMA).

System parameter	Microsoft Exchange	PDC/ BDC	WINS	File/ Print*	Web*	SQL*
Generic NT Objects						
Browser						
Cache						
ICMP (NMA required)						
IP (NMA required)						
LogicalDisk						
Memory	X	X	X	X	X	X
NBT connection						
Network interface (NMA required)	X	X	X	X	X	X
Objects						
Paging file	X	X	X	X	X	X
Physical disk	X	X	X	X	X	X
Process						
Processor	X	X	X	X	X	X
Redirector						
Server						
Server work queues						
System						
TCP (NMA required)						
Thread						
UDP (NMA required)						

Microsoft Exchange objects (all)	Microsoft Exchange	PDC/ BDC	WINS	File/ Print*	Web*	SQL*
MSMicrosoft ExchangeDB	X					
MSMicrosoft ExchangeDS	X					
MSMicrosoft ExchangeIMC	X					
MSMicrosoft ExchangeIS	X					
MSMicrosoft ExchangeIS Private	X					
MSMicrosoft ExchangeIS Public	X					
MSMicrosoft ExchangeMTA	X					
MSMicrosoft ExchangeMTA Connections	X					
WINS Server Objects						
WINS server			X			
Web Server Objects *						
FTP server					X	
Gopher server					X	
HTTP server					X	
Internet information services global					X	
SQL Server Objects *						
SQLServer						X
SQLServer replication-published DB						X
SQLServer use-defined counters						
SQLServer-locks						
SQLServer-log						X

Microsoft Exchange objects (all)	Microsoft Exchange	PDC/ BDC	WINS	File/ Print*	Web*	SQL*
SQLServer-procedure cache						X
SQLServer-users						X

* Items marked with an asterisk are departmental servers for the support organization.

Windows NT Performance Monitor Counters

Windows NT general performance counters to be used when setting up Performance Monitor

Object	Counter	Uses
LogicalDisk	% Disk Time	The percentage of time a hard drive is either reading or writing. A sustained value over 90 percent indicates that the hard drive is a performance bottleneck. Use the **diskperf** command at the Windows NT command prompt to activate disk monitoring.
Memory	Pages/sec	Measures paging of memory from or to the virtual memory paging file. A high average value indicates the computer is short on memory. You can ignore sudden spikes in use.
Processor	% Processor Time	The percentage of time the processor is running nonidle threads. Exchange Server services can use multiple processors and each instance can be watched. An average value below 20 percent indicates the server is unused or services are down. An average value above 90 percent indicates that the server is overburdened.
Process	Elapsed Time	The number of seconds a process has been running. This provides a quick way to see if a server or service has recently been restarted without looking through the event log.
Redirector	Bytes Total/sec	The number of bytes per second sent and received by the network redirector. Compare the maximum throughput of the network card with the maximum value of this counter to see if network traffic is a bottleneck.
Redirector	Network Errors/sec	The number of unexpected errors the redirector receives. If you suspect network problems, check this counter. If it is above zero, check the system event log for details on the network error.

Exchange Performance Monitor Counters

Commonly used counters pertinent to the MTA

Object	Counter	Description
Microsoft ExchangeMTA	**Messages/ Sec**	A continuous average of the number of messages the MTA sends and receives each second. This is a good way to measure traffic sent to other servers, but because it is a sampling you should also use a tool that reads the message tracking logs for exact traffic measurement.
Microsoft ExchangeMTA	**Work Queue Length**	A current count of messages in MTA queues awaiting delivery to other servers or processing by the MTA. Divide this value by Messages/Sec for a rough estimate of message delay in this queue before they are delivered or sent. A high number indicates a problem either in performance or in transmitting to other servers.
Microsoft ExchangeMTA Connections	**Queue Size**	MTA connections object counters display information for each connection established by the MTA. The Queue Size counter shows the number of objects in MTA queues to and from each connection.

Counters pertinent to directory replication

Object	Counter	Description
Microsoft ExchangeDS	**Pending Replication Synchronization**	A current count of unanswered synchronization requests sent by this directory. Check after choosing the **Update Now** button in the directory **General** property page. This value should start high and decrease slowly as synchronization messages arrive.
Microsoft ExchangeDS	**Remaining Replication Updates**	A current count of synchronization updates waiting to be applied to the directory. When this and the previous counter reach zero, directory synchronization is complete.

Counters pertinent to the information store

Object	Counter	Description
Microsoft ExchangeISPriv Microsoft ExchangeISPub	Average Time for Delivery	The average length of time the last 10 messages waited in the information store queue to the MTA. Make note of this delay time when the load is low. A high value could indicate a performance problem with the MTA.
Microsoft ExchangeISPriv Microsoft ExchangeISPub	Average Time for Local Delivery	The average length of time the last 10 local delivery messages waited for transport to a mailbox in the same information store. Make note of this delay time when the load is low. A high value could indicate a performance problem with the private information store.
Microsoft ExchangeISPriv Microsoft ExchangeISPub	Logon Count	A current count of clients logged on to the information store.
Microsoft ExchangeISPriv Microsoft ExchangeISPub	Logon Active Count	A current count of clients logged on to the information store that have initiated some server activity within the last 10 minutes.
Microsoft ExchangeISPriv Microsoft ExchangeISPub	Messages Delivered/Min	A continuous average of the number of messages delivered to the information store per minute. This includes messages submitted directly to the information store from clients on this server and messages delivered to the information store by the MTA.
Microsoft ExchangeISPriv MSMicrosoft ExchangeISPub	Message Recipients Delivered/Min	A continuous average of the number of messages sent per minute divided by the number of recipients to which they were sent. Provides a clear picture of the actual number of deliveries.
Microsoft ExchangeISPriv Microsoft ExchangeISPub	Messages Sent/Min	A continuous average of the number of messages sent per minute from the information store to the MTA for transport to other servers or gateways.

Disaster and Recovery Planning

The more you rely on a messaging system the more important it is to protect against failure and to provide for speedy, certain recovery. This section offers a three-part discussion of this complex information. Chapter 9 discusses what you are trying to accomplish and available options and methods. Chapter 10 provides answers to frequently asked questions, and Chapter 11 wraps up this topic with information on error numbers and maintenance utilities.

CHAPTER 9

Disaster Recovery Concepts

Microsoft Exchange is a robust and stable enterprise messaging platform, but computers can fail, power gets interrupted, and other disasters come to pass. In short, you need a plan for restoring Exchange with minimal downtime and data loss. It is important to create a plan and have it ready. When you are in a disastrous situation, you should not be formulating a plan, you should be executing tried and trusted procedures and techniques.

This chapter is a supplement to existing online and hard copy documentation. It is a guide that helps you formulate, test, certify, and deploy your own disaster recovery plan. It does not cover third-party backup utilities.

General Notes

Microsoft Exchange is a business-critical application, one that can handle more users per server and a larger data set than previous shared-file messaging systems. As Exchange configurations have grown, each server has become more critical to the enterprise and users have come to expect 24x7 system availability. Even so, many organizations rely on inadequate maintenance or disaster recovery capabilities.

Exchange uses Windows NT security for authentication, so Exchange backup plans must incorporate Windows NT backup and restore features. Windows NT NTBACKUP.EXE provides file-based backup services and backs up the Windows NT registry. The enhanced version of NTBACKUP.EXE that ships with Exchange Server 4.0 and later allows live backups of the Exchange information store and directory that do not interrupt the messaging system.

Exchange Server was designed so that you do not have to take it offline to perform backups. In fact, remaining online reduces system traffic by obviating the re-authentication required when a server is bought back online. The entire information store, directory, MTA, and system attendant remain in service during online backup. You can automate this and schedule it using the WINAT.EXE GUI scheduler (see the *Microsoft Windows NT 4.0 Resource Kit*). The section at the end of this chapter titled Sample Batch File for Online Backup includes some examples of a batch file that shuts down and restarts Exchange services and can be used for other purposes as well.

Exchange should not be running, however, when you back up files in directories accessed by other Exchange services for Windows NT (such as directory synchronization—DX, or Microsoft Mail message transfer agent—PCMTA).

What To Back Up

Backup procedures must capture two types of data:

- **User data**—In the information store (PUB.EDB and PRIV.EDB), .PSTs, .OSTs, .PABs, and transaction logs.
- **Configuration data**—In the Exchange directory (DIR.EDB), the Windows NT registry, and various subdirectories under the Exchange Server installation path (and perhaps paths created after running the Exchange Performance Optimizer program).

The table below shows the database file default locations. From the **Database Paths** page on the server object, you can reconfigure all database file paths during installation by selecting a different path than the default shown in the table (\exchsrvr). You can also use the Exchange Performance Optimizer to put the transaction logs on a separate physical disk from the information store and directory files.

Key Management (KM) server data and the KM server startup disk generated when KM is installed are not automatically backed up by the online backup program. You must do this manually. Exchange 5.5 KM server data is located in exchsrvr\kmsdata. (In Exchange 4.0 and 5.0, it is in a directory called \Security.)

Exchange database file locations

Component	File	Default path
Information store	Private	\exchsrvr\mdbdata\PRIV.EDB
	Public	\exchsrvr\mdbdata\PUB.EDB
Directory		\exchsrvr\dsadata\DIR.EDB
Transaction logs	Information store	\exchsrvr\mdbdata*.LOG
	Directory	\exchsrvr\dsadata*.LOG
KM server	Exchange 4.0 and 5.0	C:\security
	Exchange 5.5	\exchsrvr\kmsdata

In addition to this data, you should regularly back up:

- **The Windows NT registry**—Configuration information pertaining to the Exchange services as well as the Security Accounts Manager database (SAM) containing the Exchange service account.

- **Data in the Exchsrvr subdirectories**—For example, the TRACKING.LOG directory that contains message tracking data, IMCDATA that could contain archived Internet messages, and so on.

.PST (Personal Message Store)

Be sure that backup routines include any .PSTs stored on file servers (home directories). If a .PST is lost or corrupted, recovery is as simple as restoring the .PST and adding it to an existing user profile. You can repair a damaged . PST by running the SCANPST program. Sometimes users store .PSTs on local drives that are not regularly backed up or they password-protect their .PSTs and forget the password. In either case, the data is gone forever. Make sure users understand this.

.OST (Offline Message Store)

.OST data is at risk when changes to the local .OST have not yet been replicated up to the server-based store. If a user machine crashes after replication is complete, a new .OST can be created on the replacement computer and all server-based information can be sent down to the .OST file using synchronization. You can repair a damaged .OST file by running the SCANPST program.

.PAB (Personal Address Book)

Personal address book files can be stored locally or on a server directory. The latter is safer because most servers are backed up regularly. Users who store their .PAB locally must back it up themselves. A lost .PAB can cost hours of work and productivity.

Outlook—Archive and AutoArchive

Outlook allows for automatic .PST file archiving, a feature you can incorporate in backup strategies.

As papers accumulate on your desk, you occasionally have to clean up: sort through them, storing the ones you want to keep but do not use regularly, moving some to different folders, and discarding old ones.

To clean up in Outlook, you manually transfer old items to a storage file by clicking **Archive** on the **File** menu or by using AutoArchive, which lets you specify a duration after which items are either deleted or moved. Outlook can archive any file, such as attached Excel spreadsheets or Word documents, *if* they are stored in mail folders.

AutoArchive is a two-step process. On the **Tools** menu, click **Options** and select the **AutoArchive** tab. Set the **AutoArchive** properties for each folder, determining which items are captured (specific folders, groups of folders, or all folders) and when. Each time you start Outlook, AutoArchive checks the properties of each folder, and archives or deletes them as indicated.

AutoArchive takes care of some Outlook folders by default: Calendar (6 months), Tasks (6 months), Journal (6 months), Sent Items (2 months), and Deleted Items (2 months). It does not watch Inbox, Notes, and Contacts.

Archiving maintains an existing folder structure in the new archive file. If you archive a subfolder, the process recreates the higher level folder in the archive file, but does not archive items within that folder. It is recreating only the mailbox's structure in the archive folder structure. Folders are left in place after being archived, even if they are empty.

Unlike *archiving*, which moves items to personal folders, *exporting* leaves the original items in the current folder and copies them to numerous file types.

Don't forget to include archived Outlook data in your backup strategy.

Review of Backup Types

Online versus Offline

Online backup—Requires that the respective service (information store or directory service) be running. It does not disrupt messaging on the Exchange-based server. You can include the Windows NT registry in the backup, and can back up the directory service even if the information store is not running.

Offline backup—Requires that all Exchange services be stopped. This is files based. You simply run NTBACKUP to capture all files on the drives you select, including the Windows NT registry.

Online Backup Types

Normal (Full)

This backs up the entire information store and directory databases. Transaction logs are backed up then purged, giving context to incremental and differential backups (see below).

Copy

Copy backup does not delete log files or change the context for incremental and differential backups. This takes a snapshot of the databases, without triggering or affecting other backup routines. It is handy when you want to reproduce a system state for testing.

Incremental

This backs up a subset of the information store or directory, writing only those changes made since the last full or last incremental backup (whichever was most recent). An incremental backup writes .LOG files (only) to tape, then purges them from disk, setting context for the next backup job. Typically, an incremental restore requires a tape of the last full backup and tapes for each incremental up to the point at which the system experienced the outage. For example, suppose a full backup is performed on Sunday evenings and incremental backups every weekday. If an outage occurs on Friday morning, a full restore would be performed (restoring the system through Sunday evening) and then each incremental would be performed (restoring the system through Thursday). Services should not be started until the final incremental tape has been restored.

Incremental backup is disabled when circular logging is enabled. More information on this is given in the section Log Files and Circular Logging, below.

Differential

This backs up the changes in the information store and/or directory since the last full (normal) or incremental backup, although most administrators choose not to mix differential and incremental backups in a series. A differential backup captures only .LOG files, but does not purge them from disk. If a transaction log and database restore is required, only two tapes are required: the latest full and the latest differential. If the transaction logs are intact since the last full backup, only the last full backup tape is required because the restore process plays back all logs from the last full through the current EDB.LOG file, thus restoring all transactions to date. *Do not* select **Erase Existing Data** when restoring in this case—it erases the log files to date.

Differential backup is disabled when circular logging is enabled. More information on this is given in the Database Circular Logging section below.

Log Files and Circular Logging

Logging Explained

Exchange Server maintains several database files (stores) in a structure transparent to the end user. The information store, for instance, consists of two databases: private (PRIV.EDB) and public (PUB.EDB), both managed by the information store service. The Exchange directory is stored in DIR. EDB. The Exchange Server services use transaction log files for each of these databases.

Exchange database technology implements log files to accept, track, and maintain data. To enhance performance and recoverability, all message transactions are written first to log files and memory and then to the respective database files. Client performance is boosted because log files are written to sequentially (eliminating seek time) and Exchange Server writes message transactions to log files immediately. Log files are always appended to the end of the file however, and Exchange database files (PUB.EDB, PRIV.EDB, and DIR.EDB) are written to randomly (making seek time a performance factor).

Recoverability is boosted because log files can be used to recover message transaction data if a hardware failure corrupts the information store or directory database files, provided that the logs are backed up and intact. Log files are typically kept on a separate physical disk drive from the information store and directory database files, so a failure that affects the database files probably will not affect the log files. Any data that has not been backed up but that has been recorded in the transaction logs can be "played" back to restore the database file.

The directory and information store services use transaction logs, previous logs, checkpoint files, reserved logs, and patch files.

Transaction Logs

Transaction logs can be kept on a physical drive separate from their respective .EDB files. By default, information store logs are kept in \exchsrvr\mdbdata and directory service logs are kept in \exchsrvr\dsadata. Each subdirectory contains an EDB.LOG, file that is the current transaction log file for the respective service. Both the information store subdirectory and the directory service subdirectory maintain a separate EDB.LOG file.

Log files should always be 5 MB, and files that are not this size are most likely damaged. Transactions are first written to the EDB.LOG files and then to the database, so the database size is a combination of the uncommitted transactions in the transaction log file (which also reside in memory) and the actual .EDB database file. After the EDB.LOG files fill with transaction data, they are renamed and a new EDB.LOG file is created.

Previous Logs

When EDB.LOG is renamed, the renamed log files are stored in the same subdirectory as the EDB.LOG file. The log files are named sequentially (that is, EDB00014.LOG, EDB00015.LOG, and so forth, using hexadecimal). Previously committed log files are purged during an online normal (full) backup, or an online incremental backup using NTBACKUP.EXE. Not all previous log files are purged. After every 5-MB of transactions is written, a new log is created but not necessarily committed. At any given time, there may be several previous logs that aren't committed, and these are not purged. After circular logging is enabled, a history of previous logs is not maintained and they are not purged by backup operations. In fact, incremental and differential online backups are not permitted when circular logging is enabled.

Transactions in log files are committed to the respective .EDB file when the service is shut down normally. For example, when the information store service experiences a normal shutdown (service shuts down with no errors), any transactions that exist in log files and not in the PRIV.EDB or PUB.EDB files are committed to the .EDB files. Log files should not be manually purged while services are running. In general, it is best to purge logs during the backup process.

Checkpoint Files and the Checkpoint

Checkpoint files are used for recovering (playing) data from transaction logs into .EDB files. The checkpoint is the place marker in the EDB.CHK file that indicates which transactions have been committed. The information store and directory service maintain separate EDB.CHK files. Whenever data is written to an .EDB file from the transaction log, the file EDB.CHK file is updated with information specifying that the transaction was successfully committed to the respective .EDB file. During recovery, Exchange determines which transactions have not yet been committed by reading the EDB.CHK file or by reading the transaction log files directly (in which case EDB.CHK is not required). The information store and directory service read their EDB.CHK files during startup and use the transaction logs to play any uncommitted transactions into the .EDB files. For example, if an Exchange server experiences an outage and transactions have been recorded into the transaction log but not yet to the database file, Exchange attempts recovery on startup by automatically recording transactions from the logs to the database files.

Reserved Logs

Both the directory and information store services independently maintain two reserve files, RES1.LOG and RES2.LOG in MDBDATA and DSADATA. If either service runs out of disk space while renaming the EDB.LOG file and creating a new one, it uses the reserve log files. This is a fail-safe mechanism used only in an emergency. After this occurs, the database engine sends an error to the respective service, which then flushes into the RES1.LOG (and the RES2.LOG if necessary) any transactions in memory that have not yet been written to a transaction log. The service then shuts down and records an event in the Windows NT event log. RES transaction log files are always 5 MB, as are all transaction log files.

Patch Files

During an online Exchange backup, transactions can still be entered for .EDB files. If a transaction occurs for a part of the .EDB file that has not yet been backed up, it is simply processed. If one occurs for a part of the .EDB file that has already been backed up, it is recorded in a .PAT (patch) file. A separate .PAT file is used for each database—PRIV.PAT, PUB.PAT, and DIR.PAT. These files are seen only during the backup process.

Here is how .PAT files fit into the online backup sequence:

- .PAT file is created for the current database.
- The backup for the current .EDB file begins.
- Transactions that must be written to parts of the .EDB file that have already been backed up are recorded to the .EDB and .PAT files.
- .PAT file is written to the backup tape.
- .PAT file is deleted from \MDBDATA or \DSADATA.

TEMP.EDB

This file stores in-progress transactions and is used for some transient storage during online compaction.

How Backup Purges Log Files

When circular logging is not enabled, log files accumulate on the transaction log disk drive until an online normal (full) or incremental backup is performed.

Here is how purges fit into the online backup sequence:

- The backup process copies the specified database files.
- Patch files are created as required (to maintain transactions written during the backup to an already-processed portion of the .EDB).
- Log files created during the backup process are copied to tape.
- Patch files are written to tape.
- Log files older than the checkpoint at the start of the backup operation are purged. These are not required because the transactions have already been committed to the .EDB files and the .EDB files have been written to tape.

Database Circular Logging

Circular logging (enabled by default) uses transaction log technology but does not maintain previous transaction log files. Instead, it maintains a window of a few log files, then removes the existing log files and discards the previous transactions after transactions in transaction log files have been committed to the database. This helps manage disk space and keeps transaction logs from building up, but it prevents you from using differential or incremental backups because they require past transaction log files. In fact, because circular logging purges some transaction log files, you may not be able to recover to a point of failure by playing forward through the transaction log files—one or more may be missing. For this reason it is a good idea to disable circular logging on all Exchange servers. You can manage disk space easily enough by performing regular online backups, which purge log files from the hard disk after they have been backed up.

When circular logging is enabled, you may see multiple EDBXXXXX.LOG files in the \MDBDATA or \DSADATA subdirectory. This is normal because Exchange uses several log files before setting the circular window (wrapping around). For example, logs EDB00010.LOG, EDB00011.LOG, EDB00012.LOG, and EDB00013.LOG would increment to become EDB00011.LOG, EDB00012.LOG, EDB00013.LOG, and EDB00014.LOG. The numbers are hexadecimal.

Exchange attempts to maintain a window of four log files for circular logging, but uses more if the server I/O load is large. Log files created above the initial four are not purged until the respective service (information store or directory service) is stopped and restarted.

How to Determine if Circular Logging Is Enabled

▶   **To review database circular logging settings**

1. Run the Exchange Server Administrator program.

2. Click **Site**, **Configuration**, and **Servers** object and select the desired server.

3. Click **File**, **Properties** menu.

4. Click the **Advanced** tab. Note that you can set circular logging separately for the information store and directory.

You can change circular logging settings on the fly from the Exchange Administrator program, but if you do, Exchange stops the corresponding service and restarts it.

Recovery Example—Transaction Logs

Conditions—Circular logging is not enabled and transaction logs are stored on a disk separate from the database files. The last full (normal) backup took place two days ago. A hardware failure (bad hard disk) has damaged the information store databases but has not affected the transaction log drive.

Question—Can you restore completely or will you lose two days of production data?

Answer—You don't have to lose anything. The transaction logs are complete, so they contain all transactions since the full backup and the restore hardware performs a full restore. Do not remove existing log files (that is, *do not* select **Erase All Existing Data**). The full restore writes the database files and the log files that were backed up with the full backup. Restored log files would be log files up to the first log file on the current transaction log drive. For example, the full backup copied EDB00012.LOG through EDB00014.LOG. The log files on the transaction log drive would be EDB00015.LOG and up. The full restore copies out logs EDB00012.LOG through EDB00014.LOG and the information store database files that are part of the backup set. After the information store is started, it replays transactions from EDB00012.LOG through the last log file (EDB00019.LOG) and then replays EDB.LOG, the most recent log file. The service then starts and the database is up to date. The log files contain signatures to make sure log files are part of the sequence to be replayed.

Backing Up a Key Management Server

It is a good idea to back up the KM data files (C:\SECURITY\MGRENT in version 4.0 and 5.0, and \EXCHSRVR\KMSDATA in version 5.5) separately from other data and keep these backup tapes more secure than the everyday backups. All of the actual keys in these files are 64-bit CAST encrypted, so it is extremely secure, but treat it carefully: it contains *every user's private encryption keys* and is *not* backed up by the Exchange-aware NTBACKUP program.

The problem with tape cartridges is they are *offline*: anyone who gets a hold of one can restore the files to a server and then take time trying to crack the encryption key, with no fear of detection because of online logon actions or other conditions.

For most invaders, it is technologically infeasible to crack a 64-bit key. Current estimates say that it would require more than 12 years and $300,000 worth of dedicated cryptographic hardware, much longer with PC technology. (See http://www.bsa.org/ for a discussion of key lengths, estimated decryption time, and other issues.) This is good news, but the bad news is that technology improves every year and some unscrupulous people are smart and resourceful. Treat the KM databases as one of the most secure assets in your information system.

▶ **To back up KM server data**

1. Stop the Key Management server service.

2. Back up the data:

   In Exchange 4.0 and 5.0, back up the SECURITY\MGRENT directory.

   In Exchange 5.5, back up the EXCHSRVR\KMSDATA directory.

3. Back up the KM server startup disk.

4. Start the KM server service.

Use the Windows NT Backup utility periodically to back up advanced security files and subdirectories. Users whose security files are corrupted or who forget their security logon password cannot open any encrypted messages, including all archived ones. The administrator can recover the key (the procedure is covered in the Microsoft Exchange Server documentation; look for "recovering advanced security keys") but only if advanced security data is current.

More on Database Architecture

Reliable Data Store with Transaction Logs

Borrowing an idea from relational databases such as Microsoft SQL Server, the Exchange Server information store and directory service use separate transaction log files to improve performance and data integrity. All changes are quickly recorded in sequential transaction logs, then committed to the actual underlying database file. If there is a power loss or an unexpected server shutdown, data remains intact and recoverable up to the last complete transaction. The architecture prevents the data from being left in an inconsistent or corrupted state.

The principles behind database transaction integrity have been well-understood since the 1970s, when the ACID test of database transaction integrity was developed (atomicity, consistency, isolation, and durability). The database underlying the information store supports all of these properties:

- **Atomicity**—Transaction results are either all committed or all rolled back. In Exchange Server, atomic operations are achieved by using transaction logs. As described above, transactions in the log that haven't yet been committed to the main database file are either rolled forward and committed, or rolled back if incomplete. This process happens quickly and automatically when the system re-starts.

- **Consistency**—A shared resource (such as a database) is always transformed from one valid state to another. All operations on the Exchange Server information store are atomic, ensuring that data is always in a consistent state. Updating a transaction log to indicate that a transaction has been completely committed back to the main database file is an atomic operation.

- **Isolation**—Transactions can be serialized. In a system handling multiple simultaneous transactions, the results of any transaction are the same as if it were the only transaction running on the system. This essentially means safe, concurrent access to the data by multiple simultaneous users. Simultaneous user operations cannot interfere in ways that render the database invalid. The isolation property is enforced by the database underlying the Exchange Server information store.

- **Durability**—Transaction results are permanent and survive future system and media failures. If a portion of an Exchange Server transaction log file is corrupt or unreadable (for example, because of physical drive damage), those transactions are simply rolled back. The physical format of transaction logs is carefully designed to reduce the impact, even when storage media are damaged. This is accomplished through a combination of sequential writes, the creation of new log files every 5 MB, and low-level techniques such as ping-pong logging, which helps maximize the durability of transactions even within a partially corrupted log file.

Although it might seem that transaction logs incur significant overhead, because data is written first to the log and then committed to the main database file, proper transaction log use actually *improves* overall system throughput for a number of reasons. When transaction log files are kept on a separate disk, they are written *sequentially*, rather than *random-access*. Because the disk drive head doesn't have to seek randomly, this is at least an order of magnitude faster than random-access writes to the main database file, even with today's very fast hard drive subsystems. Logged transactions are then "lazily" committed back to the main database file—and this can be done very efficiently because it is done asynchronously (when the server has idle cycles), and because the NTFS and FAT disk cache systems in Windows NT Server automatically order the writes in the most efficient manner, using classic techniques such as elevator seeking to minimize physical head seeks. Exchange Server recovery techniques work as well for large records as small ones because its transaction logs write only the changed portions of the data.

Fast Automatic Recovery Using Transaction Rollback

When an Exchange Server information store or directory service is started after abnormal server shutdown, the transaction log file is scanned to see if there were any incomplete transactions. If there are, they are rolled back automatically to their pre-shutdown state. This automatic recovery operation is relatively quick because only the most recent transactions in the log have to be checked.

These recoverability differences are analogous to those between production DBMS servers such as Microsoft SQL Server or Oracle and end-user databases such as Microsoft Access or Lotus Approach.

Single-Instance Storage with Automatic Referential Integrity

Single-instance storage is a key requirement from customers who wish to store users' mail centrally, on the server. If 100 users on the same server receive the same message, only a single instance of the message is stored on the server: pointers to the message are placed in the users' mailboxes. Single-instance storage can save space and boost server performance.

The information store design of Exchange Server has built-in single-instance storage: it is always in effect, and requires no special configuration or administration. When a message or user mailbox is deleted, messages cannot be orphaned or lost. Pointers cannot become out of synchronization between files because everything is stored in a single file and referential integrity is handled internally by the database engine. Exchange Server is optimized for efficient, reliable storage of messages on the server.

Single-Instance Storage with Per-User Storage Limits

Research shows that one of the most common reasons for mail system outages is simply the inability to limit user storage, which eventually causes servers to fill up and cease working. To prevent this, Exchange Server allows administrators to set and enforce disk quotas at any level from user to system. Users can be given a warning as well as a "hard" limit that prohibits them from sending any mail until they clean out their mailbox. This prevents users from missing critical incoming e-mail and does not penalize other users by failing to deliver mail they send to "warned" users.

Live Online Backup to Tape for 24x7 Operation

Exchange Server has built-in support for online backups directly to tape. The server does not have to be shut down, nor do users have to log off. Furthermore, Exchange Server backup is integrated with Windows NT Server backup, so you can back up both types of servers from the same location. You can perform full, incremental, or differential backups directly to a wide variety of tape devices, from ¼-inch cartridges to high-capacity DAT systems.

Data Recovery Scenarios

Three recovery scenarios are discussed below: single-item, full-server, and .PST, .OST, and .PAB.

Single-Item Recovery

Single-item refers to individual mailboxes, public folders, messages, or private folders. Here are the various methods:

- Single mailbox recovery by restoring the entire private information store.
- Single item recovery using the Exchange 5.5 Deleted Items Retention feature.
- Single item recovery using third-party brick backup programs.

Single Mailbox Recovery

Use this procedure in Exchange 4.0 and 5.0 to recover an entire deleted mailbox or individual items. In Exchange 5.5, the Deleted Items Retention feature eliminates the need to perform this procedure for messages, folders, or public folders, although you still must follow this procedure to recover a deleted mailbox.

Caution   Do not perform this procedure on a production server. It calls for restoring data to a server that is *not* part of your production Exchange site. The dedicated recovery server is installed using the same site and organization names as the production site, but you should select the option to **Create A New Site** when installing the recovery Exchange Server.

Requirements

- A dedicated server with enough capacity to restore the entire private information store database.
- A backup of the information store private database.
- Exchange client and Exchange Server installation code.
- Windows NT and Windows NT service pack installation code.

You can also use this procedure to recover a mailbox. In a centrally supported organization, affiliate offices may mail tapes to an internal "recovery center," and this can provide single mailbox recovery for any server in the organization, regardless of the server name.

You must restore the entire information store, then retrieve data from the specific mailbox. Prepare a server running Windows NT Server and install Exchange with the same site and organization name that the lost mailbox resided on. Restore the information store from a backup tape, log on with Exchange administrative privileges, and assign the Windows NT administrator ID access to the desired mailbox. Restore the data to a .PST file and attach the .PST to the user's profile.

Prepare the Recovery Server

1. Prepare a non-production recovery server (some systems keep a recovery server running and available at all times). You can install this computer as a Windows NT PDC, BDC, or member server, and it should have the appropriate Windows NT service pack installed. Make sure it has enough disk space for restoring the entire information store from the backup tape, that it is equipped with a tape drive compatible with the drives on the production servers, and that the tape drive is tested and working.

2. Create a new site (*do not join site*). The next step requires installing Exchange. When you do this, do not join the site. The recovery server should be a stand-alone computer that is not joined to your production site.

3. Log on to Windows NT as administrator and perform a complete Exchange install using the same site and organization name used on the server from which you are restoring the mailbox. *Do not join site.* The server name of the restore computer does not matter for a single mailbox restore because you are restoring only the information store, not the directory. If you have a dedicated recovery server per location, you can keep Exchange installed, but if several sites share a recovery server, keep a copy of the Exchange installation code on the hard disk so you can install based on the required site and organization. The paths for this Exchange install do not have to match the paths of the production Exchange install being recovered.

4. Install the Exchange service pack that was on the production computer when the information store was last backed up. If the production server had Service Pack 1 on it when the backup was made and you have since installed Service Pack 2, install Service Pack 1 on the recovery server before restoring the information store.

5. Install the Exchange client on the recovery server.

Restore the Information Store from Tape

This procedure uses a tape from an online backup for the restore. (You can use an offline tape, but this requires some extra steps. They are explained after this procedure.)

1. Insert the backup tape in the drive.

2. Log on to the recovery domain as administrator.

3. From the **Administrative Tools** group run **Backup**.

4. From the pull-down menu, click **Operations**, **Microsoft Exchange**.

5. Click the **Tapes** icon and double-click on the tape name. A catalog status box will be displayed stating "**Loading ….**"

6. Click "**ORG\SITE\SERVER**"**\information store** in the right side of the **Tapes** window.

7. Click the **Restore** button from the upper part of the **Backup** main screen.

8. On the **Restore Information** screen, enter the name of the destination server in destination server field (HOTSPARE).

9. Select **Erase All Existing Data**, **Private**, **Public**, **Verify After Restore**, and **Start Service After Restore**. Click the **OK** button.

10. Click **OK** on the restore message ("**You are about to restore Microsoft Exchange components. The Microsoft Exchange services on the destination server will be stopped.**")

11. Click **OK** on the **Verify Status** screen.

12. Click **Control Panel** and then **Services** and verify that the Exchange services are running.

Offline Backup Available

If you have an offline backup of the Exchange information store, follow these steps:

1. Stop all Exchange information store services.
2. Determine the location of the database and logs for the information store service from the following registry locations:

   Information store service log path:

   HKEY_LOCAL_MACHINE\System\CurrentControlSet\Services\MSExchangeI S\ParametersSystem\DB Log Path

   Private information store database path:

   HKEY_LOCAL_MACHINE\System\CurrentControlSet\Services\MSExchangeI S\ParametersPrivate\DB Path

   Public information store database path:

   HKEY_LOCAL_MACHINE\System\CurrentControlSet\Services\MSExchangeI S\ParametersPublic\DB Path
3. Move out all files from the EXCHSRVR\MDBDATA directories on all drives.
4. Copy the PRIV.EDB file to the private information store database path.
5. Copy the PUB.EDB file to the public information store database path.
6. Copy any information store log files to the information store service log path.
7. Make sure that the Exchange directory service is started.
8. From the command prompt, change to the EXCHSRVR\BIN directory and execute the following command:

   isinteg –patch
9. Start the information store service.

Recover User Mailbox

1. Log on to the recovery server using the Windows NT Administrator ID.
2. Run the Exchange Administrator program. Run the **DS/IS consistency adjuster**. Highlight the server name. From the **File** menu, click the **Properties** command to bring up the properties of the **Server** object. Click the **Advanced** tab.

   If you are running the version 4.0 or 5.0 Exchange Administrator program, click **All Inconsistencies** and then click the **Adjust** button.

   If you are running the version 5.5 Exchange Administrator program, on the **Advanced** page, click the **Consistency Adjuster** button to bring up the **DS/IS consistency adjuster** dialog box. Select all the options for the private and public information stores, click on **All inconsistencies**, and then click **OK**.

3. Select the **Recipients** container and double-click on the desired user's mailbox name.

4. From the **General** tab, click the **Primary Windows NT Account** button.

5. From the **Primary Windows NT Account** dialog box, click **Select An Existing Windows NT Account** and then click **OK**.

6. From the **Add User Or Group** screen, click **Administrator** and the **Add** button and then click **OK**.

7. Click **OK** on the **User Property** screen.

8. From the Windows NT control panel, run **Mail and Fax**.

9. Configure a profile for the desired user.

10. Add a personal folder file to the profile.

11. Run the Exchange client.

12. Select **Mailbox - <*USERNAME*>** on the left panel.

13. Select the first folder or item in the list on the right panel.

14. From the pull-down menu, click **Edit** and **Select All**.

15. From the pull-down menu, click **File** and then **Copy**.

16. In the **Copy** screen, click **Personal Folder** and then click **OK**. This copies all data to this .PST file.

17. Copy the .PST to the destination location. You can use tape backup and restore if necessary.

18. Add this .PST to the user's profile on the production server or send the .PST to the end user with instructions. You may need to send this on a tape. If you have network access, you can copy this recovered .PST to the desired server.

19. If you are trying to recover an entire mailbox for an Outlook user, it is easier to log on to Outlook and export the entire mailbox to a .PST file, using the **Import** and **Export** command on the **File** menu.

20. If the user runs the Schedule+ client (instead of the Outlook client) to schedule activities, you must recover the user's Schedule+ data. Log on to Schedule+ as the user, select the option to create a local schedule (.SCD) file, and then send the .SCD file to the user.

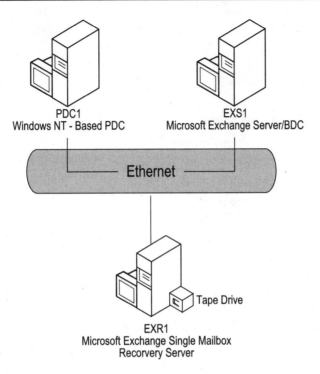

PDC1
Windows NT - Based PDC

EXS1
Microsoft Exchange Server/BDC

Ethernet

Tape Drive

EXR1
Microsoft Exchange Single Mailbox
Recovery Server

Microsoft Exchange Single Mailbox Recovery

You can maintain the single mailbox recovery server online with production servers because its name does not have to be the same as the production server running Exchange. If you keep it online, however, *do not* let it perform directory service replication with the production servers.

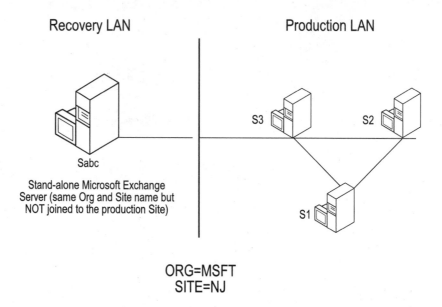

Recovery LAN

Production LAN

S3

S2

S1

Sabc

Stand-alone Microsoft Exchange
Server (same Org and Site name but
NOT joined to the production Site)

ORG=MSFT
SITE=NJ

Microsoft Exchange Single Mailbox Recovery—Example Topology

This is an example topology for maintaining a spare server for single mailbox recovery. Note that the spare server "Sabc" is *not* joined to the production site, even though it was installed using the production site's site and organization name.

Single Item Recovery in Exchange 5.5

The new Deleted Items Retention (item recovery) feature of Exchange Server 5.5 provides users with a recycle bin from which they can recover individual folders and messages from the private and public information stores. It cannot be used to undelete an entire mailbox; that requires the process outlined above.

How does Deleted Items Retention work? Deleted Items Retention associates with each object a new attribute that changes value when the object is deleted, causing the information store to hide the object from the client. The information store keeps the item for a specified number of days, then permanently purges it. The administrator can set a value that prevents permanent deletion until the store is backed up.

Configuring Deleted Items Retention

Deleted Items Retention is configured from the Exchange Administrator program, even though the recovery is performed on the client. You can configure the settings at private information store or mailbox levels, as shown in the figures below. The private information store level applies to all mailboxes on a server; the mailbox level allows you to override the information store settings.

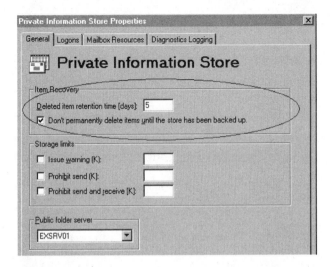

Item Recovery settings on the private information store

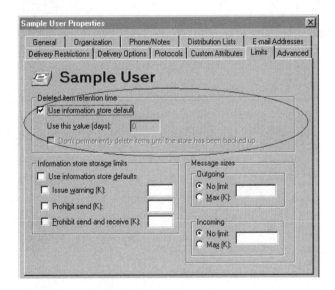

Item Recovery settings for an individual mailbox

Restoring Items from the Outlook Client

The client performs the actual recovery, using an extension available with Outlook 8.03.

To restore a deleted item from a user's mailbox, click the **Deleted Items** folder in the Outlook client, and then from the **Tools** menu, select **Recover Deleted Items**. This brings up the **Restore Deleted Item** dialog shown in the next figure.

The Restore Deleted Items dialog

The user can now select the messages or folders to recover. The items are placed in the Deleted Items folder and the user can move them to any other location.

This is a much easier way to recover deleted items than restoring the entire information store.

Note Although deleted items remain in the information store, increasing its size, they are not counted when computing a user's storage quota.

Single-Item Recovery Using Third-Party Brick Backup Programs

Some third-party vendors provide Exchange brick backup solutions, which back up and restore individual mailboxes, folders, and public folders. If you use a brick backup program, you can select and restore a damaged or deleted mailbox or public folder from tape, rather than restoring the entire information store. This is a great time saver, but brick backup solutions have some major limitations. They back up individual mailboxes or public folders, and it takes longer to back up all mailboxes or public folders on a server than it does to back up the information store. This is because the data in each mailbox or public folder is individually backed up and all single-instance storage is lost, possibly resulting in far more data than is in the information store.

Because Exchange 5.5 database sizes are limited only by hardware, it may not be feasible to use a brick backup program daily on an entire Exchange Server. Consider using a normal Exchange-aware backup program for the directory service and information store and a brick backup program for important mailboxes and public folders.

If you are thinking of using brick backup software, check its documentation for details on its features and limitations. Some products, for instance, do not back up or restore Exchange Forms and others convert .RTF messages to plain text.

Full Server Restore

Restoring an Exchange Server to a different physical computer is a special case because it requires reinstalling Windows NT, creating a new registry, and creating a new Windows NT SID (security identifier) for the recovery computer. A new SID is required only if you restore a Windows NT registry to a different server. If, for instance, you replace the hard disk on a computer and reinstall Windows NT, you do not have to create a new SID. The procedure outlined below is also useful for moving an Exchange server installation to a more powerful server.

If circumstances require you to do a full restore of the Exchange server databases (information store and directory service) you may also, depending on your environment, have to restore the Windows NT SAM database. On installation, Exchange automatically adds the Windows NT service account and the Windows NT account that was logged on to during the initial software installation. Although both of these accounts receive special privileges during installation, only the Windows NT account SID that was originally used during the installation is required to restore the Exchange directory store. This SID must exist in the Windows NT environment for the Exchange directory store to be accessible. If for any reason there are no domain controllers of the original domain available, you must restore the Windows NT PDC SAM.

Requirements

- A full backup of the information store and directory.
- Replacement PC with same hardware capacity as production server.
- Access to the original Windows NT SAM.
- Production server configuration sheet.
- Exchange installation code.
- Windows NT Server and Windows NT service pack installation code.
- Exchange production server configuration sheet.

More complex than single mailbox recovery, a full-server recovery restores an original production Exchange-based server so that all Windows NT security and configuration information as well as Exchange configuration and message data are recovered. After the recovery server is in place, users can log on to their mailboxes using their current passwords.

Where the single mailbox restore requires that only the information store be restored, a full-server recovery requires that both the information store and directory service be restored. Exchange relies on Windows NT security for providing access to mailbox data and uses Windows NT account SID information in object properties within the Exchange directory.

For a successful directory service restore, there are two key conditions:

- The directory service must be restored to a Windows NT–based server that has the same site, organization, and server name as the production server.
- The recovery server must have access from the domain in which Exchange Server was originally installed.

A full server disaster recovery involves three computers. Two are production servers (a PDC and a BDC) and a third that is non-production or non-essential, although it can be used for other production tasks if is kept available for recovery duty. The process requires a PDC/BDC/recovery-server configuration because of the way Exchange uses the Windows NT Security Accounts Manager (SAM) database to provide authentication to directory objects. A full server Exchange restore (information store and directory service) requires access to the SAM from the domain in which the Exchange-based server was first installed.

Example: Don't Do This

For example, suppose a site has one Exchange-based server that also acts as a PDC and one recovery server offline. The Exchange information store and directory are backed up nightly. If the Exchange server crashes, a hot backup PDC with Exchange can be built from scratch and the information store can be restored (as is the case for single mailbox restore). When the Exchange directory is restored, the security properties of all directory objects must match the Windows NT SAM for the accounts, but in this case they do not match because building the PDC created a new SAM. The administrator cannot log on to the Exchange Administrator program, Exchange services can't start, and restored data is not accessible. If you restore the information store without the directory, only the administrator has access to mailbox data, and this is not a full-server recovery. The original Exchange directory information is gone from the production server.

Example: Do This

Another example. Suppose there is a dedicated PDC, the production Exchange server acts as a BDC, and there is a recovery server. The production server crashes. In this case you can build a Windows NT Server domain controller from the recovery server and give it the same computer name as the crashed Exchange server. If you connect this to the domain as a BDC (you can also connect it as a member controller), you can get a copy of the SAM from the domain in which the production Exchange server resided. To do this, use server manager to delete the original computer name (BDC definition) from the PDC and then re-add it during the BDC install. (You have to do this is because each computer name gets a unique SID when it is added to the domain and the recovery computer needs a new one.) Then install Exchange using the same site and organization name; the same server name is used by default because Exchange uses the computer name to create the Exchange server name.

Note If you are recovering a server and joining an existing site, refer to the Microsoft Exchange Server documentation for more details. In this case, you install Exchange Server on the new or repaired server, but do not replicate it with the existing organization. Instead, give the server its original organization and site name, then run **Setup /R**.

Now you can restore the information store and directory from the last Exchange production server. If the original server is still available, save all transaction logs from the DSADATA and MDBDATA directories. These allow the directory and information store to play forward through any transactions applied to the databases since the last backup. If these logs are not available, you can recover only to the database state at the time of the last backup.

Example: Server Recovery from Backup Tape

Here is an example of a server recovery using a backup tape of an information store and directory service from a production server. Backup type is set to *normal*, for a full online backup of the information store and directory. During the Exchange software installation, *do not* join the site. Instead select **Create New Site**. Even though you select to create a new site, the tape backup of the Exchange directory database, upon restart, restores to the server its site identity, causing it to synchronize with other servers in the site automatically.

Prepare Recovery Computer

The recovery computer must have:

- Windows NT installed.
- The same computer name as the crashed Exchange server.
- The same role as the crashed server: if the server was a BDC, add the recovery server to the production domain as a BDC (meaning you have to delete then re-add the computer name on the PDC to create a new SID for the recovery computer).
- The same Windows NT service packs installed as the production server.
- Enough disk space to restore the entire information store and directory from the backup tape.
- A tape drive compatible with tape drives deployed on production servers.

To expedite the restore process, keep a copy of the Windows NT installation code and service pack on the recovery computer's hard disk. Keep the production Windows NT Server configuration sheet handy for pertinent settings including protocol addresses, partitioning information, protocols, options, tuning, and so forth.

Recovery server preparation process:

1. Log on to Windows NT as a domain administrator.
2. Run the Exchange Server Setup program. If you are *not* using Exchange Server 4.0, you can use **Setup /R** to recover an existing Exchange server onto new hardware.
3. Make sure the server name is the same as that of the original production computer.
4. Select **Create New Site** (*do not select* **Join Existing Site**).
5. Use the same organization and site names.
6. Select the same service account that was used on the original production server.
7. Install the same connectors that were installed on the original production server.
8. Run the Exchange Performance Optimizer to optimize Exchange for the same configuration that was used for the production server. Refer to your production server configuration documentation.
9. Install the same Exchange service pack as was installed on the original production server when the last backup was made. Again, if you are *not* using Exchange server 4.0, use **Update /R**.
10. If the Microsoft Mail (MS Mail) Connector was installed on the original server, configure it identically on the new server. The X.400 and other site connectors save their configuration information in the Exchange directory, but the MS Mail Connector saves it there *and* in the Windows NT registry. To recreate these registry entries, you must configure the MS Mail Connector before restoring the Exchange directory. If you had third-party connectors installed on the original server, they may also require configuration. Refer to your production server's documentation.
11. If the Key Management server was installed on the original server, install it on the new server.
12. Install Exchange Client or Outlook on the recovery server.

Follow the appropriate procedure below to restore Exchange data.

Run the Restore

Online Backup Available

This process assumes you are using the Exchange-aware NTBACKUP.EXE program that ships with Exchange Server. If you are using another backup program, please refer to its documentation.

If you have an online backup of the Exchange server, follow these steps:

1. Insert the restore tape.
2. From the **Administrative Tools** group, click the **Backup** icon.
3. Double-click the **Tapes** icon.
4. Double-click "**Full Backup Tape....**" This displays a **Catalog Status** screen "**...Catalog Status...Loading set list from tape.**"
5. On the right panel, select the **Directory** *and* **Information Store**.
6. Click the **Restore** button from the top of the **Backup** window. This displays the **Restore Information** dialog box.
7. If changes were made on the original production server after the last backup and you have the server's transaction logs, skip to the procedure that follows this one.

Note If your public information store is on a separate server, contact Microsoft Technical Support for assistance. The next step calls for erasing the public store; do not do this if your public information store is on a separate computer.

---

8. On the **Restore Information** screen enter the name of the destination server. Select **Erase all Existing Data**. Verify that the **Private**, **Public**, **Start Services After Restore**, and **Verify after Restore** options are all selected. Click **OK**.
9. Click **OK** on the **Restore Information** dialog to display the **Restore Status** dialog.
10. After the restore is completed click **OK** on the **Restore Status** dialog box.
11. Close the Backup program.

This restores the Exchange directory service and information store to their state as of the last backup.

If changes were made on the original production server after the last backup and you have the server's transaction logs, follow these steps:

1. On the new server, move out all files from the MDBDATA and DSADATA directories on each drive.

2. Copy the transaction log files from DSADATA and MDBDATA directories on the original server to the corresponding locations of the logs on the new server. If you are not sure where to copy the log files, check these registry entries:

   Directory service log path:

   HKEY_LOCAL_MACHINE\System\CurrentControlSet\Services\MSExchange DS\Parameters\Database log files path

   Information store service log path:

   HKEY_LOCAL_MACHINE\System\CurrentControlSet\Services\MSExchange DS\ParametersSystem\DB Log Path

3. Run the Backup program to restore the directory service and information store data. Follow steps 1 through 6 in the procedure above.

4. On the **Restore Information** screen *do not* select **Erase All Existing Data**. Select **Verify After Restore** and **Start Services After Restore**. Click **OK**. (If the directory service and information store were backed up using separate backup jobs, be sure not to start services until both have been restored.) Make sure that you *do not* select **Erase All Existing Data**—it erases all the transaction logs copied from the original server.

5. Click **OK** on the **Restore Information** dialog box to display the **Restore Status** dialog.

6. After the restore is completed click **OK** on the **Restore Status** dialog.

7. Close the Backup program.

Offline Backup Available

If you have an offline backup of the Exchange directory and information store, follow these steps:

1. Stop all Exchange services.

2. Determine the location of the database and logs for the directory service and information store service, from these registry locations:

   Directory service log path:

   HKEY_LOCAL_MACHINE\System\CurrentControlSet\Services\MSExchange DS\Parameters\Database log files path

   Directory service database path:

   HKEY_LOCAL_MACHINE\System\CurrentControlSet\Services\MSExchange DS\Parameters\DSA Database file

Information store service log path:

*HKEY_LOCAL_MACHINE\System\CurrentControlSet\Services\MSExchangeI
S\ParametersSystem\DB Log Path*

Private information store database path:

*HKEY_LOCAL_MACHINE\System\CurrentControlSet\Services\MSExchangeI
S\ParametersPrivate\DB Path*

Public information store database path:

*HKEY_LOCAL_MACHINE\System\CurrentControlSet\Services\MSExchangeI
S\ParametersPublic\DB Path*

4. Copy the DIR.EDB file (it should be in the DSADATA directory) to the directory service database path.

5. Copy any directory service log files to the directory service log path.

6. Copy the PRIV.EDB file to the private information store database path.

7. Copy the PUB.EDB file to the public information store database path.

8. Copy any information store log files to the information store service log path.

9. Start the Exchange directory service.

10. From the command prompt, change to the EXCHSRVR\BIN directory and execute:

   isinteg –patch

11. Start the information store service.

Restoring the Key Management Server Data

If the Key Management server was installed on the original server, follow these steps to restore its data onto the new computer:

1. If the KM server service has not been installed, install it.

2. Stop the KM server service.

3. Restore the KM server data:

   If you are running Exchange Server 4.0 or 5.0, restore the \SECURITY\MGRENT directory.

   If you are running Exchange Server 5.5, restore the EXCHSRVR\KMSDATA directory.

4. Restore the KM server startup disk.

5. Start the KM server service.

Review Mailboxes for Windows NT Account Association

1. Select the **Recipients** container under the site.

2. Double-click on any user.

3. Review the **Primary Windows NT Account** field to see if the Windows NT account matches the mailbox.

4. Repeat this procedure for several users.

Test User Logon from Client Workstations

1. Run the Exchange client.

2. Validate that the user password works.

3. Make sure that user mail, calendar, and so on are available.

4. Make sure that the user can send mail to other mailboxes on the same server as well as on other servers and sites.

5. Repeat this from several workstations.

Restore Microsoft Exchange Customization

Use the information on your production server configuration sheet to re-create the connectors and other services. Check the circular logging and advanced diagnostic settings, which are also stored in the Microsoft Windows NT registry.

Hardware Platforms

Most Exchange databases are hardware platform independent—you can take a PRIV.EDB, PUB.EDB, or DIR.EDB file created on an Intel server and use it on an Alpha server and vice versa. The directory (DIR.EDB), however, contains information about platform-specific components such as e-mail generators and add-ins. This information is visible through the Exchange Administrator program under *<Site>*\Configuration\Add-ins and *<Site>*\Configuration\Addressing \E-mail Addressing Generators.

Exchange 5.0 and later automatically install the add-ins and e-mail generators for all supported platforms, regardless of the platform on which the server was installed. This facilitates moving between hardware platforms. Exchange 4.0 installs only components for the platform being installed, so if you are running Exchange 4.0 you may have to follow additional steps to install new servers on different hardware platforms. Contact Microsoft Technical Support for help.

Key Information Store Articles and Notes

Note The Knowledge Base articles below outline basic procedures. Circumstances sometimes require different or altered steps. Information store recovery can lose data as well as save it, and it is always a good idea to work with Microsoft Technical Support—they are constantly gathering and refining information and can save you a lot of effort when you assess alternatives. See http://support.microsoft.com/support/ for the most up-to-date information.

Q147244, Title: XADM: Troubleshooting Information Store Start Up Problems

Revision Date: 02-03-1998

The information in this article applies to: Microsoft Exchange Server, versions 4.0, 5.0, and 5.5

Summary

The Exchange Server 4.0 information store can become corrupt and fail to start. This can be caused by such things as sudden power loss to a running Exchange Server or faulty hardware that has written information to disk incorrectly. This article outlines the steps to recover.

The steps outlined in this article will be most successful if circular logging is turned *off* and you have some type of regular backup procedures in place. If circular logging is turned *on* (default), steps 1, 2, and 6 through 9 are valid (circular logging automatically writes over transaction logs files after the data they contain has been committed to the database). If a backup is *not* available, steps 1, 2, 8, and 9 are valid. For Information and strategies on backup and restore procedures, see Chapter 12 in this book and refer to the Microsoft Exchange Server documentation.

More Information

Follow these steps in strict order to preserve as much data as possible.

1. Check the Windows NT event viewer application log for .EDB, MSExchangeIS, MSExchangePriv, and MSExchangePub messages. These error messages may give a clear reason for the problems with the information store. Two of the most common: the application log is out of disk space and you need to run **isinteg -patch**.

   For additional information, please see:

   Q128325, Title: XADM: Reclaiming Disk Space for the Information Store

   Q149238, Title: XADM: Information Store Fails to Start with -1011 Error

2. Shut down all Exchange services and reboot the Exchange server. When the information store restarts, it automatically tries to recover and return the database to a consistent state.

3. Make a full offline backup (stop all Exchange services) of the information store. This should include all .EDB and .LOG files. These may be stored on different physical drives. To find them, look in the registry under the HKEY_LOCAL_MACHINE subtree under the following subkey:

   \SYSTEM\CurrentControlSet\Services\MSExchangeIS\ParametersSystem

   Look at the DB log path parameter. This is a precautionary measure that captures the existing state of the Exchange Server before proceeding. You will need to have done this when you reach Steps 8 or 9.

4. Restore the last full online backup. *Do not* select the **Start Services after Restore** checkbox. Next restore any incremental (from the time of the last full online up to the day before the crash) online backups of the information store. Select the **Start Service after Restore** checkbox only when the last incremental backup is being restored.

   Do not select the box to erase all existing data.

   When the information store starts, it rolls forward through all the existing database logs and places the data into the restored information store. This brings the information store back to the point of the crash.

If this succeeds, no data is lost. From Step 5 on, varying amounts of data are lost.

5. If Step 4 still does not start the information store, go into the event viewer application log and review the logged messages for the source .EDB; there will be one message for each log file it replayed during the restore in Step 4. If one of these .EDB messages reports a problem replaying a particular log file, go into the MDBDATA directory and remove the corrupted log file and all log files with higher numbers, then try restarting the information store. For example, if the application log says that EDB00012.LOG could not be processed or was corrupt and in the MDBDATA directory the log files range from EDB000001.LOG to EDB000025.LOG, remove the files from EDB000012.LOG to EDB0000025.LOG and try restarting the information store. If it starts, you lose only the data stored in the log files you removed.

6. If Step 5 fails, restore the last full online backup of the information store. Select **Start Service After Restore** and **Erase All Existing Data**. This restores the information store to the point of the last online backup. Now, in the Exchange Administrator program, run the **DS/IS consistency adjuster** on the **Advanced** tab of the **Server Object** properties page.

7. If Step 6 fails, try it again with the next most recent version of either a full offline or full online backup.

8. If Step 6 will not work, delete all .EDB and .LOG files from the MDBDATA directory and restore a copy of the PRIV.EDB and PUB.EDB from the backup of the database when the problem started (Step 3). Next go into the Exchsrvr\bin directory and run **edbutil /d /r /ispriv** followed by **edbutil /d /r /ispub**. (Use ESEUTIL with Exchange 5.5.) This defragments the private and public information stores and tries to fix any database errors it encounters. If EDBUTIL.EXE is successful, try restarting the information store. If it starts, run **isinteg -fix** against both the private and public information stores to clean up any inconsistencies that may have arisen as a result of EDBUTIL. Running **edbutil /d /r** (or ESEUTIL) can delete data: use it as a last resort and work with Microsoft Technical Support when you do.

9. For additional information about the EDBUTIL and ISINTEG, refer to the Microsoft Exchange Server documentation or see Knowledge Base article Q143233, Title: XADM: Command Line Parameters for EDBUTIL.EXE.

10. If all of the above steps fail, as a last resort you can wipe the information store. As a general rule, if you must do this, wipe the public store first. If you must do both, you will understand why this process is considered drastic. Wiping PRIV.EDB *irrevocably deletes* all user mail messages and folders, and wiping PUB.EDB *irrevocably deletes* all public folders.

To wipe the public information store:

1. Ensure that you have completed Step 3 (full backup) or copy the Exchsrvr\Mdbdata directory to another location on the hard drive.

2. In the Exchsrvr\Mdbdata directory, delete all EDB*.LOG files, all RES*.LOG files, EDB.CHK, and PUB.EDB.

3. Now restart the information store service. If it starts, you have lost all public folder information (a new PUB.EDB, RES*.LOG and EDB.CHK are created automatically) and all information in the log files. You do retain, however, all the user mail messages and folders that were stored in the private information store (PRIV.EDB).

If wiping the public information store fails:

1. Remove all information in the Mdbdata directory.

2. Bring back a copy of the PUB.EDB from tape or alternate location.

3. Try restarting the information store. If it starts, public folder information is intact, but all user mail messages, folders, and log information is gone. The next time users log on, their mailboxes are recreated.

If all of the above fails, remove all information from Exchsrvr\Mdbdata and restart the information store service. This returns it to installation defaults.

Use the **DS/IS consistency adjuster** (**Advanced** tab of server object) to clear up any directory service/information store inconsistencies.

To be a recoverable system, the Exchange Server information store relies on a daily backup procedure and transaction logs. It is *highly* recommended that you put a daily backup procedure in place and verify the tapes.

Q143235, Title: XADM: Err Msg: Error -550 Has Occurred

The information in this article applies to: Microsoft Exchange Server, versions 4.0, 5.0, and 5.5

Symptoms

If the computer running Exchange Server stops responding or if it was not shut down gracefully after stopping all services properly, this error message is displayed on screen and in the event logs:

> Error -550 has occurred

After a power failure, this message may appear in the directory or information store database.

Cause

This error usually means that the database is in an inconsistent state and cannot start.

Resolution

Confirm that the state of the database is inconsistent, then try a soft recovery. Be sure to stop all services and back up all files before you run EDBUTIL.EXE.

1. Check the state of the database

   Exchange 4.0 and 5.0:

   Use EDBUTIL.EXE with the **MH** option on the problem database and dump the output to a text file:

   > **EDBUTIL /MH c:\exchsrvr\dsadata\dir.edb >c:\edbdump.txt**
   > *or*
   > **EDBUTIL /MH c:\exchsrvr\mdbdata\priv.edb >c:\edbdump.txt**
   > *or*
   > **EDBUTIL /MH c:\exchsrvr\mdbdata\pub.edb >c:\edbdump.txt**

Exchange 5.5:

Use ESEUTIL.EXE with the **MH** option on the problem database and dump the output to a text file:

ESEUTIL /MH c:\exchsrvr\dsadata\dir.edb >c:\edbdump.txt
or
ESEUTIL /MH c:\exchsrvr\mdbdata\priv.edb >c:\edbdump.txt
or
ESEUTIL /MH c:\exchsrvr\mdbdata\pub.edb >c:\edbdump.txt

2. Edit the EDBDUMP.TXT file and see if the state of the database is inconsistent.

3. If it is, run these commands:

Exchange 4.0 and 5.0:

EDBUTIL /R /DS

Exchange 5.5:

ESEUTIL /R /DS

Use /ISPRIV or /ISPUB instead of /DS for recovering the private or public information stores.

Q152959, Title: XADM: How to Remove the First Exchange Server in a Site

Last reviewed: February 3, 1998

The information in this article applies to: Exchange Server, versions 4.0 and 5.0

Summary

This article outlines the steps necessary to remove the first Exchange Server installed in a site.

In addition to any mailboxes and public folders, by default the first server in a site will contain and be responsible for the site folders, that is: the offline address book folder (.OAB), the Schedule+ free/busy information folder, and the organizational forms folder, if one exists. Servers subsequently installed rely, by default, on the first server for this information. For example, for the third server in the site to generate the .OAB, it must connect to the first server. Removing the first server in the site without performing the steps outlined below can render site folder data inaccessible.

The first server is also, by default, the routing calculation server, which is responsible for updating the site's gateway routing table (GWART). You must reassign this responsibility before removing the first server from the site. The procedure for doing this is in Knowledge Base article Q162012, Title: XADM: Unable to Change the Routing Calculation Server.

If you have removed the first server in the site before reading this article, please see Q152960, Title: XADM: Rebuilding the Site Folders in a Site.

More Information

Before removing the first Exchange Server in the site, follow these steps to avoid problems:

Important   Any users or public folders (non-site) homed on this Exchange Server must be moved to other site servers to ensure against data loss. Refer to the Microsoft Exchange Server documentation for more information.

Offline Address Book

1. Pick a server in the site to contain the .OAB.
2. Using the Exchange Administrator program, select the **Configuration** container and open the properties of the directory store **Site Configuration** object.
3. In the **Offline Address Book Server** drop-down list, select the server you chose in Step 1.
4. Click the **Generate Offline Address Book Now** button.
5. Click **OK**.

Schedule+ Free/Busy Information and Organizational Forms

1. Pick a server in the site to contain the Schedule+ information and the organizational forms.
2. Using the Exchange Administrator Program, select the **Configuration** container, the **Servers** container, and the server you chose in Step 1.
3. Double-click the **Public Information Store** object.
4. Click the **Instances** tab.
5. In the **Public Folders** list box, select the **Schedule+ Free Busy Information** and **Organization Forms** folders and click **Add**. Note that these folders should have the name of the first server in the site after the dash, for example, *Schedule+ Free Busy Information - firstserver*. This process creates a replica of these folders on the server you chose in Step 1.
6. Click **OK**.

Routing Calculation Server

1. Pick a server in the site to be the new routing calculation server.

2. Using the Exchange Administrator program, select the **Configuration** container and double-click the **Site Addressing** object.

3. Click the **General** tab.

4. In the routing calculation server drop-down list box, select the server you chose in Step 1. You must make some other change in the properties pages to activate the **Apply** button and retain the changes.

5. Click the **Routing** tab and click the **Recalculate Routing** button.

6. Click **OK**.

Note To verify that this procedure has been successful, power off or unplug the first server in the site from the network temporarily after you complete the steps. After you are sure the changes work (start an Exchange client and verify that you can access the Schedule+ free/busy information of another user and can generate an offline address book), leave the first server off the network, or powered off, and then perform the steps below to permanently remove it from the site.

---

7. Using the Exchange Administrator program, select the **Configuration** container and then the **Servers** container.

8. Highlight the first server in the site.

9. On the **Edit** menu click **Delete**, or press the DELETE key on the keyboard.

Note If an Exchange Schedule+ free/busy connector still appears in the server recipients container of the first server after all other items have been moved (re-homed) to the new server, the Schedule+ Free/Busy connector will not move automatically and will be deleted when the first server is removed from the site. To recreate this object, follow the steps listed in Q148199, Title: XCLN: Recreating a Deleted Schedule+ Free/Busy Agent.

To Include Schedule+ Free/Busy Information

The Schedule+ Free/Busy Information site folder will be repopulated as users log on to Schedule+ and generate changes. During this period, some users' free/busy information will be temporarily unavailable. Until a user logs on and makes an appointment (a "busy" time), there will be no free/busy information to view.

Q177635 XADM: How to Set Up a Disaster Recovery Server for DIR.EDB

Last reviewed: January 27, 1998

The information in this article applies to: Microsoft Exchange Server versions 4.0, 5.0, and 5.5

Summary

How to set up a Microsoft Exchange Server computer to recover information from the Exchange directory service contained in the DIR.EDB file.

More Information

The DIR.EDB file is specific to the Windows NT computer name and thus can only be restored to a server with the same computer name.

Note The following steps allow you to construct a server offline. It cannot be used in the production Exchange environment.

▶ **To build a DIR.EDB recovery server**

1. In the production domain where the Exchange service account resides, install a computer as a backup domain controller (BDC) with the same version of Windows NT Server and service pack level as the production Exchange Server computer.

2. Make sure that the recovery server computer has enough free disk space and any other devices that are necessary, such as a tape or CD-ROM drive. Take this computer offline by isolating it from the production network on a hub.

3. Promote this server to a primary domain controller (PDC) and reboot the computer.

4. In **Server Manager for Domains**, add a BDC with the same Windows NT computer name as the Exchange Server computer and rename the recovery server to the original Exchange Server computer name. (Verify that you are not on the production network first.)

   For more information, see Knowledge Base article Q150298, Title: Renaming a Windows NT PDC or BDC.

5. Reboot the server. Now the recovery server is running the same version of Windows NT Server as the production Exchange Server computer.

6. Install Exchange Server as a new site, but use the same organization and site name as the production Exchange environment. Make sure to select the same service account as the production domain to use for the Exchange services.

7. Update to the same service pack level as the production Exchange Server computer.

8. Restore from backup the previous Exchange directory store and/or the Exchange information store.

Q163686, Title: XADM: What to do if the Service Account is Deleted

Last Reviewed: October 28, 1997

The information in this article applies to: Microsoft Exchange Server, versions 4.0 and 5.0

Summary

To start, Exchange services require a Windows NT Server domain account called the Microsoft Exchange Service Account. This article explains what to do if the Service Account is deleted by mistake.

More Information

By default, the Service Account is given permissions over all objects in the Exchange directory during setup. Windows NT accounts in the directory are referred to by their SID values and not their names.

If the Service Account is deleted from the Windows NT Accounts database, no Exchange services can start. Even if this Service Account is recreated with the identical name and password, the SID value associated with it will not be the same as the value of the previous account, so the service cannot access directory objects.

Resolution

The only recommended solution to this problem is to restore the Windows NT Security Database (SAM) from a recent backup. This restores the deleted Service Account with its original SID value, and all the Exchange services will be able to start.

If a backup of the SAM is not available, the only other alternative is to reinstall Exchange Server on all servers affected by the loss of the Service Account.

You can save information from the Exchange information store (PRIV.EDB and PUB.EDB) but you must recreate the directory, resulting in the loss of all directory-specific information (custom recipients, distribution lists, mailbox details, connectors, and so forth).

Authoritative Restore

If, after you perform a restore, directory information on the restored server changes or automatically gets purged, you may be experiencing an undesired backfill state. This means previously replicated changes from the restored server are replicating back from another server because the other server's change record is more up to date than that of the restored database.

The Authoritative Restore tool (AUTHREST.EXE) allows you to force a restored directory database to replicate to other servers after restoring from a backup. You can receive assistance using this tool from Microsoft Technical Support.

Normally, a restored database is assumed to be more out of date than the collective information held on all the other directory replicas in the organization. A restored directory would normally replace its own information with the more recent data held by other servers because a restore usually recovers a lost database or server. But sometimes this is not what you want to do. For example, if an administrative error deletes thousands of mailboxes or vital configuration information, the goal of restoring from backup is not to restore one server to functionality, but to move the entire system back to its state before the undesired change.

Without Authoritative Restore, you would have to restore every server in the organization from a backup that predates the error or restore every server in the site, and then force all bridgeheads in other sites to resynchronize from scratch. If you restore only one server or restore servers one at a time, each restored server quickly overwrites its restored data with the more recent (incorrect) information held by all other servers in the site.

Using the Authoritative Restore tool, you can advance object versions and USNs on all writable objects held by that directory so that the data held on the backup appears to be more recent than any copy held by other servers. Normal replication then causes the restored information to spread to all servers. This tool allows you to restore one server (presumably the one server with the most recent pre-mistake backup) rather than all servers.

AUTHREST.EXE is on the Exchange Server CD-ROM in the directory "\Support\Utils\<*platform*>".

Restoring Service Packs

Restored databases must be run under the same version of Exchange they were originated under, so after a restore do not start services until all of the code is up to date. For example, if you are running Exchange Service Pack 2 but have the original server CD-ROM and SP2 code, you should have the SP2 code loaded before running Exchange with your restored databases from an SP2 level server.

To accomplish this, you can use the **setup /r** and **update /r** switches for the original server code and service pack installations. This tells the setup program not to start services. The **/r** switch indicates that you will provide database files from a restore. You can also run **setup** and **update** without the **/r** switches, then, when you are at the correct service pack level, you can restore your databases to replace the new databases installed by **setup**. Be sure to follow the appropriate restore procedures. **Setup** and **/r** are not for all uses:

- **Setup /r**, will not create the .DIR, .PUB, and PRIV.EDB files. Normally these files are created from the organization and site name given during setup. **Setup /r** simply copies the DIR.EDB exactly the way it is from the Exchange Server CD-ROM. You will not be able to start the directory service with this default DIR.EDB after running **setup /r**.

- If you plan to restore only the information store and not the directory store, *do not* run **setup /r**: it requires you to restore all of the database files (.DIR, .PUB, and PRIV.EDB).

- **/r** is not supported by the UPDATE.EXE program for the Exchange Server version 4.0 service packs. If you are performing a disaster recovery for an Exchange 4.0 server, do not use the **/r** option when running SETUP.EXE. After Setup has completed, run **update** (without the **/r** option) to install the required service packs and start the Exchange services with default data. Now restore the information store and/or directory service data from backup.

Restoring from an .OST After Mailbox Deletion

.OSTs are slave replicas of server-based folders. If you delete the master, the slave is orphaned.

If the original Exchange profile was not modified, you should still be able start up offline with the old .OST and recover the data by copying to a .PST file. However, if the old profile was deleted or modified (by using it to log onto the new mailbox), the data is lost.

This is caused by the security enforcement method used on .OSTs: Windows NT authentication obviously cannot be enforced while users are offline. Instead, users must prove that they're allowed to log on to the server-based master before the .OST file will grant local access. To enforce this procedure, Exchange creates an encrypted cookie from the user mailbox's unique entry ID, while the user is successfully logged onto the server, then stores it securely in the user's Exchange profile. In essence, the profile has the OST key. When a user tries to access the .OST file, the .OST checks the profile for the existence of this key.

This means .OST data cannot be recovered if the master server mailbox is deleted and the profile containing the key to the .OST is deleted or modified.

Using SCANPST.EXE to Repair .PST and .OST Files

The SCANPST program, also known as the Inbox Repair Tool, can repair both
.PST and .OST files. Similar to the MMF check capability in Microsoft Mail and
installed in the Exchange client subdirectory by default, SCANPST performs
eight checks on the selected file. During repair, you have the option to back up
the existing file prior to making the repair, although this requires that you have
available disk space equal to the .PST or .OST file size.

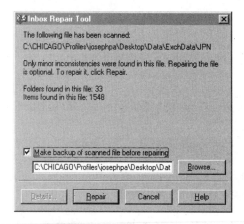

SCANPST screen

SIDs (Security Identifiers), Secret Objects, and Windows NT–Based Computer Accounts

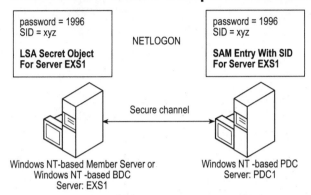

Example of Windows NT secure channel during normal production

Note that the Windows NT SID for EXS1 is *xyz*. Each Windows NT–based computer has a unique SID that is used for domain authentication. (*xyz* is not actual SID format.). To connect to the domain, the Windows NT BDC or member server must have a matching SID and LSA (local security authority) password so that authentication can take place.

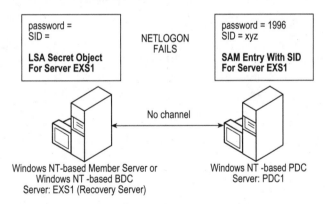

Secure channel failure

This is an example of what occurs if you do not first delete and re-add the Exchange-based server computer account before installing a recovery server. If you build a recovery server by installing Windows NT from scratch and use the same computer name, NETLOGON fails because the old computer account and SID remain in the domain SAM and can be reset only from within the Server Manager program by deleting and re-adding the computer account.

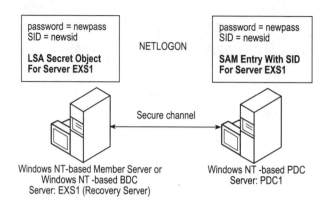

Windows NT-based Member Server or
Windows NT -based BDC
Server: EXS1 (Recovery Server)   Windows NT -based PDC
                                                Server: PDC1

A re-established computer account

This is an example of a re-established computer account. When the old computer account is deleted and re-added to the domain SAM, the SAM entry is first set to an initialize state. When the new server is added, a local LSA secret object is created along with a SID, thus synchronizing the LSA secret object (stored locally on the BDC or member server) with the SAM object for the respective computer. A password generated during this process is used whenever the BDC or member server computer logs on to the domain. This process creates a secure channel between the BDC or member server and the PDC. NETLOGON automatically changes this secure channel password to prevent the password from being discovered.

The LSA secret object is created by setup during initial installation or when a server joins a domain. The SAM computer account, however, is created by the Server Manager program. For more information, refer to Knowledge Base article Q102476, Title: Changing the Name of Windows NT Workstations and Servers.

General Practices

Create and Verify Daily Backups

Verifying backups is a critical step in disaster recovery (you can't recover data unless you have a valid backup), but many people fail to do it. Don't assume that backup tapes are being swapped and that data is being properly backed up: make sure the process is verified daily. Review all backup logs and resolve any errors or inconsistencies. Make sure to back up the registry and the Key Management server data as well. In addition to preserving valid data with which to restore the system, successful full (normal) backups reset and remove transaction logs, resulting in free disk space. If daily full backups are failing, transaction logs are not being purged and the transaction log disk drive soon fills up. Freeing disk space is less of an issue if circular logging is enabled, but freeing it through other means allows you to avoid the use of circular logging.

How to Verify Backups

1. Restore the Exchange databases from backup.

2. Run the Database Integrity Check (ESEUTIL /G) if running Exchange 5.5.

3. Defrag the databases (EDBUTIL /D) if running Exchange 4.0 or 5.0.

Perform Periodic File-Based Backup

To capture all configuration data, perform periodic full file-based backups. To make sure all Exchange-related files are closed and can be backed up, shut down services. This might be performed during the scheduled maintenance window. Online backup (not file-based) is recommended for the information store and directory databases.

Back Up Existing Log Files Before Performing any Restoration

It is a good safeguard to back up any existing log files before you restore an Exchange Server. If data is lost or an older backup set is restored by mistake, the logs help you recover.

Consider the following situation. A full online backup has been made on Sunday night and then again on Monday night. The information store runs on Tuesday, generating 50 log files. There is a problem and you need to restore from backup. You want to restore Monday night's full online backup, but by mistake you restore Sunday night's. Now you have restored a database from Sunday, but the log files on the drive were generated on Tuesday; there are no log files from Monday because they were purged by Monday night's backup. When the service starts up, the database engine detects a gap in the sequence of log files (no Monday logs) so it deletes Tuesday's log files (all log files after the gap) because they cannot be replayed and the service has to generate logs with those sequence numbers. If this happens, you have lost your only chance to recover data generated on Tuesday.

If you had backed up the existing log files before performing the restoration, you would be able to recover from this situation. As it is—sorry.

Standardize Tape Backup Formats

Recovery equipment must be compatible with production tape equipment. If you deploy a new type of tape drive, make sure that you deploy a compatible model in the recovery equipment. Always test new equipment before relying on it; periodically test installed equipment.

Deploy a UPS and Test It Periodically

Don't take the approach that if the Exchange-based server loses power, all other servers will go too. Get UPS protection if it is at all possible and verify it if it is already installed. Sometimes UPS installations do not include every outlet at a site. If you do not have a dedicated UPS, get some electricians or operations personnel to test your layout. Don't assume you are covered: if users lose all their Exchange data they won't care that someone, sometime signed paperwork that said the outlets were UPS protected. Server-class UPS system batteries can wear out every three years or so: keep track of them.

Perform a Periodic Fire Drill

A drill measures your ability to recover from a disaster and certifies your disaster recovery plans. Create a test environment and simply attempt a complete recovery. Be sure to use data from production backups and to record how long it takes to recover. This information can help you create reliable and accurate plans if there ever is a real disaster. The drill should show you that as much as a third of the total recovery time is required to gather information, map out a plan, and get the correct tools in place.

For maximum effect, provide no notice to your staff that you are performing a drill. *This will be the most valuable experience that you will have in your disaster recovery planning.*

Review the Environment when Placing Production Servers

Inspect the area when deploying servers. Make sure the environment has enough power. If possible, dedicate power lines for the Exchange equipment. Review existing amperage and new amperage requirements. Place servers in a physically secure location and make sure room temperature stays in acceptable limits. If the site has fire sprinklers (rather than a gas-based fire suppression system), don't place servers under them. As you deploy servers, perform basic preventive maintenance.

Check Windows NT Event Logs Daily

Review logs regularly. This can help you identify problems early, sometimes before they have an impact. Take advantage of the extensive logging available in Exchange and of the logging tools in the *Microsoft BackOffice Resource Kit.*

Create a Disaster Kit

Plan ahead by building a disaster kit that includes an operating system configuration sheet, hard drive partition configuration sheet, RAID configuration, hardware configuration sheet, EISA/MCA configuration disks, Exchange configuration sheet, Windows NT emergency repair diskette, Exchange Performance Optimizer settings sheet, and so forth. This material is easy enough to compile, and it can minimize recovery time—much of which can be spent trying to locate information or disks needed to configure the recovery system.

Publish a Microsoft Exchange Maintenance Window

An Exchange-based server requires check-ups and maintenance. Some organizations carefully schedule mainframes for service but overlook servers. Planned maintenance generally reduces unplanned downtime. Remember to let users know the downtime schedule—they often expect 24x7 availability. Beyond regular maintenance, there will be service packs and upgrades of hardware and software. Sometimes you have to take down the information store service to reduce the size of store files using EDBUTIL. Let users know in advance when the system will be down.

Determine Downtime Cost

Downtime cost estimates are useful when evaluating recovery equipment purchases. Models for calculating these costs vary. Some include lost orders/hour, cost of delayed financial transactions, and the cost of delayed time sensitive market decisions.

Consider Maintaining Offsite Tapes and Equipment

If for legal, security, or cost reasons you do not send backup tapes to a third-party offsite location, at least send them to an offsite location within your company.

Dedicate Recovery Equipment and Build a Recovery Lab

Dedicate some hardware to recovery. Quite often, teams are penny wise but pound foolish, scrounging test or recovery equipment and putting it into production. Keep dedicated recovery equipment, maintain it in working order, and keep it available. Besides its ongoing uses, a test lab can be a lifesaver during recovery. Using EDBUTIL for recovery and database defragmenting requires up to twice the disk space of the largest production server information store database. It is usually cost effective to maintain one recovery server with sufficient disk space.

Keep Solid Records of All Configuration Done to the Production Server

You need this information to configure the recovery server. Keep accurate records of Windows NT tuning settings, path information, protocol addresses, Exchange connector configuration, and so forth. Make them part of the disaster recovery kit.

Monitor the Information Store

Monitor the growth of the information store and server performance and be prepared with a plan to address expansion problems and logistics. Set up Windows NT disk space alerts and monitor remaining disk space. Make use of Performance Monitor's objects for the information store.

Devise an Archiving Plan

An archiving plan allows users to move server-based messages into local store files. This helps reduce the size of the server-based information store. Have users store .PSTs on local drives or on a disk or server separate from that of the information store. If necessary, dedicate a file server for .PST archiving, or you may find that data is reduced in the store but added to another area of the same disk or logical drive. This can be a significant hit because .PSTs store messages in .RTF and ASCII formats and you can't set disk space limits on .PST files. Include all sensitive data in backup strategies, including user .PST files. Use encryption when creating .OST and .PST files.

Exchange Configuration Considerations

Consider Microsoft Exchange Server Roles

If you make the Exchange server a PDC and it becomes unavailable, you have to promote an alternate domain controller to PDC. If the Exchange server is not the PDC, you need not worry about promotions and demotions of domain controllers during recovery. Don't make the Exchange server a PDC.

Some companies prefer to place the Exchange Server on a BDC in the accounts domain so that a second computer is not required for Windows NT authentication in remote offices. This saves purchasing another computer, but if you choose this tactic be sure to provide enough RAM for the Windows NT SAM and the Exchange server memory requirements. In general, Windows NT Server domain controllers require 2.5 times the RAM used by the SAM. For domain planning information, see the *Windows NT 4.0 Networking Guide* on TechNet.

If the Exchange server is a member server (neither PDC nor BDC) no additional memory overhead for the domain SAM is incurred, although companies with remote offices can save money by having the local Exchange server provide authentication (serve as a BDC) and messaging services. A proper directory service restore requires access to the original SAM. Never install an Exchange server in a domain that does not have a BDC.

An alternative is to place the Exchange servers in a large resource domain that trusts each accounts domain. In this case, you can place the Exchange servers on BDCs without incurring significant memory overhead because the SAM for the Exchange resource domain will be relatively small.

Locate Transaction Log Files on a Separate Dedicated Physical Disk

This is the single most important aspect of Exchange server performance. There are recovery implications as well. Transaction logs provide an additional recovery mechanism when they are on a separate dedicated physical disk: if you lose the drive with the databases, you can still recover using the transaction log files.

Locate Information Store on RAID5 Stripe Set or Mirrored Set

The information store uses random access, so putting it on a stripe or mirrored set provides excellent performance as well as an added level of recoverability.

Disable SCSI Controller Write Cache

You can also help avoid data loss by disabling the SCSI controller write cache. Windows NT does not use buffers if the write-through flag is set at a programming level. Thus when a program receives a write complete signal from Windows NT, it is guaranteed that the write was completed to disk. This is critical to the Exchange transaction logging process. If write cache is enabled, Windows NT thinks that a write has made it to disk and it informs the calling application of this "false" information. This can result in data corruption if there is a crash before this lazy write operation makes it to disk.

You can safely enable the write cache on SCSI controllers backed up by battery. Check with your hardware vendor for details.

Use Mirroring or RAID5 as the Operating System Partition

This provides redundancy for the underlying operating system.

Use Hardware RAID and Mirroring when Possible

After a failure, software RAID requires reconfiguration to add a new drive when bringing the system back to its original configuration. It is preferable to use hardware RAID5 wherever possible so that you can fix a disk drive failure immediately by plugging in a replacement drive. System partitions should be mirrored or RAID5 for redundancy.

Disable Circular Logging

Circular logging can help conserve disk space but it has significant drawbacks: it disables incremental and differential backups and creates a cyclical, truncated transaction log history that cannot be played back. To make sure that transaction log files are regularly purged to free up disk space, instigate a solid backup strategy that does not require circular logging.

Limit Information Store Attributes Early

Configure mailbox storage limits and maximum age of server-based messages. Limit MTA message sizes and the size of messages that users can send. This helps set user expectations and reduce server loading.

Configure MTAs Accordingly

Configure the MTA frequency so that queues are cleared quickly and queued messages do not accumulate in the information store. Design a redundant MTA path so that messages keep flowing if there is a link outage. When MTAs can keep up with the traffic that flows through them, the messages in the store are reduced and message delivery times improve.

Periodic Offline Information Store Maintenance

If you delete or move a large number of mailboxes on a server or perform a mailbox cleanup resulting in the deletion of a large number of messages, it is a good time to perform an offline defragmentation of the information store.

It is not required, but it is a good idea to periodically (say, every quarter) check the integrity of the Exchange databases by running **eseutil /g**. This allows you to assess the databases and take corrective action to resolve conditions before they become problems.

Do not run **edbutil /d /r** or **eseutil /p** to repair databases as part of the regular maintenance schedule.

Planning for Databases Larger than 16 GB in Exchange 5.5

With Exchange Server 5.5, the 16-GB limit on the size of databases has been lifted and the size of the databases is now limited only by hardware. This allows you to consolidate several servers into one, reducing hardware and administrative costs.

If you consolidate servers, keep in mind disaster recovery when you plan databases. The larger the database, the more time required to back it up, the more time required to restore it, and the more time required to perform offline maintenance.

Exchange Server 5.5 has several performance improvements for dealing with large databases. The backup APIs now support speeds over 30 GB/hour, so if there are backup bottlenecks they probably are in your hardware. The database utilities have also been enhanced. Depending on hardware and computer loading, the new ESEUTIL program can check database integrity at about 10 GB/hour, can defragment databases at about 4 to 5 GB/hour, and can repair them at about 8 to 10 GB/hour.

Keep maintenance, backup, and downtime until recovery in mind when you calculate an upper limit to information store databases. The larger they are, the longer everything takes. Set mailbox limits, control the number of mailboxes per server, set message size limits, and periodically clean mailboxes.

Deleted Items Retention is a useful Exchange 5.5 feature, but remember that the space used by deleted items is not used when calculating the storage used by a mailbox. Enabling Deleted Items Retention can increase Exchange 5.5 information store size significantly compared to Exchange 4.0 and 5.0 servers. Be careful when you set the number of days after which deleted items are purged from the information store.

Equip Servers with Sufficient Disk Space

Offline maintenance and repair routines require up to twice the disk space of the database file being administered with the EDBUTIL/ESEUTIL utilities.

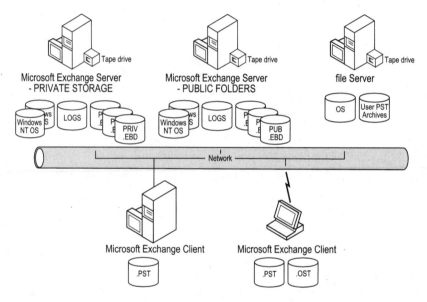

Sample configuration outlining distribution of Microsoft Exchange information and local store data

For optimal performance and recoverability, the operating system drive should be mirrored (or RAID5), transaction logs should be on a dedicated physical drive (this too can be mirrored), and the information store should be on a RAID5 stripe set. Windows NT requires that the swap file on the same partition as SYSTEM must be large enough for a memory dump. If you add more swap files to alternate drives, the system will use them to optimize disk performance.

Backup Type Strategies

Backup strategies often depend on business requirements. This section examines the characteristics of various types of backup, benefits, limitations, and tradeoffs. The time required for backup depends on type of backup being performed. A daily full backup requires the most time, but when the database moves into the gigabyte range, daily full backups can be impractical. In some cases, a combination (periodic full backups with interim incremental or differential backups) may be more practical.

Example A—Full Daily Backup

Schedule: SU:F, M:F, T:F, W:F, TH:F, FR: F, S:F

Advantages	Disadvantages
Always removes transaction log files	Impacts server performance longest
Requires only one tape restore	Requires the most tape space
Simplifies scheduling	Usually requires daily tape swaps
Allows circular logging	

Example B—Full Plus One Incremental

Schedule: SU:F, M:I, T:F, W:I, TH:F, FR: I, S:F

Advantages	Disadvantages
Always removes transaction log files	Requires two tapes to restore
Performs multiple full backups on separate tapes	Requires knowledge of backup cycle
Incremental has much less performance impact	Requires that circular logging be disabled
Has less frequent tape rotations	
At most, requires two tapes for restore	

Example C—Full Plus Two Incrementals

Schedule: SU:F, M:I, T:I, W:F, TH:I, FR: I, S:F

Advantages	Disadvantages
Always removes transaction log files	Requires full plus each incremental—in this case up to three tapes
Performs full backups relatively infrequently	Requires knowledge of backup cycle
Minimizes performance impact on server	Requires that circular logging be disabled
Incremental requires minimal tape space	

Example D—Full Plus Two Differentials

Schedule: SU:F, M:D, T:D, W:F, TH:D, FR: D, S:F

Advantages	Disadvantages
Performs full backups fairly infrequently	Differential backups do not remove log files
At most, requires two tapes for restore	Requires that circular logging be disabled
Has little performance impact on server	
Differential require minimal tape space	

A backup strategy must fit your business requirements, but a rule of thumb is to use full daily backups for small data sets and a combination of full, incremental, and differential methods for large data sets. The combination can minimize the impact to system performance and the tape space required.

The "Hot Spare" Question

Is it possible to maintain a live *hot spare* server running at all times for Exchange recovery? The answer depends on how you define *hot spare*.

Because the recovery server must be configured with the same computer name as the Exchange server (for full information store/directory service server recovery), the recovery server cannot remain online (no duplicate NetBIOS names allowed). Nor can identically named computers exist within a Windows NT Server domain. If you configure the recovery server with a different name, you will not be able to use it to restore the Exchange directory but you will be able to restore individual mailboxes easily although you will have to reconfigure Windows NT security for all objects. This can be a complex operation because it is manual. At the very least, prepare recovery equipment with copies of all required production code.

Single mailbox recovery does not include restoring the Exchange directory, and Exchange requires only that the recovery server have the same site and organization name (not the same computer name) so you can keep a Windows NT Server–based computer online. If the recovery server is servicing only one site, Exchange can be up and running but not connected to the production site.

Full server recovery requires the same site, organization, and computer name. You can maintain a recovery server doing non-critical work (serving as an additional RAS server or Microsoft Mail multitasking message transfer agent— MMTA) under a different computer name. When you need the computer for full server recovery, you can rename it or reinstall Windows NT. Keep installation code on the recovery server (\ntinstall\i386, \patches\sp4, \exchinst\i386) and make sure it has the same capacity as the production server.

Exchange Server 5.5 supports the Microsoft Cluster Server and can capitalize on the high availability that clusters provide.

Online Backup Automation Example

▶ **To perform an online backup of the information store/directory service**

1. Install the WINAT.EXE program from the *Windows NT Resource Kit* in the Windows NT directory of the local computer.

2. Create a Windows NT common group called *Microsoft Exchange Backup*.

3. Create an icon for the BACKUP.LOG file. This provides quick access to review the backup log.

4. Copy the NTBACKUP.EXE icon from the **Administrative Tools** group to the Microsoft Exchange Backup Group.

5. Create an icon for WINAT.EXE in the Microsoft Exchange Backup group.

6. From **Control Panel**, click **Services**, highlight the **Schedule** service, and click the **Startup** button. Configure for automatic startup and assign an ID that is a member of the Windows NT Backup Operators group. Be sure to enter the correct password. If the administrator ID password changes, you must change the password for the Schedule service. This account must also have "Admin" privileges within the Exchange organization site and configuration containers that you will back up. When done, start the Schedule service.

7. Create the backup batch file, name it BACK.BAT, and save it in the \winnt subdirectory. An example file is below.

8. Run the WINAT.EXE program and schedule the BACK.BAT file. You do not need to have a logon session on the computer on which WINAT is running because the Schedule service logs on to perform the operation under the defined security context. Be sure to set the batch job for **Interactive** mode.

Sample Batch File for Online Backup

```
rem ** 8/15/98  Backup Written by <Your name>
rem ** This will backup the IS and DS on both <SERVERNAME1> and
    <SERVERNAME2>.
ntbackup backup DS \\SERVERNAME1 IS \\SERVERNAME1 /v /d "SERVERNAME1 IS-
    DS" /b /t Normal /l c:\winnt\backup.log /e
ntbackup backup DS \\SERVERNAME2 IS \\SERVERNAME2 /a /v /d "SERVERNAME2
    IS-DS" /b /t Normal /l c:\winnt\backup.log /e
exit
```

Sample Batch File for Offline Backup: Example 1

You may need to experiment with the order in which you stop services. There are dependencies, and you cannot stop a service without stopping dependent services as well.

```
rem ** stop Microsoft Exchange Services
rem ** you can stop Microsoft Exchange services and restart them
    automatically to backup
rem ** files that a particular service may hold open
REM // stop all services
echo Stopping Services...
net stop MSExchangeMSMI
net stop MSExchangePCMTA
net stop MSExchangeFB
net stop MSExchangeDX
net stop MSExchangeIMC
net stop MSExchangeMTA
net stop MSExchangeIS
net stop MSExchangeDS
net stop MSExchangeSA

ntbackup backup c:\ d:\ /a /v /d "Full File Based Backup" /b /l
    c:\winnt\backup.log /e

REM edbutil OPTIONS

net start MSExchangeSA
net start MSExchangeDS
net start MSExchangeIS
net start MSExchangeMTA
net start MSExchangeIMC
net start MSExchangeDX
net start MSExchangeFB
net start MSExchangePCMTA
net start MSExchangeMSMI
```

Sample Batch File for Offline Backup: Example 2

You can start and stop PCMTA services by enclosing the service name in quotes. You can determine the service names from the Exchange Administrator program, the Windows NT Control Panel, or by looking into the Windows NT registry (HKEY_LOCAL_MACHINE\SYSTEM\CurrentControlSet\Services). Services are listed in alphabetical order.

```
rem Batch File To Stop and Restart Microsoft Exchange Services
rem For File Based Backup
echo Stopping Services ...
net stop MSExchangeMSMI
net stop MSExchangePCMTA
net stop MSExchangeFB
net stop MSExchangeDX
net stop MSExchangeMTA
net stop MSExchangeIMC
net stop MSExchangeIS
net stop MSExchangeDS

net stop "PC MTA - HUB"
net stop MSExchangeSA

ntbackup BACKUP d:\exchsrvr\mdbdata /v /d "File Based Backup" /b /l
    c:\winnt\backup.log /e

net start MSExchangeSA
net start MSExchangeDS
net start MSExchangeIS
net start MSExchangeMTA
net start MSExchangeIMC
net start MSExchangeDX
net start MSExchangeFB
net start MSExchangePCMTA
net start MSExchangeMSMI

net start "PC MTA - HUB"
```

WINAT Scheduler and the Windows NT Schedule Service

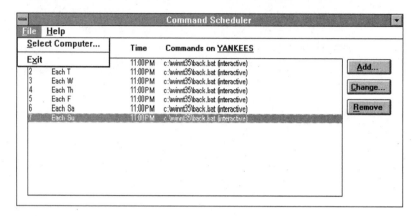

Windows AT command scheduler

NTBACKUP.EXE requires that the BACK.BAT jobs are set for **interactive**.

Jobs scheduled through the WINAT scheduler program are run by the Windows NT Schedule service. Because batch jobs are run in the context of the Schedule service, you must consider Windows NT security. When you configure the Schedule service, make the account a member of the Windows NT Backup Operators Group. This allows for a full information store/directory service backup.

Windows NT Schedule service configuration dialog box

C H A P T E R   1 0

Frequently Asked Questions

This chapter provides answers to common questions on disaster recovery, backup, and planning for both. You can find a similar list in the *Microsoft Exchange Server 5.5 Resource Guide.*

Exchange Server Database Utilities

Question 1: What are the improvements in the database utilities shipped with Exchange 5.5?

Answer: The new ESEUTIL of Exchange Server 5.5 replaces the EDBUTIL.EXE program that shipped in earlier versions. ESEUTIL includes:

- **New Integrity Checker (ESEUTIL /G)**—This checks database integrity at speeds around 10 GB/hour.

- **Enhanced Repair Process (ESEUTIL /P)**—It now includes three stages: it performs an integrity check to find corrupt pages, scans the database looking for tables that contain them, and then repairs only the corrupt tables. The first two stages are very fast, operating at speeds around 10 GB/hour. Finally, repairing only corrupt tables requires less time and disk space. An extremely conservative estimate is the ESEUTIL requires free space equal to only 20 to 25 percent of the size of database file being repaired. EDBUTIL requires 110 percent.

- **Quicker Defragmentation Process (ESEUTIL /D)**—Offline defragmentation (compaction) runs of 4 to 5 GB/hour.

  Projected speeds, of course, depend on hardware and loading. Exchange 5.5 also includes an enhanced Information Store Integrity Checker (ISINTEG.EXE) with command line switches that allow you to perform individual tests, reducing the time needed to check the information store. For more information on ISINTEG, please see the ISINTEG.RTF located on the Exchange Server 5.5 CD-ROM in the \SERVER\SUPPORT\UTILS directory.

Question 2: What are some cases where EDBUTIL/ESEUTIL should be run? Is there an article regarding information store startup problems?

Answer: You should be very careful running EDBUTIL or ESEUTIL in repair mode. Before repairing a database, always make sure you have backed up your databases and have sufficient free disk space. It is a good idea to consult Microsoft Technical Support.

The best place to look for updated Knowledge Base article information is http://support.microsoft.com/support. Search on Exchange and then enter keywords.

Question 3: What is the difference between running isinteg - fix **and** edbutil /d /r **or** eseutil /p?

Answer: First of all, **edbutil /d /r** (Exchange 4.0 and 5.0) or **eseutil /p** (Exchange 5.5) is strictly a last resort for repairing a database file: it fixes only low-level database corruption (bad pages). The **isinteg -fix** command works at the information store level, fixing objects, schemes, and other high-level data/structure problems. If for some reason you don't have a backup to restore from or log files to play forward and you have to run **edbutil /d /r** or **eseutil /p**, be sure to run **isinteg -fix** after it.

Whenever possible, you want to restore from a backup and then play logs forward because this method restores all your data. If you have no backup to restore and have to run both **edbutil/eseutil** *and* **isinteg**, you will lose the contents of any bad pages in the database—messages, attachments, folders, and so on.

Question 4: When should I use edbutil /d /r **or** eseutil /p?

Answer: This is a last resort and it can delete data; you should use it to repair databases only when you cannot restore and no other options are available.

Before running **edbutil /d /r** (Exchange 4.0 and 5.0) or **eseutil /p** (Exchange 5.5), make sure that:

- You have backed up the database files you are trying to repair.
- You have sufficient free disk space. EDBUTIL requires free space equal to 110 percent (25 percent for ESEUTIL) of the size of the file being repaired.
- You use the **/t** command line option (with either utility) to point to the drive that contains the required free disk space.
- You run **isinteg –fix** after the utility has run.

As always, it is a good idea to consult Microsoft Technical Support before attempting a complicated process that might prove harmful to your system.

Question 5: I understand that I need to run isinteg -patch **after restoring an offline information store backup to patch the GUIDs, but what is a GUID?**

Answer: A GUID is a globally unique identifier—64-bit hexadecimal string that (theoretically) uniquely tags an object in time and space. The private and public information stores have base GUIDs that they use to generate GUIDs for all other objects in the store, including folders, messages, attachments, and so forth. The **isinteg -patch** changes the information store base GUIDs. You must run the patch because when you restore an information store you are essentially rolling back time on that server. If you roll it back and don't change the base GUID, new objects created in that information store may end up with GUIDs identical to the GUIDs of other existing objects in the organization. This would cause havoc when referencing objects because they could no longer be identified accurately.

If your organization has only one server, this is not a problem because when you restore you know that there are no objects on other servers with IDs that might be assigned to new objects.

You do not have to explicitly run **isinteg –patch** after an online backup is restored because the Exchange-aware backup program automatically runs the required code to update the GUIDs after restore.

Question 6: Why do I need to run isinteg -patch **after running an offline information store restore and before starting the information store service?**

Answer: To guarantee that globally unique identifiers (GUIDs) are unique.

If you restore a copy of the information store (PUB.EDB and PRIV.EDB) from an offline backup and do not run **isinteg -patch**, you get error - 1011 when you try to restart the service. It produces an entry in the Windows NT event viewer application log (source ID 2048) displaying this message:

The information store was restored from an offline backup. Run isinteg -patch before restarting the information store.

and this command prompt DS_E_COMMUNICATIONS ERROR.

If you do not run **isinteg –patch**, the restored information store uses old GUIDs. This presents no problem if they are unique, but they can cause havoc if they match GUIDs that were left on the system. The restored information store must have a new, guaranteed-unique GUIDs.

To patch the information store, run **isinteg -patch** to replace the GUIDs. Patch mode runs it against the entire information store (PUB.EDB and PRIV.EDB), generates new GUIDs, and creates patch replication information that prevents incorrect backfilling.

▶   **To run isinteg –patch**

1. Ensure that the directory and system attendant services are running. If the either is not running, **isinteg** fails with a DS_COMMUNICATIONS_ERROR message.

2. Go into the EXCHSRVR\BIN directory and type in **isinteg -patch**. It replaces the GUIDs and notifies you when the information store is successfully updated.

3. Restart the information store service.

For more information see Knowledge Base article Q154032, Title: XADM: Error 1105 - EcBadVersion, Restoring Off-Line Store.

Question 7: When I execute the command isinteg -patch **it does not run and I receive the error message: DS_E_COMMUNICATIONS_PROBLEM. What is wrong?**

Answer: Make sure that the directory service is started before you run **isinteg - patch**.

Question 8: Do I need to run DS/IS consistency adjuster **after restoring the directory and information store?**

Answer: Not usually. Run this when you can only restore the information store. **DS/IS consistency adjuster** scans the information store and makes sure a directory object exists for each information store object (creating a directory object if one doesn't exist). It also scans the directory and makes sure there is a corresponding information store object for each directory object (deleting the directory object if one doesn't exist). It also verifies the access control list (ACL) for each object and strips any invalid entries. One good way to see what the DS/IS consistency adjuster does is to turn up DS/MDB Sync diagnostic logging to maximum and look at the application log.

If you have restored the information store onto a server that was recently added to an existing Exchange site, wait until replication has completed. At this time, the new server should be aware of all the servers and sites in the organization and its global address list should be populated. After replication has completed, run the **DS/IS consistency adjuster**. If you run the DS/IS consistency adjuster before replication has completed, public folders may be re-homed to this new server and public folder permissions will be lost.

Question 9: Should I avoid running the DS/IS consistency adjuster**?**

Answer: There are two situations in which you should be careful when running the **DS/IS consistency adjuster**.

If you have temporarily broken a directory replication connector between two sites, do not run the **DS/IS consistency adjuster** if you plan to reconnect the sites. If you run the **DS/IS consistency adjuster** when the directory replication connector is broken, any public folders homed on servers not in the current site are re-homed to the local server and any mailboxes belonging to other sites are removed from the public folder permissions list. When you re-add the directory replication connector, all changes made to the public folders in the current site are replicated throughout the organization, the public folders are re-homed, and permissions are lost.

If you have restored the information store onto a server that was recently added to an Exchange site, do not run the **DS/IS consistency adjuster** until the new server has replicated with the rest of the site and is aware of the other servers and sites in the organization.

For more information, refer to Knowledge Base articles:

- Q156705, Title: XADM: Site Tear Down Causes Public Folders to be Re-homed
- Q141342, Title: XADM: Public Folders Automatically get New Home Site/Server

Defragmentation and Compaction

Question 10: What is the difference between compaction, defragmentation, and information store maintenance?

Answer: Information store maintenance takes place between 1:00 and 6:00 A.M. It includes tombstone compression, column aging, index aging, clean per user read, and message expiration. You can change the information store maintenance times to avoid clashing with the backup process, to reduce the load on the server, or for other reasons. To view this setting from within the Exchange Administrator program, highlight the server under **Org**, **Site**, **Configuration**. Then click **File** and **Properties** from the pull-down menu and click the **IS Maintenance** tab. For more information, see Knowledge Base article Q159196, Title: XADM: Tasks Controlled by the IS Maintenance Schedule.

Compaction is offline defragmentation and disk space reclamation. It reorganizes things, consolidating data and free space. Performed with the EDBUTIL /D (ESEUTIL /D in Exchange 5.5) command, it reclaims space *and* reduces database file size, resulting in more free space on the disk. *Defragmentation* is online disk space reclamation and database defragmentation.

Question 11: What are the methods of defragmenting the information store databases?

Answer: Exchange Server automatically defragments the information store and directory databases without interrupting messaging. Online defragmentation, which always takes place in the background, marks items for deletion, and defragments database files, but does not compact files. You can also run the EDBUTIL utility (ESEUTIL in Exchange 5.5), but you must run it with the /D (defragment) option, which requires stopping the information store service. EDBUTIL /D *compacts* information store and defragments the database.

Question 12: How does the background compaction/defragmenting work?

Answer: When a user deletes a message that has no other pointers, it is marked for deletion and a background thread gives its space back to the database. For example, a message sent to five users is deleted from the private information store (and the space is marked for recovery) only when the last of its five recipients has deleted the message.

For more information see Knowledge Base article Q151495, Title: Priv.edb not smaller After Running Edbutil /D.

Question 13: Will Exchange perform information store compression on the fly? Should administrators do manual compression periodically?

Answer: No. Exchange performs defragmentation online but this differs from *compression*. (There is no compressor running all the time, but some compression takes place. Single instance message storage, for instance, uses compressed .RTF.) Compacting a database does not shrink it: if your PRIV.EDB grows to 1.2 GB and you delete some items, PRIV.EDB does not shrink even though there is new free space. Exchange reuses the space before adding to the file. So database defragmentation takes place in the background on a running server.

If you want to physically recover the free space on the disk, you must shut down a server for offline compaction. If you just want to reduce database file size, shut down services and run **edbutil** (**eseutil** in Exchange 5.5) with the **/d** option.

Question 14: How long does it take to defragment a database using EDBUTIL/ESEUTIL?

Answer: The databases are defragmented automatically as a background process, so unless you have to reduce the databases file size you should not have to run offline compaction (defragmentation with file size reduction).

For example, running EDBUTIL on an IBM 720 dual Pentium, RAID5 on a 3.4-GB private store requires about 150 minutes or approximately 45 minutes/GB. Rough calculations show: 16 GB x 45 minutes/GB = 720 minutes = 12 hours. System variables can change these numbers; 45 minutes/GB is a fast rate, derived on a high-end server, and it is a good idea to plan on a more conservative figure.

It is quite easy to run a test on your equipment and derive a more reliable figure, however.

The new Exchange 5.5 database utility, ESEUTIL, is more efficient than EDBUTIL and normally can defragment a database at the rate of 4 to 6 GB/hour.

The time to compact is a factor of how much data is in the database. A 15-GB database may have only 2 GB of data in it if there has been a recent bulk move or delete. For this database, the time to compact is based on 2 GB, not 15 GB. On some Exchange 4.0 systems, times to compact have been reported to be 6 to 10 hours for 10 to 12 GB. It depends on the fragmentation rate and other factors.

Some Exchange 5.5 systems, running on single Pentium Pro 200-MHz computers, report defrag rates of 5 GB/hour.

ESEUTIL and EDBUTIL read pages from the production database file and copy them into a temporary file. If the process is successful, the temporary file is renamed and used as the production database. You can redirect this file to another drive if disk space is required. To prevent a physical copy from one *physical* drive to another at the completion of ESEUTIL/EDBUTIL, redirect to a *logical* drive on the same physical disk as the .EDB files.

Question 15: What is the TEMP.EDB file and why is it created?

Answer: This stores in-progress long-term transactions and is sometimes used for temporary storage during online compaction.

Log Files and Circular Logging Issues

Question 16: What is the purpose of the logs?

Answer: The public and private information store and the directory service on an Exchange server have transaction logs for all transactions that occur on the database. They are for soft recovery (when the Exchange service was not shut down gracefully and the database files are inconsistent on startup), hard recovery (system crashes, hard drive failure, power fail, and so on), and restore after backup. The running server's PRIV.EDB file is always inconsistent because of the RAM database cache that is in RAM on the server. The server's consistent state is made up of the data in the .EDB file and the data in the memory cache on the server. If the server crashes and the cache is voided, the transaction logs automatically play back any transactions that had been entered but had not yet been committed to the .EDB when the crash occurred. The logs make it possible to restore the database without corruption.

A checkpoint file (EDB.CHK) keeps track of the transaction point—which transactions have been committed to disk. The process is relatively simple: the user requests an operation on the server (deliver mail, delete mail, read mail, and so on), the transactions associated with it are entered into the logs, and the operation is performed against the database memory cache. Later, the transaction is committed to disk in the background and the checkpoint for the log file is moved ahead. True database size, then, equals what is in the .EDB file *plus* those transactions in the log file *past the current checkpoint*. Shutting the server down cleanly commits all the data to the .EDB file and preserves the database at its true size.

Log files, even when they have been committed to disk, are still useful for such tasks as backup and restore. For example, suppose you took a backup yesterday and have been running ever since and you lose the database hard drive. To recover completely, you must restore yesterday's backup and then replay *all* log files from the backup forward.

Logs files consume disk space. You can ease this by doing one of the following:

- **Back up the server (online, full, or incremental)**—This writes all logs to the tape up to the checkpoint and then deletes the originals from the hard drive. You can restore the database completely by copying the database file from the tape, replaying the logs on the tape, and replaying the logs on the disk.

- **Use circular logging**—This option is not recommended. It saves disk space, but does it at the expense of recoverability. Circular logging wraps log files —a default of four—so you can restore very little of what happened since the last full backup. Most people consider this insufficient.

If you never want to lose a single bit of data, choose the first option and do frequent backups. This conserves disk space *and* allows complete recoverability.

A final point: if you look in the .EDB file directories, you will also see *.PAT (patch) files. Created during backups, these contain all changes that were entered after the backup began. The last step in the backup is to write the patch file for complete currency.

Here are the types of files you can expect to see in \exchsrvr\mdbdata:

PRIV.EDB	Private db file
PUB.EDB	Public db file
EDB.LOG	Current log file being written to
EDBXXXXX.LOG	Previous log files no longer opened or being used; new .LOG file every 5 MB
RES1.LOG RES2.LOG	Two log files reserved so that the server can be shut down cleanly even if the db or log file drive fills up
PRIV.PAT	Backup patch file for PRIV.EDB
PUB.PAT	Backup patch file for PUB.EDB
EDB.CHK	Checkpoint file

Question 17: What are the RES1.LOG and RES2.LOG files used for?

Answer: These log files are reserved for transactions that may be required to shut down the store and are used only when the transaction log hard disk fills up. They are a safety feature: if the hard disk is full, they provide enough space to record transactions from memory to disk. These files are always 5 MB each, regardless of the number of transactions in the other log files.

Question 18: How important is transaction log file redundancy?

Answer: Transactions usually are committed to the databases quickly, but on a very busy system they can accumulate as they wait to be written to the database files. If the transaction log drive crashes before they are written, they are lost. The log files are at least as important as the actual database. If a database has not been shut down cleanly (is not consistent) and the log files are lost, the database can be corrupted. In this case, even if you restore the database from backup you will lose some mail because you cannot play forward all the log files. Generally, if you are making regular backups, you are better off losing the database disk than the log files disk.

Question 19: What are lazy and non-lazy commits and how does Exchange use them?

Answer: After the transaction logs are flushed to disk, the transaction is durable and if you crash you can replay the logs and restore. *Non-lazy* commits are used for transactions that users expect will be locked down to disk quickly. For instance, when a user clicks the **Send** button, control comes back to the client and the message is locked down in the system through a non-lazy transaction. *Lazy* is used for transactions that are "expendable" if the computer crashes. An example is public folder replication—if it is lost in a crash, the out-of-synchronization state is detected and there is an automatic resend.

Question 20: When is a transaction committed to the database and how does this work? Is it first cached in memory so it is _virtually_ available, or is it necessary to read back from log files before writing to the database files?

Answer: The transactions are on both log files and fast memory pages. The log disk head is never moved back to read old data, so only sequential writes occur on log files. After transactions are written to the log file, an operation is considered complete and that data is immediately available in server memory before it is actually committed to the database files. Remember that an operation is not complete (that is, the client does not receive an acknowledgment) until all transactions are written to the transaction log (on disk).

Question 21: If an information store is in recovery after a system crash, is Exchange smart enough not to duplicate pre-existing transactions in the database and play back only uncommitted transactions?

Answer: Absolutely. Log files are read very quickly and if the transaction version number is already in the database, the transaction is not recommitted. Exchange detects if database was not shut down cleanly, and on startup it replays all transactions from the checkpoint forward.

Question 22: How can I measure transaction logging process performance?

Answer: Use Performance Monitor and select the object MSExchangeDB. Configure these counters:

- **Log Bytes Write/sec**—The rate at which byes are written to the log.
- **Log Checkpoint Depth**—A number that is proportional to the time that recovery will take after a system crash, depending on individual system performance. A data page may be cached and not flushed to the .EDB file for a long time if a lot of threads are using it. The earliest logged operations on the page may have occurred quite a while ago. The checkpoint depth is set to make sure that too many logs are not replayed when recovering from a crash. Pages are flushed if they contain operations before the checkpoint depth.
- **Log Sessions Waiting**—The number of sessions waiting on a log-commit to complete a transaction.

Question 23: With circular logging, at what point do the log files wrap around?

Answer: This default is four files, but if there is high server loading (large import/migration, public folder backfill, and so on), the checkpoint (and thus the window) can grow. They shrink back to four when the information store or directory service is stopped and restarted.

Question 24: If circular logging is enabled, can you play back logs (the ones that are present within the circular window)?

Answer: No. Circular logging on doesn't allow you to restore from a backup and play forward. You can restore only from backup, which means only to the point where that backup was taken. Exchange Server is configured with circular logging enabled by default. It is a good idea to disable it, protect disk loading through more regular backups and deletions, and provide yourself a safety margin wider than the four transactions of circular logging.

Question 25: What is the advantage of disabling circular logging?

Answer: Turning circular logging off provides additional recoverability because non-circular logging maintains a history of transaction logs for all transactions. These log files are purged only when a full or incremental online backup commits all transactions to the databases and backs up the databases. For example, say your last good backup took place on Monday and your database drive crashes on Thursday. If circular logging is turned off *and* your transaction log files are on a physical drive other than the crashed one, you can restore the Monday backup. If you *do not* select **Erase Existing Data**, the log files since the Monday backup are played back into the database, bringing it up to date to the point of the crash.

Circular logging maintains a window of transaction log files (usually four). When file4 is filled, a file5 is created and file1 is deleted. Therefore, the only transaction log files available for a restore are those in the window because the others have been purged.

Circular logging was developed to minimize hard disk loading. If you back up your system regularly (always a good idea), you don't need circular logging.

Question 26: If circular logging is disabled, how can I play back transaction log files if required?

Answer: With circular logging off, you can play back logs from the last full backup. The point to which you can play back depends on your backup schedule. For example, suppose you perform a full weekly backup on Sunday and perform incremental backups Monday through Saturday. If you lose a hard drive on Thursday, here is the best order to restore tapes:

1. Sunday full restore—don't start services.
2. Monday incremental restore—don't start services.
3. Tuesday incremental restore—don't start services.
4. Wednesday incremental restore—don't start services.
5. When you have completed all of these steps, start the information store.

If you restore all of these backup sets in one job then select **Start Services**, NTBACKUP will not start the services until all sets are restored. NTBACKUP restores the data and log files from Sunday, then adds in the log files for Monday through Wednesday. When the services restart, NTBACKUP replays all the log files from after the full backup on Sunday until the present time (Monday through Wednesday) plus any log files created after the Wednesday backup.

Incremental backups delete log files after they are backed up. *Differential* backups write the files to tape but do not then delete them. In the case above, if you had been performing differential backups you would not need to restore the Monday through Wednesday backup because you would still have those log files on the system (backup would not have deleted them).

Incremental and differential backups both copy all log files since the last backup and the EDB.CHK file; a differential backup does not delete the originals.

Question 27: What is the trade-off regarding location of log files? I have computers with a total of five disk drives. The first two are mirrored and the other three are set up in a RAID5 stripe set. Will it help performance if I do not mirror the operating system and dedicate one of those drives to transaction log files?

Answer: When it comes to concurrent users per server, the most important consideration in Exchange server performance is dedicating a physical drive for transaction log files. This is because transaction log files are written to sequentially and the read/write heads on a dedicated drive do not have to contend with other processes. However, it may not be worth sacrificing operating system drive redundancy by not using a mirror set for the first two drives. In this case it would be best to maintain the Windows NT swap file and the Exchange database files on the three-disk stripe set (RAID5) and maintain the transaction log files on the mirror set. With enough RAM in the system, there should be little disk head contention on the operating system drives and transaction log performance can be high.

Question 28: How do I clean up disk space if my log file drive fills up?

Answer: If lack of disk space prevents the information store from starting, an application event is logged in the Windows NT event viewer. The source of the event logged is EDB and the error test includes the error ID -1808. Here is how to free up disk space so that the information store can restart, and how to use Windows NT Performance Monitor to track disk space use so that this situation does not recur.

Monitoring Disk Space

Use Windows NT Performance Monitor to observe disk space usage on the drive containing the information store. The LogicalDisk object along with the "% Free Space" and "Free Megabytes" counters are used to monitor and trigger alerts when disk space is low.

Recovering Space Used by Log Files

Growing log files sometimes cause the information store or directory to run out of operating space. To prevent this, you can write the files to a different drive:

1. Open the **Server Object** properties page and click the **Database Paths** tab.

2. Change the path for the information store and directory store transaction logs and click **OK**.

3. Back up the Exchange server.

You can also use the Windows NT backup utility that ships with Exchange Server to perform either a normal (full) or incremental online backup. This automatically deletes transaction logs that have been committed to disk. If you never run the backup utility, log files continue to grow.

Circular logging conserves disk space by deleting transaction logs after they pass a checkpoint (usually four files). Typically, this deletes the majority of the potential log data. The total size of the active transactions is less than the total amount of RAM on a given computer, so circular logging affords complete system recoverability for hard and soft crashes but not for media failure. (If you lose power or the server crashes and the server can restart, the service will recover even if you had circular logging enabled. But if you lose the hard drive and need to restore from backup, you cannot recover all transactions if circular logging was enabled.) Incremental and differential backups use the transaction logs, so they are not supported on servers with circular logging enabled.

If possible, you can also delete any sample applications that you may have installed, to free up additional disk space.

For more information see Knowledge Base article Q163913, Title: IS or DS Stops Due to Lack of Drive Space for Log Files.

Backup and Restore Issues

Question 29: What are my options for single-mailbox backup and restore?

Answer:

- Use the procedures outlined in the section in Chapter 9 titled Single Mailbox Recovery. It shows how to do this by restoring the information store to a spare server.

- Use .PST files for mailbox storage and back these up.

- Use .OST files to replicate user mailboxes.

- Use a third-party brick backup program that allows single-mailbox restores.

Question 30: If I want to keep a spare server online for performing single mailbox restores, should I select Join Existing Site **or** Create New Site **when installing Exchange server?**

Answer: *Do not* select **Join Existing Site**. You must configure a single-mailbox restore server with the same organization and site name as the site from which you plan to recover single-mailbox data, but *do not* select **Join Existing Site** during install. Select **Create New Site** and use a unique computer name when installing Windows NT. If you join a site and then perform the single-mailbox restore procedures, you end up with two sets of mailbox data for the same site users after you restore the PRIV.EDB, causing undesired replication after you run the DS/IS consistency adjuster.

Question 31: I have some users who use .PST files and remain logged on at night. How can I back up their .PST files?

Answer: The client automatically disconnects from the .PST file after 30 minutes of inactivity and reconnects when activity resumes. Because of this feature, you can back up .PST files during periods of inactivity (usually at night) even while the client remains logged on to the Exchange server.

Question 32: Do I need a backup of the directory database to recover a server?

Answer: You need at least one backup of the directory service for each computer to be able to restore a server. No matter how old the backup is, the directory rebuilds itself on that computer and, after the restore, derives current information from the other directories in the site. After you have installed a new server in a site and it is replicated and up to date, it is a good idea to make a backup.

You should run **DS/IS consistency adjuster** after the directory has come back in synchronization after a restore, to make sure all objects in the information store on that server have been restored back into the directory. If you don't have a backup of the directory for a server to restore from (say the computer is destroyed in a fire) or if you lose the directory and have no backup, your only option is to delete the server from the site and reinstall it. This is not good: you lose all your information store data and a reinstall takes longer than a restore.

So it is a good idea to take a backup of the directory service as soon as you can after installing a new server. Store the backup in a safe place. Periodically (monthly, weekly, whatever you feel comfortable with) take another full backup and replace the older copy. This reduces the time it takes to re-synchronize the directory after a restore, and most users want their server back up as soon as possible.

Question 33: When restoring a server in a site, if I do not have a backup of the directory (DIR.EDB) for the server, can I backfill the directory from a replica on another server in the site?

Answer: No. You must have a backup of the directory for each Exchange server because each directory is unique. If you have the original directory backup, you can restore it and then backfill changes from another server in the site, but you must have a backup of the directory.

Question 34: If I have a good backup of the directory and information store and I am restoring a server to an existing site by reinstalling Exchange, should I select Create New Site **or** Join Existing Site **during the Exchange installation?**

Answer: Be sure to select **Create New Site**. *Do not select* **Join Existing Site**. When you restart the server after restoring the databases, the restored server automatically synchronizes with existing servers in the site—even when you select **Create New Site**. If you attempt to **Join Existing Site**, you will receive an error because other servers in the site already have knowledge of the server you are restoring (its name matches the name of the crashed server).

Question 35: Why do I need to back up the system after migrating users to the server or after an offline defragmentation or repair?

Answer: If a server crashes following a migration and you have not backed up the system, you need to redo the migration and this is time consuming.

Databases get a new log signature after they are defragmented or repaired. Thus, any logs generated after a defragmentation or repair are incompatible with a database from prior to the defragmentation or repair. If a disaster occurs between a defragmentation or repair and the next full online backup, you cannot restore the last full online backup and play forward through log files generated after the defragmentation or repair because their log signature has changed. Performing a full online backup immediately after a defragmentation or repair is a simple way to protect yourself in the event of a failure.

Question 36: I can't find the backup set on my tape. What might cause this?

Answer: Be sure to catalog the tape before using it to restore any data. Cataloging gathers information on the files on the tape and allows the restore process to take place.

▶ **To load a catalog of the backup sets on a tape**

1. In the **Tapes** window, select the tape with the catalog you want to load.

2. Choose **Catalog** by either double-clicking the tape's icon, clicking the **Catalog** button on the toolbar, or clicking **Catalog** from the **Operations** menu.

The tape is searched and a complete list of backup sets appears in the **Tapes** window with question marks (?) displayed in each of their icons to show that their individual catalogs have not been loaded.

Question 37: My tape drive is dead and I desperately need to back up the databases. How can I do this?

Answer: The method requires disk space. Shut down services. Copy PRIV.EDB and PUB.EDB from \exchsrvr\mdbdata (default installation point), and DIR.EDB file from \exchsrvr\dsadata (default installation point). You do not need to copy the transaction log files because all transactions are resolved when services are shut down normally. If you need to restore from this backup method, you should remove log files and EDB.CHK from the respective directories, copy back in the .EDB files, and follow the procedure for running **isinteg -patch**. When the services start up, a new EDB.CHK is created along with new transaction logs. Be sure to back up any files before you purge them. It is always advisable to work with Microsoft Technical Support on these matters.

Question 38: How can I back up Exchange servers from a Windows NT backup server that does not have Exchange Server or the Exchange Administrator program installed?

Answer: If you are copying files from an existing Exchange Server:

1. Rename or delete the current WINNT-WINNT-ROOT\SYSTEM32\NTBACKUP.EXE from the Windows NT backup server.

2. Copy Winnt-Winnt-Root\System32\NTBACKUP.EXE, EDBBCLI.DLL, and MSVCRT40.DLL from an Exchange mail server to the Winnt- Root\System32 subdirectory of the Windows NT backup server.

3. Copy Exchsrvr\Bin\EDBBACK.DLL from the Exchange server to the Winnt Root\System32 subdirectory of the Windows NT backup server.

If you are copying files from the Exchange Server CD-ROM:

1. Rename or delete the current Winnt-Winnt-Root\System32\NTBACKUP.EXE of the Windows NT backup server.

2. Copy NTBACKUP.EXE, EDBBCLI.DLL, EDBBACK.DLL, and MSVCRT40.DLL files in Setup\I386 (or MIPS or Alpha) on the Exchange Mail Server CD-ROM to the Winnt Root\System32 subdirectory of the Windows NT backup server.

Question 39: Is it a good idea to periodically perform a directory export?

Answer: It is not a bad idea, because it is a quick operation and it can save a lot of time if all directory backups are lost, a server is destroyed, or for some reason you cannot restore your directory database. You should never have to resort to this, but if you have to, you will be glad you have taken the time to do it.

Question 40: Should I disable SCSI controller write cache?

Answer: Yes. Unless your SCSI controller has a battery backup, this lessens the potential for data loss. If the *write through* flag is set at a programming level, Windows NT does not use buffers, so when a program receives a *write complete* signal from Windows NT, it is guaranteed that the write was completed to disk. This is critical to Exchange transaction logging. If write cache is enabled and data is placed in it, Windows NT informs the calling application incorrectly that the write has been completed. If there is a crash before write is completed, data can become corrupted.

Question 41: What is setup /r **used for?**

Answer: Setup /r allows you to recover an existing Exchange server to new hardware. It assumes that you have a valid backup of the Exchange databases and does not generate any default (empty) databases. After running **setup /r,** you must restore the Exchange databases from backup.

Setup /r is known as a *forklift upgrade*—use it to move a server to a different computer or to restore to a new computer. For example, your server is destroyed (asteroid) and you get a new computer to replace it. While you are at it, you want to move up to a newer, faster x86 or maybe to an Alpha computer. After you have the spiffy new computer, you need a full backup of the directory service and information store. If you are merely upgrading, you can shut down the original server and proceed. If your old server was indeed destroyed by a natural disaster and you don't have a full backup tape (because you kept it near the computer and it, too, was destroyed), you can just go on home.

But if you do have the full backup, you can proceed. First configure the new computer with Windows NT. Then run **setup /r** to install the Exchange software but not start any of the services or initialize the directory service into a site and so on. Now restore the backup to the new server and start the services. The new computer comes up and starts running just as the old computer did.

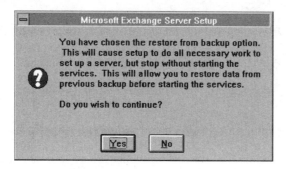

Initial screen when running setup /r

Note If you are performing a disaster recovery on an Exchange 4.0 server and need to load service packs, do not use **setup /r** to install the server. Loading service packs onto an Exchange server set up with **setup /r** requires running **update /r**, and this command is not supported by the Exchange 4.0 service packs.

Question 42: What are the implications for Windows NT when recovering an Exchange server in this scenario? The Exchange server is physically destroyed (from a natural disaster such as flooding). We have to recreate an identical computer and reload from the last backup (tapes are stored at an elevated location). The Exchange server is a member server, not a domain controller.

Answer: Refer to the Microsoft Exchange Server documentation.

You must regenerate the security identifier (SID). Each Windows NT–based computer requires a unique SID. Because flooding destroyed your original server, its SID is no longer valid. On the PDC in the domain in which the Exchange server resided, delete the crashed server definition and create one with the same name (use server manager for this.) This initializes a new SID and computer account in the domain Security Accounts Manager (SAM). When you install Windows NT on the recovery server and join the new server to the domain, a Local Security Authority (LSA) secret object is built for this recovery server and a new SID is assigned. A password for the secret object is generated and synchronized with the password for the computer account in the SAM. NETLOGON uses this password each time the server boots and connects to the domain. If you do not first delete and re-add the crashed server definition in the domain, you will not be able to join a server with the same name to the domain because NETLOGON will fail.

As long as you have access to the SAM from the original domain (you add the new computer as a server in the same domain), you can restore the Exchange directory. If the recovered server does not have access to the original SAM and you restore the directory, you will not be able to access any Exchange data after the restore because the Exchange directory uses SID information for authenticating access to objects and the restored SID information will not match SID information from the SAM in the new domain.

Refer to Knowledge Base article Q163686, Title: XADM: What to do if the Service Account is Deleted.

Question 43: Is it true that if you delete and re-add a computer name to the domain and then restore the Windows NT registry from tape, the local SID from the restored Windows NT registry will not match the new SID created in the domain?

Answer: Yes. You should delete and re-add the computer name of an Exchange-based server in the domain only if a new Exchange server is required for recovery. The Windows NT registry contains computer-specific information, so you must restore it to the same physical computer. (Restoring to a different physical computer is not supported. See Q139822, Title: How to Restore a Backup to Computer with Different Hardware.) This situation can arise if, for example, you replace the operating system hard disk (only) and then restore Windows NT.

Another issue: the Exchange directory database maintains information about Windows NT IDs in the domain (ACL information). If you cannot access the SAM from the original domain and you create a new SAM by installing a new domain and then restore the directory service, you create a disconnect between the object security in the directory (Exchange service account, user mailboxes, administrator account) and the new domain SAM. You will not be able to access any object in the Exchange directory.

Question 44: What if my Exchange server is a PDC and is destroyed or needs to be upgraded to a new computer?

Answer: In this case, promote one of the domain's BDCs to PDC. Deploy the recovery server and follow the procedures outlined in the section Full Server Restore in Chapter 9.

Question 45: Does the full server restore to a different physical computer require configuration as a BDC or PDC?

Answer: Not necessarily. The important step is to delete the computer account then re-add it to the production domain so that the recovery computer can get a new SID using the same name as the original production server.

Question 46: Is a differential restore needed only when both the transaction drive and the EDB drive require recovery?

Answer: Yes. If circular logging is disabled and transaction logs are intact, you can restore to the last full backup. When the service is started, logs from the point of the last full backup are played through the current EDB.LOG file to bring the database up to date. In this case, *do not* select **Erase Existing Data** during the restore—it erases the transaction logs and you will need to restore the last differential backup set.

Question 47: Why can't I start services between restoring a full and a differential or incremental tape or between sequential tapes being restored?

Answer: At the end of a restore, Exchange plays back all logs in sequential order and then sets the database to a new state. Suppose you are building forward and are going to run a Monday incremental tape restore followed by one from Tuesday. If you start the services after the Monday tape, a new state is set. Now if you try to run the Tuesday incremental restore, it fails because it requires that the database state be exactly what it was at the point of the Tuesday backup, and this is no longer true because a new state was set when you started the services. This Exchange feature prevents a restore from overwriting operations that have occurred on the database after services have been started.

General Questions

Question 48: How can I quickly shut down Exchange services without going into Control Panel? Sometimes services take a long time to shut down.

Answer: You can issue commands from a command line prompt to shut down services or you can use the batch file example below. To shut down the entire system from a batch file, call the *Windows NT Resource Kit* shutdown command (found in the *Microsoft Windows NT Resource Kit*) from the batch file. The idea is to shut down services in reverse dependency order. To shut down an MTA service that has spaces in the name, use quotes.

```
REM // stop all services
echo Stopping Services...
net stop MSExchangeMSMI
net stop MSExchangePCMTA
net stop MSExchangeFB
net stop MSExchangeDX
net stop MSExchangeIMC
net stop MSExchangeMTA
net stop MSExchangeIS
net stop MSExchangeDS
net stop MSExchangeSA
REM - call the shutdown command here (requires Windows NT Resource Kit)
```

Question 49: When I shut down services they keep trying to start themselves. Why is this and what can I do?

Answer: This is most likely caused by a server monitor session configured for the server in which you are trying to shut down services. Enabling **admin /t** (maintenance mode) at least one polling interval before you stop services notifies server monitor that subsequent polls of the server in maintenance mode will not result in alerts or alarms. You can then stop services and perform maintenance. When you are done, run **admin /t** again to re-enable monitoring. For a list of administrator program switches, run the command **admin /?** from the exchsrvr\bin subdirectory.

Question 50: Exchange 5.5 supports databases larger than 16 GB. Will I be able to reduce servers by consolidating?

Answer: Most definitely. Consolidation simplifies administration and allows users to have larger storage quotas, but consider these factors as you plan:

- Backup and restore time required using your existing hardware.
- Offline database maintenance time required (integrity check, defragmentation, and repair).

These also affect the amount of downtime in case of a disaster. Test your hardware to determine time requirements, and use them to determine optimum database size.

Finally, when you calculate users per server keep in mind Deleted Items Retention (the "Recover Deleted Items" feature in Outlook), which allows users to recover deleted messages. By keeping messages around after they have been marked for deletion, Item Recovery causes private and public information store databases to grow. Exchange does not count these messages when it calculates the amount of storage used by a mailbox.

Question 51: What is the impact of making Exchange Servers BDCs?

Answer: Configuring Exchange servers as BDCs can increase recoverability and reduce costs. It also, however, increases the Exchange server memory requirements.

Consider these scenarios:

- In a one-server environment, the Exchange server is a PDC and requires replacement. You can rebuild a Windows NT Server domain controller and restore the information store, but you cannot restore the directory service to a domain that does not have the original SAM.

- In a two-server environment, there is a PDC and the Exchange computer is a member server. The PDC crashes. There is no SAM. Same situation as above: you cannot restore the SAM (registry) to a different physical computer from a tape backup because each Windows NT registry is computer-specific.

- In a two-server environment, there is a PDC and the Exchange computer is a BDC. The PDC crashes. You can promote the Exchange server to PDC. If the Exchange server crashes, you can build a new BDC or member server with same name as the Exchange server and restore the information store and directory because you will be able to access the original SAM.

Configuring the Exchange server as a BDC can degrade memory performance, but it still may be an effective tactic for remote offices: it increases recoverability and can reduce costs because the Exchange server can authenticate Windows NT users and provide messaging services. Refer to the *Microsoft Windows NT Server 4.0 Networking Guide* (part of the Resource Kit) for information on domain planning and on PDC and BDC memory requirements.

Question 52: What are the third parties doing and what value do they add?

Answer: You can search for third-party solutions for Exchange at http://www.microsoft.com/exchange/partners/default.asp

C H A P T E R   1 1

Error Numbers and Maintenance Utilities

This chapter is a resource for your disaster recovery planning. It includes a reference list of error messages, details on command line switches, and sample server configuration worksheets.

Microsoft Exchange Error Numbers

In case you are wondering, we got this information by running the ERROR.EXE program located on the Exchange CD-ROM in \support\utils\i386. No, we didn't do it manually. We wrote a program to iterate!

Error number (decimal hexadecimal)	Error message
0 0x00000000	JET_errSuccess
-1 0xFFFFFFFF	JET_wrnNyi

System error number	Error message
-100 0xFFFFFF9C	JET_errRfsFailure
-101 0xFFFFFF9B	JET_errRfsNotArmed
-102 0xFFFFFF9A	JET_errFileClose
-103 0xFFFFFF99	JET_errOutOfThreads
-105 0xFFFFFF97	JET_errTooManyIO

Buffer manager error number	Error message
200 0x000000C8	WrnBFCacheMiss
-201 0xFFFFFF37	ErrBFPageNotCached
-202 0xFFFFFF36	ErrBFLatchConflict
-250 0xFFFFFF06	ErrBFIPageEvicted
-251 0xFFFFFF05	ErrBFIPageCached
-252 0xFFFFFF04	ErrBFIOutOfOLPs
-253 0xFFFFFF03	ErrBFIOutOfBatchIOBuffers
-254 0xFFFFFF02	ErrBFINoBufferAvailable
-255 0xFFFFFF01	JET_errDatabaseBufferDependenciesCorrupted

Version store error number	Error message
275 0x00000113	wrnVERRCEMoved

Directory manager error number	Error message
-300 0xFFFFFED4	errPMOutOfPageSpace
-301 0xFFFFFED3	errPMItagTooBig
-302 0xFFFFFED2	errPMRecDeleteded
-303 0xFFFFFED1	errPMTagsUsedUp
304 0x00000130	wrnBMConflict
-305 0xFFFFFECF	errDIRNoShortCircuit
-306 0xFFFFFECE	errDIRCannotSplit
-307 0xFFFFFECD	errDIRTop
308 0x00000134	errDIRFDP
-309 0xFFFFFECB	errDIRNotSynchronous
310 0x00000136	wrnDIREmptyPage
-311 0xFFFFFEC9	errSPConflict
312 0x00000138	wrnNDFoundLess
313 0x00000139	wrnNDFoundGreater
314 0x0000013A	wrnNDNotFoundInPage
-312 0xFFFFFEC8	errNDNotFound
-314 0xFFFFFEC6	errNDOutSonRange
-315 0xFFFFFEC5	errNDOutItemRange

Directory manager error number	Error message
-316 0xFFFFFEC4	errNDGreaterThanAllItems
-317 0xFFFFFEC3	errNDLastItemNode
-318 0xFFFFFEC2	errNDFirstItemNode
319 0x0000013F	wrnNDDuplicateItem
-320 0xFFFFFEC0	errNDNoItem
321 0x00000141	JET_wrnRemainingVersions
-322 0xFFFFFEBE	JET_errPreviousVersion
-323 0xFFFFFEBD	JET_errPageBoundary
-324 0xFFFFFEBC	JET_errKeyBoundary
-325 0xFFFFFEBB	errDIRInPageFather
-326 0xFFFFFEBA	errBMMaxKeyInPage
-327 0xFFFFFEB9	JET_errBadPageLink
-328 0xFFFFFEB8	JET_errBadBookmark
329 0x00000149	wrnBMCleanNullOp
-330 0xFFFFFEB6	errBTOperNone
-331 0xFFFFFEB5	errSPOutOfAvailExtCacheSpace
-332 0xFFFFFEB4	errSPOutOfOwnExtCacheSpace
333 0x0000014D	wrnBTMultipageOLC
-334 0xFFFFFEB2	JET_errNTSystemCallFailed
335 0x0000014F	wrnBTShallowTree
-336 0xFFFFFEB0	errBTMergeNotSynchronous

Record manager error number	Error message
400 0x00000190	wrnFLDKeyTooBig
-401 0xFFFFFE6F	errFLDTooManySegments
402 0x00000192	wrnFLDNullKey
403 0x00000193	wrnFLDOutOfKeys
404 0x00000194	wrnFLDNullSeg
405 0x00000195	wrnFLDNotPresentInIndex
406 0x00000196	JET_wrnSeparateLongValue
407 0x00000197	wrnRECLongField
408 0x00000198	wrnFLDNullFirstSeg
-408 0xFFFFFE68	JET_errKeyTooBig

Logging/recovery error number	Error message
-500 0xFFFFFE0C	JET_errInvalidLoggedOperation
-501 0xFFFFFE0B	JET_errLogFileCorrupt
-502 0xFFFFFE0A	errLGNoMoreRecords
-503 0xFFFFFE09	JET_errNoBackupDirectory
-504 0xFFFFFE08	JET_errBackupDirectoryNotEmpty
-505 0xFFFFFE07	JET_errBackupInProgress
-506 0xFFFFFE06	JET_errRestoreInProgress
-509 0xFFFFFE03	JET_errMissingPreviousLogFile
-510 0xFFFFFE02	JET_errLogWriteFail
-514 0xFFFFFDFE	JET_errBadLogVersion
-515 0xFFFFFDFD	JET_errInvalidLogSequence
-516 0xFFFFFDFC	JET_errLoggingDisabled
-517 0xFFFFFDFB	JET_errLogBufferTooSmall
-518 0xFFFFFDFA	errLGNotSynchronous
-519 0xFFFFFDF9	JET_errLogSequenceEnd
-520 0xFFFFFDF8	JET_errNoBackup
-521 0xFFFFFDF7	JET_errInvalidBackupSequence
-523 0xFFFFFDF5	JET_errBackupNotAllowedYet
-524 0xFFFFFDF4	JET_errDeleteBackupFileFail
-525 0xFFFFFDF3	JET_errMakeBackupDirectoryFail
-526 0xFFFFFDF2	JET_errInvalidBackup
-527 0xFFFFFDF1	JET_errRecoveredWithErrors
-528 0xFFFFFDF0	JET_errMissingLogFile
-529 0xFFFFFDEF	JET_errLogDiskFull
-530 0xFFFFFDEE	JET_errBadLogSignature
-531 0xFFFFFDED	JET_errBadDbSignature
-532 0xFFFFFDEC	JET_errBadCheckpointSignature
-533 0xFFFFFDEB	JET_errCheckpointCorrupt
-534 0xFFFFFDEA	JET_errMissingPatchPage
-535 0xFFFFFDE9	JET_errBadPatchPage
-536 0xFFFFFDE8	JET_errRedoAbruptEnded
-550 0xFFFFFDDA	JET_errDatabaseInconsistent
-551 0xFFFFFDD9	JET_errConsistentTimeMismatch
-552 0xFFFFFDD8	JET_errDatabasePatchFileMismatch
-553 0xFFFFFDD7	JET_errEndingRestoreLogTooLow

Logging/recovery error number	Error message
-554 0xFFFFFDD6	JET_errStartingRestoreLogTooHigh
-555 0xFFFFFDD5	JET_errGivenLogFileHasBadSignature
-556 0xFFFFFDD4	JET_errGivenLogFileIsNotContiguous
-557 0xFFFFFDD3	JET_errMissingRestoreLogFiles
558 0x0000022E	JET_wrnExistingLogFileHasBadSignature
559 0x0000022F	JET_wrnExistingLogFileIsNotContiguous
-560 0xFFFFFDD0	JET_errMissingFullBackup
-561 0xFFFFFDCF	JET_errBadBackupDatabaseSize
-562 0xFFFFFDCE	JET_errDatabaseAlreadyUpgraded
-563 0xFFFFFDCD	JET_errDatabaseIncompleteUpgrade
564 0x00000234	JET_wrnSkipThisRecord
-900 0xFFFFFC7C	JET_errInvalidGrbit
-1000 0xFFFFFC18	JET_errTermInProgress
-1001 0xFFFFFC17	JET_errFeatureNotAvailable
-1002 0xFFFFFC16	JET_errInvalidName
-1003 0xFFFFFC15	JET_errInvalidParameter
1004 0x000003EC	JET_wrnColumnNull
1006 0x000003EE	JET_wrnBufferTruncated
1007 0x000003EF	JET_wrnDatabaseAttached
-1008 0xFFFFFC10	JET_errDatabaseFileReadOnly
1009 0x000003F1	JET_wrnSortOverflow
-1010 0xFFFFFC0E	JET_errInvalidDatabaseId
-1011 0xFFFFFC0D	JET_errOutOfMemory
-1012 0xFFFFFC0C	JET_errOutOfDatabaseSpace
-1013 0xFFFFFC0B	JET_errOutOfCursors
-1014 0xFFFFFC0A	JET_errOutOfBuffers
-1015 0xFFFFFC09	JET_errTooManyIndexes
-1016 0xFFFFFC08	JET_errTooManyKeys
-1017 0xFFFFFC07	JET_errRecordDeleted
-1018 0xFFFFFC06	JET_errReadVerifyFailure
-1019 0xFFFFFC05	JET_errPageNotInitialized
-1020 0xFFFFFC04	JET_errOutOfFileHandles
-1022 0xFFFFFC02	JET_errDiskIO
-1023 0xFFFFFC01	JET_errInvalidPath

(continued)

Logging/recovery error number	Error message
-1024 0xFFFFFC00	JET_errInvalidSystemPath
-1025 0xFFFFFBFF	JET_errInvalidLogDirectory
-1026 0xFFFFFBFE	JET_errRecordTooBig
-1027 0xFFFFFBFD	JET_errTooManyOpenDatabases
-1028 0xFFFFFBFC	JET_errInvalidDatabase
-1029 0xFFFFFBFB	JET_errNotInitialized
-1030 0xFFFFFBFA	JET_errAlreadyInitialized
-1031 0xFFFFFBF9	JET_errInitInProgress
-1032 0xFFFFFBF8	JET_errFileAccessDenied
-1034 0xFFFFFBF6	JET_errQueryNotSupported
-1035 0xFFFFFBF5	JET_errSQLLinkNotSupported
-1038 0xFFFFFBF2	JET_errBufferTooSmall
1039 0x0000040F	JET_wrnSeekNotEqual
-1040 0xFFFFFBF0	JET_errTooManyColumns
-1043 0xFFFFFBED	JET_errContainerNotEmpty
-1044 0xFFFFFBEC	JET_errInvalidFilename
-1045 0xFFFFFBEB	JET_errInvalidBookmark
-1046 0xFFFFFBEA	JET_errColumnInUse
-1047 0xFFFFFBE9	JET_errInvalidBufferSize
-1048 0xFFFFFBE8	JET_errColumnNotUpdatable
-1051 0xFFFFFBE5	JET_errIndexInUse
-1052 0xFFFFFBE4	JET_errLinkNotSupported
-1053 0xFFFFFBE3	JET_errNullKeyDisallowed
-1054 0xFFFFFBE2	JET_errNotInTransaction
1055 0x0000041F	JET_wrnNoErrorInfo
1058 0x00000422	JET_wrnNoIdleActivity
-1059 0xFFFFFBDD	JET_errTooManyActiveUsers
-1061 0xFFFFFBDB	JET_errInvalidCountry
-1062 0xFFFFFBDA	JET_errInvalidLanguageId
-1063 0xFFFFFBD9	JET_errInvalidCodePage
1067 0x0000042B	JET_wrnNoWriteLock
1068 0x0000042C	JET_wrnColumnSetNull
-1069 0xFFFFFBD3	JET_errVersionStoreOutOfMemory
-1070 0xFFFFFBD2	JET_errCurrencyStackOutOfMemory
-1071 0xFFFFFBD1	JET_errCannotIndex

Logging/recovery error number	Error message
-1072 0xFFFFFBD0	JET_errRecordNotDeleted
-1101 0xFFFFFBB3	JET_errOutOfSessions
-1102 0xFFFFFBB2	JET_errWriteConflict
-1103 0xFFFFFBB1	JET_errTransTooDeep
-1104 0xFFFFFBB0	JET_errInvalidSesid
-1105 0xFFFFFBAF	JET_errWriteConflictPrimaryIndex
-1108 0xFFFFFBAC	JET_errInTransaction
-1109 0xFFFFFBAB	JET_errRollbackRequired
-1201 0xFFFFFB4F	JET_errDatabaseDuplicate
-1202 0xFFFFFB4E	JET_errDatabaseInUse
-1203 0xFFFFFB4D	JET_errDatabaseNotFound
-1204 0xFFFFFB4C	JET_errDatabaseInvalidName
-1205 0xFFFFFB4B	JET_errDatabaseInvalidPages
-1206 0xFFFFFB4A	JET_errDatabaseCorrupted
-1207 0xFFFFFB49	JET_errDatabaseLocked
-1208 0xFFFFFB48	JET_errCannotDisableVersioning
-1209 0xFFFFFB47	JET_errInvalidDatabaseVersion
-1210 0xFFFFFB46	JET_errDatabase200Format
-1211 0xFFFFFB45	JET_errDatabase400Format
-1212 0xFFFFFB44	JET_errDatabase500Format
1301 0x00000515	JET_wrnTableEmpty
-1302 0xFFFFFAEA	JET_errTableLocked
-1303 0xFFFFFAE9	JET_errTableDuplicate
-1304 0xFFFFFAE8	JET_errTableInUse
-1305 0xFFFFFAE7	JET_errObjectNotFound
-1307 0xFFFFFAE5	JET_errDensityInvalid
-1308 0xFFFFFAE4	JET_errTableNotEmpty
-1310 0xFFFFFAE2	JET_errInvalidTableId
-1311 0xFFFFFAE1	JET_errTooManyOpenTables
-1312 0xFFFFFAE0	JET_errIllegalOperation
-1314 0xFFFFFADE	JET_errObjectDuplicate
-1316 0xFFFFFADC	JET_errInvalidObject
-1317 0xFFFFFADB	JET_errCannotDeleteTempTable
-1318 0xFFFFFADA	JET_errCannotDeleteSystemTable

(continued)

Logging/recovery error number	Error message
-1319 0xFFFFFAD9	JET_errCannotDeleteTemplateTable
-1320 0xFFFFFAD8	errFCBTooManyOpen
-1321 0xFFFFFAD7	errFCBAboveThreshold
-1322 0xFFFFFAD6	JET_errExclusiveTableLockRequired
-1323 0xFFFFFAD5	JET_errFixedDDL
-1324 0xFFFFFAD4	JET_errFixedInheritedDDL
-1325 0xFFFFFAD3	JET_errCannotNestDDL
-1326 0xFFFFFAD2	JET_errDDLNotInheritable
1327 0x0000052F	JET_wrnTableInUseBySystem
-1328 0xFFFFFAD0	JET_errInvalidSettings
-1329 0xFFFFFACF	JET_errClientRequestToStopJetService
-1401 0xFFFFFA87	JET_errIndexCantBuild
-1402 0xFFFFFA86	JET_errIndexHasPrimary
-1403 0xFFFFFA85	JET_errIndexDuplicate
-1404 0xFFFFFA84	JET_errIndexNotFound
-1405 0xFFFFFA83	JET_errIndexMustStay
-1406 0xFFFFFA82	JET_errIndexInvalidDef
-1409 0xFFFFFA7F	JET_errInvalidCreateIndex
-1410 0xFFFFFA7E	JET_errTooManyOpenIndexes
-1411 0xFFFFFA7D	JET_errMultiValuedIndexViolation
-1412 0xFFFFFA7C	JET_errIndexBuildCorrupted
-1413 0xFFFFFA7B	JET_errPrimaryIndexCorrupted
-1414 0xFFFFFA7A	JET_errSecondaryIndexCorrupted
1415 0x00000587	JET_wrnCorruptIndexDeleted
-1501 0xFFFFFA23	JET_errColumnLong
-1502 0xFFFFFA22	JET_errColumnNoChunk
-1503 0xFFFFFA21	JET_errColumnDoesNotFit
-1504 0xFFFFFA20	JET_errNullInvalid
-1505 0xFFFFFA1F	JET_errColumnIndexed
-1506 0xFFFFFA1E	JET_errColumnTooBig
-1507 0xFFFFFA1D	JET_errColumnNotFound
-1508 0xFFFFFA1C	JET_errColumnDuplicate
-1510 0xFFFFFA1A	JET_errColumnRedundant
-1511 0xFFFFFA19	JET_errInvalidColumnType
1512 0x000005E8	JET_wrnColumnMaxTruncated

Logging/recovery error number	Error message
-1514 0xFFFFFA16	JET_errTaggedNotNULL
-1515 0xFFFFFA15	JET_errNoCurrentIndex
-1516 0xFFFFFA14	JET_errKeyIsMade
-1517 0xFFFFFA13	JET_errBadColumnId
-1518 0xFFFFFA12	JET_errBadItagSequence
-1519 0xFFFFFA11	JET_errColumnInRelationship
1520 0x000005F0	JET_wrnCopyLongValue
-1521 0xFFFFFA0F	JET_errCannotBeTagged
1522 0x000005F2	wrnLVNoLongValues
1523 0x000005F3	JET_wrnTaggedColumnsRemaining
-1524 0xFFFFFA0C	JET_errDefaultValueTooBig
-1601 0xFFFFF9BF	JET_errRecordNotFound
-1602 0xFFFFF9BE	JET_errRecordNoCopy
-1603 0xFFFFF9BD	JET_errNoCurrentRecord
-1604 0xFFFFF9BC	JET_errRecordPrimaryChanged
-1605 0xFFFFF9BB	JET_errKeyDuplicate
-1607 0xFFFFF9B9	JET_errAlreadyPrepared
-1608 0xFFFFF9B8	JET_errKeyNotMade
-1609 0xFFFFF9B7	JET_errUpdateNotPrepared
1610 0x0000064A	JET_wrnDataHasChanged
-1611 0xFFFFF9B5	JET_errDataHasChanged
1618 0x00000652	JET_wrnKeyChanged
-1619 0xFFFFF9AD	JET_errLanguageNotSupported
-1701 0xFFFFF95B	JET_errTooManySorts
-1702 0xFFFFF95A	JET_errInvalidOnSort
-1803 0xFFFFF8F5	JET_errTempFileOpenError
-1805 0xFFFFF8F3	JET_errTooManyAttachedDatabases
-1808 0xFFFFF8F0	JET_errDiskFull
-1809 0xFFFFF8EF	JET_errPermissionDenied
-1811 0xFFFFF8ED	JET_errFileNotFound
1813 0x00000715	JET_wrnFileOpenReadOnly
-1850 0xFFFFF8C6	JET_errAfterInitialization
-1852 0xFFFFF8C4	JET_errLogCorrupted
-1906 0xFFFFF88E	JET_errInvalidOperation

(continued)

Logging/recovery error number	Error message
-1907 0xFFFFF88D	JET_errAccessDenied
1908 0x00000774	JET_wrnIdleFull
-1909 0xFFFFF88B	JET_errTooManySplits
-1910 0xFFFFF88A	JET_errSessionSharingViolation
-1911 0xFFFFF889	JET_errEntryPointNotFound
2000 0x000007D0	JET_wrnDefragAlreadyRunning
2001 0x000007D1	JET_wrnDefragNotRunning

Utilities and Command Line Switches

NTBACKUP

Microsoft Exchange Server utility

Note Limit batch file command lines to 256 characters. Exceeding this limit can stop the process without warning or result in files not being backed up.

Syntax

ntbackup *operation path* [**/a**][**/v**][**/r**][**/d** *"text"*][**/b**][**/hc**:{**on** | **off**}] [**/t**{option}][**/l** *"filename"*][**/e**][**/tape**:{n}]

Parameters

Operation: Specifies the operation, **backup**.

Path

If you are backing up a drive, specifies one or more paths of the directories to be backed up.

If you are backing up Microsoft Exchange Server components, specifies the component and the server using the following format:

{DS *server* /IS *server*}
Server is the name of the server you are backing up preceded by two backslashes (for example, \\berkeley). *DS* indicates that you are backing up the directory, and *IS* indicates that you are backing up the information store.

/a

Causes backup sets to be added after the last backup set on the tape. When **/a** is not specified, the program reuses the tape and replaces previous data. When more than one drive is specified but **/a** is not, the program overwrites the contents of the tape with the information from the first drive selected and then appends the backup sets for the remaining drives.

/v
Verifies the operation.

/r
Restricts access.

/d *"text"*
Specifies a description of the backup contents.

/b
Specifies that the local registry be backed up.

/hc:on or **/hc:off**
Specifies that hardware compression is on or off.

/t {option}
Specifies the backup type. Option can be one of the following:

      normal – All selected files or Exchange Server components are backed up and marked as such on the disk.

      copy – All selected files or Exchange Server components are backed up, but they are not marked as such on the disk.

      incremental – Among the selected files or Exchange Server components, only those that have been modified are backed up and marked as such on the disk.

      differential – The selected files or Exchange Server components that have been modified are backed up, but they are not marked as such on the disk.

      daily – Among the selected files, only those that have been modified that day are backed up, but they are not marked as such on the disk. This can be useful if you want to take work home and need a quick way to select the files that you worked on that day. This option is not available when backing up Exchange Server components.

/l *"filename"*
Specifies the filename for the backup log.

/e
Specifies that the backup log include exceptions only.

/tape:{n}
Specifies the tape drive to which the files should be backed up. "n" is a number from 0 to 9 that corresponds to the tape drive number listed in the registry.

EDBUTIL

Description: Maintenance utilities for Exchange Server 4.0 and 5.0 databases.

Modes of operation:

Defragmentation: EDBUTIL /d *<database name>* [options]

Recovery: EDBUTIL /r [options]

Consistency: EDBUTIL /c *<database name>* [options]

Backup: EDBUTIL /b *<backup path>* [options]

Upgrade: EDBUTIL /u *<database name>* /d*<previous.DLL>* [options]

File dump: EDBUTIL /m[mode-modifier] *<filename>*

Defragmentation/Compaction

Description: Performs off-line compaction of a database.

Syntax

EDBUTIL /d *<database name>* [options]

Parameters

<database name> – Filename of database to compact, or one of /ispriv, /ispub, or /ds (see Notes below)

Options

None, or one or more of the following switches, separated by a space:

/l*<path>* – location of log files (default: current directory)

/s*<path>* – Location of system files (for example, checkpoint file; default: current directory)

/r – Repair database while defragmenting

/b*<filename>* – Make backup copy under the specified name

/t*<filename>* – Set temporary database name (default: TEMPDFRG.EDB)

/p – Preserve temporary database (that is, don't instate)

/n – Dump defragmentation information to DFRGINFO.TXT

/o – Suppress logo

Notes

The switches **/ispriv**, **/ispub**, and **/ds** use the registry to automatically set the database name, log file path, and system file path for the appropriate Exchange store.

Before defragmentation begins, soft recovery is always performed to ensure the database is in a consistent state.

If instating is disabled (**/p**), the original database is preserved uncompacted, and the temporary database contains the defragmented version of the database. Instating is running the process on the actual database. If it is disabled, the process does not touch the state of the original data.

Recovery

Description: Performs recovery, bringing all databases to a consistent state.

Syntax

EDBUTIL /r [options]

Options

None, or one or more of the following switches, separated by a space:

> **/is** or **/ds** – (See Notes below)
>
> **/l<*path*>** – Location of log files (default: current directory)
>
> **/s<*path*>** – Location of system files, (for example, checkpoint file; default: current directory)
>
> **/o** – Suppress logo

Notes

The special switches **/is** and **/ds** use the registry to automatically set the log file path and stem file path for recovery of the appropriate Exchange stores.

Consistency

Description: Verifies consistency of a database.

Syntax

EDBUTIL /c <*database name*> [options]

Parameters

<database name> – Filename of database to verify, or one of /ispriv, /ispub, or /ds (see Notes below)

Options

None, or one or more of the following switches, separated by a space:

> **/a** – Check all nodes, including deleted ones
>
> **/k** – Generate key usage statistics
>
> **/p** – Generate page usage information
>
> **/t<*name*>** – Performs a check on the specified table only (default: checks all tables in the database)
>
> **/o** – Suppress logo

Notes

The DS/IS consistency checker (replaced by the DS/IS consistency adjuster in Exchange 5.5) performs no recovery, and always assumes that the database is in a consistent state, returning an error if this is not the case.

The special switches **/ispriv**, **/ispub**, and **/ds** use the registry to automatically set the database name for the appropriate Exchange store.

Upgrade

Description: Upgrades a database (created using a previous release of Exchange Server) to the current version.

Syntax

EDBUTIL /u *<database name>* **/d<***previous***.DLL>** **[options]**

Parameters

<database name> – Filename of the database to upgrade

/d<*previous***.DLL>** – Pathed filename of the .DLL that came with the release of Exchange Server from which you're upgrading

Options

None, or one or more of the following switches, separated by a space:

/b<*filename*> – Make backup copy under the specified name

/t<*filename*> – Set temporary database name (default: TEMPUPGD.EDB)

/p – Preserve temporary database (ie. Don't instate)

/n – Dump upgrade information to UPGDINFO.TXT

/o – Suppress Exchange Server logo

Notes

This utility should be used only to upgrade a database after an internal database format change has taken place.

If necessary, this will usually only coincide with the release of a major, new revision of Exchange Server.

Before upgrading, the database should be in a consistent state or an error is returned.

If instating is disabled (**/p**), the original database is preserved unchanged, and the temporary database will contain the upgraded version of the database.

File Dump

Description: Generates formatted output of various database file types.

Syntax

EDBUTIL /m[mode-modifier] <*filename*>

Parameters

[mode-modifier] – An optional letter designating the type of file dump to perform. Valid values are:

h – Dump database header (default)

k – Dump checkpoint file

<*filename*> – Name of file to dump. The type of the specified file should match the dump type being requested (for example, if you are using **/mh**, then <*filename*> must be the name of a database).

ESEUTIL

Description: Maintenance utilities for Exchange Server 5.5 databases.

Modes Of Operation:

Defragmentation: ESEUTIL /d *<database name>* [options]

Recovery: ESEUTIL /r [options]

Integrity: ESEUTIL /g *<database name>* [options]

Upgrade: ESEUTIL /u *<database name>* /d*<previous.DLL>* [options]

File Dump: ESEUTIL /m[mode-modifier] *<filename>*

Repair: ESEUTIL /p *<database name>* [options]

Note log file path must be specified explicitly unless using /is or /ds options.

Defragmentation

Description: Performs off-line compaction of a database.

Syntax
ESEUTIL /d *<database name>* [options]

Parameters
<database name> – Filename of database to compact, or one of **/ispriv**, **/ispub**, or **/ds** (see Notes below)

Options
None, or one or more of the following switches, separated by a space:

/l*<path>* – Location of log files (default: current directory)

/s*<path>* – Location of system files (for example checkpoint file; default: current directory)

/b*<path>* – Make backup copy under the specified location

/t*<filename>* – Set new compacted database name (default: TEMPDFRG.EDB)

/p – Preserves old, uncompacted database in original location, and saves temporary database in default file (that is, don't instate)

/o – Suppress Exchange Server logo

Notes

The switches **/ispriv**, **/ispub**, and **/ds** use the registry to automatically set the database name, log file path, and system file path for the appropriate Exchange store.

Before defragmentation begins, soft recovery is always performed to ensure the database is in a consistent state.

If instating is disabled (**/p**), the original database is preserved uncompacted, and the temporary database will contain the defragmented version of the database.

Recovery

Description: Performs recovery, bringing all databases to a consistent state.

Syntax

ESEUTIL /r [options]

Options

None, or one or more of the following switches, separated by a space:

/is or **/ds** – (See Notes below)

/l<*path*> – Location of log files (default: current directory)

/s<*path*> – Location of system files (for example, checkpoint file; default: current directory)

/o – Suppress Exchange Server logo

Notes

The special switches **/is** and **/ds** use the registry to automatically set the log file path and system file path for recovery of the appropriate Exchange stores.

Integrity

Description: Verifies integrity of a database.

Syntax

ESEUTIL /g <*database name*> [options]

Parameters

<*database name*> – Filename of database to verify, or one of **/ispriv**, **/ispub**, or **/ds** (see Notes below)

Options

None, or one or more of the following switches, separated by a space:

/t<*filename*> – Set temporary database name (default: INTEG.EDB)

/v – Verbose output

/x – Give detailed error messages

/o – Suppress Exchange Server logo

Notes

The DS/IS consistency adjuster performs no recovery and always assumes that the database is in a consistent state, returning an error if this is not the case.

The special switches /ispriv, /ispub, and /ds use the registry to automatically set the database name for the appropriate Exchange store.

Upgrade

Description: Upgrades a database (created using a previous release of Exchange Server) to the current version.

Syntax

ESEUTIL /u <*database name*> /d<*previous*.DLL> [options]

Parameters

<*database name*> – Filename of the database to upgrade.

/d<*previous*.DLL> – Pathed filename of the .DLL that came with the release of Exchange Server from which you're upgrading.

Options

None, or one or more of the following switches, separated by a space:

/b<*filename*> – Make backup copy under the specified name

/t<*filename*> – Set temporary database name (default: TEMPUPGD.EDB)

/p – Preserve temporary database (that is, don't instate)

/o – Suppress Exchange Server logo

Notes

Use this only to upgrade a database after an internal database format change has taken place. If necessary, this will usually only coincide with the release of a major, new revision of Exchange Server.

Before upgrading, the database should be in a consistent state. An error will be returned if otherwise.

If instating is disabled (**/p**), the original database is preserved unchanged, and the temporary database will contain the upgraded version of the database.

File Dump

Description: Generates formatted output of various database file types.

Syntax

ESEUTIL /m[mode-modifier] *<filename>*

Parameters

[mode-modifier] – An optional letter designating the type of file dump to perform. Valid values are:

> **h** – Dump database header (default)
>
> **k** – Dump checkpoint file

<filename> – Name of file to dump. The type of the specified file should match the dump type being requested (for example, if you are using **/mh**, then *<filename>* must be the name of a database).

Repair

Description: Repairs a corrupted or damaged database.

Syntax

ESEUTIL /p *<database name>* **[options]**

Parameters

<database name> – Filename of database to compact, or one of **/ispriv**, **/ispub**, or **/ds** (see Notes below)

Options

None, or one or more of the following switches, separated by a space:

> **/t<filename>** – Set temporary database name (default: REPAIR.EDB)
>
> **/d** – Don't repair the database, just scan for errors
>
> **/v** – Verbose output
>
> **/x** – Give detailed error messages
>
> **/o** – Suppress logo

Notes

The switches **/ispriv**, **/ispub**, and **/ds** use the registry to automatically set the database name for the appropriate Exchange store.

Recovery will not be run.

ISINTEG

Microsoft Exchange Information Store Integrity Checker (ISINTEG) finds and gets rid of errors from the public and private information store databases. For additional information on using **Isinteg**, please see ISINTEG.RTF located on the Exchange Server 5.5 CD-ROM in the \SERVER\SUPPORT\UTILS directory. You can also refer to the chapter on troubleshooting in the *Microsoft Exchange Server 5.5 Resource Guide.*

Usage

isinteg -pri|-pub [-fix] [-detailed] [-verbose] [-l logfilename] [-test testname [, testname]...]

> **-pri** – Private store
>
> **-pub** – Public store
>
> **-fix** – Check and fix (default: check only)
>
> **-detailed** – Detailed mode performs additional tests than default test mode (default: non-detailed mode)
>
> **-verbose** – Report verbosely
>
> **-l** *<filename>* – Log file name (default: ISINTEG.PRI or ISINTEG.PUB)
>
> **-t** *<RefDBlocation>* – Location of temporary reference database that ISINTEG builds (default: the location of the store)
>
> **-test** *<testname1, testname2,...>* – Specifies tests to perform. (You can refer to the chapter on troubleshooting in the *Microsoft Exchange Server 5.5 Resource Guide* for a detailed list of test name parameters.)

isinteg -patch – Repair information store after an offline restore

isinteg -pri|-pub -dump [-l logfilename] – Verbose dump of store data

Sample Server Configuration Sheets

Hardware

Hardware item	Description
Computer model	
Display model	
S/N	
BackPlane	
CPU	
Hard disk(s)	
Floppy disk	
RAM	
NIC	
SCSI card	
CD-ROM	
Tape backup	

Windows NT Installation

Item	Description
Windows NT Server version	
Windows NT Server role	
Domain name	
Computer name	
Install directory	
Swap file	
Protocols	
Disk configuration	
Licensing	
Printer	
Special groups	

Item	Address
This machine IP	
Subnet mask	
Default gateway	

Microsoft Exchange Server Installation

Item	Data
Org name	
Site name	
Computer name	
Service account	
Service account password	
Connectors	

Exchange Performance Optimizer

During recovery, the Performance Optimizer ensures that the recovery server is tuned properly. Hardware being equal, performance should be similar after a full restore that reinstalls Exchange to a recovery server. Note that the Performance Optimizer log stored in c:\winnt\system32\perfopt.log does not reveal the specific settings chosen during optimization.

Server Name: _____

Estimated # users	X	Type of server	X	# in organization	X	Limit memory usage
1–25		Private store		Less than 100		____MB
26–50		Public store		100–999		
51–100		Connector/directory import		1,000–9,999		
101–250		Multiserver		10,000–99,999		
251–500				100,000 or more		
More than 500						

Component	Location
Private information store	\exchsrvr\mdbdata
Public information store	\exchsrvr\mdbdata
Information store logs	\exchsrvr\mdbdata
Directory service	\exchsrvr\dsadata
Directory service logs	\exchsrvr\dsadata
Message transfer agent	\exchsrvr\mtadata
Internet Mail Service files	\exchsrvr\imcdata

PART 4

Optimizing and Tuning the System

This section includes a collection of helpful ideas and procedures:

- A quick overview of backup/restore basics—Although this material is covered in several other places, this discussion looks at this important topic in the context of setting up regular procedures.
- How to prevent and handle the rare problem of a message storm.
- An examination of Exchange client optimization.
- How to assess, plan for, and deploy hot fixes, service packs, and upgrades.

C H A P T E R   1 2

Backup and Restore Basics

Backup and recovery of all or part of an Exchange server requires a basic understanding of where the data is, how it is backed up, and how it is restored. Recovery means restoring or rebuilding from backup files both static data, such as operating systems and application software, and dynamic data, such as databases and message logs. The preceding chapters have dealt with backup and recovery as elements of capacity calculation and disaster recovery. This chapter is an overview of the basics.

What to Back Up

This discussion is based on a Windows NT server that is dedicated to Exchange. This doesn't mean that the techniques and procedures discussed here are not relevant for servers supporting mixed loads, just that a certain amount of interpretation and adjustment are called for. (Configuration assumptions are outlined in the Partitioning Exchange Servers section below.)

You should back up two types of data.

Relatively Static Data

- The operating system, which in this case is Windows NT plus any service packs or hot fixes.
- Packaged application software (Exchange).
- Supporting software, such as third-party backup software, system management software, and so on.
- User application software, such as ASP applications, mailbox agents, and workflow software.
- Management scripts.

Dynamic Data

- Exchange databases and supporting files, such as directory and information store databases, transaction log files, and checkpoint files.

- The MTA "database."

- Message tracking logs.

Partitioning Exchange Servers

The Exchange Server configuration used in this discussion is a common structure widely used for dedicated Exchange servers. It involves three basic disk areas:

- **The system disk**—Supports Windows NT, swap file, Exchange binaries, other application software, and sometimes dynamic Exchange data, such as work areas or MTA database.

- **Transaction log disk**—A spindle entirely dedicated to supporting the Exchange database transaction logs. This is a fundamental piece of performance tuning advice, widely adopted in practice.

- **An extended database partition**—Frequently using hardware RAID5 to provide a large contiguous Windows NT partition that is protected against single-disk failures.

This type of partitioning is not a fixed rule, and details of where particular components are placed (MTA database, directory and store "work areas," and message tracking logs) depends both on individual preference and on the need to balance the load across the available disks.

Note This is a simple configuration that can be enhanced to use advanced hardware features to provide a high degree of protection for the different data areas. If you are concerned with availability of Exchange servers, consider protecting all disk areas using some form of hardware RAID, such as mirrored system and transaction log disks, and a RAID5-database partition.

Main Exchange Components

Here is the sample, partitioned Exchange server:

C:\ <System Disk>

D:\ <Transaction Logs>

E:\ <Exchange Databases>

The following table shows the distribution of some of the main Exchange components across these disks.

Description	Location	Files
Exchange binaries, templates, add-ins, and so on	C:\exchsrvr	
Directory database	E:\exchsrvr\dsadata	DIR.EDB
Information store databases	E:\exchsrvr\mdbdata	PRIV.EDB, PUB.EDB
Directory transaction log files	D:\exchsrvr\dsadata	EDB.LOG, EDBXXXXX.LOG
Information store transaction log files	D:\exchsrvr\mdbdata	EDB.LOG, EDBXXXXX.LOG
MTA database	C:\exchsrvr\mtadata	
Directory checkpoint file	C:\exchsrvr\dsadata	EDB.CHK
Information store checkpoint file	C:\exchsrvr\mdbdata	EDB.CHK
Directory work files	C:\exchsrvr\dsadata	TMP.EDB
Information store work files	C:\exchsrvr\mdbdata	TMP.EDB
Message tracking log files	C:\exchsrvr\tracking.log	

Other Components

An Exchange installation contains many other components that are not described above, such as Internet Mail Service data (including work area, logging area), directory synchronization agent (DXA) data, Microsoft Mail Connector postoffice, and others. Backup and restore of an Exchange server is a complex subject that involves a series of components that must fit together. This discussion intentionally focuses on the central components that are key to backing up and recovering the data held in user mailboxes and public folders.

Advantages of Partitioning

Partitioning an Exchange server is generally beneficial for performance and recovery. With proper backups, the partitioning structure described above can preserve all user data if any one partition is lost. Here are some examples:

- If the system disk is destroyed, it must be rebuilt before Exchange will work again, but user data is protected. If the system crashes, the databases will be inconsistent. However, a replay of all transaction logs will return the databases to a consistent state because the transaction log disk is secure. Because the checkpoint file, EDB.CHK, is presumed lost along with the system disk, *all* logs must be replayed.

- If the transaction log disk is destroyed, you lose the ability to roll forward from the previous online backup. However, you should not have to roll forward unless the database is also damaged, so no data is lost.

- If the database partition is damaged, then as long as the transaction logs are intact the databases can be restored from the most recent backup and all transactions replayed. The checkpoint file should also be intact (on the system disk), ensuring that only the "correct" log files are replayed, which guards against potential corruption involving a mismatch between restored database and log files on disk.

This layout also increases security, but you must understand the relationships between the different components. If you don't, you can inadvertently lose data when attempting to recover all or part of an Exchange server.

Exchange Backup Methods

Online versus Offline

Online   Requires that the respective service (information store or directory service) be running. It does not disrupt messaging on the Exchange-based server. You can include the Windows NT registry in the backup and can back up the directory service even if the information store is not running.

Offline   Requires that all Exchange services be stopped. This is files-based. You simply run NTBACKUP to capture all files on the drives you select, including the Windows NT registry.

Online Backup Types

Normal (Full)

This backs up the entire information store and directory databases. Transaction logs are backed up then purged, giving context to incremental and differential backups (see below).

Copy

This does not delete log files or change the context for incremental and differential backups. It takes a snapshot of the databases, without triggering or affecting other backup routines. It is handy when you want to reproduce a system state for testing.

Incremental

This backs up a subset of the information store or directory, writing only those changes made since the last full or last incremental backup (whichever was most recent). An incremental backup writes .LOG files (only) to tape, then purges them from disk, setting context for the next backup job. Typically an incremental restore requires a tape of the last full backup and tapes for each incremental up to the point at which the system experienced the outage. For example, suppose a full backup is performed on Sunday evenings and incremental backups every weekday. If an outage occurs on Friday morning, a full restore would be performed (restoring the system through Sunday evening) and then each incremental would be performed (restoring the system through Thursday). Services should not be started until the final incremental tape has been restored.

Differential

This backs up the changes in the information store and or directory since the last full (normal) or incremental backup, although most administrators choose not to mix differential and incremental backups in a series. A differential backup captures only .LOG files but it does not purge them from disk. If a transaction log and database restore is required, only two tapes are required: the latest full and the latest differential. If the transaction logs are intact since the last full backup, only the last full backup tape is required because the restore process plays back all logs from the last full through the current EDB.LOG file, thus restoring all transactions to date. *Do not* select **Erase Existing Data** when restoring in this case—it erases the log files to date.

Online Backup

The best way to secure Exchange databases is online backup, which should be an important part of your overall database management routine. It is the only regular procedure that systematically accesses every page in the database and detects any physical level corruption.

Internally, at the lowest level, each Exchange database is made up from 4-KB "pages," each with an associated checksum that the database engine checks every time it accesses the page.

Offline backup copies the physical file to the backup medium without checking for corruption. This can be troublesome: Exchange users sometimes detect a physical corruption and then find that it has been copied in every recent offline backup. Online backup detects corruption immediately, and you can go back to the previous backup and restore a working database.

Exchange Databases

To understand how online backup works, you need to know what an Exchange database looks like during normal running. Three main components are involved:

- The database (for example, PRIV.EDB).
- A sequence of transaction log files (the current log file EDB.LOG, plus a continuous numbered sequence of previous log files, EDBXXXXX.LOG).
- The checkpoint file (EDB.CHK).

"Normal" State of an Exchange Database

During normal running the database file itself (PRIV.EDB) is never "up to date." The store service manages a large in-memory buffer of store data and periodically flushes "dirty" or modified pages to disk. The details of the process are not important here. The key point is that there is a lag in updating the database file on disk.

This lag endangers database integrity if there is a sudden system failure. To protect against this, the dirty or modified pages are secured to disk by dumping the data into the transaction log files. This is much faster than updating the database (which incurs the overhead of updating multiple indexes, random disk access, and so forth) and allows Exchange to deliver consistently high performance even under heavy loads.

When the store service terminates gracefully, all dirty pages in the database buffer are written to the database file, bringing it to a "consistent" state before the service shuts down. If the store service terminates ungracefully (crashes), the database is left in an inconsistent or unknown state but all the information required to bring it back into a consistent state exists in the transaction logs. Replaying these logs against the database brings it back to the state it would have been after a clean shutdown.

Reading the Checkpoint File

The checkpoint file, key to the replay process, maintains information on the log files' sequence and their corresponding databases, and it points to where the data needs to be replayed to bring the store to a consistent state.

To dump the checkpoint file, use **eseutil /mk edb.chk**. Make sure you reference the right EDB.CHK. The current checkpoint reads out as three numbers—the first refers to the log generation (log file), and the second two refer to an offset within that file.

The offset numbers are not important here. The log generation number, however, is used to construct the log file name (for example, EDB020CA.LOG). If the generation number is one unit higher than the highest numbered log file, the checkpoint is within the current log file (EDB.LOG), which will be renamed using that generation number when it fills. In most systems, the checkpoint generation number will typically be several log generations behind the current log file.

Understanding Online Backup

Online backup works by streaming all the pages out of the database through the backup API. The system continues to operate while the backup is running, allowing normal user access, transaction log updates, and so forth. To prevent the loss of changes made to database pages that have already been backed up, modifications are recorded in temporary patch (.PAT) files (for example, PRIV.PAT) that are in turn backed up and then applied to a restored database before transaction replay begins.

Here's the online backup process:

1. Save the current checkpoint into another location in the checkpoint file: backup checkpoint.

2. Copy the database.

3. Copy the .PAT file.

4. Force a transaction log rollover by creating a new transaction log file.

5. Back up all transaction logs from the one pointed to by the backup checkpoint up to the one before the current one.

6. Delete all transaction log files before the one pointed to by the backup checkpoint.

The result is a sequence of log files on disk beginning with the first file needed to replay transactions into a restored database.

Restoring Exchange Databases

Typically, restoration fits one of two scenarios: restoring all databases if the whole disk partition is destroyed or restoring one database because of some less-disastrous hardware corruption.

If the PRIV.EDB file is the only one damaged on an Exchange server, for example, you can restore it in two basic steps:

1. Put everything on tape back on the disk.

2. Call Exchange to initiate recovery procedures.

This second step is triggered automatically by most backup and restore products. However, before you initiate the recovery it's best to carefully check that everything is where you expect it on disk. Restoring the wrong data in a recovery can cause irksome problems, so a quick check is worthwhile.

Immediately after the restore portion of the recovery operation, these files should be on disk:

- PRIV.EDB, restored from tape.
- PRIV.PAT, restored from tape.
- EDB.CHK, the checkpoint file, unaffected by the restore operation.
- EDBXXXXX.LOG files restored from tape.
- Sequence of log files right up to the current EDB.LOG, unaffected by the restore.

When the store service starts it initializes the database software, which checks the status of the data on disk. The "restore in progress" flag tells the database software that the database has been restored from tape.

The database software applies the modifications recorded in the .PAT file to the database, looks in the checkpoint file to find the checkpoint value *at the time of the last backup,* and then tries to open the log file referenced by the checkpoint. If successful, it begins to replay the transaction logs into the store until it reaches the last committed transaction in the current transaction log file (EDB.LOG). The database is now consistent and initialization of the store can continue.

Note This procedure varies depending on which parts of the Exchange server have been damaged and which files are restored. These variations are discussed in Chapter 9.

Backup Software

Exchange installs a version of NTBACKUP that allows you to back up Exchange databases online as described above or restore an online backup from tape. Some vendors sell Exchange modules (agents) that satisfy the requirements of the BackOffice logo program at the time of this chapter's writing. The list below is not exhaustive.

- Cheyenne ARCserve
- Seagate BackupExec
- Legato NetWorker

Advantages of Third-Party Solutions

There are some good reasons to choose one of these third-party solutions to back up your production Exchange servers:

- **Administration and management**—Some third-party products manage backup operations from a central location and provide extensive facilities for managing tape cycles, media pools, and so forth. In addition, they offer ready-made frameworks for managing Exchange backups that would have to be developed from scratch if you were using only NTBACKUP.

- **Performance**—There are significant performance differences between NTBACKUP and some third-party offerings, although these should diminish with advances in future Windows NT releases. At this time, however, the large store sizes possible with Exchange 5.5 can significantly impact backup performance. For example, compare backup rates on a high-end Intel (multiprocessor) server with Exchange databases striped across a seven-disk RAID5 partition and a single DLT 35/70 backup device (using Exchange 5.5 running on Windows NT 4.0 Service Pack 3 with DLT hardware compression turned on):

  - Using NTBACKUP: 6 GB/hour

  - Using ARCserve or BackupExec: Close to 30 GB/hour

- **Functionality**—You also should assess how the tools handle transaction log files managed by online backup. NTBACKUP backs up the Exchange databases and all log files from the checkpoint at the time the backup started. It then deletes all log files older than this file, leaving the system in a state where it can roll forward transactions after a restore of the backup. If the restore fails because of media corruption or some other reason, you must go back to the previous backup to get a consistent database, but you can no longer replay transactions because NTBACKUP deleted the files. If you use NTBACKUP, you should implement some additional processing and logic to back up the log files that may be deleted.

  Third-party solutions generally back up all the log files before deleting those older than the one pointed to by the checkpoint at the beginning of the backup. The restore operation puts all these files back, so if the restored database is corrupt (again, most likely because of media problems) a full roll-forward of transactions is possible after the previous backup is restored.

Backup and Restore Performance

Here's a recap of basic principles. After you select the software, backup and restore performance depends on two hardware configuration choices.

Select High-Performance Hardware

Start by choosing fast backup hardware (which in today's environment generally means DLT 35/70 drives) and a high-performance disk subsystem (hardware RAID implemented by a caching controller, bearing in mind that the cache must be properly protected by battery backup and ECC).

Fast backup hardware and a fast disk subsystem must be connected with plenty of bandwidth for backup and restore to work efficiently. For very high-capacity requirements this generally means that all the hardware will be in the same server or part of the same cluster (using the term loosely). You probably cannot maintain high backup rates (>30 GB/hour) over any form of network connection.

Balance Backup and Restore

There's no point buying fast backup hardware if the disk subsystem can't keep up. To maintain optimum performance, balance both sides of the backup and restore process by making it possible to read and write to multiple devices in parallel. For example, you can achieve better throughput with a 12-disk array than a 6-disk array. Hardware vendors have techniques for calculating throughput capabilities, so make sure they will support your backup and restore performance requirements.

Strategy for Online Backups

What role should the different types of online backups (full, incremental, and differential) play and how frequently should they be performed?

The first element of this strategy is to disable circular logging: it keeps only a sliding window of log files, enough to be able to make the database consistent after a crash. It discards older log files, which means you can never roll-forward from a backup. Circular logging has its uses. If you know that you will never need to back up an Exchange server (for example, because it is part of a test rig or is dedicated as a connector server) circular logging prevents the disk from filling up.

There are two basic approaches to online backup:

- Take a full online backup every night.
- Take a regular (weekly) online backup plus incremental or differential backups.

Regular Online Plus Differential

By themselves, incremental backups are insufficient. If they are all you have, recovery involves too many individual restore operations, increasing the risk that you will end up with a gap in the sequence of log files you need to replay.

A more workable scheme is to take a full online one night per week (say, Sunday night, when system usage probably is minimal) and a differential backup every other night. To recover using this material, you restore the online backup, restore last night's differential (which puts back all log files between Sunday and last night), then replay transaction log files.

Benefits:

- This usually uses fewer tapes.
- It decreases the chances that the backup contains a logical corruption of a store-level entity. (This method does not protect against a physical corruption of a database page.) Because a store-level corruption often takes a few days to become evident, detecting it with a periodic differential backup can prevent capturing it in a full backup.

Drawbacks:

- If your online backup detects a physical corruption (bad page), you must go back to the last online backup (from the previous week) and replay a full week's transaction logs. This takes a long time.
- Servers that host large user populations or that are very busy can build up large numbers of transaction log files (up to several hundred per day). Replay time varies with the number and type of transactions recorded in the log files, but a common replay rate is between 1 and 2 minutes per log file. (Test on one of your own systems to find your rate.) Replaying one day's transaction log files can take longer than restoring the full database!

Daily Online

The simplest strategy: take a full online backup of all Exchange databases every night.

Benefits:

- It is simple. Every backup is the same; every restore operation is the same.
- It offers the fastest way to detect and fix a physical corruption. If last night's backup worked, you know there was no corruption. If tonight's backup fails, you know the corruption was introduced today; all you need to do is restore last night's backup and replay today's log files.

Drawbacks:

- You could use a lot of tapes, especially if backing up to an array of DLT drives.

- If you detect a *logical* corruption, you may have to go back several days before you find a backup that does not contain it, then roll forward several days' transaction logs (assuming your backup software saved the log files). Overall this is likely to take longer than with a differential scheme.

Overall, daily online backups are the easiest and most useful method.

Restoring Exchange Server Components

This section offers sample techniques and discusses the issues involved in restoring different parts of an Exchange server. Most of the time, recovering a server does not require rebuilding the entire server from scratch, just fixing one component such as a system disk or database partition. Under these circumstances, try to restore service using the minimum number of steps. For example, if the system disk becomes corrupt but the database partition is intact, you can save a lot of time if you can recover without restoring the databases. If you do need to rebuild a server from scratch, refer to the procedure in the section Recovery of a Complete Server below.

A Thorough Restore Procedure

First you must understand exactly what needs to be restored. It is extremely unlikely that all partitions will have to be restored, and even if a server does have to be rebuilt it may be that most (if not all) disks can be moved across from the old server.

To decide what needs to be restored, you must know what is installed on the different partitions and how these relate to each other.

System Disk

The most important things on the system disk are:

- Windows NT (and all its configuration details).

- Exchange binaries plus some work files (for example the MTA "database" files may be on this disk).

- Third-party backup software, including configuration and state information.

Damage (soft corruption) to any one of these components (even Windows NT) probably will not require a complete restore of the system disk.

Transaction Logs

If your server is configured for optimum performance, the transaction log disk should contain nothing but the Exchange transaction logs. To recover, install an error-free disk, create the basic directory structure, and restart the Exchange services.

Together with the appropriate Exchange online backup tapes, the transaction logs enable you to roll-forward the day's transactions restoring a database without losing messages. Because the logs are used solely for Exchange database backup, they are managed by the backup software. After a successful online backup, the "old" transaction logs (those relating to the previous online backup) are purged. If the transaction logs partition becomes corrupt (because of something like a fault in the disk subsystem), you lose the ability to roll-forward after a database restore. This is not an issue, however, because you have to roll-forward only if there is database corruption or some other issue.

The important thing to understand is that transaction logs have no long-term value: they are useful only if they were created since the most recent online backup. There is no reason to backup or restore the transaction log files independently of the databases to which they relate.

Database Partition

The databases are the part of the backup most likely to require restoration. This is not because they are more likely to become corrupt than any other part of the system, but because a restore (plus transaction roll-forward) is generally the only (or the easiest) way to recover the databases after a corruption.

The procedure to recover a database on its own (that is, not as part of a complete system recovery) is extremely simple. For a very large store or a very busy server, however, it may take a long time to do two things:

- **Restore the database files to disk**—The time required depends on the database partition structure, but most current RAID5 controllers do not seem to be optimized for restore operations, providing restore rates of no more than 20 to 25 GB/hour.

- **Transaction log roll-forward**—The transactions' number and complexity depend what type of work users do. Test your system to get an idea of what sort of performance to expect. Roll-forward can take 1 to 2 minutes/log and on large servers (more than 1,000 users) hundreds of log files can be written in a day. It can take hours to roll forward a full day's log files.

You may have heard of "alternatives" to restore, such as running database repair utilities. These often are slower and cannot ensure a successful restore. To maintain Exchange database integrity, use systematic, verified backup and restore.

System Disk

If the system disk is completely corrupt and must be rebuilt from scratch, but the Exchange transaction log disk and database partition are both intact, you must restore the system disk so that it can come back up and "pick up where it left off" running the Exchange services.

This section is a discussion of issues specific to an Exchange server, not an exhaustive discussion of Windows NT disaster recovery techniques.

There are several approaches. The traditional one is to rebuild the system disk from scratch, by reinstalling and reconfiguring Windows NT, reinstalling Exchange, and so forth. If you are moving to new hardware, this may be the only approach that will work because of server naming, Windows NT user IDs, and so forth. Basically, this entails installing a server with the same organization and site name, but selecting **Create New Site**. This installs Exchange in preparation for a "reunion" with the existing or backed up databases, without premature interaction with existing site servers. Keep these two ideas in mind at all times:

- **Do not use the setup /r option**—Before reconnecting to the existing databases, you must apply all previous service packs and hot fixes to the replacement Exchange server. You can't do this using **setup /r**.

- **Never delete the failed server from the Exchange site**—This makes it impossible for the "same" server (that is, the new server running the old databases) to rejoin, forcing you to install again as a new server and then follow a (lengthy) process to recover user mailboxes.

A faster (and generally safer) technique involves restoring the system disk from a recent backup. Here is an example of this approach:

- Do a basic install Windows NT plus backup software that allows you to do little more than read the tape units.

- Using this installation, do a complete restore of the system partition off the most recent backup.

- Reset one or two things on the new system image.

- Reboot, automatically starting Exchange services.

You can do this only if your software backs up the Windows NT registry along with the system disk.

Before you boot to the restored image, you must do some housekeeping:

- If you have database work areas on the system disk, you must delete the directory and store service checkpoint files (c:\exchsrvr\dsadata\edb.chk and c:\exchsrvr\mdbdata\edb.chk) before starting the services. This prevents Exchange from trying to play the wrong transaction back into the directory and store databases, which might cause database corruption.

- Reset your MTA database files if they are on the system disk. Although you could probably omit this step, you should do it to prevent the MTA from trying to re-process data it was busy with at the time the server was backed up. Any messages in the database at that time will have been sent already, and a reset can avoid confusion (to the MTA and to users).

Transaction Log Disk

If the transaction log disk is totally destroyed or otherwise corrupted, the current transaction logs are lost. If this happens, Exchange probably is no longer running as a result.

These log files were created since the last backup, so no backup of them exists and there is no way to restore. This may or may not be a problem, depending on the state of the information store databases. If the store databases have not been corrupted by the event that damaged the log file disk, you can "fix" the transaction log disk and restart the store. This initializes a new set of logs and no data should be lost, although until you take another online backup you will not be able to restore and roll-forward transactions. (If you restore from the most recent backup, there is a gap at the start of the transaction log sequence, which would prevent replay.)

The process to "fix" the transaction log partition is simple: set up a new drive, map to the same drive letter, format it, and create the dsadata and mdbdata directories.

If for some reason you don't want to repair the log disk right away, you can use the Exchange Performance Optimizer to temporarily point the Exchange services at a different log file destination. As a rule, it is better to fix the transaction log disk immediately, to avoid having to take the server down later.

Exchange Databases

If there is a hardware failure, you may have to restore an information store database from an online backup onto an Exchange server that is still running. The process below assumes that the database work areas exist on the system disk.

The following parts of the system are involved:

- **System disk: c:\exchsrvr\mdbdata**—The store "work area." This directory contains EDB.CHK (the checkpoint file), which is very important because it contains a pointer indicating which log file the transaction roll-forward should start with, and TMP.EDB, which is not important because it contains temporary information used by the store service while it is running. TMP.EDB is not backed up and is deleted when the store service is shut down gracefully.
- **Transaction log disk: *<drive letter>*:\exchsrvr\mdbdata**—Contains log files. EDB.CHK contains a pointer to the log file containing the transaction most recently committed to the store database(s). Note this may not be the "current" (open) log file (which is always EDB.LOG) because the store service usually runs "behind" the transaction logs in committing things to disk. The transaction log disk should contain a continuous sequence of log files from the current file back to the file that contained the most recently committed transaction at the time of the last backup (as indicated by EDB.CHK).

  For example (a somewhat compressed sequence):

  EDB.LOG

  EDB0002B.LOG

  EDB0002A.LOG ➞ EDB.CHK points to last transaction in the store

  EDB00029.LOG

  EDB00028.LOG

  EDB00027.LOG

  EDB00026.LOG ➞ this was EDB.LOG at last backup

  EDB00025.LOG

  EDB00024.LOG ➞ EDB.CHK points to last transaction in store at time of last backup

  This directory also contains the files RES1.LOG and RES2.LOG, which act as reserved space to allow the store to shut down gracefully if the disk becomes full.
- **Database disk: *<drive letter>*:\exchsrvr\mdbdata**—Contains the store databases, PUB.EDB and PRIV.EDB.

Restore Using Third-Party Backup Software such as ARCserve or BackupExec

The restore operation is simple. Select the appropriate Exchange database as the source, leave the destination to default to the original location, and start the restore process. Generally, you should leave the backup software's restore defaults alone: *do not* select **Erase All Existing Data** or **Start Services After Restore**. The restore may take some time (even assuming a maximum restore rate of 20 to 25 GB/hour), after which the following should have happened:

- **No change to the system disk**—Nothing is restored here, EDB.CHK is untouched.

- **All the transaction log files backed up with the database are restored to the transaction log disk**—This would mean there is now an extended sequence starting from (say) EDB0001E.LOG (all the files from EDB0001E.LOG to EDB00025.LOG have been restored from tape):

  EDB.LOG

  EDB0002B.LOG

  EDB0002A.LOG   → EDB.CHK points to last transaction in store

  EDB00029.LOG

  EDB00028.LOG

  EDB00027.LOG

  EDB00026.LOG   → this was EDB.LOG at last backup

  EDB00025.LOG

  EDB00024.LOG   → EDB.CHK points to last transaction in store at time of last backup

  EDB00023.LOG

  EDB00022.LOG

  EDB00021.LOG

  EDB00020.LOG

  EDB0001F.LOG

  EDB0001E.LOG

- In addition, two files PAT.PRI and PAT.PUB are restored. They contain modified pages written to parts of the database already backed up by the backup software.

- Finally, one or both of the database files (PRIV.EDB or PUB.EDB) will have been restored to the database partition.

Finally, check the restore job logs to ensure that everything worked, and restart the information store service to trigger replay of the transaction log files (starting with the transaction in EDB00024.LOG pointed to by EDB.CHK).

Potential Complications

Loss of EDB.CHK

For example, if the system disk has also been rebuilt, it is likely that either you will not have EDB.CHK or you will have an inappropriate EDB.CHK (that is, a copy of the file not associated with the online backup you are restoring from). The wrong EDB.CHK is worse than no EDB.CHK because it provides the soft recovery function with the wrong pointers. In fact if you doubt the status of EDB.CHK, the best thing to do is to delete it.

If there is no EDB.CHK, soft recovery starts from the oldest log file it finds. Recovery processing checks every log entry as it goes, checking first to see whether the entry has already been committed to the store, before actually replaying anything. In other words recovery still works, it's just a little slower.

Gaps in the Sequence of Log Files

Recovery replays log files only until it comes to a break in the sequence. Never attempt to fool the system into "jumping" over a gap. Although procedures for doing this have been discussed on some public discussion groups, they *will* result in serious data corruption.

Under some circumstances, you may be faced with a gap at the *beginning* of a sequence of log files. This situation is actually very difficult (sometimes impossible) to detect, and if it exists, an attempt to replay logs will almost certainly result in database corruption. The only course under these circumstances is to delete all log files before attempting to start the store.

Need To Return to Older Backup

If the newly restored database is corrupt, you probably need to return to an older backup. As long as you return (each time) to the previous backup, you should still be able to replay the transaction logs (because with each restore your backup software restores all the log files deleted during the backup operation, maintaining a complete sequence). To get the logs to replay, you must delete EDB.CHK *before* starting the information store service (you get only one attempt at this).

If you "jump" backups (for example, go back two or more days, missing one or more online backups), you end up with a gap in the log file sequence and cannot replay past this gap.

Recovery of a Complete Server

A complete rebuild that involves restoring data from tape is likely only after a major disaster destroys the original server or prevents you from getting to the site. If a server is being rebuilt in place (for example, because of failure of a central component such as the motherboard), you should usually expect to be able to move all disks over from the old server and would not expect to restore anything from tape.

If you are rebuilding onto 100 percent identical hardware, the restore could be a simple rollup of the procedures discussed above. But if you are rebuilding on new hardware at a new location, there likely are some differences and the system image from the failed server will not work if restored directly to the new hardware. Here is a generalized procedure that has been tested under a wide variety of circumstances. You can also use this technique if the procedure described above for rebuilding a system disk does not work (because of a change in the underlying hardware or some other reason).

Here are the basic steps. (The procedure is described in more detail in Chapter 9):

1. Remove the failed server from the Windows NT domain.

2. On the new hardware install Windows NT, using the same server name as the failed server and joining the domain as a "new" BDC or member server.

3. Install any Windows NT service packs or hot fixes.

4. Install any necessary third-party backup software.

5. Install Exchange, creating a *new* organization and site with the same name as the existing site. If there were no service packs or hot fixes on the failed server, you can use the **setup /r** option. If there were service packs and other fixes, run a "normal" setup and *do not use* **setup /r.**

6. Apply any Exchange service packs or hot fixes.

7. Stop all Exchange services except the system attendant.

8. Delete all checkpoint files and transaction log files.

9. Restore the Exchange databases (directory plus both information store databases) from the backup.

10. Start the Exchange services and check that they run normally.

11. Install any additional software.

Note Under no circumstances should you delete the failed Exchange server from the Exchange site: it causes serious problems getting the replacement server back online.

Third-Party Procedures

A number of third-party products include "disaster recovery" modules for Windows NT. Typically these involve creating one or two diskettes to add to a set of Windows NT boot diskettes so that you can restore a system disk or entire server by simply booting off diskette and kicking off a recovery operation.

Be careful. It is unlikely you will find a product that synchronizes the disaster recovery backup with an Exchange online backup, so you will not be able to restore an entire Exchange server using this type of product. If you plan to use this type of software to recover a system disk (only) you should either:

- Make sure no database work areas or other Exchange dynamic data are on the system disk.
- Set all Exchange services to manual startup before taking the backup that will be used in conjunction with the disaster recovery product.

The danger is that you may automatically start Exchange and feed it "bad" data, which can stop soft recovery processing and corrupt the database.

CHAPTER 13

Preventing and Correcting Large Distribution List Message Storms

A message storm can start simply and completely innocently: a user sends a single message to a large distribution list. From this point, things can happen quickly. Recipients grind the messaging system down by using *Reply to All*. Frustrated by overflowing inboxes, users send *Reply to All* messages telling everyone to *stop*, which, of course, only makes things worse.

If you've ever experienced a message storm, you probably understand why it is often called *bedlam*. You probably also know that while it is going on it disrupts productivity system-wide and when it is over it ties up support staff as they clean it up. This chapter discusses how to prevent message storms on Exchange Server and what to do if one occurs.

Forms and Causes of Message Storms

Companies most at risk are those with more than one server and a large distribution list of more than 10,000 recipients. However, companies with under-powered servers and medium-size lists (5,000 or so recipients) are also at risk, especially if the links are slow and the users vocal. The Exchange configuration also affects how the problem spreads: in a single, big site, a message storm bogs down everything; in a distributed architecture, bridgehead servers usually bog down, effectively isolating the problem.

Message storms are not caused by sending a message to one or several large distribution lists (DLs). It is caused by a combination of large, unrestricted DLs and human nature. Users who would never consider sending a message to a DL such as *All Employees Worldwide* don't hesitate to use *Reply to All* against the same list to send messages such as:

- "Remove me from this list."
- "Please quit *Replying All* to this message."

Another form of message storms occurs when someone sends a message with *delivery* or *read* receipts to a large DL. Sent to unsecured DLs, this can lead to the worst form of message storms, one that generates enormous quantities of mail. To prevent this, clear the **Report To Message Originator** check box on your system's DLs.

Securing a Distribution List

You can educate users to reduce knee-jerk *Reply to All* messages, but human nature being what it is, the best answer is to lock down or restrict the largest DLs to those with a clear business need to use them.

▶ **To secure a distribution list**

1. In the DL's property page, click the **Delivery Restrictions** tab.
2. Add the mailboxes (or DLs containing the mailboxes) of the users who are allowed to send mail to this DL to the **Accept messages from** box.
3. Click the **Advanced** tab.
4. Clear the **Report To Message Originator** check box under Distribution List options.

Refinements

Other safeguards you can implement for large distribution lists:

- Restrict access to large DLs by creating security DLs. (This process is similar to using groups to assign Windows NT permissions.) This also reduces the amount of data that is replicated automatically whenever a DL is changed by restricting changes to smaller DLs.

- Add a DL into the **Accept Messages From** box of its own property page to restrict its use to its own members. This also prevents outsiders from spamming it. Security DLs (described above) should always be self-secured.

- Keep DLs to 5,000 or fewer recipients to improve DL processing. If you need a larger list of recipients, break it into sub-DLs and embed them in a master DL. The Microsoft Information Technology Group, which manages network and messaging traffic, has found that servers perform best at about 3,000 members per sub-DL. Use the ONDL tool found in the *Microsoft BackOffice Resource Kit* to split DLs.

- Place large DLs on the BCC line so that recipients who use *Reply All* won't be sending a message to the DL.

Cleaning Up After Message Storms

If you do experience a message storm, you must purge the messages from the system. Unfortunately, there is no way to globally remove all the redundant message copies from public or private information stores.

The Basic Concept

Each message (and all of its reply branches) contains a unique ID. The easiest way to intercept traffic and reduce a message storm is to use this ID to catch messages and replies while they are queued in message transfer agent (MTA) databases.

The Basic Process

1. Locate a copy of the problem message in a mailbox.
2. Log out of the MAPI client you are using (such as Exchange or Outlook).
3. Run MDBVU32.EXE (located on the Exchange Server CD-ROM in the Support\Utils\I386 directory).
4. Using the same profile from Step 1, log on to the identified mailbox.
5. Open the mailbox and drill down to the individual message.
6. Find the first 22 bytes of the message's PR_CONVERSATION_INDEX property.
7. Create a batch file to use with **FINDBIN.EXE** and the first 22 bytes of the property found in Step 6. You can find the **FINDBIN.EXE** tool on the companion CD-ROM under the \FindBin directory. More information is included below.
8. Use the batch file and FINDBIN to remove all queued copies of the message from backlogged servers. Repeat periodically until you have the storm under control.

Step-by-Step

Step 1

Find a copy of the problem message in your server mailbox using one of the Exchange or Outlook clients. If you didn't receive any copies of the problem mail, perform Steps 1 through 6 using another user's account.

Note the specific folder, such as the Inbox or Deleted Items folders, where a copy of the message resides.

Step 2

Exit and log off the Exchange or Outlook client.

Step 3

Open MDBVU32.EXE, which can be found on the Exchange Server CD-ROM (\SERVER\SUPPORT\UTILS\<*platform*>\MDBVU32.EXE).

This opens two windows: a minimized **MDB Viewer** window (which you can ignore) and an **MDB Viewer Test Application** window along with a modal dialog box.

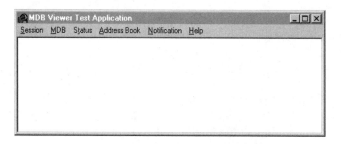

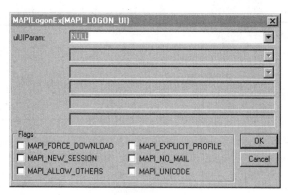

Step 4

Leave everything at the defaults and simply click **OK** on the **MAPILogonEx(MAPI_LOGON_UI)** dialog box. You are prompted to select a logon profile. Do so, then click **OK**.

Step 5

Select **OpenMessageStore** from the **MDB** menu.

If **OpenMessageStore** is unavailable (dimmed), press ESC and try again. It may take a little while before the option is available.

A dialog box prompts you to select a message store. Select your mailbox, then click **Open**.

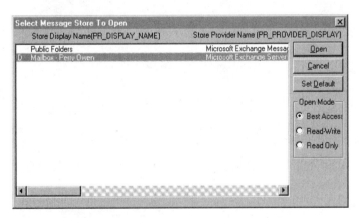

Select **Open IPM Subtree** from the **MDB** menu.

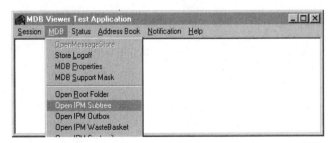

A **MAPI_FOLDER – IPM_SUBTREE** window is displayed. Double-click your **Inbox** (or whatever folder contains a copy of the message) in the **Child Folders** box.

A **MAPI_FOLDER – Inbox** window is displayed. Double-click a copy of the message in the **Messages in Folder** box.

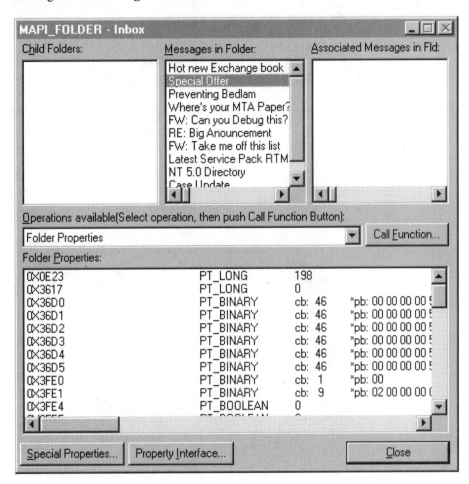

Step 6

After the **MAPI_MESSAGE** screen is displayed, scroll down and select
PR_CONVERSATION_INDEX in the **Message Properties** box.

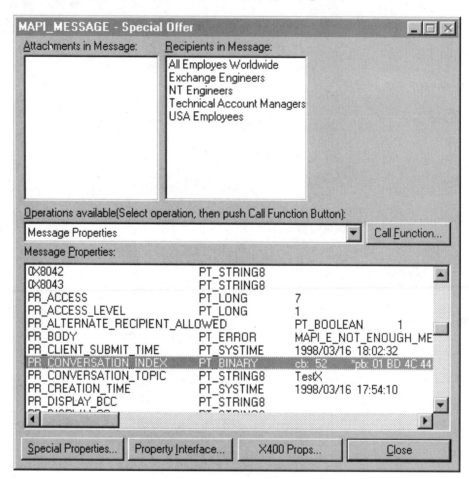

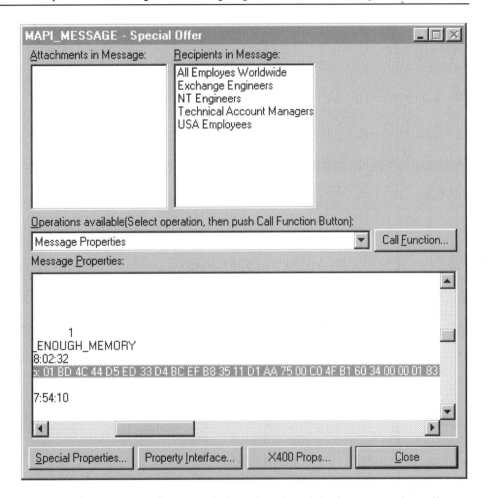

No matter how many replies or reply branches the original message takes, all copies start with the same 22 bytes in the PR_CONVERSATION_INDEX property.

Open Notepad or some other text editor and very carefully type in a copy of the first 22 bytes (44 characters in all) of the binary value in the PR_CONVERSATION_INDEX property. Do not include spaces. Double-check it carefully for mistakes. In the example above, the recorded value is: 01BD4C44D5ED33D4BCEFB83511D1AA7500C04FB16034.

Notice the *cb: 52* in the example PR_CONVERSATION_INDEX line above (Step 6, left figure). It shows that this copy of the message has been replied to six times. A message's PR_CONVERSATION_INDEX begins with 22 bytes; each reply appends 5 bytes. Subtract 22 from 52, divide 30 by 5, and you get 6, meaning that by the time this message branch arrived in your Inbox it had been replied to 6 times.

Step 7

Use a text editor and the binary value you recorded in Step 6 to construct a batch file (you can call it BEDLAM.BAT) similar to this example:

```
@ECHO OFF
IF NOT EXIST BEDLAM ECHO Creating BEDLAM directory.
IF NOT EXIST BEDLAM MD BEDLAM
IF NOT EXIST FINDBIN.EXE ECHO Can't find FINDBIN.EXE file in current
    directory.
IF EXIST FINDBIN.EXE FINDBIN
    01BD4C44D5ED33D4BCEFB83511D1AA7500C04FB16034 DB*.DAT BEDLAM
```

The FINDBIN Utility

FINDBIN syntax is as follows:

FINDBIN *<binary string> <files-to-search> [directory-to-move-files-to]*

FINDBIN searches files matching the pattern specified in the second parameter for binary content matching the string specified in the first parameter. If no third parameter is given, FINDBIN simply reports the results to the screen. If you include a directory as the third parameter, files matching the first two parameters are moved to that directory.

Using FINDBIN

FINDBIN is easy to use. If you run into problems, check your syntax, double-check your binary string, and be patient. If the cursor hasn't come back, it's still working.

Step 8

Perform the following sequence periodically on your system's MTAs until most replies to the problem message have been eliminated and users have been educated to avoid *Reply All.*

1. Identify your MTA's database directory. Inspect the server's registry for the **MTA database path** found at this registry key:

    HKEY_LOCAL_MACHINE\SYSTEM\CurrentControlSet\Services\MSExchangeMTA\Parameters\

2. Copy the FINDBIN.EXE and BEDLAM.BAT files to the MTADATA directory identified in this path

3. Stop the MTA and any dependent services.

4. Run the batch file from a Command box. This finds any files with the targeted message's PR_CONVERSATION_INDEX thread. When the cursor returns to the command box, the process has finished moving these files to the BEDLAM directory. You can now delete them.

5. Run MTACHECK. You can use switches other than /rp.

6. Restart the MTA.

Periodically repeat Steps 3 through 6 to remove new replies that have arrived at the MTA since the last time you ran the procedure.

CHAPTER 14

Client Optimization

This chapter focuses on one area of system optimization: Exchange client performance. All optimization tactics have in common the challenges presented by the extent and complexity of the Exchange messaging system, but they also are alike in that the mesh of relationships and interdependencies can be sorted out and approached logically. This chapter explains how to identify and define your needs and limitations, how to assess trade-offs, and how to boost client performance by fine-tuning a system that is already up and running. To help you accomplish these tasks, it details tools, techniques, and field observations that establish a foundation for optimization efforts.

The Big Picture—Consider the Entire Infrastructure

Before you can develop a plan to optimize client/server messaging performance within an existing Exchange system, consider the current environment, its overall performance, and any current issues with Exchange clients or servers:

- What are the levels of guaranteed service (the time it takes an e-mail message to travel between users)?
- Do any existing issues affect these service levels?
- Are there any current issues or user complaints with messaging client performance?
- Have all clients been upgraded to the latest versions of messaging clients?

Current Network Bandwidth Usage Trends

To optimize Exchange server responsiveness and performance, start by considering the current network environment and usage trends. The "Exchange Implementation: Client Traffic Analysis" white paper, located on TechNet and as a chapter in the companion book *Deploying Microsoft Exchange 5.5,* explains how to obtain and analyze this sort of data.

You can sometimes quickly resolve issues found by analyzing network e-mail. For example, suppose a large group of Exchange users at a remote office access their Exchange server mailboxes over a WAN link to corporate headquarters. If network usage analysis indicates that the link frequently becomes saturated during peak messaging activity, you can quickly improve performance by configuring a new Exchange server at the remote location.

Determining Message Volume Averages

To simplify load estimation and performance benchmarking, Microsoft has defined three basic user types, based on data collected on current mail systems.

User types and system requirements

Parameter	Light user	Medium user	Heavy user
Maximum Inbox size (in messages)	20	125	250
Other old mail processing (per day)	5x	15x	20x
Total sends per day (computed average)	7	20	39
Total receipts per day (computed average)	20	56	119

Load Simulator (LoadSim), a multi-client messaging emulation tool for the MAPI protocol, is available from the Microsoft download Web site at http://backoffice.microsoft.com/downtrial/.

Use it to study server capacity by testing servers under various message loads. The data you gather can help you evaluate server hardware performance, determine the optimum number of users per server (see Chapter 3), and identify performance bottlenecks.

Assessing the Current User Population

You need to create a description (profile) of Exchange users to identify and meet their needs. Users typically rely on e-mail mostly for messaging, but how much scheduling do they do, and how much public folder discussion do they participate in? Which groups of users communicate with each other the most? This evaluation requires that you understand how your organization is structured so you can identify permanent workgroups and provide for temporary ones. You also need to know what types of desktop hardware/software configurations exist and what applications are used by what proportion of the user base. All this information goes into an overall user profile.

Organizing Exchange Server Users into Workgroups

You can start by grouping Exchange users by organizational and network location to make sure that the users who e-mail each other the most are located on the same server—the same network segment wherever possible. After you verify the organization and network grouping, analyze each group to see what kind of information they generate and exchange. For example, how do they schedule meetings or share information? Do they use public folders? If so, how much? What are their performance requirements for mail storage and message delivery? Are there regular (predictable) hours of peak performance? For instance, do most users arrive at about the same time every day and download mail first, resulting in an intense load? You should also assess how knowledgeable they are about Exchange and, if possible, how receptive they are to retraining. Do they let mail folders grow? Can you get them to change this and other habits?

Understanding your user base can show you how to enhance performance, balance loading on servers and the network, and create a more stable system.

The first step in setting up workgroups is to look at your organizational chart and survey each LAN segment. Estimate the number of users in each group as you add it to your layout and name it. You should try to group users in ways that are easy to change, to provide you with flexibility later when you plan your servers and later still if you decide to revamp or expand your layout. The trick is to make groups large enough to ease the administrative and loading burdens, but small enough to be manageable segments of the user population. If you can achieve consistent sizes, that is good, but it may simply not be possible. Organizations usually grow and change over time, and you someday may have to reassess and redesign your workgroup structure to maintain an optimal Exchange infrastructure.

Client-Side Optimization Techniques

32-bit Operating System Workstations and Clients

For the most concise guide to optimizing Outlook clients in Windows NT and Windows 95, see the *Microsoft Outlook 97 Administrator's Guide* on TechNet.

Running Outlook with Exchange Server 5.5

Optimized for use with Exchange Server 5.5, Outlook 8.03 is not a maintenance release and does not contain new features, but it does allow Outlook to take advantage of Exchange Server 5.5 enhancements.

For more information on Outlook 8.03, see Knowledge Base article Q163743, Title: OL97: Information About Outlook Version 8.01. (The Knowledge Base is at http://support.microsoft.com/.)

For more information on Outlook 98 enhancements and performance improvements, go to http://www.microsoft.com/outlook.

Clean Up Existing Outlook Configurations

If it is not maintained and occasionally cleaned up, Outlook information can become cluttered and messy, affecting client performance. The table below lists some command-line switches you can use to clean up erroneous information and perform other tasks from the command line.

Outlook 32 startup switches

Command-line switch	Description
/CleanFreeBusy	Cleans and regenerates free/busy information
/CleanReminders	Cleans and regenerates reminders
/CleanViews	Restores default views
/ResetFolders	Restores missing folders for the default delivery location
/ResetOutlookBar	Rebuilds the Outlook Bar
/CleanSchedPlus	Deletes all Schedule+ data (free/busy, permissions, and .CAL file) from the server and allows the free/busy information from the Outlook Calendar to be used and viewed by all Schedule+ 1.0 users

> **Note** Microsoft provides the following command-line switch documentation
> without warranty of any kind, either express or implied, including but not limited
> to the implied warranties of merchantability and/or fitness for a particular
> purpose.

▶ **To use Outlook command-line switches**

1. In Windows 95 or Windows NT Workstation 4.0, right-click the **Outlook**
   icon, click **Properties**, and then click the **Shortcut** tab. In Windows NT
   Workstation 3.51, click the **Outlook** icon and then on the **File** menu click
   Properties.

2. In the **Target** box or the **Command Line** box, type the path to the Outlook
   application file, type a space after the path, and then type one or more of the
   command-line options listed in the table.

3. Paths are case-sensitive, and you must enclose in quotes any paths that contain
   spaces (such as C:\Program Files) with the switch *outside* the closing quotation
   mark. For example:

   "c:\program files\outlook\outlook.exe" /cleanfreebusy

16-Bit Operating System Workstations and Clients

The Win16 client runs under Windows 3.1 or Windows for Workgroups 3.11,
but because these operating systems do not natively support remote procedure
call (RPC) mechanisms, the client install includes the additional libraries needed
for RPC support.

Older client systems can present problems. Make sure Microsoft Windows and
Windows for Workgroups clients are running the most current TCP/IP protocol
stack and update client software. The most current updates for Windows 3.*x*
networking client software are on the Windows NT Server CD-ROM.

On Windows 3.*x* systems, the most common client performance issues are
memory constraints and the RPC binding order.

16-Bit Exchange/Outlook Client and Memory Issues

Most common symptom for 16-bit clients with insufficient memory: they start up
but cannot run any applications simultaneously. In Windows 3.1*x* and Windows
for Workgroups 3.1*x,* this problem usually indicates that there is not enough
memory below 640 KB (conventional memory) for the virtual machine to create
a task database (TDB), initiating "**Out of memory**" or "**Insufficient memory**"
messages.

When running Outlook under various combinations of Windows 3.1 and LAN Manager version 2.1 or 2.2, if you close enough applications to free up at least 490 KB of memory, Outlook will be able to save new messages larger than 2 KB.

Low-memory errors are more prevalent on Windows 3.*x* computers running IPX/SPX. Conventional memory is even more restricted on computers using Token Ring network cards. Computers running TCP/IP or NetBEUI have much lower conventional memory requirements. In most cases, you can eliminate memory problems by optimizing the configuration (loading network drivers high, using a memory optimization utility, and so forth).

How to Troubleshoot Windows 3.*x* Memory Issues

Follow these tips to reduce **"Out of memory"** errors when starting the Exchange Client.

- **Optimize conventional memory**—If you have MS-DOS version 6.0 or 6.2, use MemMaker or a similar utility.

- **Change the loading order for programs or drivers**—This can minimize memory fragmentation by changing where the fixed code is placed in the computer's memory address space.

- **Disable any applications that start automatically when you start Windows**—Check the WIN.INI file Load= & Run= lines and StartUp group.

- **Run Windows Setup and change to standard generic Windows drivers (VGA, no mouse).**

- **Use Program Manager (PROGMAN.EXE) as the Windows shell.**

- **Remove any third-party Windows drivers or virtual device drivers (VxDs).**

- **On Windows for Workgroups computers uncheck the option to use Network DDE**—This saves about 60 KB of conventional memory. (Click **Control Panel**, **Networks**, and **Startup**.)

- **Configure the computer to use TCP/IP or NetBEUI**—They use less memory than IPX/SPX.

- **Test a single computer using the Memory Valet utility**—See below.

How to Obtain and Use Memory Valet (MemValet)

If you optimize conventional memory and the 16-bit client still returns "**Out of memory**" errors, you might consider using the MemValet utility to force-load Windows 3.*x* .DLLs in upper, instead of conventional, memory, but do so only after normal troubleshooting methods have failed.

Note When you consider using MemValet, remember that it has not yet been specifically tested with Exchange or Outlook Windows 3.*x* clients and is considered an *unsupported utility*.

You can obtain Memory Valet at
ftp://ftp.microsoft.com/bussys/exchange/exchange-unsuped/Memval.zip.

How Memory Valet Works

Each Windows-based application that is initiated on a Windows 3.*x* system needs a task database (TDB) that has 512 bytes of fixed, contiguous memory and is in the low or conventional memory area (below 640 KB). When the Windows loader can't find space for a TDB it returns an "**Out of memory**" message.

When Windows starts, Memory Valet allocates a block of memory below 640 KB and "stripes" it with alternating 512-byte and 32-byte allocations. The 512-byte allocations are free, contiguous spaces available for use by applications. During operation, Windows memory manager puts non-TDB requests in the lowest address space possible, and when these allocations threaten the reserved TDB space, MemValet forces them into higher address spaces.

Memory and Using Microsoft Word for E-mail Messages

Windows 3.1 also sometimes returns low-memory warnings (or simply sends a blank file) when Microsoft Word is used to create Outlook messages. When this happens, close as many applications as possible and attempt to re-send the message.

RPC Files Installed for the Windows 3.*x* and MS-DOS Clients

Here are the necessary RPC network support files installed with the MS-DOS and Windows 3.*x* clients for Exchange server:

RPC network support files

RPC transport	MS-DOS client	Windows 3.*x* client
Named Pipes	RPC16C1.RPC	RPC16C1.DLL
TCP/IP	RPC16C3.RPC	RPC16C3.DLL
SPX	RPC16C6.RPC	RPC16C6.DLL
UDP	RPC16DG3.RPC	RPC16DG3.DLL
IPX	RPC16DG6.RPC	RPC16DG6.DLL
NetBIOS	RPC16C5.RPC	RPC16C5.DLL
DECNet	RPC16C4.RPC	RPC16C4.DLL
Banyan Vines	N/A	RPC16C8.DLL

Where:

- The letter "C" after the 16 indicates that the file is for client-side RPC using the listed transport.
- "DG" indicates data grams.
- The last number in the file name indicates the transport.

You can use this table to locate the RPC files on Windows NT and Windows 95. If one of the client-side RPC files is deleted, the client may not be able to use the listed transport to communicate with the Exchange Server by way of RPC.

Macintosh System Workstations and Clients

Memory and System Considerations

A Macintosh must have at least 12 MB of RAM (16 MB recommended) and 16 MB of virtual memory (more is recommended) to run Outlook and Outlook Calendar. Setting up Outlook requires a minimum of 8 MB of RAM and if this is all you have and the system consumes more than 3 MB, you need to remove Macintosh system extensions to run Outlook.

It is recommended that you use the Macintosh operating system 7.6 or later. For the Power Macintosh, you should set virtual memory to **ON** and to at least 1 MB more than the installed physical memory. For example, if a Power Macintosh has 16 MB of memory installed, set virtual memory to 17 MB.

Upgrading from a Previous Release of the Macintosh Client

The **Show Schedule** button sometimes disappears from the toolbar when you upgrade Macintosh clients. If this happens, pull down the **Tools** menu, click **Customize Toolbar** and then **Reset**.

Memory Problems When Using 24-Bit Color Display

Macintoshes using 24-bit color displays, sometime encounter **"Out of memory"** errors when using the **Print Preview** command in Outlook Calendar. Although there is no solution available for this problem, you can sometimes work around this by lowering the display resolution.

Connect Macintosh Clients to Exchange Server Using AppleTalk or TCP/IP

Both AppleTalk and TCP/IP are supported. With TCP for the Macintosh, use MacTCP version 2.06 or Open Transport version 1.0 or later. With dynamic host configuration protocol (DHCP) Open Transport 1.1 or later is recommended.

In environments where the Exchange server is local to the users and local network bandwidth constraints are not a concern, AppleTalk is a faster protocol and easier to configure on the client. When Macintosh clients access their server over congested or slow network links, they get better performance and fewer network timeouts with TCP/IP.

▶   **To connect Macintosh clients through AppleTalk**

1. Run Windows NT Services for Macintosh on the Exchange Server computer and establish an AppleTalk zone for that computer. Ensure you have installed the latest Windows NT service packs and updates. See the Windows NT Server documentation for more information on configuring Windows NT Services for Macintosh and establishing AppleTalk network zones.

2. Ensure Macintosh users know which AppleTalk zone to connect with.

3. Verify that the Windows NT MacFile name is the same as the Exchange Server name.

For Macintosh clients connecting through TCP/IP, verify that the Macintosh client can find the Exchange Server IP Address and NetBIOS name by using Macintosh-supported TCP/IP utilities.

Network Configurations and RPC Binding Order

When a Microsoft messaging client is installed, it sets the default RPC protocol binding order, which determines the protocol sequence the client will use to communicate with Exchange Server. When the client starts up, it tries to communicate with the Exchange server using the first protocol in the RPC binding order. If this attempt fails, the client tries the next and so on until it establishes communication with the server or runs out of protocols, at which point it displays an error message stating the fact and offers the user the option of working offline.

How you configure RPC binding order affects startup time and can improve it significantly. For example, suppose the client uses NetBEUI, IPX/SPX, and TCP/IP to communicate on the network, but only TCP/IP when connecting to Exchange server. Putting TCP/IP first in the binding order can noticeably improve client start-up performance.

The next table lists the protocol strings used in setting RPC binding order. *Ncacn* = Network Computing Architecture Connection.

RPC binding order strings

Protocol name	RPC protocol string
Local RPC	Ncalrpc
TCP/IP	Ncacn_ip_tcp
SPX	Ncacn_spx
Named pipes	Ncacn_np
NetBIOS	Netbios
VINES IP	Ncacn_vns_spp

This example string attempts to establish connections in this order: SPX, TCP/IP, NetBIOS:

RPC_Binding_Order=ncacn_spx,ncacn_ip_tcp,netbios

Clients Running Windows 95, Windows NT Server, and Windows NT Workstation

By default, Microsoft messaging clients on 32-bit operating systems attempt to connect to a server using this RPC binding order for Windows 95, Windows NT Server, and Windows NT Workstation:

1. TCP/IP
2. SPX
3. Named pipes
4. NetBIOS
5. VINES IP (Windows NT Server and Windows NT Workstation only)

    Use the registry editor to modify the binding order (remove any references to protocols not used) in this registry key:

    HKEY_LOCAL_MACHINE\SOFTWARE\Microsoft\Exchange\Exchange Provider.

    For example, use this string to direct the client to attempt connection in the order TCP/IP, SPX, NetBIOS:

    RPC_Binding_Order= ncacn_ip_tcp,ncacn_spx,netbios

Clients Running Windows 3.1 and Windows for Workgroups

By default, Microsoft messaging clients for Windows 3.*x* attempt to connect to a server using this RPC binding order:

1. Named pipes
2. SPX
3. TCP/IP
4. NetBIOS
5. VINES IP

In the EXCHNG.INI file (located in the \Windows directory), edit the [Exchange Provider] section listing the protocols used by the Exchange server and removing any protocols not used. For example, this EXCHNG.INI entry attempts to establish connections through TCP/IP then NetBIOS:

[Exchange Provider]

RPC_Binding_Order=ncacn_spx,ncacn_ip_tcp,netbios

Clients Running MS-DOS

The Exchange Client for MS-DOS attempts to connect to a server using this default RPC binding order:

1. Local RPC
2. Named pipes
3. SPX
4. TCP/IP
5. NetBIOS

Edit the RPC_BINDING_ORDER line in the MLSETUP.INI file to streamline the binding order. This file is installed automatically on the client or on a network share. For example, this directs the client to attempt connection in this order: local RPC, named pipes, TCP/IP, NetBIOS:

RPC_Binding_Order=ncalrpc,ncacn_np,ncacn_ip_tcp,netbios

A Few Notes on RPC Binding Order

You do not have to reboot the workstation after you modify the RPC binding order; just restart the messaging client and it will reread the binding order. To troubleshoot 32-bit clients, you can change the binding order in the registry (make sure the key has been fully committed to the registry) and then attempt a *check names* from the properties for the Exchange Server Service (by clicking **Control panel** and **Mail**). You do not have to exit REGEDIT or REGEDT32 when trying different bindings.

You *must* use commas between binding order entries. If you use "ncacn_ip_tcp;netbios" and attempt a "check names" as described above, you get this error:

The name could not be resolved. The Microsoft Address Book was unable to log on to the Microsoft Exchange Server computer. Contact your system administrator if the problem persists. <ok>

If you delete the entire RPC_binding_Order subkey or INI entry, the client reverts to the default binding order.

Using 16-Bit Outlook with IPX/SPX and NWLink

If a Windows for Workgroups computer has the IPX/SPX-compatible transport installed and the Exchange Server computer is running NWLink, Outlook cannot connect to the server using named pipes.

▶ **To solve this problem**

1. Copy the updated Windows for Workgroups redirector files to the Windows for Workgroups system directory and restart the computer. The files are included on the Windows NT Server 3.51 compact disc in the \Clients\Wfw\Update subdirectory and on the Windows NT Server 4.0 compact disc in the \Clients\Update.wfw subdirectory.

2. In the Windows for Workgroups SYSTEM.INI file, set DirectHost=Off in the [NETWORK] section, and then restart Windows.

You might see "**Out of Memory**" error messages when you start Schedule+ after a Microsoft messaging client for Windows 3.*x* has been started and vice versa. In some cases, "**Out of Memory**" or "**Insufficient Memory**" error messages might also occur in other applications after the client for Windows 3.*x* has been started, particularly in networked applications. Three conditions can cause this:

- The NET.CFG file has not yet been edited to include the entries as suggested in the README.WRI file on the Exchange Server CD-ROM.

- NET.CFG is improperly configured.

- The NET.CFG file you edited is not the one being used by the Novell NetWare real mode networking components.

To resolve, verify that the following lines are present in the correct NET.CFG file:

```
[PROTOCOL IPXODI]
IPX SOCKETS 50
SPX CONNECTIONS 50
```

Reboot the computer and either manually load the NetWare components or step through the lines in the AUTOEXEC.BAT file. After the computer loads the IPXODI drivers, the screen should acknowledge that IPXODI has been loaded with the above parameters.

Using 16-Bit Outlook with TCP/IP Stacks

If you are having performance issues with TCP/IP on Windows 3.*x* computers, try adjusting any of the tuning parameters related to sockets, window size, or buffer size. For example:

> Protocol TCP/IP:
>
> > tcp_window 8192
>
> Link Support:
>
> > Buffers 8 1500
>
> > MemPool 8192

After modifying TCP/IP parameters, restart the Windows 3.*x* computer for these changes to take affect.

Client Storage Options

Optimizing a user's mail storage configuration is highly dependent upon how the messaging clients are used. This section discusses the different mail storage options, as well as ideas on how to optimize them for user messaging needs.

Private Information Stores

User mailbox information is kept in the private information store on the server. This is good in that it is accessible to network backup software. But this benefit can be offset by an overburdened server if users have no limits on how much information they can keep.

Exchange messages sometimes are larger than messages sent with other messaging systems: they can use rich text formatting and attachments of OLE objects and documents. Consider this when you set private information store limits during a migration, especially from a text-only messaging system. As you obtain and analyze client usage data (such as percentages of messages addressed to multiple users and the average number of multiple users per message), you can develop more realistic storage quotas and refine the use of private information store.

If you allow users to keep mail indefinitely, you should encourage them to use personal folders on their local drives (where they are responsible for backing up their mail). If you allow them to store messages on the server, you should manage their accounts and enforce expiration dates for old messages. Encourage users to clean up their private information storage space to improve server performance. Here are some tips for users:

- Create a Personal Folder (.PST) file on your hard disk to archive folders/items that you do not accessed regularly. To set up this personal folder, click the **Tools** menu, and then click **Services**. Add a **Personal Folders** entry to the existing list of services, providing a path and filename *.PST. Then, create the folders in the .PST file, and manually copy or move items from your server mailbox to the file.

- If you are not using the Outlook Journal, make sure that you turn off the AutoJournal feature: On the **Tools** menu, click **Options**, and then click **Journal**.

- Delete items that are old or no longer relevant, including mail, calendar information, and tasks.

- Delete attachments from mail, and save only relevant attachments to your hard disk.

- Install the StorStat utility from your Outlook or Office CD. It analyzes your server store (or any .PST or .OST file) and gives complete statistics, including the number of items and folders and the size of your mail store.

▶ **To install StorStat**

1. Copy the entire StorStat folder from the Outlook or Office CD-ROM to your hard disk.

2. Quit Outlook.

3. Click **Start**, then **Run**.

4. In the **Open** box, type: **c:\storstat\storstat.exe_/email name**

Personal Folder Storage

The personal folder storage (.PST) file can contain folders, messages, forms, files, and other items. You can create any number of .PSTs for use within a single user profile, place them on the user's local drive or a network share, and designate them to receive incoming mail. An advantage is that users can store as many messages as they like without enlarging a private information store on the Exchange Server. Users generally are more aware of space limitations on their computers than on a network server, and the .PST file size shows them how much space they are using.

One disadvantage with .PST files has to do with the .PST being on the user's hard drive: it may not get backed up. If the hard drive fails, the user loses everything in the .PST. This can be avoided by storing the .PST on a network drive that is regularly backed up. Another disadvantage is that the .PST is password protected: if the user forgets the password, the contents cannot be recovered. Microsoft Premier Support recommends that users not set a .PST password. The information below is from Knowledge Base article Q150247, Title: Cannot Recover the Password of an Exchange .PST:

> Corporate IS policies often dictate where .PST files are stored. The files usually are captured in regular backups when stored on a file server, but this location becomes a disadvantage (the .PST becomes inaccessible) if the network connection is lost or the file server goes down. Network inaccessibility may also cause problems with the client, especially if new mail deliveries are attempted to the .PST.

> When the .PST is stored locally, access is never a problem but the file probably is not caught in scheduled backups and is not recoverable after a disaster. Users keeping local .PST files should be informed of this danger, and provided with a local backup mechanism or a procedure for copying the file to a network share periodically. Either way, backups become the user's responsibility.

> Security issues arise when more than one user uses locally stored .PSTs. Password protection is discouraged, so locally stored .PSTs become available to anyone using Exchange or Outlook. Of course, .PSTs on a file server also require that network or domain security allow access only to the authorized user.

> Even with these restrictions, personal information stores (.PSTs) are a good idea. If for example users have portable computers that they regularly use outside of the office, they will probably want to have access to their mail messages without being required to either dial in and work online or synchronize with a server (offline store/.OST file). For portable users, the best solution is usually to set up a .PST as their default message store.

Client storage options—advantages and disadvantages

Storage option	Advantages	Disadvantages
Private store	Universal storage method; user can access from multiple clients.	Complicated to restore single mailbox or specific messages (requires separate server); system administrators usually implement storage size limits.
.PST on server	Can archive file through network backup; recoverable.	Slower responsiveness; higher network load; .PST cannot be backed up if the user is connected and using the file.
.PST on local drive	Faster performance; storage flexibility for the user.	Difficult to automate backup; cannot recover data if user forgets password.

Storage quotas, disk space, and users per server

Storage strategy	Advantages	Disadvantages
Increase disk capacity of computers running Exchange Server.	Users can maintain most of their messages on the Exchange Server. Easier to maintain and back up critical user data. Users can create offline storage replicas (.OSTs) of server-based folders.	Requires adding and configuring hard disks on computers running Exchange Server. Must restore a backup of the server's entire private information store to recover a single mailbox.
Decrease number of users per server.	Users can maintain most of their messages on the server. Easier to maintain and back up critical user data. Users can create offline storage replicas (.OSTs) of server-based folders.	Requires buying additional computers to run Exchange Server. (Same number of users but fewer users per server means more servers.) Must restore a backup of server's entire private information store to recover a single mailbox.

(continued)

Storage quotas, disk space, and users per server   *(continued)*

Storage strategy	Advantages	Disadvantages
Maintain majority of mail messages in personal store (.PST) files.	No additional hardware expense on computers running Exchange Server. Providing that .PST files are stored on a file server and regularly archived, you can recover a single user's data without restoring the entire Exchange private information store.	Users must keep all data beyond their 20- to 30-MB storage quota in .PST files. Users must maintain their own .PST files locally or store them on a network file server. There is no single-instance storage so more total disk space is used within the organization (across the computer running Exchange Server and .PST host computer). There is no way to create offline storage (.OST files) for .PST files maintained on a network file server. If .PST is password protected and the user forgets the password, the file is unrecoverable.

Offline Folder Storage

An offline folder storage (.OST) file contains a local replica of a user's Exchange folders (private and public) and forms. The .OST is stored on the user's local drive and is synchronized with the Exchange Server copy for use offline. An .OST is specific to a particular mailbox and cannot be accessed by other Exchange users.

An .OST can contain a subset of the folders available to a user while logged on to the Exchange Server. When users are no longer connected to the server (as occurs when they use laptops outside the office), the .OST allows access to any public folders and folders in their private information store. Users can add messages to public folders, and send or delete mail from the private information store folders. The next time they log onto the server, the .OST and the server information stores on the server are synchronized but .PST files are not.

When to Use an .OST or a .PST

An .OST is the preferred method for offline storage, because it allows you to use public folders and organizational forms while working offline. Because an .OST acts as a copy of Exchange folders, the data is captured during standard Exchange Server backup procedures. In contrast, a local .PST in most cases can be backed up only by the owner. .PSTs allow you to use Exchange client remote e-mail features: download headers, move or copy messages, delete unwanted messages before downloading, and read new messages while others are downloading. The .OST synchronization process is not multithreaded.

Common .OST Procedures

The .OST benefits users who regularly take their portable computers away from the office. They should store their .OST on their local drive and learn the process for manually synchronizing .OST information with the information stores. Other procedures useful for .OST users are explained below:

New Client Installation

When the Exchange client is first installed, users are asked if they commonly work remotely. If the answer is yes, an offline store provider is set up and the file EXCHANGE.OST is created.

Existing Client Installation

If the Microsoft Exchange client already is installed, you can create an offline store using the **Offline Folder File Setting** button in the **Advanced** tab of the Exchange Server driver property page. .OST files are profile-specific, so if a computer has multiple users each needs an .OST file.

▶   **To add a folder to an .OST**

1. Open the folder property sheet by selecting the folder and clicking **Properties** on the **File** menu.

2. Click the **Synchronization** tab and select **Available Offline or Online**.

After a folder is made available offline, it can be synchronized with Exchange server by using the commands found under **Synchronize** on the **Tools** menu.

▶ **To disable an .OST**

1. Open the **Mail Control Panel**.
2. Select the Microsoft Exchange Server service and click **Properties**.
3. Click the **Advanced** tab, and then click **Offline Folder Settings**.
4. Click **Disable Offline Use**.

▶ **To compress an .OST**

1. Open the **Mail Control Panel**.
2. Select the Microsoft Exchange Server service and click **Properties**.
3. Click the **Advanced** tab, and then click **Offline Folder Settings**.
4. Click **Compact Now**.

▶ **To compress a .PST**

1. Open the **Mail Control Panel**.
2. Select the Personal Folders service and click the **Properties** button.
3. Click the **Compact Now** button.

The .OST Synchronization Log:

When .OST synchronization completes, a log file is placed in the Deleted Items folder. This file is useful when you are looking for synchronization details and errors. Here are some of errors and possible causes:

.OST error codes and typical causes

8004010f	The user has changed the language of the organization forms registry after the .OST was created.
	There are two Exchange Server sites: the first has an organization forms registry and the second does not. Unless public folder affinity is set correctly, users in the second site receive this error when they try to open the organization forms registry.
	The user added an organization forms registry, but it was later removed.
80030070	There is no space left on the disk. Free up hard drive space and try again. Can occur when trying to synchronize large attachments.
80040115	A network error prevented successful completion of the operation. Perform basic RPC network troubleshooting.

User's Mailbox Deleted from Microsoft Exchange Server

An .OST is stamped with a mailbox's unique ID, so if a user's mailbox is deleted and new one is created on the computer running Exchange Server, the .OST file will not synchronize with the new mailbox. To recover the data in the .OST you must follow the steps immediately *before starting the client online:*

1. Start the Exchange client in offline mode, using the same profile that was used before with the .OST.

2. Add a .PST to the profile.

3. Copy the messages to the .PST.

4. Create a new profile that connects to the new mailbox.

5. Move the messages from the .PST to the new mailbox.

Server-Side Optimization Techniques for Clients

Network Configurations

Ensure You Have the Latest Windows NT Server Service Packs Installed

Several known issues with earlier builds of Windows NT network support files can affect Exchange messaging client performance. Two such issues are detailed in Knowledge Base articles:

- Q161938, Title: Slow Exchange Client Logons Due to Resource Deadlock

- Q149819, Title: RPC Causes Exchange Server to Hang All Connected Clients

Using IPX/SPX for Client Connectivity to Exchange Server

In environments where Novell NetWare networking components are prevalent and most workstations are already configured and optimized for IPX transport, using IPX/SPX as the Exchange messaging protocol can be the best choice. Here are a few tips to consider when configuring Exchange servers and clients in this type of networking environment.

Exchange server name resolution within a Novell network:

When a Microsoft messaging client tries to locate the computer running Exchange Server on a Novell network, it tries to locate a file server for the Exchange Server name resolution. To do this, it sends out an SAP *Nearest Service Query* packet to get the nearest NetWare file server. There are two ways it should get a response:

- If the file server is on the same subnet as the client, it will respond.
- A router responds on behalf of the servers on a different subnet, if and only if the router believes that no servers exist on the client subnet.

After a NetWare file server is located, its bindery is used to translate the name of the computer running Exchange Server into an IPX address.

When an Exchange server is on the same subnet as the client but there is an internal IPX network number defined on this Windows NT/Exchange server, the Windows NT server acts as if it is on a different subnet. In other words, the Windows NT server running Exchange server acts as an IPX router and responds to the *Nearest Service Query* packet.

For more information, see Knowledge Base article Q162010, Title: XCLN: Exchange Server Name Resolution on a Novell Network.

Configuring the Exchange Server for IPX/SPX support

When configuring NWLink IPX/SPX on an Exchange Server to support more than one frame type, you must configure IPX to have a unique Internal Network Number. If you do not, Exchange clients using IPX/SPX can have trouble connecting to the server, especially when sending or saving messages with attachments.

▶ **To configure the Internal Network Number in Windows NT Server 3.51**

1. In **Control Panel**, double-click the **Network** icon.
2. Select **NWLink IPX/SPX Compatible Transport** in the **Installed Network Software** list.
3. Click **Configure**.
4. Type a unique 8-digit number in the **Internal Network Number** box.
5. Click **OK**.
6. Restart the Windows NT Server.

▶ **To configure the Internal Network Number in Windows NT Server 4.0**

1. In **Control Panel**, double-click the **Network** icon, and then click the **Protocols** tab.

2. Select **NWLink IPX/SPX Compatible Transport** in the **Network Protocols** list.

3. Choose **Properties**.

4. Type a unique 8-digit number in the **Internal Network Number** box.

5. Click **OK**.

6. Restart Windows NT Server.

Public Folder Server and Client Access Considerations

A Microsoft messaging client (that is a recipient of an Exchange server located in Site A), may temporarily stop responding or you may be prompted several times for domain credentials for the domain containing the Exchange site that owns the organization forms folder (Site B). The domain credentials dialog box also appears when you attempt to open a read receipt, delivery receipt, or non-delivery report (NDR).

You are prompted for domain credentials when all of these conditions are met:

1. An organization forms folder has been created.

2. A public folder affinity has been established between the sites.

3. No local instance of the organization forms folder exists.

Other symptoms include:

- Clients in Site A (remote to Site B) are slow when attempting to open a read receipt, delivery receipt, or non-delivery report, but clients in Site B can open these receipts at normal speed.

- When affinity is set to Site B, but clients in Site A have no physical LAN connection to servers in Site B, clients in both sites are slow when attempting to open a read receipt, delivery receipt, or non-delivery report.

- When the server containing the only instance of the organization forms folder is not available on the network, clients in Site A are prompted for domain credentials but Site B clients are not.

- When a trust does not exist between Windows NT domains in Site A and Site B and, a Site A client attempts to access the organization forms folder on a server in Site B, it is prompted for domain credentials for a valid Windows NT account in Site B.

This behavior is by design. To avoid it, ensure that each site has an instance of the organization forms folder for each site. For more information see Knowledge Base Q157632, Title: XADM: Client Hangs or Prompts for Domain Credentials.

Exchange Server, Internet Information Service, and OWA Clients

Clients using the Outlook Web Access components (Internet browsers accessing their mailboxes rendered into HTML) have performance considerations different than those discussed for Exchange and Outlook MAPI-based clients. Because most of the actual processing work is being done on the Exchange and Internet Information Service (IIS) servers, performance and optimization must also take place on the server side.

Outlook Web Access Network Traffic Considerations

- Initial client logon traffic is heavier than the MAPI-based client suite: approximately 65.195 KB per client logon is required.
- Send mail traffic generates a 30-KB response from IIS server regardless of message size (1, 10, or 100 KB) and message bodies are not compressed at the client.
- Very little item caching takes place on the client: no messages, only screen items (as per the browser defaults).

Outlook Web Access Advantages

- **No installation of client software**—Reduces administrative costs and resources substantially.
- **No configuration maintenance at the client end**—Reduces time and resources needed to administer the messaging environment.
- **Profiles are created as needed**—Easier to implement remote and roving client configurations.

Remember that client memory resources may be an issue (for example, many browser windows/session).

Outlook Web Access Server Sizing

IIS server can be configured separately from Exchange server, and multiple IIS servers can host access to a single Exchange Server. Servers perform all actions for clients (for example, HTML rendering), so a relatively low user/IIS server ratio is recommended. Here are some rules-of-thumb recommendations on the numbers of *light* users (sending 1 to –3 messages a day and replying to 5) per Exchange IIS server running OWA:

- Exchange 5.0 with IIS 3.0—300 concurrent users.
- Exchange 5.0 SP1 with IIS 3.0—600 concurrent users.
- Exchange 5.5 with IIS 4.0—800 concurrent users.

These figures were derived from this test configuration: P166 dual processor computer; 256-MB RAM; IIS and Exchange Server running together on the same computer. Running IIS and Exchange on separate servers lowers processor usage slightly.

Concurrent OWA users/server is limited by the addressable memory space available to Windows NT. Each MAPI session is allocated x amount of address space whether it is all being used or not. About 800 concurrent users will generally use all available space.

The figures above are for *light* users. Increasing the number of IIS servers increases the overall number of users, but not in direct proportion. Testing has shown that OWA can handle up to 800 light users/server; experience has shown that *heavy* users should be limited to about 100.

When you install Outlook Web Access, you should install the Windows NT hot fix that addresses problems with secure sockets layer (SSL) and memory leaks. You can download it at:

ftp://ftp.microsoft.com/bussys/iis/iis-public/fixes/usa/ASP/asp-memfix/.

The self-extracting zip file is called ASP-MEMFIX.EXE. For more information, see Knowledge Base articles:

- Q176245, Title: XWEB: VBScript Error when Accessing Outlook Web Access Server
- Q176246, Title: XWEB: Unexpected Behavior when Accessing Outlook Web Access

Server Capacity Planning

The good resource on Exchange server capacity planning is the white paper "Microsoft Exchange Performance: Concurrent Users Per Server" on TechNet. It defines the factors that influence Exchange server capacity planning and explains how they can affect an existing infrastructure. The white paper also shows examples of several basic user/server configurations and provides data (derived from tests run by the Exchange performance team) that you can apply to capacity planning projections or to comparative evaluation of your own concurrent users/server data.

Server Tuning and Maintenance

System performance under load varies greatly depending on hardware, operating system, and Exchange Server system parameters. For instance, your hardware configuration may allow you to enable or disable a secondary processor cache, or to configure disk striping, mirroring, and parity. Windows NT Server allows you to change various settings such as the amount of virtual memory available from the system page file, foreground and background application-tasking options, and network protocol settings, among others.

The best tool for verifying your optimization efforts is the Exchange Performance Optimizer. It runs automatically at the end of Exchange Server Setup, but it is extremely important that you rerun it every time changes are made to your server hardware, system settings, or usage patterns. For example, if you add RAM to a server, Exchange Server won't take advantage of it until you rerun Performance Optimizer. Refer to the *Microsoft Exchange Server 5.5 Resource Guide* for more information on using the Performance Optimizer.

C H A P T E R   1 5

Strategies for Service Packs and Version Upgrades

This chapter offers tips on deploying hot fixes and service packs, and on how to decide when to upgrade to a newer version of software. The discussion explains how to enhance, correct, or extend your system functionality while minimizing adverse impact to the Windows NT Server and Exchange Server messaging environment.

The Three Types of Enhancement

Service Packs

Service packs correct known problems and provide tools, drivers, and updates that extend product functionality, including enhancements developed after the product released. Exchange and Windows NT Server service packs can be released several times per year, and Exchange service packs can contain server and client updates. Exchange service packs go through broad regression testing on Microsoft's internal Exchange network, which handles about 3 million messages a day.

Hot Fixes

Hot fixes solve problems reported by customers. Before being released, hot fixes are extensively reviewed and tested by Microsoft and verified by the users who reported the problem. They are not regression tested. Hot fixes are very specific: you should apply one only if you experience the exact problem they address and are using the current software version with the latest service packs.

If Microsoft finds a significant problem affecting a wide range of customers, the hot fix is widely publicized with the suggestion that everyone upgrade. All hot fixes released after a service pack has been released are incorporated into the next service pack.

New Version/Release

New releases of Windows NT and Exchange Server are available about every 12 to 18 months, with service packs and .5 releases in between. These contain many new features as well as all fixes and features delivered in previous service packs.

Exchange Server and client versions interoperate completely, although older versions may require a service pack before an upgrade. For example, Exchange 4.0 requires SP2 to interoperate with Exchange 5.0 and 5.5, but Exchange 5.0 does not require a service pack to interoperate with Exchange 5.5. Exchange 5.5 servers will support Outlook 8.01 and 8.02 clients. Outlook version 8.03 is optimized for use with Exchange Server 5.5, but will operate with Exchange versions 4.0 and 5.0. Upgrade requirements and information on interoperability are always published in the product documentation and release notes. A new version of Exchange may require that you apply a Windows NT Server service pack before installing the new version of Exchange.

Strategies for Service Pack Deployments and Version Upgrades

Given the release schedule for service packs and version upgrades for both Windows NT Server and Exchange, you may decide it is unrealistic to perform constant testing and enterprise-wide updating of production server. This section outlines a strategy for balancing the need to keep the production environment up to date against the allocation of testing and operations resources.

General Guidelines

Strategies for software and hardware upgrades are central to managing and maintaining your production environment. Set aside time to test and evaluate service packs and new releases. Build a deployment schedule using the projected dates of new software version releases and service packs, which you can get from the Microsoft Web site (http://www.microsoft.com/exchange/) or from your Microsoft account team, including local sales representatives, system engineers, and Microsoft Consulting Services (MCS). Remember to be flexible when you plan, because release dates are subject to change. The point is to start assessing the impact of new releases and service packs as soon as possible so you can stay up to date.

If there are strong business requirements for deploying the latest release into your environment, you can proceed to testing. The process below assumes you have a test lab fully equipped to model your production infrastructure. You can refer to the companion book *Deploying Microsoft Exchange Server 5.5,* Chapter 3, for details on setting up a test environment. If you do not have a lab, the TechNet article "Tips for Deploying MS Windows NT Server 4.0 Service Pack 3" explains how to introduce service packs directly into production. It also has tips on how to obtain service packs and how to deploy them.

Evaluating Service Packs

If you report a problem to Microsoft Technical Support (MTS) that has already been fixed in a service pack, the solution is pretty obvious. You should review and evaluate every service pack in a lab as soon as it is released, even if you don't plan to deploy it immediately. Source of information on service packs include: TechNet, MTS e-mail, the support Web site http://support.microsoft.com/support/, and the Premier NewsFlash—if you have Microsoft Premier support—a newsletter that previews hot fixes, new releases, and service packs.

If you have neither MTS support service contract nor TechNet, you can get up-to-date information from http://support.microsoft.com/support/, and the latest service packs from ftp://ftp.microsoft.com/bussys/.

Evaluating New Releases

When new releases are announced, you should assess the effort of upgrading against the effort of deploying the latest service pack. Microsoft previews new software using Beta and Release Candidate programs. Although beta versions do not always have fully implemented functionality, Beta program subscribers can still use them to evaluate features and assess the degree of change the new release represents. The Release Candidate (RC) is very close to final code, and you can use it for integration testing in the lab and in-depth evaluation of the new features and functions.

The goal is to understand what the latest release of a product offers and determine if there are business reasons for deploying it. A test lab is a great advantage in this process. You can use a test lab to assess a new release for your production installation *and* to see how much effort is required to implement it. Premier Support customers with critical business needs can arrange through their Technical Account Manager (TAM) to install new releases early.

Refer to the companion book *Deploying Microsoft Exchange Server 5.5,* Chapter 3, "Setting Up a Test Environment," for more information on test lab procedures.

When to Deploy Service Packs and When to Wait

The basic question is simple: should you install a service pack for Windows NT or Exchange or wait for the next new version, investing your time and resources in deployment planning?

- Each service pack has a README.TXT file that describes its contents, reprints the Knowledge Base article titles for all the fixes, describes new features, provides installation instructions, and explains any known issues. You can conduct further research into issues in the Knowledge Base, which is supplied on TechNet and Microsoft's Web site http://support.microsoft.com/support/. Study the README carefully to determine if the service pack will improve your environment or correct a critical problem, and if its benefits outweigh the risks and effort of deployment. These considerations can help you decide:

- If you are not experiencing any of the problems a service pack fixes or if the problems are low-impact, you may decide not to deploy. If you can, however, you should still install it on a couple of servers in your lab to get first-hand installation experience.

- If you are not experiencing problems and a new Exchange or Windows NT release is expected within six months, you might as well wait for the new version. New releases include service packs to date.

- If you are two or three service packs behind, you should update your environment. Schedule periodic service pack upgrades as part of your operations maintenance and try never to be more than two service packs behind.

- If you get into the habit of always installing service packs in the lab, you are better prepared to deploy them throughout your organization. For instance, if you encounter a serious problem that is not addressed in a current or coming service pack, there probably is a hot fix available. But you can't deploy a hot fix until you have all current service packs installed. Certain recovery operations require that new servers have the same service packs installed as the server they are replacing. If you have installed and tested service packs in the lab, you are ready for all contingencies.

- Chapter 3 of *Deploying Microsoft Exchange Server 5.5* contains a table that shows how to assess service pack features for functionality, effort, and risk. Proceeding feature by feature can simplify the decision process.

Testing Service Packs and New Releases

Testing Service Packs

Service packs in general are cumulative. For example, Service Pack (SP) 3 contains all the fixes in SPs 1 and 2. Always use the README file to check the service pack's contents, its installation prerequisites, and the Knowledge Base articles detailing the issues it addresses. Use this information to develop test plans.

Coordinate the testing and installation schedules for Windows NT and Exchange service packs as much as possible. Any Exchange dependencies on Windows NT service packs will be documented in the README and in the Release Notes and Exchange documentation. Introduce each service pack separately in the lab to assess its individual impact, and if there are no problems test for any issues between the Windows NT and Exchange service packs by installing them at the same time in the lab. A simultaneous installation reduces server downtime. During testing, watch for risks to your environment. Other good ideas:

- Install the service pack on at least one lab server to test coexistence with other servers even if the fixes and features are not needed immediately. Day-to-day use in the lab sometimes reveals problems better than specific tests. Lab experience makes it easier to install the service pack in the production environment, and this can be a great advantage if a critical problem requires a rapid SP installation.

- Coordinate service pack testing with other IS groups that may be affected by it. A Windows NT Server service pack may contain Exchange fixes, for example, and these can affect other areas in your organization. For example, suppose a service pack that fixes a problem Exchange has with Windows NT Backup also changes DHCP. (Studying the README file can show you this.) You need to test both the Windows NT Backup fix and the DHCP change and to coordinate testing with the group that supports DHCP so you can get their sign-off prior to deployment.

- Exchange servers can be dedicated to specific functions. Test service packs on lab servers running the appropriate services and configured identically to production servers.

- If the test cycle is successful, start deploying to non-critical servers first, if possible, and then move to the primary servers once the service pack has been in production for 10 to 14 days. Always check the README file for specific instructions and to see if there is a recommended sequence of which servers to update first.

Note Setting up "test" servers in your production environment helps ensure a successful deployment. For example, set up an Exchange server with test mailboxes and apply the service pack to this server first. For Windows NT Server, set up a test WINS server as a replication partner with the hub WINS server. This requires extra servers but reduces user impact if there is a problem. See the table in the Evaluating Risks section below for help in determining which servers to upgrade first.

Testing New Releases

New releases include features that may change the way the product operates. If the current release of a product is meeting your needs and you are not experiencing problems, you may not want to bother with a new release. You still, however, should preview new releases and plan for their implementation. If time and resources are limited, skip the Betas and save thorough testing and evaluation for the RC, which has more complete features and bug documentation.

Here are some considerations for testing new versions:

- Production Exchange Servers can be dedicated to specific functions, so you may need different upgrade procedures for different server types. For example, it is easier and entails lower risk to upgrade an Internet Mail server than a dedicated mailbox server with 1,000 users. Thoroughly test the upgrade procedure in the lab first on every type of server and client. Use the results to develop an upgrade plan for clients and servers that minimizes downtime and interrupts user productivity the least.

- Develop a version interoperability plan for servers and clients so older versions can coexist with newer ones as you upgrade. It can take week or even months to upgrade all servers and clients. As a general rule, upgrade servers first. Repeat the client/server test plan developed for the initial deployment, this time using the client version currently installed running against the new version servers. New features and version interoperability testing require additional test plans. You need to identify version interoperability issues and inform operations groups and business units.

- A new version must be tested against all other production operating systems, legacy mail systems and gateways, applications, and all production client types. If you have integration test plans from the original deployment, repeat them. Add tests for new features and functionality. Your lab should mirror the production environment, especially client and server types.

- Don't forget to test the Exchange Administrator program and any server monitoring tools that you will use across versions. Coordinate upgrades for servers and administrator/monitoring workstations.

- Simulate system loading with tools such as autorun scripts, LoadSim, and other utilities.

- Configure and test *all* new features, even if there is no immediate need or interest, so that you can understand how the feature works and what its implementation requires.

Evaluating Risks

Every production upgrade requires that you evaluate possible risks. Basically, you need to determine what can happen if you don't install the SP, and what can happen if the installation itself causes problems. A failed installation is rare, but you should develop a backout plan just in case. Each installation is different, and users have different business requirements and critical needs. Do your best to determine what risks an upgrade pose for you.

The table below can help you assess the risk associated with upgrading a particular server in a production environment and determine the best server upgrade sequence (if the SP has no requirements). Always check the README file for requirements or recommendations on server deployment.

The analysis process can be summarized as follows: First, review the SP's fixes and note the ones that will benefit you. Weigh the significance of the problem the service pack will fix for you against the impact on the server and your environment if the service pack installation fails. Consider server roles. Generally, servers that host mailboxes are riskier to upgrade because a failure can lose user data. Servers that run only connectors are safer because they automatically load balance, so if one goes offline another takes over and mail continues to flow.

Note Always do a full backup of the server before applying a service pack or version upgrade. For other precautions see Knowledge Base article Q165418, Title: Before Installing a Windows NT Service Pack.

Server (number of servers)	Probability of server failure without SP	Effect if SP install fails	Upgrade Priority [Scale of 1-3 with 1 being as soon as possible]
News server (2)	Low	Low: not a critical server	**2**—Install this server first after hours as a test of the SP. Run for several days before installing the next server.
Internet Mail Server (3)	High: known problem is addressed in SP	Low: no users on server; there are other Internet Mail Servers that will take up the load; connector can be moved to another server or rebuilt with minimal down time	**1**—Install on one server after hours and run for several days before installing the other Internet Mail Servers.
Public folder server (6)	Medium: folder replication performance improvements in SP could be beneficial	Medium: users without public folder access; applications use public folders	**2**—Install if performance begins to degrade below acceptable levels; install after hours
Dedicated mailbox server with 1,000 users each (15)	Low: no connectors running on server; server performance is good	High: users without mail	**3**—Wait until other servers are upgraded and the process has been validated; check on dates for new release before starting. Install over the weekend to limit user impact.
Microsoft Mail Connector (2)	High: Microsoft Mail Connector problem fixed in SP	High: all message transfer to Microsoft Mail stops	**2**—Install over the weekend to allow testing/checkout.
Bridgehead (2)	Medium: X.400 performance improvements in SP could be beneficial	Low: not much traffic between sites; downtime would have minimal impact	**1**—Install after Internet Mail Server; install after hours.

The first servers to upgrade are those with a low impact on the environment but a high probability of experiencing problems fixed in the service pack. Monitor high-risk servers for 10 to 14 days before upgrading. Test-install the SP on high-impact server types in the lab first to get a feel for the process and to uncover any issues.

New version releases may require that service packs be installed, so develop an upgrade plan for all server types. For example, you decide to deploy a service pack, but not to update the messaging servers until after all the other Exchange servers because you want to build a new production messaging server. Install the new messaging server with the latest lab-tested Windows NT and Exchange versions and service packs that you are deploying, then move mail- or test-team members to this server for a week or so for final checkout before adding users.

Using SMS to Deploy

Microsoft Systems Management Server (SMS) uses the Package Command Manager (PCM) to deploy software to workstations and servers: when a user logs on, the interactive version of PCM checks the SMS logon servers for software packages at intervals specified by the SMS administrator. The interactive version does, however, create some issues for Windows NT Servers, which are not typically used for interactive logons. Unless the target server is part of the SMS hierarchy, the SMS client with PCM won't get installed. As a result, the server will not appear as a software distribution target in the SMS administrator interface. The interactive version also must remain logged onto the network to receive the deployed software packages even with the SMS client software installed.

SMS 1.2 Service Pack 2 includes a new feature called *PCM as a Service* that performs the same functions as the interactive version of PCM, but performs installations even if no user is logged on to the server. This service was delivered with SMS prior to Service Pack 2, but was installed only on servers that were directly involved in the SMS hierarchy. The service pack update allows the PCM service to function correctly on both Windows NT Servers and Windows NT Workstations.

Another advantage of PCM as a Service is that it installs the software using the security context on the service, unlike the interactive version, which uses the logged-on user's security information. (It should install software in the security context of an account with administrative privileges on the server.) Follow the special procedures listed in the product documentation to install this feature on each machine.

Rolling Out Service Packs Using SMS

It takes only a few minutes to copy service pack files to the server and, depending on the nature of the upgrade, either reboot the server or stop and restart Exchange services. But it can take time to update each server, especially if your organization has remote locations with distributed servers.

Automating service pack deployments with SMS takes careful planning, but it can speed up production server updates and help you stay current with the latest fixes. Start by testing service pack installations in the test lab and ensuring that all servers have the necessary SMS software installed. Be sure to include all server configuration types in your testing. Check that your SMS packages and batch files are functioning correctly, and verify that the target server is updated.

After testing and running the service pack on lab servers for several days, finalize the SMS install procedures. Update local, low-impact production servers and run for 10 to 14 days, then install on some local high impact servers before you attempt to install to a remote server. Start the SMS remote deployment with a low-impact remote server. Validate that the remote server was installed correctly and then allow it to run for 10 to 14 days before attempting widespread deployment. You may want to extend the checkout periods for each step, depending on your hardware and software environment, business cycles, and the nature of the servers you are upgrading.

You can verify a successful installation by looking at the Help menu under **About** or by typing **winver** in a command line prompt window.

Install the SMS Client

If the SMS infrastructure is configured correctly, the client software is installed automatically when an interactive user logs into the machine. Installation places the machine in the SMS inventory database, which enables the machine to be targeted for software distribution. If the client software is installed on the machine but is not in the SMS database, a configuration problem might affect inventory collection. Knowledge Base article, Q126642, Title: Troubleshooting Inventory Collection Problems, addresses the most common causes of inventory problems.

If the server cannot be easily accessed to perform an interactive logon, you can remotely install the SMS client software with the Scheduler service. It normally runs using the SYSTEM security context, which is a problem because the SYSTEM account cannot easily connect to network resources. If that's the case, change the security context of the service or use a different user account when connecting to network resources.

The following batch file installs the SMS client on a remote server without changing the security context of the Schedule service. Before using this in production, test it and implement error checking.

```
SCHEDSMS.BAT

@ECHO OFF
ECHO Copying command batch file.
COPY .\INSTSMS.BAT \\EXCHSVR\C$\TEMP\INSTSMS.BAT
ECHO Remotely scheduling SMS client installation.
SOON.EXE \\EXCHSVR 5 /INTERACTIVE "C:\TEMP\INSTSMS.BAT"
ECHO Completed scheduling.


INSTSMS.BAT

@ECHO OFF
ECHO Connecting to the SMS site server.
NET USE X: \\SMSSVR\SMS_SHR PASSWORD /USER:CORP\USER1
ECHO Installing the SMS client software
X:\X86.BIN\RUNSMS.BAT
ECHO Removing the connection from the SMS site server.
NET USE X: /DELETE
ECHO Complete
```

After installing the SMS client software, add PCM as a Service by creating a user account with administrative privileges for the PCM service. For example, if the server is in the CORP domain, you must put the service account named PCMSVC into the CORP\Domain Admins security group.

The software for the PCM service is located on the Systems Management Server Service Pack 2 or higher CD-ROM in the \support\pcmsvc32 directory. Install the service using the RSERVICE.EXE utility, which remotely installs, configures, and starts most types of Windows NT services. RSERVICE is configured using an *.INI file. The installation documentation located at \SUPPORT\PCMSVC32\INSTALL.DOC has specific usage instructions.

Here is an example RSERVICE.INI file and the command line to execute the RSERVICE utility. This example targets only one server for the installation.

```
[domain name]
CORP=LISTED
[machine list]
EXCHSVR=INCLUDE
[service account]
*=CORP\PCMSVC
[service name]
*=SMS_PACKAGE_COMMAND_MANAGER_NT
[executable file]
*=PCMSVC32.EXE
[installation directory]
*=c:\pcmsvc\x86.bin
[startup parameters]
[source directory]
*=\\SMSSVR\d$\SMS\SITE.SRV\X86.BIN
[other files]
[access permissions]
*=Administrators:FULL smsuser:READ
[automatic start]
*=yes
[registry settings]
*=key:HKLM\Software\Microsoft\SMS\Identification SZ:"Installation
Directory=C:\PCMSVC" key:HKLM\Software\Microsoft\SMS\TRACING
DWORD:Enabled=1
key:HKLM\Software\Microsoft\SMS\TRACING\SMS_PACKAGE_COMMAND_MANAGER_NT
DWORD:Enabled=1
key:HKLM\Software\Microsoft\SMS\TRACING\SMS_PACKAGE_COMMAND_MANAGER_NT
SZ:"TraceFilename=\pcmsvc\LOGS\pacman.log"
[logfile path]
*=C:\PCMINST.LOG
```

The command line for RSERVICE using the above example file would be:

RSERVICE /INSTALL .\RSERVICE.INI /C

Once installed and started, the PCM service automatically uses the same parameters as the interactive version of PCM and rechecks the SMS logon server for new software packages on the same interval. As soon as you verify that the PCM service is functioning correctly, you can use the service to perform software installations.

Create the Service Pack SMS Package

Now, create the SMS software package by setting up the source files on a network share and defining the package in SMS. The following procedure illustrates how to create the SMS software package for an Exchange service pack. See the SMS product documentation for specific instructions.

▶ **To create the SMS package**

1. On the network share used as the source for your SMS packages, create a directory for the service pack files, such as \EXCH.SP.

2. Copy all of service pack files to the newly created directory.

3. Using the SMS Administrator tool, open the **Packages** window and click **New** from the **File** menu.

4. Assign the package a name and useful description.

5. Even though this package will be applied to a Windows NT Server, click the **Workstation** button to define it as a workstation-type package.

6. In the **Source Location** box on the **Package Properties** dialog, enter the UNC path to the Service Pack source files, for example, \\SMSSOURCE\EXCH.SP.

7. In the **Command Lines** section, click the **New** button to create a command line for the installation. If different types of installation are required, multiple command lines can be configured and selected at the time of deployment.

8. Enter a descriptive name for the installation, for example, **Unattended Installation**.

9. In the **Command Line** field, enter the command and command line parameters required to start the installation. For example, to install the Exchange service pack the command line would be UPDATE.EXE /U.

10. Select the **Background Execution** check box. This determines which version of PCM will perform the installation. Checking it causes the PCM service to perform the installation. If it's not selected, the interactive version performs the installation.

11. Click **OK** to create the command line. Repeat as many times as necessary to create all of the required command lines.

12. Click **OK** to complete the creation of the SMS package.

The Service Pack SMS software package is now ready for test deployment. After you verify the package on a test server, you can use it in production without any further changes.

Deploying Hot Fixes

Hot fixes are usually collected and rolled into the next service pack. In between service pack releases, you should track which hot fixes have been applied. When a new server is built or an existing server needs the current service pack reinstalled, you must reapply all of the hot fixes that were previously installed.

To help manage these hot fixes, the service pack SMS software package can be enhanced to include the reapplication of each hot fix. Instead of directly calling the UPDATE.EXE program to install the service pack, write a batch file to include both the UPDATE.EXE and all appropriate hot fixes. As additional hot fixes are required, you can simply modify the batch file. This technique helps track hot fixes and makes it easier to apply the necessary hot fixes when a new server is installed or the service pack must be reinstalled on an existing server. Here is an example:

```
SP_HF.BAT

@ECHO OFF
ECHO Applying the Service Pack
%0\..\UPDATE.EXE /U
ECHO Applying Hot Fix #1
%0\..\HOTFIX1\HOTFIX.EXE
ECHO Applying Hot Fix #2
%0\..\HOTFIX2\HOTFIX.EXE
ECHO Copying extra files for manual Hot Fix. (example only)
COPY %0\..\XFILES\CONFIG.INI D:\EXCHANGE\CONFIG.INI
ECHO Updating Registry for manual Hot Fix. (example only)
REGEDIT.EXE /s UPDATE.REG
```

After creating a batch file, you can modify the SMS software package for the service pack to include an additional command line that applies both the service pack and the hot fixes. For example, the command line title could be "Unattended Installation plus Hot Fixes" and the command line would read: SP_HF.BAT. Because this command line also requires the PCM service to perform the installation, remember to select the **Background Execution** check box.

Appendix

A P P E N D I X   A

References and Resources

This list contains references to Microsoft support offerings and other sources of information on Exchange Server found through Microsoft Press, on the Microsoft Web site, or on TechNet.

Support and technical resources	Where found
Microsoft Support: Pointer to Support Online and support options	http://www.microsoft.com/support/
Microsoft Support Online: Access to Microsoft Technical Support's entire collection of problem-solving tools and technical information, including the Knowledge Base, troubleshooting wizards, service packs, and other downloads	http://support.microsoft.com/support /a.asp?M=F
Q155545, Title: XGEN: First Customer Contact Form for Exchange	Query TechNet using the "Q" number. Or search Microsoft Technical Support online: http://support.microsoft.com/support /a.asp?M=F
Microsoft Enterprise Services: Worldwide services and support for large organizations	http://www.microsoft.com/Enterprise /support.htm
Premier Technical Support	http://www.microsoft.com/Enterprise /support/techsupport.htm
Premier Technical Account Management	http://www.microsoft.com/Enterprise /support/TAM.htm
Basic and Enhanced Supportability Review	Consult your Microsoft Consulting Services liaison or Technical Account Manager for additional information
Microsoft Certified Solution Providers	http://www.microsoft.com/mcsp/
Microsoft Certified Professional (MCP) training	http://www.microsoft.com/mcp/

(continued)

Support and technical resources	Where found
Microsoft Training and Certification	http://www.microsoft.com/train_cert/
Microsoft Authorized Training Centers (ATECs)	http://www.microsoft.com/train_cert/train/atec.htm
Microsoft Press: Look for the following titles: *Microsoft Exchange Connectivity Guide* *Microsoft Exchange 5.0 Step by Step* *Field Guide to Microsoft Exchange* *BackOffice Resource Guide: Part One Microsoft Exchange* *BackOffice Resource Guide, Second Edition* *Microsoft Windows NT Server 4.0 Resource Kit* *Microsoft Windows NT Server 4.0 Resource Kit, Supplement 1* *Microsoft Windows NT Server 4.0 Resource Kit, Supplement 2*	1-800-MSPRESS (677-7377) http://mspress.microsoft.com/
Microsoft BackOffice Web site	http://www.backoffice.microsoft.com
Microsoft Windows NT Web site	http://www.microsoft.com/ntserver/
Microsoft Exchange Web site	http://www.microsoft.com/exchange/
Microsoft Exchange 5.5 Routing Objects	http://www.backoffice.microsoft.com/downtrial/default.asp
Sample application download	http://www.microsoft.com/ithome/resource/exchange/default.htm
Microsoft Security Advisor Web site	http://www.microsoft.com/security
Microsoft Outlook 97 Administrator's Guide	http://www.microsoft.com/outlook/adminguide/
Microsoft Developer Network (MSDN)	http://www.microsoft.com/msdn/
Microsoft TechNet: Technical information, including recent sample application information on Microsoft Exchange	http://www.microsoft.com/technet/
Worldwide Exchange Connectivity Competency Center (EC3): Microsoft Consulting Services (MCS) group that works with other MCS offices and key partners, assisting enterprise customers with Exchange connectivity and migration	E-mail EC3@microsoft.com

General information	Where found
Microsoft Solutions Framework: To help you plan an enterprise architecture that adapts to (or drives) industry change, consistently build business-driven applications, and manage your computing environment	http://www.microsoft.com/msf/ You can also find an overview article on TechNet.
"MS Exchange Server 5.5 Reviewer's Guide"	Search TechNet
"Managing Infrastructure Deployment Projects"	Search TechNet
Q163537, Title: XGEN: Exchange Whitepapers Available on WWW	Query TechNet using the "Q" number, or search: http://support.microsoft.com/support /a.asp?M=F
Q154792, Title: Exchange and Schedule+ Whitepapers	Query TechNet using the "Q" number, or search: http://support.microsoft.com/support /a.asp?M=F
Deploying Microsoft Exchange Server 5.5	For more information: http://mspress.microsoft.com/
Microsoft Exchange Installation Guide	Microsoft Exchange Server documentation (on the Exchange Server CD-ROM)
Microsoft Exchange Server documentation	Exchange Server CD-ROM
Microsoft Exchange Books Online	Exchange Server CD-ROM
Microsoft Exchange Server 5.5 Resource Guide	*(Microsoft BackOffice Resource Kit, Second Edition)* For more information: http://mspress.microsoft.com/ Available on TechNet
Microsoft Outlook 97 Administrator's Guide	http://www.microsoft.com/outlook /adminguide/
Microsoft Outlook 98 Deployment Kit	On TechNet, May 1998 issue or later

(continued)

General information	Where found
"MS Exchange Server Migration and Coexistence: Planning Considerations and Components"	Search TechNet
"MS Exchange Server Host-Based Migration and Coexistence"	
"MS Exchange and Mail Coexistence and Migration with LAN and Host Mail Systems"	
"Module 5: Post Office Protocol 3 (POP3) Service"	Search for this title on TechNet, and then use **Sync Contents** (CTRL+S) to see the table of contents
"Module 6: Lightweight Directory Access Protocol (LDAP)"	
"MS Exchange Forms Designer Fundamentals"	Search TechNet
"Extending MS Exchange Forms"	
"Introduction to Collaboration Data Objects"	
"Active Directory Services Interface in the MS Exchange 5.5 Environment"	
"Active Directory Service Interfaces—The Easy Way to Access and Manage LDAP-Based Directories (Windows NT 4.0)"	
"Integrating Client Applications with MS Exchange"	
"Interoperability with MS Exchange, MS Mail 3.x, MS Schedule+ 95 and 1.0"	

Building support infrastructure	Where found
"Saving Time, Money, and Expertise with a Self-help Support System"	Search TechNet
"Helping the Help Desk During a Product Rollout"	
"Constructing A Help Desk - Avoiding Common Pitfalls"	
"The HelpDesk Model"	
Microsoft Sourcebook for the Help Desk, Second Edition	For more information: http://mspress.microsoft.com/

Exchange optimization and tuning	Where found
"Disaster and Recovery Planning"	Search on TechNet
Q182505, Title: XADM: Memory Usage of Store.exe Is Higher in Exchange 5.5	Query TechNet using the "Q" number.
Q178779, Title: XADM: Exchange 5.5 Upgrade Fails with -1011 (Out of Memory)	*For the most up-to-date collection of Knowledge Base articles, search Microsoft Technical Support online:*
Q183057, Title: XADM: Private Information Store Has High Disk Size Item Numbers	*http://support.microsoft.com/support /a.asp?M=F*
Q179065, Title: XADM: Changes to Primary Windows NT Account Do Not Take Effect	
Q176163, Title: XADM: Restart Services Disabled After Performance Optimizer Use	
Q177762, Title: XADM: Access Violation (0xc0000005) During Exchange Setup	
Q173345, Title: XADM: PerfWiz Allows Memory Limit to be Set to Less than 16 MB	
Q173481, Title: XADM: PerfWiz Reports Multiple Errors when Moving Files	
Q173706, Title: XADM: Performance Optimizer Sets Store Threads Differently	
Q174033, Title: XFOR: Performance Tuning a 16Mbps Token Ring Network for PROFS	
Q183614, Title: XADM: Cannot Run Performance Optimizer From An Unattended Setup	
Q182901, Title: XADM: Optimizer Error: One or More File Locations Are Not Valid	
Q183924, Title: XADM: Slow Client Performance While Performing Store Operations	
Q181922, Title: XADM: Performance Optimizer Display Control Settings	
Q184186, Title: XADM: Recovering Exchange from a Corrupted Directory	

Exchange administration troubleshooting, backup, and recovery	Where found
"Disaster and Recovery Planning"	Search on TechNet
Q155269, Title: Microsoft Exchange Administrator's FAQ	Query TechNet using the "Q" number.
Q150564, Title: XADM: How to load Exchange Symbols for DR. Watson	*For the most up-to-date collection of Knowledge Base articles, search Microsoft Technical Support online: http://support.microsoft.com/support /a.asp?M=F*
Q161495, Title: XADM: Setting Up Exchange View-Only Administrators	
Q159485, Title: XADM: Troubleshooting Setup Problems Joining an Existing Site	
Q170334, Title: XADM: Troubleshooting Intrasite Directory Replication	
Q159298, Title: XADM: Analyzing Exchange RPC Traffic Over TCP/IP	
Q162012, Title: XADM: Unable to Change the Routing Calculation Server	
Q147704, Title: XCON: Troubleshooting Tips for: Exchange MTA Not Starting	
Q147244, Title: XADM: Troubleshooting Information Store Start Up Problems	
Q159196, Title: XADM: Tasks Controlled by the IS Maintenance Schedule	
Q170361, Title: XADM: Troubleshooting a Rapidly Growing Information Store	
Q128325, Title: XADM: Reclaiming Disk Space for the Information Store	
Q149238, Title: XADM: Information Store Fails to Start with -1011 Error	
Q163913, Title: XADM: IS or DS Stops Due to Lack of Drive Space for Log Files.	
Q154032, Title: XADM: Error 1105 - EcBadVersion, Restoring Off-Line Store	
Q163686, Title: XADM: What to do if the Service Account is Deleted	
Q139822, Title: How to Restore a Backup to Computer with Different Hardware	
Q177635, Title: XADM: How to Set Up a Disaster Recovery Server for DIR.EDB	

Exchange administration troubleshooting, backup, and recovery	Where found
Q143233, Title: XADM Adm: Command Line Parameters for Edbutil.exe	Query TechNet using the "Q" number.
Q151495, Title: PRIV.EDB not smaller After Running Edbutil /D	*For the most up-to-date collection of Knowledge Base articles, search Microsoft Technical Support online:*
Q152960, Title: XADM: Rebuilding the Site Folders in a Site	*http://support.microsoft.com/support /a.asp?M=F*
Q156705, Title: XADM: Site Tear Down Causes Public Folders to be Re homed	
Q141342, Title: XADM: Public Folders Automatically get New Home Site/Server	
Q152959, Title: XADM: How to Remove the First Exchange Server in a Site	
Q143235, Title: XADM: Err Msg: Error -550 Has Occurred	
Q148199, Title: Recreating a Deleted Schedule+ Free/Busy Agent	
Q150298, Title: Renaming a Windows NT PDC or BDC.	

Client troubleshooting	Where found
"MS Outlook Interoperability: Digging Deeper"	Search TechNet
Q163576, Title: XGEN: Changing the RPC Binding Order	Query TechNet using the "Q" number.
Q148284, Title: XCON: When and How to use the Mtacheck Utility	*For the most up-to-date collection of Knowledge Base articles, search Microsoft Technical Support online:*
Q159298, Title: XADM: Analyzing Exchange RPC Traffic Over TCP/IP	*http://support.microsoft.com/support /a.asp?M=F*
Q177763, Title: XADM: Troubleshooting Failure to Generate Offline Address Book	
Q163743, Title: OL97: Information About Outlook Version 8.01	
Q136516, Title: XCLN: Improving Windows Client Startup Times	
Q155048, Title: XCLN: Troubleshooting Startup of Windows Client Using TCP/IP	
Q182444, Title: NBF MaxFrameSize Calculated Incorrectly on Token Ring	

(continued)

Client troubleshooting	Where found
Q181619, Title: OL98: Outlook Starts Slowly with Dial-Up Adapter DNS Enabled	Query TechNet using the "Q" number. *For the most up-to-date collection of Knowledge Base articles, search Microsoft Technical Support online: http://support.microsoft.com/support /a.asp?M=F*
Q161973, Title: OL97: Troubleshooting Outlook Configuration Problems	
Q150247, Title: XCLN: Cannot Recover the Password of an Exchange PST nor Contents of OST	
Q161938, Title: Slow Exchange Client Logons in Due to Resource Deadlock	
Q149819, Title: RPC Causes Exchange Server to Hang All Connected Clients	
Q162010, Title: Exchange Server Name Resolution on a Novell Network	
Q157632, Title: XADM: Client Hangs or Prompts for Domain Credentials	
Q176245, Title: XWEB: VBScript Error when Accessing Outlook Web Access Server	
Q176246, Title: XWEB: Unexpected Behavior when Accessing Outlook Web Access	
Memory Valet	ftp://ftp.microsoft.com/bussys/exchange /exchange-unsup-ed/Memval.zip

Windows NT Server support	Where found
Q129845, Title: Blue Screen Preparation Before Calling Microsoft	Query TechNet using the "Q" number. *For the most up-to-date collection of Knowledge Base articles, search Microsoft Technical Support online: http://support.microsoft.com/support /a.asp?M=F*
Q123750, Title: Debugging Windows NT 3.5 Setup STOP Screens	
Q148954, Title: How to Set Up a Remote Debug Session Using a Modem	
Q158744, Title: How to Automate Network Captures with Network Monitor	
Q164931, Title: Using Regedit to Backup Your Windows NT Registry	
Q130928, Title: Restoring a Backup of Windows NT to Another Computer	
Q102476, Title: Changing the Name of Windows NT Workstations and Servers	
"Tips for Deploying MS Windows NT Server 4.0 Service Pack 3"	Search TechNet

Exchange traffic analysis	Where found
"MS Exchange Performance: Concurrent Users Per Server"	Search TechNet
Q149217, Title: XCLN: Microsoft Exchange Message Size Limitations	Query TechNet using the "Q" number.
Q163576, Title: XGEN: Changing the RPC Binding Order	*For the most up-to-date collection of Knowledge Base articles, search Microsoft Technical Support online:*
Q136516, Title: XCLN: Improving Windows Client Startup Times	*http://support.microsoft.com/support /a.asp?M=F*
Q167100, Title: XCLN: Out of Memory Errors with Microsoft Exchange 5.0 16-Bit Client	
Q155048, Title: XCLN: Troubleshooting Startup of Windows Client	
Q161626, Title: XCLN: Troubleshooting IPX/SPX Connections	

Key Management server and security	Where found
Basic security and algorithm information	http://www.rsa.com
Q177492, Title: XADM: Key Management Server Fails to Reissue Key	Query TechNet using the "Q" number.
Q148432, Title: XADM: Location of the Key Management Server Software	*For the most up-to-date collection of Knowledge Base articles, search Microsoft Technical Support online:*
Q177309, Title: XADM: Setup Cannot Initialize the Key Management Database	*http://support.microsoft.com/support /a.asp?M=F*
Q177734, Title: XADM: KM Server Features Not Supported in Exchange 5.5 release	
Q176737, Title: XADM: Key Management Server Fails to Start and Logs Event 5060	
Q174743, Title: XADM: Cannot Install 4.0/5/0 KMS After Installing 5.5 Server	
Q156713, Title: XADM: KM Server Stops Intermittently on Alpha Servers	
Q154531, Title: XADM: Moving the KM Server to Another Server in the Site	
Q153394, Title: XADM: Error When Selecting Security Tab for Mailbox	
Q152849, Title: XADM: How to Recover from a Lost Key Management Server	

(continued)

Key Management server and security	Where found
Q151689, Title: XADM: Error Starting Key Management Server	Query TechNet using the "Q" number.
Q149333, Title: XADM: The Basics of Advanced Security	*For the most up-to-date collection of Knowledge Base articles, search Microsoft Technical Support online: http://support.microsoft.com/support /a.asp?M=F*
Q152498, Title: XADM: Unable to Enable Advanced Security on User Account	
Q169519, Title: XADM: Exchange 5.5 Remove All Option Removes Database Files	
Q146464, Title: XCLN: Err Msg: Unable to Obtain a Valid…Revocation List	
Q152686, Title: XCLN: How Expired Encryption Key Pairs Work	
Q154089, Title: XCLN: Cannot Send Sealed Message when Offline	
Q147421, Title: XFOR: How Exchange Encryption is Disabled on French Servers	
Q176681, Title: XGEN: Description of Microsoft Exchange Server 5.5	
Q146463, Title: XGEN: KMS Cannot Write Certificate Revocation List	
Q143380, Title: XGEN: Exchange Server Services and Their Dependencies	
Q170908, Title: INFO: Key Management Server Functions not Exposed to Developers	

Information and resources for cc:Mail	Where found
Microsoft Outlook 97 Administrator's Guide	http://www.microsoft.com/outlook /adminguide/
Q169259, Title: OL97: New Nickname Features in Outlook 8.02	Query TechNet using the "Q" number, or search: http://support.microsoft.com/support /a.asp?M=F
CCREGMOD program	Look on the cc:Mail software CD-ROM or search: http://www.ccmail.com
MESA MailBox Converter for cc:Mail	http://www.mesa.com
ComAxis Technology Web site	http://www.comaxis.com

More information on Microsoft Mail	Where found
Microsoft Exchange Server Migration Guide.	Exchange Server CD-ROM
Exchange Forms Designer (EFD) 1.0 compatibility	*Microsoft Exchange Server Migration Guide*, (Exchange Server CD-ROM)
Microsoft Mail for PC Networks Administrator's Guide, Chapter 14	Microsoft Mail for PC Networks server setup diskettes
DIRSYNC.TXT	Microsoft Mail for PC Networks server setup diskettes
Q114119, Title: PC Gen: Application Notes and Replacement Files for PC Mail	Query TechNet using the "Q" number.
Q158308, Title: XFOR: Err Msg: Initialization of Dynamic Link Library Failed [exchange]	*For the most up-to-date collection of Knowledge Base articles, search Microsoft Technical Support online:*
Q108831, Title: PC DirSync: Err Msg: Fatal [203] GAL Rebuild Problem	*http://support.microsoft.com/support /a.asp?M=F*
Q99117, Title: PC DirSync: Err Msg: Fatal [203] GAL Rebuild Problem	
Q148389, Title: XFOR: How to Backbone MSMail 3.x over Exchange	
Q147698, Title: XADM: Configuring the Schedule+ Free/Busy Connector	
Q155897, Title: OL97: Using Schedule+ as the Primary Calendar in Outlook 97	
Q158694, Title: XFOR: DirSync: Map Template Info Between MSMail & Exchange	
Q152231, Title: XFOR: How To Reset Microsoft Exchange DirSync Numbers	
Q166545, Title: XFOR: DXA Appends 001 Only When Needed [Exchange]	
Q156545, Title: XFOR: How to Set Up a 2nd MS-type Proxy Address for MSMail Users	
Q149284, Title: XADM: PC Mail Shared Folders not Converted To Public Folders	
Q175978, Title: XFOR: List of Reserved Microsoft Mail Network Names	
Q152231, Title: XFOR: How To Reset Microsoft Exchange DirSync Numbers	

(continued)

More information on Microsoft Mail	Where found
PODIAG.EXE	Microsoft Mail for PC Networks version 3.5 installation software, or in application note WA0883 (see Q114119)
	Download this from: ftp://ftp.microsoft.com/Softlib/Mslfiles
WA0940.EXE	In application note WA0940 (see Q114119)
	Download this from: ftp://ftp.microsoft.com/Softlib/Mslfiles
Application note WA0725 on directory synchronization	Query TechNet using "WA0725"
	Download the executable from: ftp://ftp.microsoft.com/Softlib/Mslfiles

AppleTalk, Quarterdeck /StarNine Connectivity	Where found
Q154619, Title: XFOR: Export Menu Disabled on Exchange Connection DER	Query TechNet using the "Q" number.
Q156961, Title: XFOR: Mac Connection Gateway Will Not Install on System 7.5.3	*For the most up-to-date collection of Knowledge Base articles, search Microsoft Technical Support online: http://support.microsoft.com/support /a.asp?M=F*
Q160664, Title: XFOR: Cannot Configure Microsoft Mail Connector (AppleTalk)	
Q169659, Title: XFOR: Err Msg: AppleTalk Mail Connector Service Not Created	
Q152477, Title: XFOR: Handshake Files Moved to BADMAIL Directory	
Q171259, Title: XFOR: How to Move the Microsoft Mail Connector Postoffice	

More information on Lotus Notes	Where found
Migrating from Lotus Notes to Microsoft Exchange Server	You can find an abstract of this service guide on TechNet, April 1998 issue or later: "Migrating from Lotus Notes to MS Exchange Service Guide Abstract."
	MCSPs can order service guides by calling 1-800 SOL PROV.
	Other customers can order by calling 1-800-255-8414.
	For more information about service guides, e-mail SGQuest@microsoft.com.
"Connector for Lotus Notes"	Search TechNet
"MS Exchange Server Migration and Coexistence: Planning Considerations and Components for Lotus cc:Mail"	Search TechNet
Q175746: Title: XFOR: Specifying the Container for Propagated Users	Query TechNet using the "Q" number.
Q180517, Title: XFOR: Customizing Dirsync Between Exchange and Notes	*For the most up-to-date collection of Knowledge Base articles, search Microsoft Technical Support online: http://support.microsoft.com/support/a.asp?M=F*
Q174207, Title: XFOR: Notes Proxy Domain Name Over 31 Characters Stripped	
Q169393, Title: XFOR: Messages Containing Doclinks Are Getting Stuck in Exchange	
Q174730, Title: XFOR: Lotus Notes Invitations Result in NDR	
Q179057, Title: XFOR: Exchange-Notes Dirsync Fails with Truncated Person Doc	
Q177597, Title: XFOR: Delivery and Read Reports Do Not Appear in Lotus Notes	
Q177598, Title: XFOR: RTF Always Sent from Exchange Server to Lotus Notes	
Q175836, Title: XFOR: Lotus Notes Low Delivery Priority Message Not Delivered	
PROFGEN.EXE	*Microsoft Exchange 5.0 Resource Kit (BackOffice Resource Kit)*
CHNGINBX.EXE	Valuepack directory on the Outlook CD-ROM

Information on SMS and unattended setup	Where found
SMS Installer download	http://backoffice.microsoft.com /downtrial
"Advanced Techniques of Software Distribution with the SMS Installer"	Search TechNet
Microsoft Outlook 97 Administrator's Guide	http://www.microsoft.com/outlook /adminguide/
Q181864, Title: XADM: Setup/Q Prompts for Service Account	Query TechNet using the "Q" number.
Q175115, Title: XADM: Err Msg: There is Something Wrong with the INI File	*For the most up-to-date collection of Knowledge Base articles, search Microsoft Technical Support online: http://support.microsoft.com/support /a.asp?M=F*
Q180404, Title: XADM: Silent Mode Setup Does Not Support Upgrade Mode	
Q176243, Title: XADM: Batch Setup-Setup /r /q Options Combined Unsupported	
Q168490, Title: XADM: Unattended Exchange Server Setup	
Schema properties and attributes	See *Microsoft Exchange Books Online* (Exchange Server CD-ROM)

Knowledge Base articles on upgrading to Exchange 5.5	Where found
"Microsoft Exchange Server 5.5 Upgrade Procedures"	Search TechNet
	For the most up-to-date collection of Knowledge Base articles, search Microsoft Technical Support online: http://support.microsoft.com/support /a.asp?M=F
Q179258, Title: XADM: Considerations When Upgrading to Exchange Server 5.5	Query TechNet using the "Q" number.
Q170280, Title: XADM: Upgrading From Exchange Standard Edition to the Enterprise	*For the most up-to-date collection of Knowledge Base articles, search Microsoft Technical Support online: http://support.microsoft.com/support /a.asp?M=F*
Q152659, Title: XADM: Importing Exchange Accounts from Another Organization	
Q153121, Title: XADM: Migrating from WGPO to Exchange	
Q170337, Title: XADM: User Manager Can Cause File in Use Errors	
Q174254, Title: XADM: GroupWise Users must Grant Access Rights to be Migrated	

Knowledge Base articles on upgrading to Exchange 5.5	Where found
Q174729, Title: XADM: Err Msg: No Mapping Between Account Names and Security IDs	Query TechNet using the "Q" number.
Q175098, Title: XADM: Unexpected Error Occurs During Upgrade or Installation	*For the most up-to-date collection of Knowledge Base articles, search Microsoft Technical Support online: http://support.microsoft.com/support /a.asp?M=F*
Q175100, Title: XADM: Unexpected Error 0xc0040000 Upgrading to Exchange 5.5	
Q176757, Title: XADM: Administrator Program Column Settings Lost After Upgrade	
Q177221, Title: XADM: Errors Occur During Exchange Service Pack Upgrade	
Q177735, Title: XADM: Unable To Access Exchange Administrator Program	
Q177959, Title: XADM: Information Store Does Not Start, Error -1022	
Q178302, Title: XADM: Upgrade to Exchange 5.5 Fails If Virus Software Is Enabled	
Q178303, Title: XADM: Chat 5.5 Err Msg: Unable To Start Microsoft Chat Service	
Q178779, Title: XADM: Exchange 5.5 Upgrade Fails with -1011 (Out of Memory)	
Q178857, Title: XADM: Setup.exe Not Found On Premier Select CD-ROM	
Q178919, Title: XADM: Exchange Event Service Not Installed During Upgrade	
Q179927, Title: XADM: KCC Site Teardown Blocked by Site-Proxy-Space Attribute	
Q180009, Title: XADM: Exchange 5.5 Upgrade Fails With ID No: c106fdda	
Q180403, Title: XADM: Error Message Trying to Install Exchange 5.5 Upgrade Only	
Q180404, Title: XADM: Silent Mode Setup Does Not Support Upgrade Mode	
Q180876, Title: XADM: Err Msg: Invalid Home Server Definition in User List File	
Q182320, Title: XADM: Unable to Upgrade from Exchange Server 4.0 to 5.5	

(continued)

Knowledge Base articles on upgrading to Exchange 5.5	Where found
Q182665, Title: XADM: Exchange Migration Wizard Fails with 7026 error	Query TechNet using the "Q" number.
Q182903, Title: XADM: Eseutil Utility Replaces Edbutil from Earlier Versions	*For the most up-to-date collection of Knowledge Base articles, search Microsoft Technical Support online:*
Q183105, Title: XADM: Dr. Watson While Upgrading from 4.0 SP4 to 5.5	*http://support.microsoft.com/support /a.asp?M=F*
Q183312, Title: XADM: SFS Mail Not Migrated When Custom Recipient Is Converted	
Q145964, Title: XCLN: Upgrade Fails; Err Msg: Application(s) Are Running	
Q168182, Title: XCLN: Wizard Doesn't Migrate Schedule+ Info to Outlook Calendar	
Q173597, Title: XCLN: Migrating PAB Entries From Microsoft	
Q178124, Title: XCLN: Microsoft Outlook for Macintosh and Windows 3.1x	
Q181694, Title: XCLN: How to Upgrade Shared Workstation Installations of Exchange	
Q181939, Title: XCLN: Macintosh Mail Migration Fails to Import SMTP PAB Entries	
Q183531, Title: XCLN: How to Update Exchange Forms Designer Forms	
Q166567, Title: XCON: How to Enable Lowest Cost Routes Only	
Q164456, Title: XFOR: Migrated MS Mail Users May Not Receive Messages in Inbox	
Q169130, Title: XFOR: MS Mail Migration Fails When User List File Is Specified	
Q169659, Title: XFOR: Err Msg: AppleTalk Mail Connector Service Not Created	
Q173895, Title: XFOR: Migration Process is Faster on an Intel Processor	
Q174037, Title: XFOR: OLE Objects Larger Than 1 MB Not Migrated into Exchange	
Q174153, Title: XFOR: Incorrect Character Mappings when MSFS32.DLL Doesn't Match	
Q174167, Title: XFOR: Forum Password Security Lost After Collabra Migration	

Knowledge Base articles on upgrading to Exchange 5.5	Where found
Q174168, Title: XFOR: GroupWise Messages Missing After Migration	Query TechNet using the "Q" number.
Q174253, Title: XFOR: MAC Binary Attachments not Migrated from GroupWise	*For the most up-to-date collection of Knowledge Base articles, search Microsoft Technical Support online:*
Q174725, Title: XFOR: Packing List Code Page 10000 or 437 May Cause Mismatch	*http://support.microsoft.com/support /a.asp?M=F*
Q174738, Title: XFOR: Migrated Users Assigned Random PST Password	
Q174740, Title: XFOR: Error When Migrating Version 6 cc:Mail Post Office	
Q174749, Title: XFOR: cc:Mail Migration Does Not Create PST File	
Q175103, Title: XFOR: Migration Wizard Contains Inaccurate Help File Option	
Q176740, Title: XFOR: Migrated GroupWise Users Cannot See Migrated Messages	
Q177998, Title: XFOR: IMAP/POP3 Clients Cannot Reply to Migrated Messages	
Q179980, Title: XFOR: DBCS Messages Not Migrated Correctly from GroupWise	
Q180907, Title: XFOR: Unable to Send Bitmap in Body of Message	
Q181125, Title: XFOR: Bcc Recipients Visible in Migrated cc:Mail Messages	
Q181130, Title: XFOR: Additional Characters Appear in Migrated cc:Mail Messages	
Q181636, Title: XFOR: Rule For Forwarding To Internet Address Does Not Work	
Q182279, Title: XFOR: Incorrect Cc: List When Resending or Forwarding From PROFS	
Q166349, Title: XGEN: Microsoft Exchange Version Numbers	
Q168735, Title: XGEN: README.TXT: Microsoft Exchange 5.0 U.S. Service Pack 2	
Q175203, Title: XWEB: Pine 3.96 Cannot Handle IMAP DRAFT Flag	

(continued)

Knowledge Base articles on upgrading to Exchange 5.5	Where found
Q179895, Title: XWEB: Err Msg. Object Moved When Accessing Active Server	Query TechNet using the "Q" number.
Q182440, Title: XWEB: Err Msg: Unable to Render This View424Object Required	*For the most up-to-date collection of Knowledge Base articles, search Microsoft Technical Support online: http://support.microsoft.com/support /a.asp?M=F*
Q175676, Title: OL97: Summary of Changes in Outlook 8.03	

Third-party information	Where found
MoreMem (Gamma Research Inc.)	http://www.moremem.com

Index

Symbols and Numbers

A

C

G

GAL (global address list)
    distribution lists in, 150, 151
    recipients not in, 158
    two entries for a mailbox in, 158
Gateway Address Resolution Table. *See* GWART
gateways
    checking speed across, 180
    effect on server performance, 54
global address list. *See* GAL
global groups
    changing for users, 143
    creating, 181
globally unique identifiers. *See* GUIDs
global public folder administrator group, 42
graceful termination of the store service, 356
Green Book, 237
green up arrow on the Exchange monitor screen, 152
GUIDs
    patching, 307–8
    replacing with isinteg -patch, 215
GWART
    effect of "shortcut" messaging connectors on, 78
    server responsible for updating, 282

H

Handle exceptions MTA registry parameter, 112
hard disk space, insufficient available, 214
hard drives. *See also* disk drives; physical drives
    checking for errors, 210
hard recovery, 311
hardware
    configuration choices for backup and restore, 360
    configuration for Windows NT Server, 228
    issues with servers, 220–21
    platforms, restoring information specific to, 276
    RAID and mirroring, 296
    resources, affecting performance, 49
    server configuration sheet for, 347
heavy usage user, 47
heavy user classification, 62
heavy user, system requirements for, 384
helpdesk. *See* Tier 1 helpdesk
helpdesk calls, scripts for handling, 136–39
helpdesk duties, 125–26
helpdesk personnel. *See also* Tier 1 personnel
    changing global groups for users, 143
    changing logon scripts for users, 144
    disabling user accounts, 144
    qualifying scripts for Tier 1 support, 136–37
    resetting user accounts, 143
    responsibilities of, 125

helpdesk personnel *(continued)*
    steps for assigning new passwords, 142
    steps for creating new user accounts, 142–43
Hewlett-Packard NetServer LXr Pro8, Load Simulator (LoadSim) results, 66–67
Hide From Address Book attribute, 166
hierarchy change replication, reducing the frequency of, 102
hierarchy replication of public folders, 101–2
hierarchy status messages for public folders, 102–3
high-end servers, 63, 64
high-level logging, 211
high-performance hardware, selecting for backup, 360
HOSTS file, checking for Internet Mail Service startup problems, 33
hot fixes, 409
    deploying, 422
hotfix software, obtaining, 76
hot spare server, maintaining, 300–301
How-do-I...? questions, sources of information on, 133
hub-and-spoke architecture versus mesh, 74–75
hub-and-spoke environment, staggering directory replication times, 79
hub directory, replication of, 109
hub servers, directory update request messages from, 109
hub sites, 75
    centralized, 75
    distributed, 75
    losing, 236
hub site server room, losing, 235
hub-to-spoke address book views, replication of, 110

I

IBM Netfinity 7000, Load Simulator (LoadSim) results, 67–68
Idle state timer MTA registry parameter, 115
Idle state working set size (Kbytes) MTA registry parameter, 115
IIS
    placing on a different computer from Exchange Server, 51
    sizing, 407
IMAP4 clients, effect on Exchange server loads, 51
immediate severity level, 130
inactive mailboxes, removing, 182
inbound mail, not reaching recipient's inbox, 160
Inbox Repair Tool, 288
incident reporting in the daily log system, 40–41
incident tracking and escalation section of the messaging operations audit, 9–10
incoming calls, categorizing, 131–35
incomplete transactions, rolling back automatically, 259
inconsistent state, confirming, 280

Design.

Roll out.

Support.

U.S.A. **$199.99**
U.K. £187.99
[V.A.T. included]
Canada $289.99
ISBN 1-57231-632-2

Troubleshoot.

Achieve.

Master.

Now you can take Microsoft® BackOffice®
to new heights of performance—and do
likewise for your professional knowledge,
skills, and career. Just start applying the
authoritative information and tools in this
exclusive Microsoft collection. You get four
substantial volumes and a CD full of
valuable tools. All of which makes this kit
the essential resource for computer
professionals who aim to get the most
from their enterprise systems.

Impress.

Succeed.

Microsoft*®*Press

MICROSOFT LICENSE AGREEMENT

(*Managing and Maintaining Microsoft Exchange Server 5.5* - Book Companion CD)

IMPORTANT—READ CAREFULLY: This Microsoft End-User License Agreement ("EULA") is a legal agreement between you (either an individual or an entity) and Microsoft Corporation for the Microsoft product identified above, which includes computer software and may include associated media, printed materials, and "online" or electronic documentation ("SOFTWARE PRODUCT"). Any component included within the SOFTWARE PRODUCT that is accompanied by a separate End-User License Agreement shall be governed by such agreement and not the terms set forth below. By installing, copying or otherwise using the SOFTWARE PRODUCT, you agree to be bound by the terms of this EULA. If you do not agree to the terms of this EULA, you are not authorized to install, copy or otherwise use the SOFTWARE PRODUCT; you may, however, return the SOFTWARE PRODUCT, along with all printed materials and other items that form a part of the Microsoft product that includes the SOFT-WARE PRODUCT, to the place you obtained them for a full refund.

SOFTWARE PRODUCT LICENSE

The SOFTWARE PRODUCT is protected by United States copyright laws and international copyright treaties, as well as other intellectual property laws and treaties. The SOFTWARE PRODUCT is licensed, not sold.

1. GRANT OF LICENSE. This EULA grants you the following rights:

   a. Software Product. You may install and use one copy of the SOFTWARE PRODUCT on a single computer. The primary user of the computer on which the SOFTWARE PRODUCT is installed may make a second copy for his or her exclusive use on a portable computer.

   b. Storage/Network Use. You may also store or install a copy of the SOFTWARE PRODUCT on a storage device, such as a network server, used only to install or run the SOFTWARE PRODUCT on your other computers over an internal network; however, you must acquire and dedicate a license for each separate computer on which the SOFTWARE PRODUCT is installed or run from the storage device. A license for the SOFTWARE PRODUCT may not be shared or used concurrently on different computers.

   c. License Pak. If you have acquired this EULA in a Microsoft License Pak, you may make the number of additional copies of the computer software portion of the SOFTWARE PRODUCT authorized on the printed copy of this EULA, and you may use each copy in the manner specified above. You are also entitled to make a corresponding number of secondary copies for portable computer use as specified above.

   d. Sample Code. Solely with respect to portions, if any, of the SOFTWARE PRODUCT that are identified as sample code in the Readme file that forms a part of the SOFTWARE PRODUCT (the "SAMPLE CODE"):

      i. Use and Modification. Microsoft grants you the right to use and modify the source code version of the SAMPLE CODE, *provided* you comply with subsection (d)(iii) below. You may not distribute the SAMPLE CODE, or any modified version of the SAMPLE CODE, in source code form.

      ii. Redistributable Files. Provided you comply with subsection (d)(iii) below, Microsoft grants you a nonexclusive, royalty-free right to reproduce and distribute the object code version of the SAMPLE CODE and any modified version of the SAMPLE CODE, other than SAMPLE CODE, or any modified version thereof, designated as not redistributable in the Readme file that forms a part of the SOFT-WARE PRODUCT (the "Non-Redistributable Sample Code"). All SAMPLE CODE other than the Non-Redistributable Sample Code is collectively referred to as the "REDISTRIBUTABLES."

      iii. Redistribution Requirements. If you redistribute the REDISTRIBUTABLES, you agree to: (i) distribute the REDISTRIBUTABLES in object code form only in conjunction with and as a part of your software application product; (ii) not use Microsoft's name, logo, or trademarks to market your software application product; (iii) include a valid copyright notice on your software application product; (iv) indemnify, hold harmless, and defend Microsoft from and against any claims or lawsuits, including attorney's fees, that arise or result from the use or distribution of your software application product; and (v) not permit further distribution of the REDISTRIBUTABLES by your end user. Contact Microsoft for the applicable royalties due and other licensing terms for all other uses and/or distribution of the REDISTRIBUTABLES.

2. DESCRIPTION OF OTHER RIGHTS AND LIMITATIONS.

- **Not For Resale Software.** If the SOFTWARE PRODUCT is labeled "Not For Resale" or "NFR," then, notwithstanding other sections of this EULA, you may not resell, or otherwise transfer for value, the SOFTWARE PRODUCT.

- **Limitations on Reverse Engineering, Decompilation, and Disassembly.** You may not reverse engineer, decompile, or disassemble the SOFTWARE PRODUCT, except and only to the extent that such activity is expressly permitted by applicable law notwithstanding this limitation.

- **Separation of Components.** The SOFTWARE PRODUCT is licensed as a single product. Its component parts may not be separated for use on more than one computer.

- **Rental.** You may not rent, lease or lend the SOFTWARE PRODUCT.

- **Support Services.** Microsoft may, but is not obligated to, provide you with support services related to the SOFTWARE PRODUCT ("Support Services"). Use of Support Services is governed by the Microsoft policies and programs described in the user manual, in "on line" documentation and/or other Microsoft-provided materials. Any supplemental software code provided to you as part of the Support Services shall be considered part of the SOFTWARE PRODUCT and subject to the terms and conditions of this EULA. With respect to technical information you provide to Microsoft as part of the Support Services, Microsoft may use such information for its business purposes, including for product support and development. Microsoft will not utilize such technical information in a form that personally identifies you.

- **Software Transfer.** You may permanently transfer all of your rights under this EULA, provided you retain no copies, you transfer all of the SOFTWARE PRODUCT (including all component parts, the media and printed materials, any upgrades, this EULA, and, if applicable, the Certificate of Authenticity), **and** the recipient agrees to the terms of this EULA.

- **Termination.** Without prejudice to any other rights, Microsoft may terminate this EULA if you fail to comply with the terms and conditions of this EULA. In such event, you must destroy all copies of the SOFTWARE PRODUCT and all of its component parts.

3. **COPYRIGHT.** All title and copyrights in and to the SOFTWARE PRODUCT (including but not limited to any images, photographs, animations, video, audio, music, text, SAMPLE CODE, REDISTRIBUTABLES, and "applets" incorporated into the SOFTWARE PRODUCT), and any copies of the SOFTWARE PRODUCT are owned by Microsoft or its suppliers. The SOFTWARE PRODUCT is protected by copyright laws and international treaty provisions. Therefore, you must treat the SOFTWARE PRODUCT like any other copyrighted material **except** that you may install the SOFTWARE PRODUCT on a single computer provided you keep the original solely for backup or archival purposes. You may not copy the printed materials accompanying the SOFTWARE PRODUCT.

4. **U.S. GOVERNMENT RESTRICTED RIGHTS.** The SOFTWARE PRODUCT and documentation are provided with RESTRICTED RIGHTS. Use, duplication, or disclosure by the Government is subject to restrictions as set forth in subparagraph (c)(1)(ii) of the Rights in Technical Data and Computer Software clause at DFARS 252.227-7013 or subparagraphs (c)(1) and (2) of the Commercial Computer Software—Restricted Rights at 48 CFR 52.227-19, as applicable. Manufacturer is Microsoft Corporation/One Microsoft Way/Redmond, WA 98052-6399.

5. **EXPORT RESTRICTIONS.** You agree that you will not export or re-export the SOFTWARE PRODUCT, any part thereof, or any process or service that is the direct product of the SOFTWARE PRODUCT (the foregoing collectively referred to as the "Restricted Components"), to any country, person, entity or end user subject to U.S. export restrictions. You specifically agree not to export or re-export any of the Restricted Components (i) to any country to which the U.S. has embargoed or restricted the export of goods or services, which currently include, but are not necessarily limited to Cuba, Iran, Iraq, Libya, North Korea, Sudan and Syria, or to any national of any such country, wherever located, who intends to transmit or transport the Restricted Components back to such country; (ii) to any end-user who you know or have reason to know will utilize the Restricted Components in the design, development or production of nuclear, chemical or biological weapons; or (iii) to any end-user who has been prohibited from participating in U.S. export transactions by any federal agency of the U.S. government. You warrant and represent that neither the BXA nor any other U.S. federal agency has suspended, revoked or denied your export privileges.

DISCLAIMER OF WARRANTY

NO WARRANTIES OR CONDITIONS. MICROSOFT EXPRESSLY DISCLAIMS ANY WARRANTY OR CONDITION FOR THE SOFTWARE PRODUCT. THE SOFTWARE PRODUCT AND ANY RELATED DOCUMENTATION IS PROVIDED "AS IS" WITHOUT WARRANTY OR CONDITION OF ANY KIND, EITHER EXPRESS OR IMPLIED, INCLUDING, WITHOUT LIMITATION, THE IMPLIED WARRANTIES OF MERCHANTABILITY, FITNESS FOR A PARTICULAR PURPOSE, OR NONINFRINGEMENT. THE ENTIRE RISK ARISING OUT OF USE OR PERFORMANCE OF THE SOFTWARE PRODUCT REMAINS WITH YOU.

LIMITATION OF LIABILITY. TO THE MAXIMUM EXTENT PERMITTED BY APPLICABLE LAW, IN NO EVENT SHALL MICROSOFT OR ITS SUPPLIERS BE LIABLE FOR ANY SPECIAL, INCIDENTAL, INDIRECT, OR CONSEQUENTIAL DAMAGES WHATSOEVER (INCLUDING, WITHOUT LIMITATION, DAMAGES FOR LOSS OF BUSINESS PROFITS, BUSINESS INTERRUPTION, LOSS OF BUSINESS INFORMATION, OR ANY OTHER PECUNIARY LOSS) ARISING OUT OF THE USE OF OR INABILITY TO USE THE SOFTWARE PRODUCT OR THE PROVISION OF OR FAILURE TO PROVIDE SUPPORT SERVICES, EVEN IF MICROSOFT HAS BEEN ADVISED OF THE POSSIBILITY OF SUCH DAMAGES. IN ANY CASE, MICROSOFT'S ENTIRE LIABILITY UNDER ANY PROVISION OF THIS EULA SHALL BE LIMITED TO THE GREATER OF THE AMOUNT ACTUALLY PAID BY YOU FOR THE SOFTWARE PRODUCT OR US$5.00; PROVIDED, HOWEVER, IF YOU HAVE ENTERED INTO A MICROSOFT SUPPORT SERVICES AGREEMENT, MICROSOFT'S ENTIRE LIABILITY REGARDING SUPPORT SERVICES SHALL BE GOVERNED BY THE TERMS OF THAT AGREEMENT. BECAUSE SOME STATES AND JURISDICTIONS DO NOT ALLOW THE EXCLUSION OR LIMITATION OF LIABILITY, THE ABOVE LIMITATION MAY NOT APPLY TO YOU.

MISCELLANEOUS

This EULA is governed by the laws of the State of Washington USA, except and only to the extent that applicable law mandates governing law of a different jurisdiction.

Should you have any questions concerning this EULA, or if you desire to contact Microsoft for any reason, please contact the Microsoft subsidiary serving your country, or write: Microsoft Sales Information Center/One Microsoft Way/Redmond, WA 98052-6399.

Register Today!

Return this
*Managing and Maintaining Microsoft®
Exchange Server 5.5*
registration card today

Microsoft®Press

mspress.microsoft.com

0-7356-0528-9

Managing and Maintaining Microsoft®
Exchange Server 5.5

FIRST NAME   MIDDLE INITIAL   LAST NAME

INSTITUTION OR COMPANY NAME

ADDRESS

CITY   STATE   ZIP

(   )

E-MAIL ADDRESS   PHONE NUMBER

U.S. and Canada addresses only. Fill in information above and mail postage-free.
Please mail only the bottom half of this page.

For information about Microsoft Press®

products, visit our Web site at

mspress.microsoft.com

Microsoft®*Press*

BUSINESS REPLY MAIL
FIRST-CLASS MAIL   PERMIT NO. 108   REDMOND WA

POSTAGE WILL BE PAID BY ADDRESSEE

MICROSOFT PRESS
PO BOX 97017
REDMOND, WA 98073-9830

NO POSTAGE
NECESSARY
IF MAILED
IN THE
UNITED STATES

‖‖‖‖‖‖‖‖‖‖‖‖‖‖‖‖‖‖‖‖‖‖‖‖‖‖‖‖‖‖‖